## Also in Plains Histories

# LAW A⚖ LITTLE BIG HORN

# LAW A⚖ LITTLE BIG HORN

## DUE PROCESS DENIED

Charles E. Wright

Foreword by Gordon Morris Bakken

Texas Tech University Press

This book is typeset in Minion Pro. The paper used in this book meets the minimum requirements of ANSI/NISO Z39.48-1992 (R1997). ∞

Cover photograph/illustration Kicking Bear's *Battle of the Little Big Horn (Custer Massacre)*, circa 1896. Southwest Museum of the American Indian Collection, Autry National Center, Los Angeles; 1026.G.1

Library of Congress Cataloging-in-Publication Data
Wright, Charles E. (Lawyer)
    Law at Little Big Horn : due process denied / Charles E. Wright ; foreword by Gordon Morris Bakken.
        pages cm. — (Plains histories)
    Includes bibliographical references and index.
    ISBN 978-0-89672-912-4 (hardback) — ISBN 978-0-89672-913-1 (e-book)
1. Dakota Indians—Wars, 1876—Law and legislation 2. Cheyenne Indians—Wars, 1876—Law and legislation 3. Dakota Indians—Legal status, laws, etc.—History—19th century. 4. Cheyenne Indians—Legal status, laws, etc.—History—19th century. 5. Dakota Indians—Wars, 1876. 6. Cheyenne Indians—Wars, 1876. 7. Little Bighorn, Battle of the, Mont., 1876 I. Bakken, Gordon Morris, writer of foreword. II. Title.
    KF7221.W75 2016
    342.7308'72—dc23                                   2015028640

16 17 18 19 20 21 22 23 24 / 9 8 7 6 5 4 3 2 1

Texas Tech University Press
Box 41037 | Lubbock, Texas 79409-1037 USA
800.832.4042 | ttup@ttu.edu | www.ttupress.org

# CONTENTS

# ILLUSTRATIONS

# FOREWORD

This is not just another Custer book. Its contents will surprise even the most accomplished Little Big Horn scholar. Though other authors have analyzed George Armstrong Custer's tactics and equipment, Charles E. Wright is the first to do so against the legal and constitutional questions surrounding United States strategy in attacking the American Indians camped at the Little Big Horn.

Charles E. Wright analyzes the treaty relations with American Indian tribes as backdrop to the Great Sioux War. He asks the hard questions of how treaties were to be honored by the parties and how the United States government failed to abide by its sovereign word. Regardless of treaties, in 1876 the United States launched the Great Sioux War without a declaration of war by Congress. Congress had declared war against Great Britain in 1812 and against Mexico in 1846. It would declare war against Spain in 1898, Germany in 1917, Austria-Hungary in 1917, Japan in 1941, Germany in 1941, Italy in 1941, Bulgaria in 1941, Hungary in 1942, and Rumania in 1942. But no such declaration preceded the Great Sioux War.

Short of declaring war, presidents had also called upon Congress for authorization of military force. Congress authorized John Adams to use force against France in 1798 and Thomas Jefferson to use force in Tripoli in 1802. When Congress refused to declare war against the Regency of Algiers in 1815, it did grant President James Madison authority to use the United States Navy against the Algerian navy, expressly to protect American vessels from attack and to further United States policy regarding freedom of the sea. In 1819, when petitioned by private parties, Congress acted once again to protect American ships at sea, this time authorizing American ship captains to use force. The March 3, 1819, legislation was broad in that it authorized the use of "public armed vessels" or privateers. Congress told American ship captains not only to use force if attacked but also to seize the pirates and their vessels.[1] There was money to be made in this venture under the law of prize. A declaration of war and the authorization of the use of force today triggers a long list of standby statutory authority giving the president extensive power. Could the legal and constitutional ramifications of the Great Sioux War have been so different that no authorization was required from Congress?[2]

The Battle of the Little Big Horn generated hundreds of books and several massive bibliographies. Starting with Colonel Graham's 413-page book *The Custer Myth* (1953), scholars have stalked libraries and archives in search of every shred of evidence on Custer and the battle.[3] Every aspect of the ground and personnel seems covered, but the books keep finding print. Joan Nabseth Stevenson's *Deliverance from Little Big Horn* focused on Doctor Henry Porter, the sole surviving physician at the Little Big Horn.[4] Novelist Larry McMurtry's *Custer* gave a far more readable version of the man and his last battle.[5] They are the most recent of hundreds of titles on Custer, Crazy Horse, Gall, Sitting Bull, Reno, Benteen, Crook, and dozens of others.

Given the thousands upon thousands of words devoted to Little Big Horn and Custer, it is surprising that no legal and Constitutional history of the battle exists. There have been narrow monographs on the court martials that followed, but until now no sufficient attention has been focused on how this major event in the history of Western conflict has impacted American law. Charles E. Wright brings a level and form of analysis previously untried.

You must read this thought-provoking book cover to cover. It is more than worth your time.

Gordon Morris Bakken

# ACKNOWLEDGMENTS

My road to Little Big Horn and Custer was long and full of turns, halts, and backtracking. During the late 1930s and early 1940s, Cub Scout rituals and *The Leatherstocking Tales* stimulated my early interest in the American Indians, and Ernest Thompson Seton's *Wild Animals at Home* and *Wild Animals I Have Known* brought out awareness of the relationships between humans and the wild animals of the Great Plains. During World War II the movies *What Price Glory* and *Sergeant York* (watched five times), Ernie Pyle's *Brave Men*, and *Guadalcanal Diary* by Richard Tregaskis created and stimulated my lifelong interest in military history. Arthur Conan Doyle and his *Complete Sherlock Holmes* shed light upon the world of deductive reasoning. After I started law school, 90 percent of my reading was related to my legal education and law practice. In 1962 I had the good fortune to read *The Guns of August* by Barbara Tuchman, and shortly thereafter I chanced upon two volumes of Winston Churchill's splendid *The World Crisis*. This was powerful stuff, written by writers whom I understood and admired, and I decided that when I reached a stage in life where I would be able to read what I pleased, I would write about the Great War. To prepare for this I assembled and read more than 300 books, toured the western front on two occasions, visiting battlefields and military cemeteries from Menin Gate in Ypres, Belgium, to Xivray south of Verdun, including the battles of Messines in 1914, 1917, and 1918, the British memorial for the Accrington Pals Regiment at Serre, the Canadian battlefield at Vimy Ridge, Belleau Wood, and the Aisne-Marne Cemetery. I visited world-famous museums such as the Imperial War Museum in London, the Cloth Hall in Ypres, the Douaumont Ossuary, the Verdun Memorial Museum at Fleury, the Tranchée des Baïonnettes, the Meuse-Argonne American Cemetery at Montfaucon, as well as the splendid National World War I Museum in Kansas City. From these tours, which supplemented my reading and my active duty as a line officer with the U.S. Navy in the Western Pacific, I learned about the necessity of strategic and tactical planning, the need for adequate communications and continuous, thorough, and accurate reconnaissance, the paramount importance of intelligent leadership and rational thought processes, and the necessity for timely courageous decisions by tactical leaders who were in the front lines giving on-the-spot orders to deal with rapidly developing situations that could change from minute to minute. Everything was falling in place for me to commence writing about the Great War when, during the summer of 2000, my wife and I pulled off interstate highway I-90 in southeastern Montana to visit the Little Bighorn Battlefield National Monument. I wandered into the visitors' center and purchased two or three books about Custer and the Little Big Horn. Whoa! Stop all engines! All back full!

I was hooked—postponed my efforts on World War I and set out to learn what I could about the Plains Indian wars and, of course, George A. Custer. The Custer books from the visitors' center were interesting, but I was not comfortable with many of the conclusions. So, having discovered Amazon and the ability to acquire specific works quickly, I began accumulating books and acquiring information from discussions with other historians, studying the battlefield, and reviewing documents in collections from other museums and various historical societies. The Nebraska Game and Parks Commission and the Nebraska State Historical Society were presenting biennial seminars on the Indian Wars at historic Fort Robinson, which is located near the former Red Cloud and Spotted Tail agencies in the heart of Sioux and Cheyenne country in the Pine Ridge area of northwest Nebraska. Attending several of these seminars, I heard excellent presentations by National Park Service historians such as John D. McDermott, Jerome Greene, and Paul Hedren, as well as scholars and writers such as James Hanson, Michael Tate, Paul Hutton, and Brian Dippie. Some of the best presentations were given by Douglas D. Scott, then chief of the Rocky Mountain Research Division, Midwest Archaeological Center, National Park Service, who also prepared the detailed aerial photographs utilized in maps 15 through 19 of this book.

After examining numerous documents and maps, the Little Big Horn battlefields, the Rosebud and Fetterman battlefields, and what is now believed to be the Crow's Nest, I would ask questions of just about anyone who would speak with me. During this process I developed certain conclusions of my own that I believed would add clarity to the Custer fight, assign responsibility for Custer's defeat, and explain the cause and effect of the Great Sioux War on the culture and subsequent existence of the Indian tribes that were involved.

My early drafts focused heavily upon Custer and the tactical movements of his regiment prior to and during his actual battle. It soon became apparent that, except for attacking unarmed Indian women and children with their pistols and sabres, cavalry troopers with single-shot carbines had to dismount in order to fight Indian warriors. However, when they dismounted, they lost their mobility and often lost their horses as well. Slowly but surely I began to realize that the real story was not about Custer—it was about what the United States government was taking from its Native American citizens despite the fact that they were living on lands granted to them by the 1868 Treaty of Fort Laramie, approved and ratified by Congress, who were jointly and severally entitled to all the rights and protection provided for them in the United States Constitution. More precisely, the lives, liberty, and property to which they (as "persons") were entitled in the due process clause of the Fifth Amendment. My research indicated that these rights were being violated, with impunity, by the president of the United States (Grant), his general-in-chief (Sherman), and a senior field commander (Sheridan) and were being executed by the book's protagonist, none other than Lt. Col. George A. Custer. These crimes included premeditated murder, genocide, the taking of liberty, and the destruction of property. For information about the Indian Wars, I relied heavily on the writings of John D. McDermott. I found his report on Gen. George Crook's 1876 campaigns, which he prepared for the American Battlefield Protection Program, to be the best of the whole lot. His research was thorough and accurate. While he did not always agree with my conclusions, he was helpful and sometimes relentless in his observations and critique. In addition, I am greatly impressed by several of his observations that were favorable to General Crook and the actions taken by him to assist in restoring the memory of and promoting a decent burial for Maj. Marcus Reno—actions demonstrating honor and decency on the part of McDermott.

Douglas Scott was extremely helpful in explaining his archaeological findings at the battlefield and gracious and generous in preparing for me the aerial battlefield exhibits identifying the Indian and army shell casings and spent bullets in relation to the marble headstones, which provide a credible, detailed and scientifically generated illustration of the battle and what actually happened to Custer's troopers. Scott also assisted in converting the aerial maps in maps 12 through 19 from color to black and white. Dick Harmon, who participated in the archaeological studies, provided valuable information about the army and Indian firearms that were fired during the battle. The first and second editions of the *Atlas of the Sioux Wars*, published by the Combat Studies Institute at Fort Leavenworth, Kansas, in 1992 and 2006, were invaluable in describing much of the Indians' fighting with the U.S. Army on the northern plains and provided information for use in maps 2, 3, and 4.

I relied heavily on information provided by Dr. John S. Gray (*The Sioux War of 1876*), the discussion of Edward Lazarus about the illegal taking of the Sioux 1868 "treaty lands" (*Black Hills/White Justice*), the U.S. Supreme Court's record and opinion in *United States v. Sioux Nation of Indians*, 448 U.S. 371 (1980), and the materials prepared by Professor John LaVelle (*Rescuing Paha Sapa*) describing, piece by piece, the disgraceful conspiracy involving President Grant and his generals, Sherman and Sheridan, to wage the illegal war against the Sioux and Cheyennes on their treaty lands.

The treatises on strategic and tactical warfare by Sun Tzu, Clausewitz, and Jomini, and the nineteenth-century army officers August Kautz and Emory Upton, the army's laws of war (General Orders No. 100) drafted by General Halleck, Franz Lieber, and other generals, and the works of William Winthrop (*Military Law and Precedents*) were valuable in analyzing Custer's actions before and during the battle and in applying the army's laws of war to its conduct throughout the Great Sioux War.

*The Sherman Letters*, published in 1898 by Gen. William T. Sherman's daughter, Rachel Thorndike Sherman, express the strong affection that existed between the members of the general's family and are primarily letters between the general and his brother, United States Senator John Sherman, and other family members. However, they are of great probative value to establish beyond question that William Tecumseh Sherman was an unmitigated racist who had absolutely no regard for the legal rights of not only the American Indians, but of Mexicans, Negroes, and all the Confederate noncombatants in the vicinity of a war zone.

Professor John Wunder, who has written extensively on the legal rights of Indians, was not only helpful but instrumental in convincing me that I must bring American law into the story. Thus, I have brought the due process clause out of the closet, where it was ignored by President Grant with impunity and continues to this day to struggle for consideration and enforcement by the United States Supreme Court.

Two employees of the Nebraska State Historical Society, Thomas R. Buecker (*Fort Robinson and the American West, 1874–1899*) and Richard E. Jensen (*The Indian Interviews of* [Judge] *Eli S. Ricker*) produced detailed books that were particularly useful in describing the Cheyenne outbreaks from the Fort Robinson barracks and the hard-hitting and unequivocal opinions of deceased Judge Eli Ricker with respect to the treatment of the Sioux and Cheyenne Indians by the U.S. Army and the federal government during the nineteenth century. Martha Miller, a curator for references and photographs at the Nebraska State Historical Society, provided exceptional assistance in locating and selecting nineteenth-century photographs of Sioux and Cheyenne Indians. Steve Petteway, curator of the Supreme Court of the United States, located and provided excellent photographs of justices of the court.

Judi Gaiashkibos, director of the Nebraska Commission on Indian Affairs, has shared valuable information about the sovereign status of the Nebraska tribes and issues impacting the current lives of tribal members.

I am grateful to the following authors for their recent works that will, or should, change the way Americans think about their individual constitutional rights and the ability of the American government on certain occasions to act in ways that ignore or violate these rights. The first is the magnificent book by John M. Barry entitled *Roger Williams and the Creation of the American Soul: Church, State, and the Birth of Liberty,* which demonstrates the difficulties that Williams and other European settlers had in protecting individuals' liberties without the benefit of constitutional rights. The second book, authored by Eve LaPlante, and entitled *American Jezebel: The Uncommon Life of Anne Hutchinson, the Woman Who Defied the Puritans,* demonstrates why certain individual rights need to be protected from the tyranny of a majority that attempts to deprive one of life, liberty, or property without due process. The third book, by Bernard Bailyn, entitled *The Barbarous Years: The Peopling of British North America: The Conflict of Civilizations, 1600–1675,* describes the world of the indigenous Americans before the influx of the European settlers and how the settlers "clashed at times savagely with the indigenous peoples whose worlds they exploited but did not understand."

Finally, there is the forceful and brilliant winner of the Pulitzer Prize, *A Problem from Hell: America and the Age of Genocide,* authored by Samantha Power, the current United States ambassador to the United Nations, which provides a compelling argument for prompt and vigorous efforts to stop genocide whenever and wherever it occurs—regardless of the perpetrators.[1]

Because I lack a mastery of Internet technology, I relied heavily upon my personal assistant, Jane Casey. I am indebted to Bob Hanna and Darrel Stevens for their exceptional efforts in the design of the book's cover and the maps that appear throughout the text.

Finally, I would be remiss if I failed to thank my good friend and fellow law student at the University of Nebraska, James W. Hewitt, for his candid comments and wise counsel as my writing progressed.

For her patience and constant encouragement, I dedicate this work to Suzy, my partner for life.

# INTRODUCTION

*All wanton violence committed against persons in the invaded country, all destruction of property not commanded by the authorized officer, all robbery, all pillage or sacking, even after taking a place by main force, all rape, wounding, maiming, or killing of such inhabitants, are prohibited under the penalty of death, or such other severe punishment as may seem adequate for the gravity of the offense. A soldier, officer or private, in the act of committing such violence, and disobeying a superior ordering him to abstain from it, may be lawfully killed on the spot by such superior.*

Instructions for the Government of Armies of the United States in the Field, General Orders No. 100, Art. 44. Approved by President Abraham Lincoln, as promulgated and published by the Adjutant General's Office by order of the Secretary of War on April 24, 1863.

History is replete with reprisals and war crimes perpetrated by sovereign nations against defenseless noncombatants because of their race, religious beliefs, or because they happen to be in the wrong place at an unfortunate time. Many readers have read about the horrible reprisals from biblical times when entire cities were put to the torch and their inhabitants put to the victors' sword—acts for which there was seldom any justification and that created unspeakable misery, death, and terror. Within our lifetimes we have been told about the killing of Nazi war criminal Reinhard Heydrich in 1942 by a Czech assassination squad, which resulted in the Nazi government's destruction of the entire village of Lidice and the execution of more than 1300 Czech men, women, and children who had no part in the Heydrich assassination. The purpose of the Nazi reprisal was to spread terror among the conquered citizens of Czechoslovakia and serve as a symbolic punishment of innocent souls for the assassination.[1]

Why was it that certain U.S. Army officers felt the need or were ordered on numerous occasions to use their military force to commit outrageous crimes against helpless and generally innocent Indians, mostly noncombatants, for reasons related to minor misdemeanors, past transgressions by others not present, or for no reason other than they were believed to be Indians? Was it a lust for power sustained by the terror achieved by killing, or was it simply an exercise of military power by the U.S. Army to force removal or utilize genocidal acts of reprisal on Indians who had never been indicted or convicted of any crimes? Some officers boasted of their deeds orally and in writing. Other officers and enlisted men were sickened by such behavior, writing about it in personal correspondence and subsequent official reports. Nearly all of these atrocities fall into the category of "war crimes" that violated not only the Indians' due process rights under the Fifth Amendment to the Constitution, but the U.S. Army's "laws of war," which were drafted under the direction of President Abraham Lincoln and ordered into effect as General Orders No. 100, "for the Government of the Armies of the U.S. in the Field, effective from [and thereafter] April 24, 1863."[2] General Orders No. 100 were known as the "Lieber Code" because they were drafted by a committee of four Union generals chaired by Franz Lieber, a Prussian immigrant who once fought in the Prussian army at Waterloo and taught history and law at Columbia College. The Lieber Code contains 157 separately stated and numbered orders, protecting due process rights under the Fifth Amendment to the U.S. Constitution, prohibiting internecine wars, infliction of intentional wounds, assault of an already disabled person, murder, theft, rape, and unnecessary or revengeful destruction of life. When these war crimes were committed by U.S. soldiers, they were often committed under the orders or explicit compulsion of their commanding generals—such as William T. Sherman, Philip Sheridan, John C. Fremont, and William S. Harney—on vulnerable Indian villages located in remote areas where there was no judicial, congressional, or military oversight, upon persons who were unable to read or write and were totally unaware of their individual rights under the Fifth Amendment and the Lieber Code. When these war crimes were perpetrated, they were generally preapproved by these senior officers and subsequently covered up by these same officers—thus war crimes could be perpetrated with impunity because the soldiers directly involved were never punished and their crimes had been approved in advance by senior officers who were not at the scene of the crime.

The Lieber Code was so well drafted and universally accepted as the "international laws of war" that it was thereafter adopted verbatim during the Civil War by the Confederate States of America and subsequently recodified into the Hague Conventions, which in turn formed the basis for the Geneva Conventions, the "Convention on the Prevention and Punishment of the Crime of Genocide" (adopted by the General Assembly of the United Nations on December 9, 1948) and thereafter the famous Resolution 1674 on the "protection of civilians in armed conflict," adopted by the Security Council of the United Nations on April 28, 2006.[3]

Between 1840 and 1900 there were numerous acts of genocide perpetrated by soldiers of the United States Army and volunteer militia upon noncombatants of tribes and smaller camps of Native Americans at various locations between the Mississippi River and the Pacific Coast. As defined in the Convention on the Prevention and Punishment of the Crime of Genocide, genocide is any of the following acts, committed with intent to destroy, in whole or in part, a national, ethnical, racial, or religious group by (1) killing members of the group, (2) causing serious bodily or mental harm to members of the group, (3) deliberately inflicting on the group conditions of life calculated to bring about its physical destruction, in whole or in part. Genocide, conspiracy to commit genocide, direct and public incitement to commit genocide, attempt to commit genocide and complicity in genocide are each separate criminal offenses punishable by law.[4]

The term "genocide" was created by Raphael Lemkin in the 1940s to define and prescribe punishment for intentional acts intended to damage or destroy a national, ethnical, racial, or religious group. The prohibited acts would include, inter alia, killing, causing serious bodily or mental harm to members of the group, and deliberately inflicting on the group conditions of life calculated to bring about its physical destruction, in whole or in part. Persons subject to punishment would include not only the perpetrators of genocide, but conspirators—those who incite the commission of genocide, attempt, or are complicit in a genocidal act. Born to Jewish parents in eastern Poland in 1900, Lemkin witnessed a "panorama of destruction of the Armenians," which alerted his moral interests in protecting vulnerable racial, national, ethnical, and religious groups. He obtained a doctorate in law while studying in Germany in the 1920s. When the Nazis approached Warsaw in 1939, he fled to the countryside, where he was interrogated by the Russians. In 1940 he fled to Lithuania, then to Latvia, and thereafter to Sweden. Academic connections landed him a teaching position at Duke Law School in 1941. All the while, Lemkin was accumulating facts about the horrible Holocaust that was occurring throughout central and eastern Europe. Shortly thereafter, while speaking about prior and current genocides at a prestigious academic dinner, he stated: "If women, children and old people would be murdered a hundred miles from here wouldn't you run to help? Then why do you stop this decision of your heart when the distance is five thousand miles instead of a hundred?"[5]

Lemkin's questions were prescient because the United States did not take immediate steps to deter the ongoing holocaust in Poland and Germany until the invading Allied armies reached the Nazi extermination camps. Samantha Power describes the American responses to the "atrocities in Bosnia" as consistent with prior American responses to genocide:

Raphael Lemkin. Courtesy
American Jewish Historical
Society.

Early warnings of massive bloodshed proliferated. The spewing of in-
flammatory propaganda escalated. The massacres and deportations
started. U.S. policymakers struggled to wrap their minds around the
horrors. Refugee stories and press reports of atrocities became too
numerous to deny. Few Americans at home pressed for intervention.
A hopeful but passive and ultimately deadly American waiting game
commenced. And genocide proceeded unimpeded by U.S. action and
often emboldened by U.S. inaction.[6]

These more recent American responses are similar in most respects to the response by Congress to the Great Sioux War initiated in 1876 by President Grant
and his generals Sherman and Sheridan, with the exception that Grant's campaign was begun in the heart of the United States against persons who were
entitled to protection under the U.S. Constitution.

Lemkin moved to New York, where he enjoyed an outstanding career serving
and consulting with prestigious universities, government offices, and as advisor

to U.S. Supreme Court Justice Robert Jackson when he served as chief counsel at the Nuremberg trials of Nazi war criminals. Working for the U.S. Board of Economic Warfare in Washington, he was shocked to learn of Axis plans for mass destruction of racial, national, and religious groups throughout Europe. This caused him to author the book *Axis Rule in Occupied Europe*, in which he began to use the term "genocide." For the balance of his life, he devoted most of his waking hours to persuading the United Nations and its General Assembly to adopt the Convention on the Prevention and Punishment of the Crime of Genocide. This convention was adopted by the General Assembly on December 9, 1948, and entered into force on January 12, 1951.

Genocide had not been defined or codified into law in the 1860s and 1870s, but the numerous actions by President Grant and his generals against various groups of Indians involved premeditated murder, false imprisonment, intentional wounding, and destruction of property—each of which constituted felony crimes against persons who were entitled to due process and which would now, under the United Nations convention, constitute punishable genocide.[7]

Within the army's officer corps there were a few men who would instinctively, impulsively, or when ordered, without regard to due process, carry out premeditated murder, wanton destruction of food and shelter, and other acts of genocide and extermination in the name of reprisal for real or imagined wrongs by Indians. Among these officers were William S. Harney, Grenville Dodge, Philip Sheridan, William T. Sherman, and Winfield Scott Hancock, as well as lesser officers Lt. Col. George Custer, Brevet Capt. Nathaniel Lyon, Brevet 2nd Lt. John Grattan, Capt. Ben Wright, Maj. Eugene Baker, Maj. John C. Fremont, and Brevet Gen. Christopher Houston ("Kit") Carson. However, there were also senior army officers, such as Generals George Crook,[8] Ranald Mackenzie, Nelson Miles, John Pope, and also including General Harney (who organized and led the massacre at Blue Water Creek), who in certain instances made good-faith efforts to observe treaty covenants and oral promises made to the Sioux and Cheyennes and levied severe criticism on the Interior and War Departments when the covenants and promises were violated, including numerous instances when food rations were not delivered and Indians on reservations lacked sufficient other resources to avoid starvation.

In the 1870s and 1880s Col. William W. Winthrop, acclaimed by the U.S. Supreme Court as the "Blackstone of Military Law," noted the army's concern for justice and humanity in the interaction between officers and soldiers and friendly Indians:

(6) *Relations in General of the Military Toward Peaceable Indians.* It remains to remark that the relations of the military with the friendly

Indians should be distinguished by a particular and scrupulous justice, humanity and discretion, for the reason that the former specially represent to the latter the power of the United States. For an officer or soldier to fail in his duty toward such Indians is a peculiarly serious offence, since it materially compromises the government and sensibly impairs its authority over this class of its subjects, and moreover tends to induce them to lapse into hostility. In a case, in the Department of the Columbia, of an aggravated injury inflicted by a soldier upon an Indian, the offence was characterized by the Department Commander, (Gen. [Edward] Canby,) [who was later murdered by Modoc Chief Captain Jack] as a graver one than if committed by a civilian, because— as it was expressed—"the Army has been made, under the direction of the President, an important agent in the execution of the laws regulating intercourse with the Indian tribes, and such acts by soldiers are not only violations of the statute but gross breaches of discipline and of trust."[9]

Commencing July 2, 1862, every officer of the U.S. Army was required to take an oath to support and defend the Constitution of the United States[10]—a Constitution that prohibited taking the life, liberty, or property of any person without due process.[11] Articles of War adopted by Congress in 1806 provided that any officer who "shall disobey any *lawful command* of his superior officer shall be punished" (emphasis supplied).[12] In later times the term "lawful order" was defined in the army's Uniform Code of Military Justice as follows: "An order requiring the performance of a military duty may be inferred to be lawful and it is disobeyed at the peril of the subordinate. This inference does not apply to a patently illegal order such as one that directs the commission of a crime."[13] It is therefore rational and logical to believe that a subordinate officer has not only the right but the sworn duty to refuse the orders of a superior officer to commit murder and other genocidal acts against persons entitled to Fifth Amendment protection of life, liberty, and property. In many instances the Indian victims were guilty of no transgressions. In others, the victims were misidentified by the officer in charge. Virtually all were noncombatants, and many of them were defenseless women and children. Similarly, many incidents were perpetrated on fabricated transgressions or minor misdemeanors totally unworthy of genocidal retaliation. Strategic objectives of the reprisals could be, and often were, to kill or conquer and terrorize the victims, destroy their villages, strip them of their horses and firearms, and force them to vacate their treaty lands and live on remote areas of arid land, where they would have to depend upon the U.S. government for all or a substantial portion of their support. In other instances the sole object was to kill, wound, maim, pillage, and spread terror.

On May 10, 1846, a particularly vicious and wanton reprisal was inflicted on innocent members of the Klamath tribe when army forces under the command of Maj. John C. Fremont and his guide, Kit Carson, sprang a surprise attack on a small village of Klamath Indians while the Klamath men were away on a hunt. Carson's soldiers fell upon the innocent village and slaughtered twenty-one Indians—mostly women and children.[14]

In May of 1850, Brevet Captain Nathaniel Lyon attacked several villages of helpless Pomo Indians in the vicinity of Clear Lake, in Lake County, California. These attacks were in retaliation for the killing of two degenerate white farmers who had enslaved Pomo Indians and sexually abused their young daughters. Lyon's men killed more than one hundred Pomos, none of whom had anything to do with the murder of the two white farmers. Captain Lyon described this premeditated mass murder as a "perfect slaughter pen."[15]

In August of 1854, near Fort Laramie on the banks of the North Platte River in Nebraska Territory, Brevet 2nd Lt. John Grattan, a recent graduate of West Point, with a force of twenty-nine soldiers and a drunken and arrogant interpreter named Auguste, on his own volition and against the advice of soldiers and traders in the area, marched boldly into a large village of Brulé Lakota Indians led by Chief Conquering Bear and demanded that Conquering Bear arrest and hand over a Minneconjou warrior, High Forehead, who had allegedly killed a cow belonging to a Mormon wagon train moving west along the river valley. After Chief Conquering Bear told Grattan that High Forehead was not subject to his command and he could not deliver him to Grattan, Grattan's soldiers fired two small cannons and their own muskets into the huge Brulé camp of 4,800 Indians, containing more than 1,000 warriors, killing Chief Conquering Bear. The Brulé warriors returned fire in short order, killing Grattan and his entire force of twenty-nine.[16]

In September of 1855, more than one year after Grattan's small force was killed, 500 mixed cavalry and infantry soldiers commanded by Brig. Gen. William S. Harney, acting in reprisal for the killing of Grattan and his troops, sought out and attacked two villages containing 250 Brulé and Oglala Sioux led by Chief Little Thunder. The Indians were camped on Blue Water Creek, located on the north bank of the North Platte River, a few miles northwest of what is now the small town of Lewellen, Nebraska. In a punitive reprisal against the Brulés, who had recently been certified as "peaceful" by Indian agent Thomas S. Twiss, Harney's forces killed eighty-six Brulé and Oglala Sioux Indians and took seventy-three women and children as prisoners, having laid waste to two Indian villages and left the battlefield strewn with dead and wounded Indian warriors, women, and children.[17]

Harney had no evidence that any of those he killed or injured had participated in the fight in which Lieutenant Grattan and his twenty-nine soldiers were killed—he was exacting his reprisal on Little Thunder and his camp simply because they were Indians living in tepees. After the battle 2nd Lt. Gouverneur Kemble Warren and other officers assisted several wounded Indian survivors to a makeshift shelter to provide rudimentary medical treatment for their wounds. These included a woman shot in both legs, with a bullet that also killed the baby she was holding, a twelve-year-old girl lying face down in a ravine with bullet wounds in both legs, a small boy with leg wounds, a little girl shot in the right breast, and a boy with bullet wounds in both an arm and a leg.

> As [1st Lt. Richard] Drum and Company G returned to the villages after their pursuit of the Sioux, they came across a small girl. Drum asked a sergeant to pick her up, but she scratched and bit him when he tried. After a drink from his canteen filled with whiskey and lemonade, the girl soon calmed down. For several days, Drum looked after her before turning the girl over to her people. Only later did Drum learn that the little girl was Spotted Tail's daughter. She died within days of the battle.[18]

On November 29, 1864, some nineteen months after the U.S. Army enacted the Lieber Code (General Orders, No. 100), which prohibit, inter alia, "all wanton violence against persons in the invaded country . . . all robbery, pillage or sacking" and "all rape, wounding, maiming or killing of such inhabitants, are prohibited under penalty of death." U.S. Army Col. John M. Chivington, with 700 soldiers of the Colorado and New Mexico militia, attacked the camp of Cheyenne peace chief, Black Kettle, killing dozens of innocent men, women, and children and destroying their food and shelter.

> Most of the dead, including women and children, were scalped. Fingers were cut off hands to get rings, ears taken as trophies, and noses cut off. The genitals of men and women had been removed, those of the former for use by soldiers in making tobacco pouches.[19]

Capt. Silas Soule, who commanded Company D of the First Colorado Cavalry, refused to take part in the massacre, calling any man who did "a low lived cowardly son of a bitch."[20] Verifying Soule's opinion of their immoral character, Charles Squires and William Morrow, soldiers serving in the Second Colorado Cavalry Regiment, ambushed Soule and shot him to death in the presence of his wife on April 23, 1865.[21]

In late November of 1868, Gen. Philip H. Sheridan ordered Lt. Col. George Custer (whom he had recently paroled from a one-year sentence by an army general court-martial) to seek out and punish Indians in the vicinity of the Canadian and Washita rivers in what is now the state of Oklahoma. Custer's orders from Sheridan were to destroy (unspecified) Indian "villages and ponies, to kill or hang all warriors and bring back all women and children."[22] Such acts—premeditated and intentional killing and kidnapping aimed at a particular race of people—constituted murder and the currently recognized crime of genocide. These were the orders of a general of the United States Army, who had taken an oath to support the Constitution. By Custer's own count (Custer tended to exaggerate his achievements), 140 Indians living in the camp of the same unfortunate Cheyenne peace chief, Black Kettle, were killed, others were wounded, and 53 women were taken prisoner and brought to Camp Supply where General Sheridan was located. Following the killing, the Indians' lodges and food were destroyed, and 650 of their ponies were slaughtered and left to rot on the ground where they fell. Prior to the attack Custer had no knowledge of the identity of his victims, their tribe, or whether any of the occupants had ever committed a transgression against anyone. He was unaware that a few days earlier, on November 20, Black Kettle and Arapaho chief Spotted Wolf, who occupied the camp, had attempted to surrender their followers to Col. William Hazen at Fort Cobb.

In January of 1870, General Sheridan ordered Maj. Eugene Baker and his Second Cavalry Regiment to locate the camp of Piegan Blackfoot chief Mountain Chief and to punish Blackfoot warrior Owl Child and other Piegan warriors who had killed a white trader in a dispute involving horses stolen by Owl Child. Baker's troops chanced upon the innocent village of Piegan peace chief Heavy Runner, camped on the banks of the Marias River in what is now northwest Montana. Heavy Runner's camp was starving, and many of its occupants were dying of smallpox. In the dead of a severe winter in subzero temperatures, most of Heavy Runner's warriors were away from camp, hunting for food. As Baker's troops approached the camp, Heavy Runner ran out to meet him, attempting to plead the innocence of his people. Ignoring the evidence, Baker, reportedly drunk at the time, launched a brutal attack on the "friendly and defenseless village," killing Heavy Runner, along with 170 others, including ninety women and fifty children.[23] The camp was torched, and some Piegans died inside burning lodges. All food was destroyed, and their ponies were taken. This was another outrageous act of genocide, arson. and first-degree murder—perpetrated by the U.S. Army pursuant to orders from General Sheridan.[24]

In the spring of 1873, Kickapoo Indians operating from Mexico near the Texas border were raiding ranches along the Texas side of the Nueces River. General Sheridan and Secretary of War William Belknap met with Col. Ranald Mackenzie and other Army officers to discuss strategy. Sheridan, indicating his specific attitude toward genocide, premeditated murder, and terrorism, ordered Mackenzie to cross the border and destroy a Kickapoo village, stating:

> "I want you to be bold, enterprising, and at all times *full of energy*, when you begin, let it be a campaign of *annihilation, obliteration* and *complete destruction*, as you have always in your dealings done to all the Indians you have dealt with. . . . I think you understand what I want done, and the way you should employ your force."
>
> Mackenzie asked, "Gen. Sheridan, under whose orders and upon what authority am I to act? Have you any plans to suggest, or will you issue me the necessary orders for my actions?" Sheridan exploded, pounding his fist on the table. "Damn the orders! Damn the authority! . . . You are to go ahead on your own plan of action, and your authority and backing shall be Gen. [President] Grant and myself. With us behind you in whatever you do to clean up this situation, you can rest assured of the fullest support. *You must assume the risk.* We will assume the *final responsibility* should any result."[25]

Shortly thereafter, Mackenzie crossed the border and attacked a small Kickapoo village while its warriors were not present, killing nineteen Kickapoo women, children, and elders, taking forty prisoners back across the border to the United States, meanwhile destroying the Kickapoo village and two nearby Lipan and Mescalero Apache villages. Prior to the attacks Mackenzie had no knowledge that any of the victimized Kickapoos or Apaches had ever participated in any of the prior Indian raids in U.S. territory.[26]

The attack on the Kickapoo Indians took place more than ten years after the U.S. Army had adopted a detailed set of rules (General Orders No. 100) that were in direct conflict with Sheridan's orders. These words of Sheridan, with which General Sherman and President Grant acquiesced, lowered the bar for punitive reprisals by the U.S. Army and unprovoked genocide perpetrated against the Indians located west of the Mississippi River from April of 1873 through the Great Sioux War of 1876–1877, and continuing until after the horrible atrocities perpetrated at the Battle of Wounded Knee on December 29, 1890.

Late in 1875 President Ulysses S. Grant was confronted with the need to remove the Sioux and Cheyenne Indians from the ownership and occupancy of treaty lands consisting of vast areas located in Dakota, Wyoming, and Montana territories in order to provide a railroad right of way and adjoining plots of land for thousands of westbound settlers. Instead of acting in good faith toward the Indians and their treaty rights, Grant fell in step with Generals Sherman and Sheridan and ordered the U.S. Army to ignore the Fifth Amendment and the 1868 Treaty of Fort Laramie and forcibly remove all Sioux and Cheyenne Indians from their treaty lands without any due process or just compensation. The army's strategy of total war, against noncombatants as well as Confederate soldiers, had possibly hastened the final surrender of the Confederate states. Sherman and Sheridan were fully aware of the army's rules of engagement (the Lieber Code); had each taken an oath to support the Constitution; and each had been complicit in several genocidal actions against the Indians during and subsequent to the Civil War. Therefore, they were more than willing to proceed with the Great Sioux War because they believed they were covered by President Grant's orders. Sherman was ruthless in exercising the army's superior military might to trample the Indians' constitutional and treaty rights. Sheridan, perhaps more aggressive and less cautious than Sherman, was only too willing to cooperate. However, throughout the Great Sioux War, each of them refrained from on-site command of tactical combat units and distanced themselves from direct control of the genocidal attacks on the Indians. General Alfred H. Terry commanded the "northern army" to which Lieutenant Colonel Custer and his Seventh Cavalry Regiment were attached. Terry intentionally avoided commanding the Seventh Cavalry at the Battle of Little Big Horn—and for the balance of the entire year of 1876 was never personally present at any of the numerous battles between the units he commanded and the Indians.

Custer himself relished commanding the Seventh Cavalry in combat with the Indians. He had no compunction about surprise attacks on vulnerable Indian villages where innocent warriors and their families would be killed and wounded, their food and shelter destroyed, and their liberty terminated. Prior to the commencement of the Great Sioux War, Custer received strong support from Generals Terry and Sheridan when they successfully interceded with President Grant to reinstate Custer after Grant had removed him from command because of his derogatory testimony before a congressional investigation committee.

As will be detailed in the subsequent chapters, the ruthless and illegal strategies of General Sheridan (and General Sherman) became the standard of conduct for the U.S. Army units assigned to carry out President Grant's overall strategic objective in the Great Sioux War—to attack the Indians and either kill or

force them to relinquish their treaty lands and move them onto designated reservations—death or loss of liberty and their treaty lands—actions that involved
the rights of the Sioux and Cheyenne Indians under the Fifth Amendment of the
Constitution and the 1868 Treaty of Fort Laramie, which were also prohibited
by the army's General Orders No. 100 and constituted the crimes of premeditated murder and genocide.

More detail regarding the Indians' due process rights and the army's General
Orders No. 100, governing the conduct of its armies in the field, is provided in
the glossary.

## Chapter One
# George Armstrong Custer, The Man and His World

*There is scarcely an individual in our service who has contributed more to bring about this desirable result than your gallant husband.*

—*Major General Philip Sheridan to Elizabeth Custer, April 10, 1865*

The tactical choices, the multitude of decisions made before and during the shattering moments at the Little Big Horn, had long roots extending back through three decades. Born in New Rumley, Ohio, on December 5, 1839, George Armstrong Custer was the third child born into the second marriage of both Maria Kirkpatrick and Emanuel Henry Custer, who went on to parent four more children.[1] Emanuel, a devout Presbyterian turned Methodist[2] and a blacksmith by trade, was an outspoken Democrat who supported Andrew Jackson.

Custer enjoyed a rough-and-tumble boyhood with his brothers, who loved to tease their father and make him the butt of outlandish practical jokes. There is little about Custer's early years or his relationship with his parents or siblings to indicate that he acquired any abilities as a leader, was a good student, or developed any respect for authority. He was, however, bright, ambitious, independent, and crammed full of impulsive mischief—which often got him into trouble and for which he seemed immune to feelings of guilt or shame.

During one of his early school years, Custer was confronted by one of his teachers for misbehavior:

"I know I was wrong," Custer said, "but I could not help it."

"Could not help it?" the teacher replied.

"No Sir, I wanted to do it."

"But could you not restrain your impulses?"

"Don't know Sir—never tried."[3]

His habit of making hasty decisions, often ill advised, would later impact his career as a tactical cavalry commander in the Indian Wars.

At age ten Custer went to live with his married half-sister Lydia Ann (Reed) in Monroe, Michigan. He left her home for McNeely Normal School in Hopedale, Ohio, when he was fourteen and dropped out at the age of sixteen to teach school in Locust Grove, Ohio. He was attracted to a young lady named Mary Jane Holland who lived in Cadiz, Ohio. Custer was not favored by Mary Jane's father, and his infatuation with Mary Jane came to nothing when he obtained an appointment to West Point Military Academy in January of 1857. Mary Jane's father, Alexander Holland, helped Custer obtain the appointment, supposedly so that Custer would not be around to court his daughter. Custer said goodbye to Mary Jane and took the train to Albany, New York, where he traveled by boat down the Hudson River to West Point. Custer was one of sixty-eight (of 108) applicants who were accepted into the class of 1857.[4]

Custer entered West Point on July 1, 1857, and graduated on June 24, 1861. His academic career was undistinguished, and his grades were uniformly bad. One source indicates that, after his first year, Custer never checked a book out of the library.[5] Among other things, he had bad marks in ordnance, gunnery, and cavalry tactics in his second- and first-class years.[6] As a fifth-classman (1858) he stood fifty-eighth out of a class of sixty-two. Among his instructors was Lt. Col. W. J. Hardee, who wrote manuals and provided theoretical instruction on the tactics of artillery and infantry.[7] As a fourth-classman (1859) Custer stood fifty-sixth out of fifty-eight and received more instruction in tactics from Hardee. In his third-class year (1860) Custer found his ultimate "order of merit" when he stood fifty-seventh out of fifty-seven. There was more instruction in the tactics of artillery, cavalry and infantry. As a second-classman (1861) Custer stood thirty-fifth out of thirty-five, received further instruction in tactics as well as strategy, and studied from Dennis H. Mahan's *Treatise on Advance Guards and Outposts*[8] and Baron Antoine Henri de Jomini's *Art of War*.[9] As a first-classman at graduation (also 1861), Custer stood thirty-fifth out of thirty-five. During his final year he received instruction concerning the "rules for the exercise and maneuvers of the United States infantry, practical instruction in the schools of the soldier, company and battalion, and practical instruction in artillery and cavalry."[10] In a candid self-evaluation Custer later noted, "My career as a cadet had but little to commend it to the study of those who came after me, unless as an example to be carefully avoided."[11]

Indeed, Custer constantly flirted with disaster at the academy. He wore long golden curls, then shaved his head, and thereafter wore a wig until his hair grew out. He enjoyed socializing with fellow cadets and had not yet taken his vow of sobriety. Extroverted and gregarious, he formed strong friendships with both southern and northern classmates.

Custer demonstrated little respect for authority. He was a cut-up in and out of class who played pranks on everyone, including the officer instructors. He stole test questions from an instructor's personal living quarters (a flagrant breach of the cadet's code of honor),[12] accumulated demerits for such behavior as keeping cooking utensils in the chimney, unkempt hair and beard (his nickname, "Fannie," was due to his long hair), maintaining food items in his quarters, keeping a messy room, drawing graffiti on the walls, throwing snowballs and bread, and "highly unmilitary and trifling conduct." Many of the demerits were for actions indicating that he lacked rational judgment, was not reliable, and had little respect for rules and authority. He was frequently late for parade and for breakfast, supper, and dinner. Such was Custer's well-publicized conduct that he became a legend at West Point in his own time—perhaps in his own mind as well.[13] Two hundred demerits in a one-year time frame were grounds for dismissal from the academy. For the years 1859, 1860, and 1861, he flew near the flame, accumulating 192, 191, and 192 demerits, respectively.[14] By the time he graduated, his grand total was 726.[15] This number was not unique, as it was common for cadets in each class to have more than 150 demerits in a given year.

On June 24, 1861, Custer was commissioned a second lieutenant and assigned to the Second U.S. Cavalry Regiment. In Washington, while awaiting his assignment to the Second Cavalry, Custer had an opportunity to meet the aging Gen. Winfield Scott, hero of the Mexican War. General Scott asked Custer if he wanted to remain in Washington training recruits, or accept an assignment in the field with the cavalry stationed near Centreville, Virginia, about forty miles southwest of the capital. Custer chose combat with the cavalry. Scott told him to obtain his own horse and report back to pick up dispatches for delivery to Gen. Irvin McDowell at the front. After borrowing a horse from an enlisted man, Custer rode all night, delivered the dispatches to General McDowell, and was able to locate his Second Cavalry Regiment by dawn.

On July 21, 1861, Custer's regiment went into battle at Bull Run (Manassas, Virginia). Gen. Pierre G. T. Beauregard (the same Beauregard who was active with Robert E. Lee at Cerro Gordo and Mexico City during the war with Mexico) commanded the Confederates. The Rebels thrashed the Yanks, and many of the Union troops, officers and men, broke and ran, abandoning their equipment. Custer got his first taste of hissing cannon balls and fought hard until the Second Cavalry retreated from the field. Post-battle reports mentioned him for bravery.[16] Four days after the battle, General McDowell was sacked by President Abraham Lincoln and replaced by Maj. Gen. George B. McClellan, who assumed command of the U.S. Army and the Department of the Potomac. The Second Cavalry was redesignated the Fifth Cavalry Regiment and attached to a brigade commanded by Brig. Gen. Philip Kearny, who lost his left arm during the Mexican War. Custer served on his staff and acquired Kearny's penchant for the cavalry charge.

In October of 1861, Custer took a four-month leave of absence (due to illness) and returned to Monroe, Michigan. There he first met Elizabeth "Libbie" Bacon, the daughter of Judge Daniel Stanton Bacon. Carousing with some old friends, Custer overdosed on applejack and was unable to hold his liquor. He gave an exhibition of public drunkenness on the street in front of the Bacon residence that was observed by Libbie and the judge. They were unimpressed.[17] Following this incident, perhaps in order to redeem himself with Libbie, Custer took a vow of sobriety (administered by his half-sister Lydia Ann), which he maintained for the balance of his life.[18]

On June 5, 1862, Custer was promoted to brevet captain and selected by General McClellan to serve as his aide-de-camp. This brevet promotion and staff selection were due to an extraordinary individual reconnaissance by Custer, enabling a safe Union crossing at the Chicahominy River. Custer admired McClellan and served him with distinction. On July 17, 1862, he was promoted to first lieutenant in the regular army.[19] He had earned a reputation for unbridled energy and absolute courage.[20]

In March of 1862, Custer was selected to lead a small cavalry patrol to scout the Confederate pickets of Gen. Joseph Johnston, who was pulling his army back from northern Virginia to prepare for an anticipated

Union offensive. Leading his company, Custer encountered mounted Rebel sentries whom he immediately charged, causing them to flee from their posts. Shortly thereafter, he made several scouting missions in a hydrogen balloon. At Williamsburg he led Col. Amassa Cobb and his Fifth Wisconsin Regiment through an obscure trail, crossing a stream to turn the enemy's left flank. On September 14 and 17, he was engaged in the famous battles of South Mountain and Antietam. In each instance he showed bold initiative and a lack of concern about his personal safety. Custer feared nothing and could endure long periods of time without sleep.

In November of 1862, Lincoln sacked McClellan, replacing him with Maj. Gen. Ambrose Burnside, and Custer was given a furlough. He returned to Monroe to await further assignment. While there, he was formally introduced to Libbie and she "flung a craving on him." In turn, Libbie began to show interest in Custer. Like Mary Jane Holland's father, Judge Bacon disapproved of Custer and did what he could to dampen Libbie's ardor. After a lengthy courtship the judge relented, and Custer married Libbie in February of 1864. After their honeymoon Libbie often accompanied Custer to his post and traveled with him in the field.

Burnside resigned on January 26, 1863, and was replaced by Maj. Gen. Joseph Hooker, who held command until shortly after Lee defeated him at Chancellorsville in the first week of May 1863. Custer was thereupon assigned to the staff of Brig. Gen. Alfred Pleasonton, a hardworking and efficient general with eight years' experience in Indian fighting. Pleasonton was given command of the entire Union Cavalry Corps, and Custer was both fortunate and pleased to be on his staff. Pleasonton in turn treated Custer well. In Custer's own words, "I do not believe a father could love his son more than Genl. Pleasanton loves me. He is as solicitous about me and my safety as a mother about her only child."[21]

On June 9, 1863, Custer distinguished himself and received a citation from General Pleasonton for gallantry during the Battle at Beverly Ford. Custer asked Pleasonton for command of a cavalry regiment. Pleasonton responded by recommending three captains—Custer, Wesley Merritt, and Elon Farnsworth—for appointment to the brevet rank of brigadier general. Thus, Custer became a brevet brigadier general of the volunteers on June 29, 1863, at the age of twenty-three.[22] It should be noted that an officer could receive a promotion attributable to either the U.S. Volunteers or the regular U.S. Army. A promotion could be a brevet promotion (which was not a permanent rank)[23] for gallant and meritorious services, or a promotion to a permanent rank in either the volunteer or the regular army.

Custer was promoted directly from the rank of captain, bypassing the intervening ranks of major, lieutenant colonel, and colonel. This event occurred again in September of 1906, when President Theodore Roosevelt promoted John Joseph Pershing from captain to brigadier general, jumping him over 862 regular U.S. Army officers who were senior in either rank or point of time.[24] While this seems incredible, Custer's rapid promotion was due partly to merit and partly to a severe shortage of trained officers with leadership aptitude. At that time there were approximately 900,000 officers and enlisted men in the Union army, most of whom served in state volunteer regiments that, with their own officers, reported for duty under command of the federal army. State volunteer regiments could be formed by anyone who chose to form the regiment. Many officers and men of the volunteer units, as well as enlistments in the regular army, lacked prior military experience, knew little about riding, and had never fired a gun. Under these circumstances the Union army was desperate for officers who had any knowledge of military drill and tactics and any penchant for leading troops in battle. Custer, Merritt, and Farnsworth all emanated from the military academy and had demonstrated qualities of leadership and bravery.

Custer was one of the youngest brigadier generals in the Union army. The boy general sported long golden curls, a navy-blue shirt, a red cravat, worn with a soft black felt hat, matched up with high boots and spurs. He was given command of the Second Michigan Volunteer Cavalry Brigade, consisting of the First, Fifth, Sixth, and Seventh Michigan Cavalry Regiments. On July 3, 1863, he received a brevet as major in the regular U.S. Army for gallant and meritorious services at the Battle of Gettysburg, where he demonstrated superior ability in initiating and leading cavalry charges. Custer and his Michigan Cavalry Brigade distinguished themselves in several encounters with the Confederate cavalry, and Custer's reputation continued to grow. His aggressive tactics on the battlefield, often leading sabre charges, were generally successful, resulting in significant victories and the capture of prisoners and equipment.[25]

Custer was promoted to the permanent rank of captain in the Fifth

U.S. Cavalry on May 8, 1864 (after having been promoted to the rank of brevet brigadier general in the U.S. Volunteers on June 29, 1863), and on May 11, 1864, he was breveted to the rank of lieutenant-colonel in the regular U.S. Army for gallant and meritorious services at the battle of Yellow Tavern, Virginia. On September 19, 1864, he was promoted to brevet colonel of the U.S. Army for gallant and meritorious services at the battle of Winchester, Virginia. Shortly thereafter, he was given the brevet commission of major general of the U.S. Volunteers for gallant and meritorious services at the battles of Winchester and Fisher's Hill, Virginia. On March 13, 1865, he was given a brevet brigadier general's commission in the U.S. Army for gallant services at the battle of Five Forks, Virginia. Finally, on March 13, 1865, he was breveted a major general in the U.S. Army for meritorious services during the campaign that ended with the surrender of Lee's insurgent army of Northern Virginia.

In a biographical sketch maintained at West Point, Custer himself summarized his accomplishments during the final six months of the war. He noted that his troopers had captured 111 pieces of field artillery, 65 battle flags, and upwards of 10,000 prisoners of war, including several general officers.[26]

In the spring of 1864, Ulysses S. Grant became general-in-chief of the Union army and achieved a series of crushing victories over the Confederates. Grant sacked General Pleasonton, with whom Custer had formed a strong bond of friendship, and replaced him with Maj. Gen. Philip H. Sheridan, a short, stocky, aggressive leader with whom Custer also developed a strong and permanent connection. Sheridan played a major role in Custer's military career for the balance of his life. Whenever Custer's luck turned sour, he could turn to Phil Sheridan for rescue.

During 1864 and 1865 the Union forces gradually wore down the Confederate army. Custer continued to function as a tactical field commander, fighting well at Cold Harbor and Front Royal. His actions at Winchester in August of 1864, where he made a brilliant attack on the Confederate artillery and infantry, brought him and his Michigan Brigade additional accolades. General Pleasonton called him the best cavalry commander in the world. At this point, as far as tactical maneuvers under oversight of a superior officer were concerned, this was reasonably accurate.

In 1864 Sheridan selected Custer to command the Third Cavalry Division as he reorganized the entire U.S. Cavalry Corps. Custer joined the Third Division at Harrisonburg, Virginia. At Sheridan's direction, the Third Division carried out much of the Union's new slash-and-burn policy in Virginia, similar to what Sherman was undertaking in Georgia and North and South Carolina. Custer's first action at Tom's Brook, later dubbed the "Woodstock Races," was highly successful, routing the Confederates and pushing them back while taking prisoners and equipment.[27] Additional distinction was obtained in the Shenandoah Valley campaign in October of 1864, where Custer's aggressive leadership of the Third Division stopped the Confederate advance. The Union forces were able to turn the tables on the Confederate cavalry, inflicting severe losses that they could not replace. Confederate morale continued to decline during the winter and spring of 1865.

By the end of the Civil War, Custer's record with the army was one of rapid promotion and highly meritorious service. In slightly less than four years, he had risen from a newly commissioned second lieutenant to a brevet major general in command of a volunteer cavalry division when he was but the age of twenty-five. Many Union officers held him in high regard. His first biographer and eulogist, Frederick Whittaker, believed that "there is no spot on his armor."[28] General Sheridan paid him the ultimate tribute when he wrote the following note to Custer's wife, Libbie: "I respectfully present to you the small writing table on which the conditions for the surrender of the Army of Northern Virginia were written by Lt. General Grant—and permit me to say, madam, that there is scarcely an individual in our service who has contributed more to bring about this desirable result than your gallant husband."[29] Custer historian Robert Utley aptly summarized Custer's Civil War record when he stated, "Had Confederate shrapnel struck him dead at Appomattox Station on April 8, 1865, he would be remembered as the great cavalry general that he was, second in the union army only to Sheridan."[30]

But there is a more complicated, foreboding picture of Custer as a military commander that emerges from the Civil War. At times his bravery and tendency for the aggressive charge created problems. While Custer served much of his Civil War career as a brigadier and later as a major general (commanding a brigade and later a division), he seldom operated for any length of time away from the oversight of a superior officer who could restrain or rescue him from the consequences of his impulsive and high-risk behavior. When Custer was out of sight and control of a superior officer, he could get himself and his regiment into trouble. In June of 1863, while acting as adjutant for Gen. Judson Kilpatrick (nicknamed "Kill Cavalry" for his aggressive behavior that led to heavy Union casualties), in a skirmish around a group of farmhouses known as Aldie, Custer's mount (a black horse named Harry) took the bit in his teeth and carried Custer well behind the Confederate lines. At the time Custer's hair was long, and he was wearing oversized boots and a straw hat, rather than traditional military clothing.[31] The Confederates mistook him for one of their own and he was able to school Harry into behaving and race back to the Union lines unscathed. This would not be the last time that Custer was unable to control his horse.

In October of 1863, at the Battle of Buckland Mills, Custer led his cavalry unit into a trap, where they were pinned down and attacked by Confederate infantry. Custer himself escaped but lost his headquarters wagon with a tent and various papers. Part of this predicament was due to his lack of advance reconnaissance.[32]

On June 11, 1864, (then Brig. Gen.) Custer's Michigan Brigade (comprised of the First, Fifth, Sixth, and Seventh Michigan Cavalry regiments) was involved in a major engagement with Maj. Gen. Wade Hampton's Confederates at Trevilian Station in central Virginia. It was one of the largest and bloodiest cavalry battles of the war. Sheridan ordered Custer to guard his left flank and approach Trevilian Station from the east. Custer's brigade flanked the Confederate forces that were opposing Sheridan's approach from the north. Custer's advance scouts discovered a large Confederate concentration of supply wagons moving westward out of Trevilian Station. Without further reconnaissance he sent his Fifth Regiment ahead to seize the supply wagons. The Fifth Michigan's chase was successful, and it captured 1500 horses and 800 prisoners, along with large numbers of supply wagons. Meanwhile, Confederate regiments on the north of the railway tracks reversed course and commenced surrounding not only the Fifth Michigan but Custer's remaining three Michigan regiments on the north side. Simultaneously, Confederate forces under Custer's friend from West Point days, (then Brig.) Gen. Thomas L. Rosser, were closing in from the east, and a large contingent under Maj. Gen. Fitzhugh Lee closed in from the southeast. As they would be at the Little Big Horn on June 25, 1876, Custer's forces were surrounded and taking Confederate fire from all sides. After surrounding Custer, the Confederates reclaimed their wagons and supplies and rescued the Confederate prisoners from Custer's forces. Due to Custer's monumental effort in maneuvering his regiments and battalions, aided by the efforts of other elements of Maj. Gen. Philip Sheridan's corps and a combination of the efforts of other Union forces under the direction of Brig. Gen. David M. Gregg, Custer and the survivors of his Michigan Brigade were extricated from what could have been a complete disaster. Custer's brigade suffered 416 casualties, of which some 300 were captured by the Confederates. Custer had placed his entire brigade at risk and sustained heavy losses. However, his leadership skills and aggressive tactical maneuvers prevented the destruction and capture of his entire brigade.[33]

Much of Custer's praise during the Civil War resulted from his instantaneous reaction to sudden encounters. Instead of seeking safety or considering the security of his command, he favored an immediate attack—a tactic that was often successful in blunting Confederate movement, forcing them to retreat or run for cover. Custer often functioned as a company grade officer, under oversight and support from a superior officer with other Union troops in the vicinity. Thus, the positive results of Custer's aggressive action would be preserved. If Custer's unit was in trouble, he could be rescued in some instances—while in others he could fight his way out.

While rational planning, logistics, and conventional maneuvers were not always critical to Custer's success in the Civil War, they would become issues of absolute necessity on the Great Plains, where the Indians used nontraditional and highly mobile guerrilla tactics, logistics were a major restriction on mobility, there was scant oversight by superior officers, and it was necessary to utilize cavalry for close-in fighting in situations where infantry was better suited. Sound and timely decisions would be required.

There can be no doubt that Custer was actively involved in offensive combat throughout the Civil War, leading sabre charges, blunting Confederate advances, engaging in flanking maneuvers, and pursuing routed Confederates. However, he gained little experience in defensive tactics. Even when surrounded, he would charge and fight his way out rather than stand fast, parry a thrust, or await an attack.

In the decade that followed the Civil War, General Sherman and the armies he commanded on the western frontier were continually looking for experienced and aggressive officers to lead expeditions to punish and subjugate those Plains Indians who continued to hunt buffalo and refused to live on their designated reservations. The army, because of the Indians' inherent mobility, relied heavily on its cavalry regiments to assist in the policing and settlement of the vast western frontier, which extended from New Orleans to the West Coast. To meet this need, Congress passed the Military Peace Establishment Act in 1867, which created four new cavalry regiments that were numbered seven through ten.

The postwar officer corps was composed primarily of West Point graduates and officers who had served with volunteer regiments. A few enlisted men rose up through the ranks to become officers, and an occasional foreign officer was able to obtain a commission. Some effort was made to apportion officers equitably from the states that had supplied the most volunteer regiments during the war.[34]

Custer was mustered out of the volunteer army on February 1, 1866, and reverted to his permanent U.S. Army rank of captain, a rank that would lower his duties to that of a company commander. He was assigned to the Fifth U.S. Cavalry Regiment effective July 28, 1866.[35] Custer wanted to remain in the army, but he had a lucrative offer from the Mexican government to serve as a military advisor. He sought a leave of absence from the army to serve the government of Mexico, but his request was denied. Custer thereafter lobbied hard for a permanent position and an advanced rank in the regular U.S. Army; however, he declined a permanent rank of colonel and command of the all-black Ninth Cavalry Regiment. In August of 1866, with Sheridan's help, Custer was tendered a commission as lieutenant colonel (second in command) of the newly created Seventh Cavalry Regiment that was being organized at Fort Riley, Kansas.[36]

And so in the fall of 1866, Custer and Libbie, together with an entourage of four horses and several hounds, journeyed into the American West, riding the train to Fort Riley, where Custer reported for duty with the Seventh Cavalry—a new command keeping order on the western frontier, an ancient land filled with hunter-gatherers, some of whom had lived there for centuries.

Two officers who served under Custer at the Little Big Horn were

Maj. Marcus A. Reno (the second in command) and Capt. Frederick W. Benteen (the third-ranking officer). Both were decorated and breveted officers from the Civil War. Captain Benteen joined the Seventh Cavalry at Fort Riley in January of 1867, and Major Reno was promoted to the permanent rank of major and assigned to the Seventh Cavalry in December of 1868. Each officer commanded a separate battalion and took an active part in the events that determined the outcome of the battle.

Reno's early life had certain similarities to Custer's. He obtained a political appointment to West Point in the summer of 1851 and, as a fourth-classman in May of 1852, stood thirty-fifth out of his fifty-two classmates. For the next two years he was also in the bottom quarter of his class and drew a sizeable number of demerits. He should have graduated with his class in 1855, but he was suspended for insubordination. Allowed to return and retake his first-class year, Reno was again suspended for disobedience of orders, forcing him to endure a third year as a first-classman. He was able to move his class standing up to number twenty out of thirty-five when he graduated in 1857. Along the way he had little difficulty in finding trouble for himself, particularly while drinking.

On graduation from West Point, Reno served three years in the Northwest, where he had several encounters with Indians and white settlers. During the Civil War he commanded the First U.S. Cavalry Regiment, which fought at Antietam and Crampton's Gap. In March of 1863, at the Rappahannock River (in Virginia), he was recommended for the brevet rank of major. On October 19, 1864, following the battle of Cedar Creek (Virginia), he was breveted a lieutenant colonel for gallant and meritorious services. He assumed command of the Twelfth Pennsylvania Cavalry in December 1864. On March 13, 1865, he was breveted to a full colonel and on the same day, to a brigadier general in the U.S. Volunteers for "gallant and meritorious services during the rebellion." On March 21, 1865, he skirmished with John Mosby's guerillas near Harmony, Virginia.[37]

After the war Reno was assigned to teach infantry tactics at West Point. He disliked teaching so, at his request, he was reassigned to New Orleans as part of the Union occupation forces.

In January of 1889, Reno wrote a lengthy letter to his son Ross that had this to say about his feelings for Custer: "Any stories you might have heard about Custer and me being enemies or having trouble when our paths crossed were untrue. We got along quite well and each of us respected the other's strong points. Such accounts were fabricated, mostly by some officers who did not like Custer and were content to paint me or anyone else as his enemy."[38]

In 1869 Reno was promoted to major in the regular U.S. Army and assigned to the Seventh Cavalry. Among company commanders who served under Reno in the Seventh Cavalry were Thomas B. Weir, a partisan supporter of Custer; Frederick Benteen, who had no use for Custer; and Custer's younger brother Tom, whom Reno liked and respected.

In 1872 Reno was appointed as the cavalry's representative to a select "board for selecting a breech-system for muskets and carbines,"[39] along with officers representing the ordnance, infantry, and artillery departments. This board was chaired by Gen. Alfred H. Terry. A separate board (chaired by Maj. J. G. Benton) was appointed to determine the "proper caliber" for small arms. In January 1773 the Benton board recommended a .45-caliber diameter for all shoulder and handheld arms. Shortly thereafter, following dozens of meetings and endless deliberations, the Terry board recommended the retention of the trap-door breach-loading system designed by master armorer Erskine Allin. Thus, the 1873 Springfield carbine was approved and thereafter used by the Seventh Cavalry in its 1876 campaigns. One author commented that "the Board as a whole acted in gross stupidity."[40] The irony of the board's action is that it deprived the Seventh Cavalry Regiment of a repeating carbine that could be operated with one hand while mounted. To Reno's credit, he did file a minority opinion recommending the "Elliot" system, which contained a 24-round magazine carrier that would have provided Reno's regiment with a much greater rate of fire.[41] While the Elliot system would have provided an increased rate of fire, it might well have exhausted the limited amount of ammunition that each Seventh Cavalry trooper was able to carry on his person or in his saddlebag.

Reno believed that the Little Big Horn battle was a "racial battle." The Indians believed that man could coexist with nature, while whites generally felt that nature existed for their benefit. Thus, the Indian view was not rational in the mind of the *wasicu* (white person). Reno observed:

I am convinced that the Indians, on the whole, tried to avoid confrontation and killing. But when it became apparent that the two civilizations could not exist together, it became a matter of survival. The whites so outnumbered the Indians that there was never a chance for the Indians to win an armed conflict and the Indians knew that well. . . . Once they accepted the inevitable, they had at least two options. One was to fight as long as possible, and if any survived, to accept whatever the white man gave them. The other was to avoid fighting an impossible war and to make the best of a loser's hand. Some chose each option.[42]

Reno also noted that the executive branch of the government turned the resolution of the Indian problem over to the army, specifically to Generals William T. Sherman and Philip H. Sheridan, who set about addressing matters in the army's most efficient way—use of force. Reno lamented, "My own duty as a soldier would be to carry out their orders."[43]

Following the Little Big Horn battle, Reno requested a court of inquiry to review charges of cowardice leveled against him by the press and certain officers. He was absolved by the court and continued to serve honorably as second in command of the Seventh Cavalry. His inability to handle liquor led to numerous incidents in which his unacceptable behavior made him new and lasting enemies. In 1880 he was cashiered by the army and lived the balance of his life in disgrace, finally succumbing in March of 1889 to a painful bout with a cancer located on his tongue. Reno was buried in a pauper's grave in the District of Columbia. On May 31, 1967, as a result of lengthy proceedings by an army board for the correction of military records, Reno was awarded an honorable discharge from the service as a major of the U.S. Army, was restored to his brevet ranks of colonel and brigadier general of the U.S. Volunteers, and his remains were disinterred from the unmarked grave in which he had been buried in 1889. On September 9, 1976, he received a hero's burial at the Custer Battlefield National Cemetery.[44]

Linked forever with Reno after the Little Big Horn battle, Capt. Frederick W. Benteen commanded Company H and was third in command of the Seventh Cavalry during the battle. From the time of their first meeting at Fort Riley in January of 1867 (during which Benteen concluded that Custer was a braggart) until Custer's death in 1876, there was bad blood between the two. Matters did not improve with age. Benteen told others of his low opinion of Custer and disparaged him to his face in front of the officers of the Seventh Cavalry. Benteen's feelings included both lack of respect and an unmitigated dislike of his commanding officer.

Early in 1869 Benteen claimed authorship of an anonymous letter, published after the dawn attack on Chief Black Kettle at the Washita River, asserting that Custer had abandoned Maj. Joel Elliott and eighteen troopers who were missing when Custer ordered his stealthy retreat at sundown on the evening of the massacre. When Custer complained of this letter to the officers of the Seventh Cavalry, Benteen claimed authorship and humiliated Custer by daring him to do anything about it.

Custer often detailed Benteen and his company to undesirable assignments detached from the regiment. At the June 22, 1876, officers' call, three evenings prior to the Little Big Horn battle, Custer raised issues about loyalty among his officers, and Benteen challenged him to name the offenders. Custer refused but felt compelled to say that Benteen was not one of them. These bad feelings between Benteen and Custer set the stage for Custer's subsequent order initiating Benteen's famous scout to the left shortly before the Battle at the Little Big Horn.

Like Reno and Custer, Benteen had a distinguished record in the Civil War. After the war Benteen chose to remain a career U.S. Army officer, but he was discharged in 1866. He requested a permanent commission from the secretary of war and was offered the rank of captain with the newly created Seventh Cavalry Regiment—in which he served until 1882 without promotion.

And so, the military careers of Custer, Reno, and Benteen came together as each was assigned to serve with the Seventh U.S. Cavalry Regiment, which spent much of its duty in the 1860s and 1870s fighting Indians on the central and northern plains.

## Chapter Two
# Custer and the Seventh Cavalry Regiment

*Taking my direction accordingly, I set out on foot, abandoning, of course, my saddle, bridle, etc. I had the pleasant satisfaction of knowing that if I failed to strike the command, I would be at least one hundred miles from any other civilized beings, and would have nothing before me but the almost certain prospect of being picked up by some one or other of the many bands of hostile Indians infesting that region.*

—Lt. Col. George A. Custer, September 9, 1867[1]

On July 28, 1866, President Andrew Johnson signed a law creating four new cavalry regiments, the Seventh through the Tenth. As part of the permanent U.S. Army, the Seventh Cavalry performed much of its service assisting in revising the settlement and occupation of the Great Plains. Emigrant settlers were displacing the Indians. For military activity along the frontier, the army was authorized to hire up to one thousand Indian scouts. In addition to enforcing law and order during the reconstruction of the South, it was the responsibility of the postwar army to police the entire western frontier because, in most areas, state and territorial militia or other local law enforcement were not available. This is how the original author and compiler of the history of the Seventh Cavalry Regiment perceived its "sole duty" on the post-Civil War frontier:

In this inevitable struggle between the aborigines and an advancing civilization, many wrongs were committed by the whites but there were also atrocities committed by the Indians. Irrespective of the merits of any controversy, the sole duty of the Army in this situation was to protect the citizens of the United States who, as immigrants, settled upon Western lands their right to which was guaranteed by the government.[2]

This statement is partially and historically accurate. However, settlers' rights that were protected by President Grant and his army were often in violation of the U.S. Constitution and the terms of treaties approved by Congress.

The frontier army (west) was organized into two geographical divisions—the Division of the Missouri and the Division of the Pacific. The latter had responsibility for all territories on the western slope of the Rocky Mountains, extending west to the Pacific Ocean. The Division of the Missouri included three departments titled Missouri, Platte, and Dakota.[3] Ulysses S. Grant continued to serve as General of the Army and Lt. Gen. William Tecumseh Sherman[4] was placed in command of the Division of the Missouri. From this position Sherman was instrumental in developing government policies for the regulation and control of the Plains Indians, policies that continued for the balance of the nineteenth century. At birth, Sherman's father gave him the name "Tecumseh" out of admiration for the famous Shawnee chief who spent most of his adult life fighting for Indian rights and resisting the cession of Indian lands. When Sherman was five, he was baptized by a Catholic priest who required that he take the name of a saint. Thus "Tecumseh" was moved to the middle and thereafter, Sherman used "William" as his first name. It is ironic that Sherman, who betrayed the Indian treaties that he helped to negotiate and who advocated Indian extermination, carried the name Tecumseh for the balance of his life and responded to the nickname "Cump." The Department of Dakota included Minnesota and land that is now the states of North and South Dakota and Montana.

When Ulysses S. Grant became president in 1869, Sherman was elevated to general in chief of the United States Army. This required him to relinquish his command of the Division of the Missouri headquartered in St. Louis. The new frontier army was molded around the strategies of Sherman, who favored the use of military force to control the Indians and to force them to live on designated reservations. Having served under him during the Civil War, Sherman was well respected by President Grant. By limiting appropriations in the 1870s, Congress reduced the permanent army to 27,000. Statutory numerical limitations were misleading because the army seldom recruited sufficient enlisted men to fill its quota, and infantry and cavalry companies often operated at about 50 percent of their authorized complement. In addition, cavalry regiments operating on the frontier consistently lost up to 20 percent of their en-listed men in any given year through desertion. This robbed the cavalry regiments of trained horsemen and experienced fighters.[5]

In the postwar army, after an officer was assigned to a regiment, his primary opportunity for promotion would be the death, retirement, or reassignment of a senior officer within the regiment. Replacement was by seniority. Occasionally a line officer serving with a regiment would obtain appointment as a staff officer serving under the chief of staff and the secretary of war.

At the end of the Civil War, Custer's annual pay as a brevet major general exceeded eight thousand dollars. Ten years later his salary as a lieutenant colonel of the Seventh Cavalry Regiment was less than three thousand dollars per year. In the postwar army, officers were not promot-ed on experience, examination, or merit. There was an overabundance of officers, many of whom, by reason of their age and physical infirmities, were physically incapable of vigorous activity in the field, particularly on the frontier, where long, strenuous field campaigns in rain, snow, sleet, and hail were involved. There was competition and bickering among the officer corps. Complaints and court-martials were frequent. Much of an officer's time was spent serving on court-martial boards, few of which produced anything beneficial for the operation of the army.[6]

Custer reported for duty with the Seventh Cavalry on November 3, 1866, and served as its lieutenant colonel for the balance of his life. The regiment's first commanding officer was Col. Andrew Jackson Smith, a seasoned veteran with prior service on the plains and in the Civil War. Smith did not concern himself with details and left much of the regimen-tal management to Custer. Under U.S. Army regulations at that time, as second in command, Custer had no specified duties other than to assist the regimental commanding officer, who was a full colonel.[7] Among oth-er things, Custer had to train green troops, a task he disliked.[8]

Life was not easy for enlisted men. The pay was penurious. A private received thirteen dollars a month, corporals fifteen, ordinary sergeants seventeen, and a first sergeant twenty-two.[9] To compound their meager pay, enlisted men had to purchase additional food and other necessaries from sutlers and traders out of their own pockets at inflated prices.

In the field an individual trooper had to endure long rides, look for-ward to caring for his horse at the end of each ride, and take his turn at guard duty. On longer expeditions, unless wagons or sufficient pack mules were available, each trooper had to carry part of his own food, grain for his horse, and if the commanding officer permitted, a small canvas tarpaulin for protection from the elements. In rain and snow the enlisted men often slept on the ground in the open with virtually no protection.

While campaigning in the field, the trooper's basic diet consisted of varying amounts of salt pork, hardtack, sugar, and coffee. The recipe for hardtack required but two ingredients—flour and water. A little salt could be added if available. Sometimes the rations were short and were infested with worms, rodent pellets, and other deleterious matter. Troopers on the trail were underfed and malnourished. From time to time scurvy appeared. On occasions when they ran out of meat and game was not available, it was necessary to butcher and eat their own horses and mules.[10]

The enlisted man complained that he was given so many common duties unrelated to training and fighting that he spent little time as a soldier. Among their chores enlisted men were required to build quarters, stables, storehouses, bridges, roads, and telegraph lines. They cut and carried logs, made lumber, worked in stone quarries, and made adobe and bricks. They burned lime, performed masonry chores, plastered, and did carpentering tasks. Some worked as blacksmiths, while others had to perform field tasks such as chopping wood and putting up hay. They also had their customary guard duty; care of their horses, arms, and equipment; cooking and baking; policing the quarters and grounds; and moving stores, all in addition to performing the ordinary drills that were expected of troopers and infantrymen.[11] To save money, gardening, farming, and animal husbandry were introduced at certain frontier stations, with adverse reactions from the enlisted men who were ordered to perform these chores. Pvt. Augustus Meyers, of German lineage, balked when he was ordered to take care of a sow and her farrow. He told his sergeant: "To hell mit der piggins, I'm no swiney doctor."[12]

Frontier soldiers seldom had decent quarters. They lived in places that were hot and fly infested in the summer and cold in the winter. A trooper shared his bunk with another soldier who was known as his "bunkie." General-issue clothing was often too hot in the summer and provided insufficient protection from the cold, rain, and persistent wind that prevailed on the high plains. Shoes were made of poor leather, and burlap was commonly used to protect the feet. To supplement their inadequate clothing, soldiers had to use their meager salary to purchase other items of nontraditional clothing that, in some regiments (including the Seventh Cavalry), were permitted. Soldiers were issued rubber ground cloths to sleep on while out in the field.[13] Toilet and latrine facilities were primitive, and bathing facilities were nonexistent.

Boredom was always a problem. There was little to do with spare time except to drink (when booze was available), gamble (if you had any money left), read (if reading material was available), write home, or visit a nearby town or encampment in search of a little excitement.

Discipline was a significant problem in the enlisted ranks. Company officers would disregard bullying by corporals and sergeants. Troopers were hung by their wrists, arms, or thumbs, whipped, paraded until exhausted while carrying a heavy load, confined to a sweat box, dunked in a stream, in addition to being beaten up with fists or struck with hard objects. A private had little or no means to protect himself from a bully who had tied the can to his tail. Bullying was not limited to noncommissioned officers. Certain officers, including Custer, also developed reputations for excessive punishment.[14]

Between October 1, 1866, and October 1, 1867, more than 500 troopers deserted the Seventh Cavalry. In the year 1867 alone, 1400 men deserted from the U.S. Army, and between 1867 and 1891, one-third of all army recruits deserted. Deserters were flogged. When flogging was banned, they were branded on the right hip. In some regiments they were subjected to thumb hooks, leg irons, horizontal crucifixion, and other cruel and unusual punishments.

Compounding Custer's problems were his junior officers. Some were older than he and had gold-braid brevet ranks from the Civil War. Several disliked Custer with varying degrees of severity. Among his early detractors were Maj. Wycliffe Cooper, a brevet brigadier general[15] who drank heavily and subsequently committed suicide in the summer of 1867 while serving under Custer in the field; Capt. Robert M. West, a brevet brigadier general who brought charges for which Custer was court-martialed in 1867; and Capt. Frederick Benteen, a breveted colonel in the Civil War who harbored strong animosity and a lack of respect for Custer that he carried to his grave. Benteen had no compunctions about challenging Custer behind his back and to his face, nor did he refrain from embarrassing him in front of his own troopers.[16]

Custer could count on support from several officers, including Capt. George Yates; his brother, Capt. Tom Custer; Capt. Louis Hamilton; Capt. Myles Keogh (who drank frequently and heavily); Myles Moylan, who advanced from the enlisted ranks with Custer's help; and Custer's adjutant, 1st Lt. William W. Cooke, another "mustang" (from the enlisted ranks) who wore heavy sideburns and served as Custer's adjutant.[17] On both sides of the issue was the heavy-drinking captain of Company D, Thomas B. Weir, to whom Libbie Custer paid undue attention. Custer criticized Libbie for her judgment and had a raging confrontation with Weir in 1867. By the 1870s Weir was overtly supportive of Custer.[18] The friction among the regimental officers was disquieting to Custer, Libbie, and the regiment's troopers.[19]

The officers came from diverse backgrounds, which may have caused increased friction. Some were volunteers, some came up through the ranks, others originated in the military academy, a few were Custer's relatives, and a handful were amateur officers from civilian life. Capt. William Thompson was a former congressman from Iowa who had served with Custer in Texas. Capt. Louis Hamilton was the grandson of Alexander Hamilton. Lieutenants Henry Jackson and Henry J. Nowlan had served in the British army, while Captain Moylan had served with the Pope's forces in Italy. Lieutenant Cooke was from Canada, and Lt. Edward G. Mathey hailed from France. Lt. Donald McIntosh was half-Scotch and half-Indian. Clearly, Custer lacked unified loyalty and friendship among his officers.

Custer, only two months shy of twenty-seven and never having served significant time at a company rank in the Civil War, found it difficult to administer discipline. "Things are becoming very unpleasant here," Capt. Albert Barnitz wrote to his wife Jennie from Fort Hays on May 15, 1867. "General Custer is very injudicious in his administration, and spares no effort to render himself generally obnoxious. I have utterly lost all the little confidence I ever had in his ability as an officer—and all the admiration for his character, as a man, and to speak the plain truth I am thoroughly *disgusted* with him."[20] Two days later Custer administered a half-shave to the scalps of six enlisted men who went to a sutler's post to purchase canned fruit without a pass from camp. The miscreants were then paraded about the camp, to the "disgust of all right-minded officers and men in camp."[21]

Custer not only needed to learn how to command the troopers of the Seventh Cavalry, but he had to learn, by trial and error, how to fight Indians. Unfortunately, the tactics that were successful during the Civil War seldom worked in opposing the mobile hit-and-run and the decoy-and-ambush tactics utilized by Plains Indians. In addition Custer was rarely involved in a defensive stand against rebel troops—thus he had little experience with essential defensive tactics.

There were at least three critical factors in plains warfare that were not encountered by Custer during the Civil War. The first was the problem of extended supply lines to reach the vast and distant plains where the Indians were located. During the 1860s and 1870s, it was difficult to extend a plains expedition into areas where the railroad had not been constructed and steamships could not travel. The rough terrain, severe weather conditions, and the inability of the army to live off the land made military expeditions, encumbered by supply wagons and pack mules, a slow-moving, labor-intensive, and clumsy venture. On an extended march when grass was not available it was difficult for the pack mule to carry sufficient grain to feed itself—let alone the troopers and their mounts.[22]

Second, while Custer served much of his Civil War career as a brevet brigadier and later as a major general (commanding a brigade and later a division), he seldom operated for any length of time away from the oversight of a superior officer who could restrain or rescue him from the consequences of his impulsive and high-risk behavior. When Custer was out of sight and control of a superior officer, he could get himself and his regiment into trouble. Prior to Robert E. Lee's surrender at Appomattox, Custer displayed an amazing ability to extricate himself from these predicaments. It was not all luck. His instincts during the Civil War had served him well.

Finally, the Indians had greater mobility and more area in which to maneuver than the Confederate Army. While the cavalry lacked adequate weapons for effective offensive operations and was ill equipped to defend itself while mounted, it was the only branch of the army that had sufficient mobility to pursue and bring the mounted Plains Indians to battle. However, the Indian pony, with a lighter load to carry, was generally able to outrun and outmaneuver the cavalry mounts.[23]

Custer was hampered from the start by inherent limitations in the weaponry of his cavalry troops. At the Little Big Horn each trooper was armed with a .45-caliber Model 1873 Springfield single-shot carbine and a .45-caliber Colt revolver. The traditional sabre was of little use in combat with Plains Indians and was not carried by Custer's troopers at the Little Big Horn. Unfortunately, many recruits were poorly trained to shoot and ride at the same time, and some were unable to control their mounts during a charge. One month before the regiment departed from Fort Lincoln in May of 1876 for the summer campaign against the "hostiles," the regiment received 125 untrained recruits. A sergeant from A Company testified after the Little Big Horn battle that some of the men in his company were unfit to take into action, that "it is very seldom that you can ever find so many poor horsemen as we had," and that "they were not well enough drilled in horsemanship."[24]

In the spring of 1867, Custer experienced his first independent command involving direct combat with Plains Indians. Until March he had been living with Libbie at Fort Riley, Kansas. At the direction of Gen. William T. Sherman, Gen. Winfield Scott Hancock, commanding the Department of the Missouri, headed west through Kansas with a force that included Custer and elements of the Seventh Cavalry. They were ordered to pursue a "get tough" policy with the Indians, notably the Cheyennes and Lakotas, who were resisting the western movement of white settlers through their hunting grounds.[25]

In April of 1867, General Hancock encountered and initiated a brief parley with a mixed band of Cheyennes and Lakotas west of Fort Larned in west-central Kansas. Fearing another Sand Creek massacre, the Indians deserted their camp under cover of darkness before Hancock and his troops arrived and Custer was ordered out in pursuit.[26] While the Indians were evading Custer, Hancock burned their camp and all of their possessions,[27] an act that not only violated the due process rights of these Indians but increased the tension between the army and those Cheyenne Indians who survived the Sand Creek Massacre.

Custer's chase was frustrating, tiring, and totally unsuccessful. While leading his battalion in pursuit of the Indians, Custer rode off ahead with one attendant and six hounds to chase antelope. After several miles of futile antelope chasing, having left his attendant far behind, Custer spotted his first buffalo. Impulsively, he and his dogs set off in hot pursuit, chasing it for three miles before Custer attempted to shoot it with his Savage revolver. Instead of hitting the buffalo, Custer shot his mount between the ears, killing Libbie's favorite stallion in its tracks and launching Custer to the ground. He was alone and afoot on the prairie, out of the sight and knowledge of his battalion and confronted by an angry buffalo. While he was alone, lost, and in dangerous circumstances, his luck held. The buffalo "moved off," and Custer was located and rescued by more responsible troopers of his regiment.

Unchastened and unabashed, Custer made light of his situation in an article that he authored for a magazine:

> Taking my direction accordingly, I set out on foot, abandoning, of course, my saddle, bridle, etc. I had the pleasant satisfaction of knowing that if I failed to strike the command, I would be at least one hundred miles from any other civilized beings, and would have nothing before me but the almost certain prospect of being picked up by some one or other of the many bands of hostile Indians infesting that region. This consideration undoubtedly did not check my speed. After a walk of over two miles, I saw the dust of the cavalry moving toward me. Sitting down, I passed the time, until their arrival, in considering the uncertainty of all human calculations.[28]

Historian Brian W. Dippie noted:

> Custer had ample cause for sober reflection, not only because of his predicament—unhorsed, alone, and potentially lost in hostile Indian country—but also because of the whole course of action that had landed him there. . . . But his superiors might not be so understanding, especially if they knew the full particulars. At the outset of the expedition, General Hancock had issued a strict injunction against "straggling" and the discharging of firearms "without authority." . . . But he [Custer] was supposed to be pursuing Indians, and, while he had all but abandoned the chase the previous evening, his reports to superiors concealed that fact and instead gave the distinct impression that his command had pressed on after the foe and put in an arduous day marching and countermarching.[29]

As Dippie noted, Custer's behavior placed both himself and his regiment in jeopardy.[30] Custer was off on his own on an ill-considered chase, out of the sight and control of General Hancock. His behavior was not that of a responsible officer commanding troops in the field—he was attempting to shoot a buffalo for his own amusement. The irony of the situation is the fact that Custer had no prospect of killing the 1500-pound buffalo with a pistol bullet less than one inch in length and three-eighths of an inch in diameter—unless he happened to hit its brain or damage its spine. The bullet, if it pierced the hide, would have caused suffering but would not have been sufficient to bring the animal down. If he had succeeded in bringing it down alone in an isolated location, he would not have been able to salvage anything of value from its pitiful carcass.

Any experienced cavalry officer who makes frequent use of his horse in combat will see to it that it is well trained to respond to his commands so that he will not endanger his life—and the lives of his troopers—with a horse that he is unable to control. This incident in which Custer accidentally shot his own mount was due (in his own description of the incident) to a sudden and unexpected movement by his horse. This was the third time in seven years that Custer had placed his life, and the lives of others in his proximity, in needless danger as a result of his inability to control his horse. The first was when "Harry" ran wild with Custer, carrying him well behind the Confederate front line in full view of Rebel troops. The second was during a victory parade on May 23, 1865, before President Johnson and a huge crowd. Passing a reviewing stand in front of the White House, while riding with the Army of the Potomac, in full parade regalia, Custer, with a "fair and ruddy complexion—a sunrise of golden hair which ripples upon his blue shoulders," with an evergreen wreath on his left arm and wearing white gauntlets and a red kerchief, reached for a wreath tossed his way by an "overwrought woman." His horse ran away with him while his hat blew off and his long golden locks streamed behind him.[31] Careless use of a poorly trained horse endangered Custer's life in each of the three incidents.

On May 3, 1867, Custer and his regiment returned to Fort Hays in northwest Kansas for resupply, having encountered no Indians. Adequate supplies were not available, so his men and horses languished for a month at the fort, during which time Custer brought Libbie out from Fort Riley to be with him. On June 1 General Hancock ordered out Custer and six companies of the Seventh Cavalry on a search-and-punish mission. Cutting corners, Custer spent an extra day with Libbie and then raced out to join his battalion, which had left a day earlier.[32] After leaving Fort Hays, Custer's companies rode 160 miles northwest to Fort McPherson in southwest Nebraska.[33]

This mission was both strenuous and frustrating, and it tested the mettle of Custer's men and horses. On June 8 Custer's number-two officer, Maj. Wycliffe Cooper, committed suicide in his tent with his pistol while the officers were at evening mess. Custer stated that Cooper was "another of rum's victims."[34] The life of Custer's troopers on the frontier was hard and discouraging.[35] Troopers were deserting the Seventh Cavalry on a daily basis.[36] Custer increased disciplinary punishment, and troopers continued going over the hill. He sent a squad of officers and men to run down a group of fifteen deserters with instructions to shoot them "where you find them."[37] Five deserters, including three with wounds, were captured, and Custer allegedly denied two of them medical treatment.[38]

At Fort McPherson Custer met with General Sherman on June 17. Sherman gave him orders to scour the Republican Valley for Indians and then report to Fort Sedgwick in Colorado for resupply and more orders. Fort Sedgwick was one hundred miles west and slightly south of Fort McPherson. Leaving Fort McPherson, Custer's search wandered in all directions of the compass, covering over 500 miles in a fruitless quest for Lakotas and Cheyennes. His regiment rode in a semicircle around the west, south, and east sides of Fort Sedgwick but never came within forty miles of it. By keeping his distance from Fort Sedgwick, he avoided direct contact and the receipt of new orders from Sherman. Custer displayed both his lack of respect for orders and his own self-centered immaturity when he told Libbie in a letter dated June 17, "I am on a roving commission, going nowhere in particular, but where I please."[39] This letter was written before Custer left Fort McPherson under Sherman's orders to search for Indians between the South Platte and the forks of the Republican rivers—a specific area that Custer interpreted to mean "anywhere he pleased."

Custer was missing Libbie. He had the urge to have her join him in the field.[40] She had "flung another craving" on him. His subsequent actions were heavily oriented toward reunion. He wrote and told her to join him at Fort Wallace, which was more than 250 miles west of Fort Riley and 135 miles southeast of Fort Sedgwick.

Instead of resupplying at Fort Sedgwick in northeastern Colorado (in proximity to Fort Sidney and the migration trails), as ordered by General Sherman, Custer sent his supply wagons and two of his companies 150 miles south to Fort Wallace for supplies, with orders to return with Libbie. Fort Sedgwick (where Sherman directed) was supplied directly from the main line of the Union Pacific Railroad, while supplies at Fort Wallace (where Custer expected Libbie to be) had to be hauled by wagons traveling from Fort Harker located 200 miles to the east. Custer's travels made no sense to General Sherman.[41] Keeping his distance from Fort Sedgwick and Sherman, Custer dispatched his second in command, Maj. Joel Elliott, back to Fort Sedgwick to inquire for his orders from Sherman. Thus, Custer avoided direct contact with his commanding officer while he was traveling "where he pleased" on the desolate prairie of northeastern Colorado.

However, Custer's supply train was somehow able to find Indians They had to run a perilous gauntlet as they rumbled to Fort Wallace and returned with supplies. The supply train returned to Custer at the Republican River on June 27. To Custer's disappointment, Libbie was not with them. Seeking Libby, Custer headed due south, straight back to Fort Wallace, from which his supply train had just made a 260-mile round trip.[42]

Custer reached Fort Wallace on July 13, thus ending the 700-mile expedition (sixteen miles per day) that had commenced at Fort Hays on June 1. En route to Fort Wallace, Custer was rejoined by Major Elliott, returning from Fort Sedgwick, from which he had departed one day prior to the arrival of Custer's orders from Sherman. Custer, in turn, was riding around the barren hills of the Republican Valley out of control. He was also avoiding the settlers' trails along the Smokey Hill and Platte River routes where Indians were actively raiding.

Sherman was attempting to get a handle on him. When Custer failed to show at Sedgwick, new orders from Sherman were dispatched to him with Lt. Lyman Kidder and ten troopers of the Second Cavalry. When Sherman returned to St. Louis, he was informed that Custer was attempting to locate the Indians on the Republican River and was replenishing his supplies at Fort Wallace instead of reporting to Fort Sedgwick as Sherman had ordered. Sherman sent the following order to Custer through Col. Henry Litchfield, Gen. Christopher Augur's chief of staff in Omaha, stating:

I don't understand about General Custer being on the Republican awaiting provisions from Fort Wallace. If this be so and all the Indians be gone south, convey to him my orders that he proceed with all his command in search of the Indians toward Fort Wallace and report to General Hancock, who will leave Denver for same place today.[43]

Oglala war leader Pawnee Killer and his war party had discovered and killed Lieutenant Kidder and his squad of ten, whose naked and mutilated bodies were discovered by Custer en route to Fort Wallace.[44] Custer was not only wearing down his men and horses, but his actions were responsible for the loss of Kidder and his men. Not even the battle-hardened William Tecumseh Sherman could control him.

At Fort Wallace Custer received a letter from Libbie, then in Fort Riley, Kansas, stating that cholera had reared its dreadful head.[45] His impulses taking control, Custer, without orders, set out for Fort Riley, 300 miles to the east, with six dozen troopers mounted on seventy-five of the best of the regiment's jaded horses. He was one jump ahead of General Hancock with fresh orders from Sherman. While en route, several horses, including a spare mare of Custer's, strayed from his battalion. Custer sent a patrol of seven troopers to find them, while he continued moving east. Two of the search party were shot by Indians and later found by soldiers from a nearby mail station, one dead and one wounded. Custer moved on, abandoning five of them to their fate. Twenty of his escort party deserted.[46] While Custer had ordered deserting troopers to be shot "on sight," he had no reluctance to desert his entire regiment while it was campaigning in the field. Ordering the shooting of troopers without a trial constituted a serious violation of their Fifth Amendment due process rights.

When Custer did not find Libbie at Fort Hays, he rode eastward another seventy miles and arrived at Fort Harker in the middle of the night. There he awakened his superior officer, Col. Andrew J. Smith, and told him that he was continuing on east to Fort Riley. Boarding the night train and reaching Fort Riley, Custer had a joyous one-day reunion with Libbie. However, when Colonel Smith awoke the next morning and gathered his wits about him, he ordered Custer arrested, charging him with "absence without leave from his command and conduct to the prejudice of good order and military discipline,"[47] pursuant to the 1863 Articles of War. *The 1865 Customs of Service for Officers of the Army* points out that punishment should not only intimidate the offender but should be administered with a view to reform him.[48]

Custer's actions reflect heavily on a primary issue—his fitness for command. When off on his own, out of sight and verbal control, he could be so irrational and self-centered that he became a danger to his troops. His actions had no relationship to his mission—his sense of duty and purpose had vanished. Would he possibly learn from experience and improve—as he had done with his drinking? History would tell.

On orders from Gen. Ulysses S. Grant, Custer was tried by a court-martial board consisting of officers who were currently serving under Gen. Philip Sheridan. On October 11, 1867, Custer was found guilty of all three charges and all seven specifications (as modified by the court). Among the specifications were abandoning his regiment without leave, overworking and damaging his horses, misuse of government property, failure to take measures to protect a small search party, ordering deserters to be shot without trial, denial of medical treatment for troopers who were wounded pursuant to his orders, and the murder of trooper Charles Johnson without a trial. He was suspended from rank and command and ordered to forfeit all pay for one year. On November 18, 1867, General Grant approved the findings of guilt and the sentence, noting that the sentence was lenient. With no hard time or discharge from service, Custer was free to go where he chose and do whatever he pleased. He would be restored to duty at full pay and rank after one year. His sentence made a mockery of the U.S. Army and those who sat in his judgment at the court-martial. On November 19, 1867, Sheridan wrote to Custer, "I presume the court made everything right for you from what I have heard from some of the members—If not I feel certain that General Grant will."

Custer historian Lawrence Frost wrote, "It would appear that some of the members of the Court were 'polishing the apple,' for Major General Sheridan was the superior of every member of the Court. Custer was his favorite, and it wouldn't do to appear in Sheridan's eyes as one who went out of the way to prosecute his protégé."[49]

After the sentence was imposed, Sheridan offered Custer and Libbie the use of his personal quarters at Fort Leavenworth. Custer received his sentence on November 25, 1867. He took Sheridan up on his offer, living in Sheridan's quarters until he and Libbie returned to Michigan in September of 1868. In his autobiographical book about his experiences with the Seventh Cavalry and the Indians of the southern plains, Custer referred to his comfortable quarters at Fort Leavenworth in "the winter of 1867–68" but neglected to mention that he was able to languish in Sheridan's comfortable quarters because of his court-martial and the sentence relieving him from active duty for one year.[50]

Custer's next experience in leading the Seventh Cavalry revealed inadequacies in his aptitude for command that would hinder his performance during the balance of his military career. In the fall of 1868, General Sheridan sought an aggressive field commander to punish the Indians who were raiding in Indian territory. While Custer was serving the balance of his sentence in Michigan, Sheridan arranged to have him reinstated and report to Fort Hays to lead an expedition in the southern plains.[51] Sheridan's carriage met Custer at Fort Leavenworth and conveyed him to Fort Hays, where Sheridan awaited.[52] Sheridan was planning a punitive winter campaign on the southern plains, where he believed the Indians (primarily young Cheyenne dog soldiers and Sutaio warriors) had been raiding, stealing, and getting out of hand. Sherman and Sheridan were impatient with and frustrated by the inability of the Indian bureau and a congressional peace committee to put an end to Indian depredations in Texas and Indian territory. Present in the area were Indians from various tribes, including Cheyennes, Arapahos, Kiowa-Apaches, Comanches, Kiowas, Kaws, and Osages. Sheridan wanted to attack Indian villages (on an indiscriminate basis) when the snow was heavy and their ponies were weak from lack of grass. He believed that Custer had the unique ability to lead a campaign in the brutal winter weather that was certain to make life difficult for trooper and Indian alike.

Custer was ordered to join the Seventh Cavalry at Fort Dodge, Kansas, obtain supplies, assemble a wagon train and establish a supply camp ("Camp Supply") 200 miles south of Fort Dodge on the south side of the Canadian River in Indian territory. Custer immediately started training his regiment for a winter expedition and selected some of its best marksmen to form a group of forty "sharpshooters." He hired several white and Osage scouts. Among the white scouts (who were paid one hundred dollars a month) were Ben Clark, an intelligent and experienced frontiersman who was highly respected for his ability and judgment, and Moses Milner ("California Joe"), a favorite of Custer who proceeded to lose his title as chief of scouts when he got drunk the night before the expedition commenced.[53]

One of the objects of the punitive expedition was the Southern Cheyennes, who remained enraged by the cowardly and brutal attack of Col. John Chivington and his Colorado militia at Sand Creek, Colorado, in 1864. Additional animosity was generated by the outrageous actions of Gen. Winfield Scott Hancock when he burned the Cheyenne and Oglala villages at Pawnee Fork on April 19, 1867. Historian William Chalfant noted, "But his [General Hancock's] flawed and arrogant reasoning failed to take into account the character of his targeted enemy. The Cheyennes were good and honest people who loved their country and way of life every bit as much as Hancock loved his."[54]

Following his escape from the Sand Creek Massacre, Southern Cheyenne peace chief Black Kettle continued to advocate peace, but he lacked influence and authority among young Cheyenne dog soldiers. Reassembled in Indian territory, Black Kettle and his small band were participating in a "peace council" organized by Indian Agent Edward W. Wynkoop, who was doing everything that he could to maintain peace among the Indians, the settlers, and the U.S. Army. Agent Wynkoop also negotiated with some peaceful Cheyenne chiefs to turn over the perpetrators of an attack on Maj. George Forsythe at the Republican River in Colorado. While Wynkoop was distributing rations and making peace with the Indians, Sheridan (at another location) was organizing his unconstitutional punitive expedition against them. Sherman and Sheridan were determined to punish all Indians on the southern plains (whether peaceful or hostile) and force them to remain permanently within the boundaries of their relatively new reservations.[55]

Both Sherman and Sheridan had little sympathy for Wynkoop's strenuous efforts to differentiate the peaceful from the vengeful culprits. Due process be damned! Sheridan believed in both corporal and company punishment for all Indians. He wanted to make a coordinated attack, with multiple columns converging from different points where the Indians could be located.[56] According to Sherman's strategy, "there would be 'no terms with the hostile Indians except unconditional surrender.'" The objective of the operation was "to strike the Indians a hard blow and force them on to the reservations set apart for them [by the Medicine Lodge Treaty of 1868], and if this could not be accomplished to show to the Indian that the winter season would not give him rest, and that he and his villages and stock could be destroyed; that he would have no security, winter or summer, except in obeying the laws of peace and humanity."[57] Sherman was consistent. He believed in genocide to subdue the Cheyennes, Arapahos, and Lakotas, whenever and wherever they could be found.

Custer set out from Camp Supply in brutally cold and snowy weather on November 26, 1868, to initiate an attack against any Indians whom he could locate, wherever he might find them. Each of his troopers was armed with a sabre, a .50-caliber Model 1865 Spencer seven-shot repeating carbine, and a .44-caliber Colt revolver. The troopers wore leggings and lined their boots and clothing with blankets; some wore buffalo skin overshoes and mittens—mittens that could hamper their ability to aim, fire, and reload their carbines and revolvers.

On November 20 Black Kettle and a delegation of Cheyenne and Arapaho chiefs had ridden to Fort Cobb (120 miles southeast of Camp Supply) to proclaim their peaceful intentions and discuss their concerns with Col. William B. Hazen, who had been designated by General Sherman to oversee Indian affairs in the southern plains. Black Kettle's camp was located on the south bank of the Washita River about sixty-five miles south of Camp Supply and eighty miles northwest of Fort Cobb. These peaceful Cheyennes were concerned that actions by their dog soldiers and other warriors in the summer of 1868 would bring forth military retaliation against all of them. Black Kettle's Cheyenne followers and Big Mouth's Arapaho warriors wanted Hazen to know that they favored peace and intended to avoid any encounter with the military. They asked for sanctuary at Fort Cobb. Hazen told Black Kettle and Big Mouth that he was not able to make peace with them, that they could not remain at Fort Cobb, that he had no control over Sheridan, who was bent on fighting the Cheyennes and Arapahos, and that it was their responsibility to attempt to make peace directly with Sheridan. They were told that their presence at Fort Cobb would cause trouble for friendly Kiowas and Comanches. Too bad for Black Kettle—Sheridan's unlawful strike force was already launched.[58]

Instead of being allowed to surrender peacefully, Black Kettle and the other peace chiefs headed back to their villages and their uncertain fate on the twenty-first and twenty-second of November. They reached their villages late on the evening of the twenty-sixth, concerned and confused about what course of conduct to pursue.[59]

Every Cheyenne winter camp required four elements—fresh water, shelter from the wind, firewood, and forage for their ponies. Food was either stored or obtained from current buffalo hunts. Black Kettle's village of fifty lodges was located on a stretch of level ground on the south bank of the Washita River, a creek little more than nine to twelve feet wide. The ground was heavily timbered on both banks, and there was a fifty-foot embankment located about one hundred yards to the south of the village. That evening, Black Kettle had assembled certain leaders in his lodge to discuss their concerns over the denial of sanctuary by Colonel Hazen at Fort Cobb and their knowledge that General Sheridan had troops in the field who were apt to attack them.[60]

Despite the fact that a small party of Kiowa warriors had warned them of Custer's trail in their vicinity, the Cheyennes in Black Kettle's village failed to mount a reliable night watch. It was easy for Custer's troopers to follow the trail to their camp and surround them during the night without detection. With no advance reconnaissance Custer was not aware that six or seven larger Cheyenne, Kiowa, and Arapaho villages were also located along the Washita a few miles east of Black Kettle's camp.[61]

Custer's strike force consisted of eleven companies of the Seventh Cavalry. There were fifty-one lodges containing 250 Indians in Black Kettle's camp. The Medicine Lodge Treaty of 1868 gave Black Kettle and his followers the right to camp and hunt at this location.

Black Kettle and his small band were fearful of reprisal. Their fears were well founded because on November 27, Custer, with his 750 troopers (an independent tactical combat unit), attacked Black Kettle's camp at dawn. Prior to the attack Custer did not know who was in the camp, which tribe was involved, or whether the camp contained any wrongdoers. All he knew was that they were Indians, and he was going to use his 750 troopers to murder some, capture the rest, burn their tepees and food, and slaughter or take possession of all the Indians' ponies. Twelve to eighteen inches of snow covered the ground, and the temperature was frigid. Surrounding the Indian village, Custer's men opened fire on the sleeping occupants at first light. To enhance Custer's notion of drama, as his troopers commenced their premeditated murder of Black Kettle and his Cheyenne campers, the regimental band played their frozen instruments, rattling out the strains of the regimental battle song, which ended with the phrase, "Of Garryowen in Glory."[62] There was little glory in the work of the Seventh Cavalry on November 27, 1868.

It was a single coordinated attack with Custer in control of all components of his detachment. Under his direction warriors, women, and children were killed and wounded.[63] When Black Kettle's daughter raised her hands to surrender, Sgt. E. F. Clear shot and killed her with his pistol.[64] Custer took fifty-three women and children captive and proceeded to loot and then burn the village, destroying food, clothing, shelter, and whatever else the Indians possessed.[65] He then proceeded methodically to slaughter 650 of the Indians' ponies by cutting their throats or shooting them, leaving them to die and rot where they fell.[66] Black Kettle and his wife were shot in the opening minutes, and their inert bodies were left in the shallow waters of the Washita. What had Black Kettle, his wife, and his daughter done to deserve such despicable and horrible deaths at the hands of the U.S. Army?

The troopers' lust for killing Black Kettle's sleeping Cheyennes is vividly described by 2nd Lt. Francis M. Gibson of Company A, who was an eyewitness:

And now we listened intently for the signal notes of "Garry Owen," our charging call, and the death march as well of many a comrade and friend. At last the inspiring strains of this rollicking tune broke forth, filing the early morning air with joyous music. The profound silence that had reigned through the night was suddenly changed to a pandemonium of tumult and excitement; the wild notes of "Garry Owen," which had resounded from hill to hill were answered by wilder shouts of exultation from the charging columns. On rushed these charging cavalcades from all directions, a mass of Uncle Sam's cavalrymen *thirsting for glory*, and feeling the flush of coming victory at every bound, and in their impetuous eagerness, spurring their steeds to still greater effort, and giving voice to their long pent up emotions. There was no hope of escape for the surrounded savages. Their pony herd had been effactually cut off, and their slumbering village entered from all sides before they had time to realize the extent of their peril; but they fought with courage and desperation (emphasis supplied).[67]

How does one properly describe a U.S. Army officer like Custer, who arranges to have a band play "inspiring strains of a rollicking tune" as he orders his officers and men to commence a genocidal attack upon innocent persons, murdering helpless men, women, and children, destroying their food and shelter, slaughtering their ponies, and thereafter taking the freedom from female prisoners, who are forced to serve as concubines for his officers? Is this officer fit to command a cavalry regiment of the United States Army?

Lieber Code Order No. 44 provided, "All wanton violence committed against persons in the invaded country . . . all robbery, pillage or sacking . . . all wounding, maiming or killing of such inhabitants, are prohibited under penalty of death or such other severe punishment as may seem adequate for the gravity of the offense."

Order No. 68 provided, "Modern wars are not internecine wars in which the killing of the enemy is the object," and "unnecessary or revengeful destruction of life is not lawful."

Following the surrender of Japan in World War II, the U.S. Supreme Court upheld the conviction and death sentence of General Tomoyuki Yamashita by a United States military commission, holding that a [military] commander's actual knowledge of unlawful actions is sufficient to impose individual criminal responsibility.[68]

Lt. Colonel Custer was present at Washita and well aware that, pursuant to Sherman and Sheridan's orders, the Seventh Cavalry troopers, as well as the Osage scouts under his direct command were murdering and wounding innocent Cheyenne Indians and committing internecine acts, while Custer himself ordered his troops to take Cheyenne women prisoners to Camp Supply. Prior to the commencement of his attack, Custer did not know the name or tribal affiliation of any person in the camps, nor did he have any basis to believe that anyone in Black Kettle's camp had ever committed a crime or an illegal act toward or upon any person in the entire Indian territory—red or white.

In a particularly vicious but vivid unsigned letter dated December 22, 1868, that found its way into the *St. Louis Democrat* and the *New York Times*, Capt. Frederick Benteen fired ridicule and sarcasm at Custer for his participation in the slaughter of dogs and ponies and the killing of Cheyenne women and children:

The day is drawing to a close and but little has been done save the work of the first hour. A great deal remains to be done. That which cannot be taken away must be destroyed. Eight hundred ponies are to be put to death. Our Chief exhibits his close sharpshooting and terrifies the crowd of frightened, captured squaws and papooses by dropping the straggling ponies in death near them. Ah! He is a clever marksman. Not even do the poor dogs of the Indians escape his eye and aim as they drop dead or limp howling away . . . Now commences the slaughter of the ponies. Volley on volley is poured into them by too hasty men, and they, limping, get away only to meet death from a surer hand. . . . The last pony is killed. The huge fire dies out; our wounded and dead comrades—heroes of a bloody day—are carefully laid on ready ambulances, and as the brave band of the Seventh Cavalry strikes up the air, "Ain't I glad to get out of the Wilderness," we slowly pick our way across the creek over which we charged so gallantly in the early morn. Take care! [D]o not trample on the dead bodies of that woman and child laying there![69]

Did Custer have these same designs on the Indians encamped at the Little Big Horn?

A Mexican called Pilan (known to the Cheyennes as "White Bear") was found hiding with his little daughter and taken prisoner. Having been ordered to "move off down the ravine," and fearing he was about to be killed, Pilan said, "Don't kill me. Me Mexican." The soldiers took the little girl and then shot Pilan in the back at a distance of thirty feet.[70] This deed was never punished; however, Pilan's daughter lived to adulthood.

The protection of the Fifth Amendment applies to all persons' lives, liberty and property. To place these incidents in perspective, all of the Indians at Black Kettle's camp, including the Mexican who was shot in the back, were persons, none of whom had ever been charged with a crime. They were also persons who could not be deprived of their lives, their property, or their freedom without due process of law. They were being attacked, pillaged, and murdered by Custer and the Seventh Cavalry that he commanded solely because they were Indians. Some of the captive women were used as concubines by Custer and his soldiers. These actions most certainly violated the due process rights of the victims—not to mention the oath of each Seventh Cavalry trooper involved.

As sunset approached Custer became aware that large numbers of mounted warriors from other bands were observing the proceedings from the surrounding high ground. Since he had neglected to conduct reconnaissance, he was unaware of nearby Indian camps located downstream with more than 6,000 Cheyennes and others. These angry Indians greatly outnumbered Custer's 750 faithful. Had these downstream Indians reacted promptly and surrounded Custer, cutting him off from his supplies, eleven companies of the Seventh Cavalry might well have been wiped out in November 1868.

On the recommendation of scout Ben Clark, Custer was able to extricate himself by mounting up and marching toward the Indian camps downstream. The nearby warriors fled back to protect their own villages. In a short while it was dark, and Custer thereupon reversed course and skedaddled out of the Washita valley, leaving behind the bodies of Maj. Joel H. Elliott and seventeen troopers who had been killed while attempting to run down escaping Indians.[71] Custer's other casualties included two wounded officers and thirteen troopers. He was unable to account for the whereabouts or the fate of Major Elliott and his men.

Tactically, Custer had successfully surprised the small camp of peace chief Black Kettle. He outnumbered Black Kettle's Cheyenne warriors by more than five to one. By attacking at dawn, with heavy snow on the ground, he was able to surround the Indian encampment on four sides. The Indians were not expecting the attack, and Custer's tactics deprived them of access to their ponies. More than half the Indians were women, children, and elderly noncombatants. The warriors in Black Kettle's camp numbered between eighty and one hundred. Despite the fact that the army achieved complete surprise and, for the most part, was fighting unarmed Indians, including women and children, well over half the Indians escaped on foot. Those who survived were left at the mercy of the winter and charity from other Indians downstream while Custer ran off with fifty-three of their women and children.

Mixed feelings followed the battle. On the morning of the twenty-eighth, Custer sent a brief message ahead to Sheridan, "We have cleaned Black Kettle and his band out so thoroughly that they can neither fight, dress, sleep, eat, or ride without sponging on their friends."[72] On receipt of Custer's first message, General Sheridan was elated—this was his kind of reprisal. However, Indian Agent Wynkoop argued strongly that it was a serious moral error to attack Black Kettle's peaceful camp. Sheridan soon became angered that Custer was unable to account for Major Elliott and had no knowledge of his whereabouts or fate. Sometime after the battle Captain Benteen readily admitted to Custer, in the presence of some of the regimental officers, that he was the author of the published letter criticizing him.[73] In his eagerness to attack the small defenseless sleeping village, Custer committed a major tactical mistake—he failed to conduct reconnaissance downstream, placing his entire regiment in danger of annihilation. Custer charged in and was successful in shooting up Black Kettle's village, but the net result was to incur the wrath of the surviving Indians and a blot on the honor of the army and his country. Custer's actions were harshly criticized by the eastern press and the commissioner of Indian affairs.[74] The army had taken matters into its own hands in violation of the Constitution and its Lieber Code and, in the process, had murdered many peaceful and innocent Indians, including noncombatants.

Custer's action, which he conducted at the direction of General Sheridan, accomplished little toward achieving a reasonable solution with the Indians of the southern plains. It also discouraged the Cheyennes' northern cousins from turning to peace. The battle of Washita in November 1868 was the last significant engagement between Custer and the Indians until his fateful and final encounter at the Little Big Horn less than nine years later.

Custer needed to take heed of the tactical lesson so aptly demonstrated at Washita. Although outnumbered three to one, taken by complete surprise and separated from their ponies, over half of Black Kettle's villagers were able to escape—on foot in the dead of winter with over twelve inches of snow on the ground. It was not easy to surround and capture Plains Indians under any circumstances.

Custer's Washita atrocities earned him a reputation among non-Indians as an aggressive "Indian Fighter"[75]—a reputation he carried to his grave. In reality Custer never enjoyed any success in fighting Indian warriors. His most notable achievements in plains warfare were the killing of noncombatants, plundering and burning their food and shelter, slaughtering ponies and taking women and children as prisoners.

On other occasions subsequent to Washita, while operating in the field in command of his regiment, Custer placed himself or his troops in unnecessary danger or failed to exercise rational judgment. On the

Yellowstone expedition in southeastern Montana during the summer of 1873, Custer had a run-in with his commanding officer, Gen. David S. Stanley, who was known to drink while on duty. Custer told Libbie that Stanley was "possessed by the fiend of intemperance."[76] In a minor but characteristic incident, Custer led his cavalry contingent four miles ahead of Stanley's main group as they approached a crossing of the Muddy River. Custer and his mounted troopers had no difficulty in crossing. Stanley needed Custer and his regiment to assist his wagons with their crossing. Instead, Custer wandered ahead fifteen miles from the crossing and sent back a note requesting General Stanley to have forage and rations delivered to him. Stanley took umbrage, told Custer to "halt where he was, to unload his wagons, and send for his own rations and forage, and never to presume to make another movement without orders."[77] For this transgression Custer was ordered to consider himself under arrest and to march at the rear of the column. Historian Edgar I. Stewart noted: "From the beginning Custer had acted as though he were in command of the expedition, much to Stanley's exasperation. It was not long before the latter recorded his conviction that Custer was a 'cold-blooded, untruthful and unprincipled man,' who was 'universally despised by all of the officers of his regiment' with the exception of his relatives and a few sycophants."[78] According to Custer, Stanley later apologized, and they made up. While this was not a major infraction, it does show the tendency of Custer to respond to his own impulses at any opportunity. Whether Stanley was drunk or sober, he had the authority to require Custer to operate within the parameters of the orders that Stanley had issued to him.

With General Terry's Dakota column en route to its rendezvous with the Montana column in the spring of 1876, Custer would occasionally separate himself from the main column. These actions took him out of the sight and control of Gen. Alfred Terry. Whatever the reason, on May 31, 1876, Custer was skylarking well ahead of the column with his brothers Tom and Boston. Custer and Tom decided to spook little brother Boston, so they ditched him while traversing over rough, hilly ground. The pranksters then circled around behind Boston and fired shots over his head. Boston got his wind up and took off at high speed, returning to the main column, where he spread the false alarm. In the meantime, the main column under Terry was wandering around lost. (Terry was not good at finding his way.) As a result, Terry had to chasten Custer for behaving like a teenage boy rather than the commanding officer of a regiment engaged in potential combat against the Plains Indians. In a manner that would make a politician blush, Custer responded with a disingenuous statement regarding his actions: "At the time I proposed to accompany the advance battalion, I was under the impression that it would probably be sufficiently far in advance of the main column to constitute a separate command [basically an intentional lie], and that I could be of more service to you and to the expedition acting with the advance than elsewhere. Since such is not the case, I will, with your permission, remain with, and exercise command of, the main portion of my regiment."[79] Chasing around ahead of and out of sight of Terry's column, discharging firearms and creating a false alarm[80] did not constitute any worthwhile service to General Terry nor provide any benefit to the entire expedition. Custer's disingenuous response was based on a false premise.

And so, during the early years of its existence, problems surfaced that would impact the Seventh Cavalry Regiment as it entered the decade of the 1870s. Congress and the Department of the Interior, with cooperation from Presidents Andrew Johnson and Ulysses Grant, were actively pursuing a peace policy through a series of negotiated treaties containing an equitable plan to share the use and occupancy of the Great Plains with the Indians. In direct conflict with the peace policy, General Sherman, who succeeded Grant as general of the army in March 1869, advocated all-out war and genocide against all the plains tribes—to the point of extermination if they failed to remove to and remain permanently on their reservations. Custer and the Seventh Cavalry were to play a pivotal role in the army's efforts to subjugate the Lakotas and Cheyennes on the northern plains. The Seventh Cavalry had an abundance of battle-tested officers from the Civil War, but new tactical doctrines had to be learned—by trial and error—to fight the highly mobile mounted warriors. There was disunity among the Seventh Cavalry officers and widespread desertion among its enlisted ranks. Between 1866 and 1870 a series of incidents in the field gave rise to legitimate questions concerning the aptitude and fitness of its officers, the adequacy of its weapons, and the training and performance of its mounted troopers. Would these problems be recognized and corrected by June of 1876?

## Chapter Three
# The Indians Who Fought at the Little Big Horn

*If I were an Indian, I often think I would greatly prefer to cast my lot among those of my people adhered to the free open plains rather than submit to the confined limits of a reservation, there to be the recipient of the blessed benefits of civilization, with its vices thrown in without stint or measure.*

—*Lt. Col. George Custer*[1]

On June 25, 1876, the "unceded Indian territory" where the Battle at Little Big Horn occurred was occupied by the Sioux and Cheyennes and a few Arapaho Indians who were hunting antelope and buffalo. They were operating from a single grand encampment located on the west bank of the Little Big Horn River. Most of the Sioux were members of the Lakota group (also known as the "Teton" Sioux), consisting of seven bands (or tribes), called Oglala, Brulé, Hunkpapa, Minneconjou, Sans Arc, Two Kettle, and Blackfeet.[2] Some of the Lakotas, mostly Hunkpapas led by Sitting Bull and certain Oglalas led by Crazy Horse, had refused to sign the 1868 Treaty of Fort Laramie. Others, who were mostly Oglalas and Brulés, were members of Lakota tribes, who had signed the treaty and had left their reservations to join in the summer hunt in order to supplement insufficient food rations at their reservations. Their Cheyenne allies were members of the Northern and Southern Cheyenne divisions.[3] Also present were certain Arikara, Shoshoni, and Crow Indians who were serving as scouts for the separate forces of Gen. George Crook and Gen. Alfred H. Terry. Prevailing treaty stipulations prohibited all "white persons" from settling upon, occupying, or trespassing through this "unceded Indian territory."[4]

American Horse and family. American Horse was a Lakota Sioux chief, shown here
with his three wives, three children, and four adult relatives.
Courtesy Nebraska State Historical Society.

During the middle of the seventeenth century, the ancestors of these
seven Lakota tribes lived in what is now northeastern Minnesota.[5] They
existed independently, without guns and horses, as hunters, gatherers,
and fur traders. These early Lakotas were constantly fighting with the
powerful Cree and Chippewa tribes (located to their north and east),
who had acquired guns from fur traders.[6] For several reasons, including their lack of firearms, these Lakotas began a slow but steady migration toward the south, where buffalo and beaver were plentiful. As
they migrated southward, they also began acquiring guns from various
traders. Around 1700 they crossed the Mississippi River and began to
split up. Five Lakota tribes (Hunkpapa, Blackfeet, Sans Arc, Two Kettle,
and Minneconjou) turned ninety degrees to the west, continuing until
they reached the Missouri River around 1780. The remaining two tribes
(Oglala and Brulé) continued south until they reached the Blue Earth
area, where they also altered their course to the west, reaching northeastern Wyoming and northwestern Nebraska between 1790 and 1810.
(See map 1.)[7]

By the mid-nineteenth century the Lakotas had cleared the other

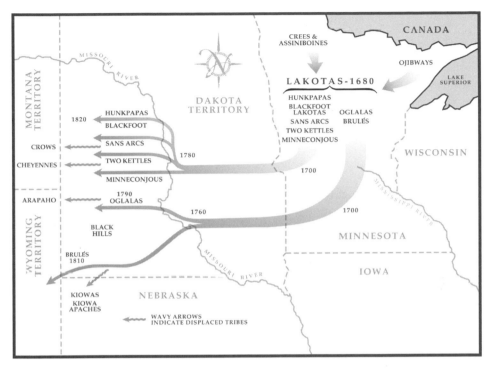

Map 1. Lakota Migrations, 1680–1820. Map copyright © Charles E. Wright.

tribes from the area north of the North Platte and west of the Missouri rivers in the Nebraska and Dakota territories, and the powerful Oglalas and Brulés developed an alliance with the Cheyennes, enabling them to dominate the northern plains.[8] As they moved west, the Cheyennes and Lakotas were able to obtain horses from southern tribes. Both tribes commenced living in portable tepees, using manpower and horses to follow the wandering buffalo herds that were their primary source of food. Throughout the period from 1740 until 1876, various white traders passed through the region, acquiring furs and buffalo hides, for which they exchanged firearms, ammunition, metallic utensils, and cloth—items that were essential to the Indians' mobile existence.

As the Lakotas continued west, thriving on buffalo and trapping beaver, they pushed aside other tribes in their path. Reaching the Missouri River in the 1760s and 1780s, they tried farming for a brief period. By this time, with their great numbers and their acquisition of horses and guns, the Lakotas were the largest tribe on the upper Missouri River.[9]

Red Cloud, the famous chief and leader of the Oglalas, who did not participate in the Battle of Little Big Horn or the subsequent Great Sioux War battles. Courtesy Denver Public Library, Western History Collection (B-115).

He Dog, a fierce Oglala warrior and follower of Crazy Horse, who fought at Rosebud, Little Big Horn, and finally surrendered with Crazy Horse in May 1877. Courtesy Nebraska State Historical Society.

Pawnee Killer, another fierce Oglala war leader who earned his name fighting against Pawnee Indians. Courtesy Nebraska State Historical Society.

Low Dog, an Oglala Lakota who fought at Little Big Horn for his right to live on the Indian treaty lands. Courtesy Denver Public Library, Western History Collection (B-106).

Abandoning farming and crossing the Missouri River, the Brulés reached the northwest corner of Nebraska by 1810, and the Oglalas reached the Black Hills and northeastern Wyoming Territory around 1790. The other five Lakota tribes had entered southeastern Montana Territory by 1820. Lured by the lucrative trading of buffalo hides with Spanish and French traders and the weakening of non-Lakota tribes resulting from smallpox epidemics and battle casualties, the Lakotas continued westward onto the northern plains at the end of the eighteenth century.

The Lakota were a "self-reliant" and "self-determined society."[10] With strength in numbers and their acquisition of firearms and horses, and with little competition from white settlers, their culture thrived and their numbers grew. By 1873 they dominated the northern Great Plains and were able to live and hunt in the area north of the North Platte River and east of the Bighorn Mountains, where buffalo were still plentiful. Young Lakota males were trained to ride and hunt at an early age.

As Lakota culture evolved, there were two types of fraternal groups— the *akicita* and the *naca*. The former were policemen and the latter a civil society of elders and ex-chiefs who were the source of tribal leadership. From the nacas came the selection of the shirt-wearers for each band. The shirt-wearers were called upon to decide matters of diplomatic concern. From the elder nacas of each band, a group of four executive chiefs was appointed. These were the supreme rulers over the entire Lakota group. As a matter of policy, the Lakotas sought consensus on all council decisions. The four supreme male virtues were bravery, fortitude, generosity, and wisdom. Another virtue, which enhanced all of the others, was humility. "Anything good that was done or said with humility carried more impact."[11] Among the women, the four virtues were bravery, generosity, truthfulness, and childbearing.[12]

During the latter half of the seventeenth century, the ancestors of the Northern and Southern Cheyennes lived along the Minnesota River in southwestern Minnesota, dwelling in pole-supported lodges covered with bundles of grass, brush, and bark. They existed by hunting, gathering, and farming. Without guns, they were at times at the mercy of the larger Cree and Chippewa tribes located to their north and east, who had obtained firearms from the French and the British.[13] The Cheyennes began migrating toward the west and northwest, crossing to the west bank of the Missouri River around 1780. There they lived in earthen lodges near friendly Arikara and Mandan villages and raised corn, beans, and squash. By this time they had acquired firearms and horses, which they used to hunt buffalo.[14] During this interval, they were joined by a closely related tribe, the Suhtaios, who spoke their language and shared their culture. Pressed at times by the migrating Lakotas, the Cheyennes moved west from their Missouri River villages, became full-time buffalo hunters, and migrated through the Black Hills into eastern Wyoming and Montana, northeastern Colorado, and western Nebraska. Along the way they formed an alliance with the Arapaho Indians, and the Suhtaios who, in 1831, had merged into and joined their camp circle.[15] It is believed that during the first half of the nineteenth century, the Cheyennes, despite their hunting ways, continued to raise crops along the Little Missouri and North Platte rivers.[16]

The Cheyennes had "warrior societies" that performed various tribal functions. One of their most significant duties was to enforce the orders of the chiefs and maintain order in the camps. When the camp moved, the "dog soldiers" were the last to leave. While moving, the "crazy dogs" would guard the flanks, and the dog soldiers would bring up the rear.[17] At times, particularly in Indian territory during 1867 and 1868, the dog soldiers assumed a militant attitude, advocating revenge against settlers and soldiers while continually resisting white encroachment into their hunting areas.

The Cheyennes at times lacked a sense of unity and purpose. Thus, some chiefs such as Black Kettle continually sought peace, while others were eager to fight. After the Battle at the Little Big Horn, a few Cheyenne warriors served as cavalry scouts for General Crook. In 1825 when the Cheyennes divided into southern and northern bands, the dog men from the southern band became the "old dog men" and from the northern band, they became the "crazy dogs."[18] The old dog men and the crazy dogs at certain times behaved as rogues, ignoring tribal consensus and taking issues with white settlers into their own hands.

Cheyenne males were honored for their bravery and hunting skills. They trained from an early age to become successful warriors.[19]

With the acquisition of horses and guns, both the Cheyennes and Lakotas had to develop new fighting strategies. While individual warriors feared neither death nor injury during combat, their strategy in fighting the army avoided direct frontal attack and needless loss of life. This made good sense because without superiority in numbers or weapons, they would be unable to retain possession of the northern plains. Before they acquired firearms, all combat was conducted at close range with the arrow and spear or hand-to-hand with a knife and club. Rifles and muskets made it possible to kill and wound at a much greater range. Their tangible symbol for bravery in combat was counting coup—literally touching your enemy and risking death.[20] Because of this Indian warriors developed their skill at decoy and ambush—declining a direct frontal attack unless the numbers or conditions were in their favor. They did not permit blind fury or impulsive aggression to prevail over common sense. Due to their tactics involving flight and ambush and their strategy of avoiding needless loss of life, the Indians never developed organized tactics for defending their village or standing fast. When their village was attacked, they would flee or counterattack. This is the situation that prevailed in June of 1876 at the Little Big Horn River.

By 1876 the Northern Cheyennes and the Lakotas were a powerful alliance, and many of their warriors owned repeating firearms. From time to time, Cheyennes from the southern division traveled north and hunted with the northern division—and vice versa. They welcomed each other's presence for the 1876 summer buffalo hunt along the tributaries south of the Yellowstone River. Raiding and hunting were their way of life. Thus, when they combined into one encampment on the Little Big Horn River in late spring, they had no reluctance to stand and counterattack the U.S. Army, particularly when the Indians' numbers were overwhelming and their hunting grounds and entire encampment were threatened.

By 1877 the population of the Mandan, Hidatsa, Arikara, Ponca, Omaha, and other sedentary Indians who lived in villages along the Missouri River had declined by 79 percent, due primarily to small pox, cholera, measles, and other imported diseases. During this same time, the population of the migratory Lakota, Cheyenne, and Arapaho tribes declined by less than 10 percent. It is believed that their dispersion and frequent movement made them less susceptible to contagious germs. In one instance a small number of Sioux were vaccinated for smallpox by doctors hired by the Office of Indian Affairs.[21] In 1866 the entire Lakota population was estimated by the commissioner of Indian affairs to be 11,520.[22] By 1877 a census revealed that the population of the Lakotas had increased to 18,100; Cheyennes numbered 3,236; and Arapahos, 2,964.[23]

By 1876 the primary diet of the Cheyennes, Lakotas, and Arapahos consisted of the buffalo and other animals they were able to trap or kill with their rifles and arrows, supplemented with the wild roots and berries they were able to gather. Most of their waking hours were spent in search of food and the hides that they used to trade for guns, ammunition, and grain. They had no written history and few, if any, could read or write.

Without farming or fishing to sustain their existence, the Sioux and Cheyennes depended upon the buffalo for most of their daily necessities. Hides were used for shields, robes, and buckets. The skull was utilized in spiritual matters. Ropes, halters, and hair pieces were made of buffalo hair. Muscles were used to make glue, thread, and arrow ties. Meat was wrapped in the haunch liner. Buckskin robes, shirts, leggings, mittens, and bridles were fashioned from the hide. Blood was used in soup and puddings. From horns the Indians made arrow points, powder horns, and spoons. Fat was used for soap, grease, and cosmetics. The tongue was considered a delicacy. Bones were used for knives, shovels, scrapes, and pipes. Meat was consumed cooked, raw, or dried and was made into jerky and pemmican. Tendons could be made into bow strings, and the bladder and scrotum could be used for rattles, pouches, and other containers. Buffalo chips made good fuel, teeth were used for ornamentation, and brains were prized for tanning and softening leather.[24]

Hunting activities required the Sioux and Cheyennes to travel over vast geographical areas in search of the buffalo. The buffalo of the northern herd gathered and fed on the grasslands adjacent to the lengthy Missouri River and its numerous tributaries. Since Plains Indians were their own providers, they were subject to starvation whenever buffalo or other food sources were not available. When the buffalo were gone, the nomadic Sioux and Cheyennes who did not live on reservations were faced with starvation unless they could find another primary food source. Rations provided by the government at their reservations were often short in quantity, lacking in quality, and uncertain of delivery. As the buffalo declined, the Cheyennes and Lakotas became more aggressive in locating the few remaining large herds and protecting them from white hunters as well as other Indians who suffered from the same predicament. In

1876 the bulk of the surviving buffalo of the northern herd were located east of the Bighorn Mountains and north of the North Platte River in the "unceded Indian territory" of southeastern Montana.

By 1876 many of the Sioux and some Northern Cheyennes had followed their leaders to reservations, where they depended upon government subsistence deliveries. When government subsistence was inadequate, there was hunger and starvation. A substantial number of the Lakotas and Cheyennes who fought at the Little Big Horn had not signed either the 1851 or the 1868 Treaties of Fort Laramie and had never voluntarily submitted themselves to life under wasicu rule on one of the reservations. These Lakotas were largely non-treaty followers of Hunkpapa holy man Sitting Bull and Oglala warrior leader Crazy Horse. They called themselves *Waziyata Oyate*, the "Northern Nation."[25]

Also present at the Little Big Horn in 1876 were certain Indians who lived on one of the reservations during the winter and rode out in the summer to hunt with the winter roamers. These "treaty Indians" consisted of both Sioux and Cheyennes. In late spring of 1876 and throughout the month of June, they left their reservations and rode to the area of the Yellowstone drainage, where they joined the huge encampment of non-treaty Indians in search of food.

With the exception of a small number of Santee Sioux, led by their intrepid war chief Inkpaduta (Scarlet Top)[26] and five Arapaho warriors, the remaining Sioux at the Little Big Horn encampment were Lakotas. Sitting Bull, the acknowledged spiritual leader of the encampment and also leader of those Lakotas who had refused to sign the Treaty of 1868, was both a *wichasha wakan* (holy man) and a war chief of the Hunkpapa band. Sitting Bull had established a brilliant record as a warrior and a respected reputation as a holy man whose dreams and visions, coupled with sound judgment and leadership, often became reality.[27] Because of his age and stature Sitting Bull did not take an active part in the fighting at the Little Big Horn, but he encouraged others to do battle and, at the same time, assisted with preparations for a hasty removal of women and children from the camp at the appropriate time.

A leading warrior at the Little Big Horn was an Oglala called Crazy Horse who excelled as a fighter and a leader in battle. He was a "thunder dreamer." Lakota tradition held that Crazy Horse possessed "thunder power," which was "a violent, eruptive force that had to be carefully harnessed to serve the people's good."[28] Rattle Blanket Woman, the mother of Crazy Horse, was a Minneconjou, a tribe led by the noted warrior Hump. As a young adult Crazy Horse spent time with Hump learning the role of a scout, which provided him with experience and training for his later role as a warrior. He was precocious as both a hunter and a warrior and earned a well-deserved reputation among his people for bravery and skill in fighting. Such were his reputation and respect among the Oglalas that he was elected as one of four new leaders to become a shirt-wearer, a prestigious office empowered to establish national policy. British historian Kingsley Bray noted that "Shirt Wearer status lay increasingly heavily on Crazy Horse's shoulders—and, scarcely eighteen months after the treaty [of 1868] Crazy Horse became terminally disenchanted with the peace process on the Plains."[29]

By the time of the Battle at the Little Big Horn, Crazy Horse was a principal war leader of the Lakotas and had no difficulty inspiring warriors from various bands to follow his direction and example. In December of 1866, he participated in a successful decoy and ambush that lured eighty-one infantry and cavalry soldiers commanded by Capt. William J. Fetterman to complete annihilation. Their tactic was to taunt the soldiers with aggressive mounted warriors, drawing them away from Fort Phil Kearny into a trap where they were surrounded and pinned down by a larger number of well-armed warriors.[30] Crazy Horse had the instinctive ability to recognize tactical opportunities and exploit them to the disadvantage of Custer's troopers. He utilized the mobility of the Indian pony to wreak havoc on the slower cavalry formations. Riding fleet Indian ponies, many of his tactical maneuvers were aimed at concentrating a rapid attack at the point where the defenders were either weak or out of position. Once he found a weak spot, he would not hesitate to engage in close-order combat.

In addition to Crazy Horse, other Oglala leaders at the encampment were He Dog and Big Man. Among the Brulé was Crow Dog. Minneconjou leaders included Hump, Fast Bull, Lame Deer, and Red Horse. Among the Hunkpapa, in addition to Sitting Bull, were Gall, Knife Chief, Black Moon, and Crow King. Blackfeet Lakota leaders were Kill Eagle and Scabby Head. Among the Cheyennes were Lame White Man, Ice, Black Moccasin, Fast Bull, Old Bear, and Two Moon. Notably absent at the Little Big Horn were Red Cloud, the most prominent and capable leader of the Oglalas, and Spotted Tail, the acknowledged leader of the Brulés. Both Red Cloud and Spotted Tail had signed the 1868 Treaty, and during the summer of 1876 they remained with large numbers of Oglalas and Brulés at their agencies located in northwest Nebraska.[31]

In military operations warrior chiefs often acted as instructors or advisors but did not issue commands. They may have taunted or challenged individual warriors, but in essence the fighting Indians had no commanding officers. Individual warriors could decide whether or not to fight or to accept advice, instruction, or taunts from any warrior chief. An individual warrior could withdraw from combat at any time, but he ought to have had a good reason for his withdrawal so that he would not be accused of cowardice.

During the 1876 spring hunt, Lakotas and Cheyennes had to move frequently in order to find grass for their extensive pony herd and to maintain sanitation within their campsite. As they continued to move west onto the Little Big Horn and Bighorn drainage, they were aware that they were moving into Crow country.

The current reservation of the Crow nation surrounds most of the Little Big Horn and Bighorn rivers, as well as the site of the Little Big Horn Battlefield. The reservation itself is an irregularly shaped rectangle, seventy miles in length at its longest point and forty-five miles in width. It was a cherished homeland of the Crow Indians, who were bitter enemies of the Cheyennes and Lakotas. Ancient Crow chief Rotten Belly (Arapooish) expressed his affection for Crow country:

> The Crow country is exactly in the right place. It has snowy mountains and sunny plains, all kinds of climates and good things for every season. When the summer heats scorch the prairies, you can draw up under the mountains, where the air is sweet and cool, the grass fresh, and the bright streams come tumbling out of the snow banks. There you can hunt the elk, the deer and the antelope when their skins are fit for dressing; there you will find plenty of white bears and mountain sheep.
>
> In the autumn when your horses are fat and strong from the mountain pastures you can go down into the plains and hunt the buffalo, or trap beaver on the streams. And when the winter comes on, you can take shelter in the woody bottoms along the rivers; where you find

buffalo meat for yourselves and cottonwood bark for your horses, or you may winter in the Wind River valley, where there is salt weed in abundance.

The Crow country is exactly in the right place. Everything good is to be found there. There is no country like Crow country. [32]

During the spring and summer of 1876, Crow warriors were serving as scouts for General Terry, Col. John Gibbon, and General Custer (and their northern force), as well as for General Crook (commanding the southern force). They performed well because they were familiar with the area, were experienced horsemen, and were bitter enemies of the Lakotas.

By January 31, 1876, the U.S. Army's policy required the Sioux and Cheyennes to remain on reservations located in Dakota Territory and Nebraska—but there were no buffalo and little farmland on these arid reservations. Thus, reservation Indians required government clothing and rations in order to survive. At various times Generals Custer, Crook, and Hatch sought permission to use army stores to feed starving reservation Indians, but in each instance permission was denied. Indian wars historian John D. McDermott noted, "Records show that no supplies worth mentioning had been issued at Red Cloud and Spotted Tail Agencies since April 10, 1876, and that the Sioux were on the verge of starvation due to the failure of Congress to vote on appropriation and failure on the part of the Indian Bureau to forward the supplies needed." [33] Gen. Edward Hatch stated, "The cavalry are in the field, but they have only power to force the Indians to starve peaceably or be killed violently." [34]

The confrontation between the Indians at the Little Big Horn and the United States Army involved the provisions of Article VI and the Fifth Amendment to the Constitution of the United States and the 1868 Treaty of Fort Laramie—a treaty that was in effect when Ulysses S. Grant was sworn in as president. Pursuant to Article VI of the Constitution, the 1868 Treaty, having been "made under the Authority of the United States" became the "supreme Law of the Land." In addition, when Montana was admitted as a territory in 1864, Congress enacted a law specifically providing that "all treaties . . . made by the government of the United States with Indian tribes inhabiting the territory [Montana] . . . shall be fully and rigidly observed."[35] Not only did President Grant lack the power to violate this treaty, but the methods that he used in perpetrating the violations were in direct violation of the Indians' Fifth Amendment rights under the Constitution.

## Chapter Four
# Laws, Treaties, and the Doctrine of Good Faith

*Before he enter on the execution of his office, he shall take the following oath or affirmation: 'I do solemnly swear that I will faithfully execute the office of President of the United States, and will to the best of my ability, preserve, protect and defend the Constitution of the United States.'*

—*Article II, Section 1, Constitution of the United States*

What does law have to do with the Battle at the Little Big Horn? The answer is simple—and compelling. The constitutional oath of office sworn by the president is mandatory—he must follow the dictates of the Constitution—and no exceptions are permitted. Whenever civil rights are suspended or ignored and martial law is utilized by the president, his cabinet, and the United States Army to deprive a small tribe of "persons" identified solely by their race, who were born and whose civilization originated in the United States, of their lives, their liberty, and their property, serious issues of law exist. These issues are easily defined but were brutally violated by President Grant and the army he commanded throughout the Great Sioux War of 1876–1877.

The applicable laws include the unanimous declaration of the thirteen United States of America proclaiming the unalienable rights of "all men" to "Life, Liberty and the pursuit of Happiness" and the doctrine of equality "to which the Laws of Nature and of Nature's God entitle them."[1] The United States Constitution creates a republican form of government (the supreme power rests in its citizens) that grants to Congress the power to enact laws and the exclusive power to declare war. Without the protection of individual human rights, our democracy would simply be another form of tyranny. Because of this, amendments were added to the Constitution by the thirteen original states, creating and preserving the basic human rights of all persons. These basic civil rights contained in the Bill of Rights apply to "persons" as well as United States citizens. Indians now qualify both as "persons" and "citizens" of the United States. Prior to 1924 the U.S. Supreme Court refused to treat American-born Indians as citizens and generally denied them the individual rights guaranteed to (all) persons in the Fifth and Fourteenth Amendments. These constitutional rights include equality, due process, and the sanctity of one's individual home. More specifically, no Indian person may be deprived of "life, liberty or property without due process of law."[2] As Justice Louis Brandeis noted, "Crime is contagious. If the government becomes a lawbreaker, it breeds contempt for the law; it invites every man to become a law unto himself; it invites anarchy."[3]

The battles between the U.S. Army and the Plains Indians in the 1860s and 1870s provide a vivid and violent example of what can happen to a well-organized government with a Constitution that protects fundamental human rights (life, liberty, property, and equality) when the president and the army he commands are corrupt and forsake the law, allowing greed and power to dominate honor and decency. At stake were the Lakotas' treaty lands and the arid grasslands west of the 100th meridian, where the Lakotas and Cheyennes lived and hunted buffalo. In this setting we are dealing with two cabinet officers (the secretaries of war and the interior), the commissioner of Indian affairs (serving under the secretary of the interior), and the General of the Army, each of whom was appointed by the president—a president who was head of the executive department and commander in chief of the U.S. Army, whose primary responsibility was to "preserve, protect and defend the Constitution of the United States." The Sioux and Cheyenne Indians were subject to the jurisdiction of the commissioner of Indian affairs and the secretary of the interior, who in turn were controlled by President Grant, who utilized the army he commanded to conquer and force the removal of these Indians in order to facilitate the construction of transcontinental railroads and non-Indian settlement. William T. Sherman (General of the Army), in turn, followed his own strategy of total war directed against Lakota and Cheyenne men, women, infants, and elders—not for military necessity, not for national security, but to kill or remove them simply because they were Indians who had the legal right to occupy their treaty lands—lands where Congress was creating a new railroad right of way from which it would also grant or sell parcels to settlers from the East. Being heavily outnumbered, with no help in sight from Congress or lawyers to represent them in the federal courts, their own firearms were the only means Indians had to protect their lives, liberty, property, and their rights under the Fifth Amendment of the Constitution and the 1868 Treaty of Fort Laramie.

There were detailed and specific laws that applied to the Great Sioux War of 1876 and the genocidal strategy of President Ulysses S. Grant (conceived and carried out by his generals, William T. Sherman and Philip H. Sheridan), who ordered the U.S. Army to attack the villages of the Lakota, Cheyenne, and Arapaho Indians (located within the Great Sioux reservation or in their "unceded Indian territory"), to confiscate their horses, firearms, and food, burn their shelters, and force them against their will to forfeit their liberty and return to their reservations. On a premeditated basis individual women, children, elders, and other noncombatants were murdered in an indiscriminate fashion without benefit of warning, a determination of guilt, or some other form of due process. Some Indians not killed by the attacking U.S. Army would subsequently die of starvation, battle wounds, and exposure to the elements. Those who were not murdered lost their freedom and their property.

The property lost by the Indians was essential to their culture and, in many cases, their very existence. Lost property included their treaty lands (which included mostly low-grade grazing lands on which hundreds of thousands of American bison lived and thrived), horses (which provided essential mobility), tepees and lodges (which provided shelter from the snow, rain, and subzero temperatures, and their firearms (which they used for hunting and self-protection).

President Abraham Lincoln deplored all forms of cruelty and inhumanity perpetrated by Americans against each other during the war of secession, much of which was inflicted on innocent noncombatants and caused in many instances by undisciplined troops and uncaring officers. Following the Great Sioux Uprising of 1862, under orders from General Henry H. Sibley, Minnesota military courts began interrogating Sioux warriors who were rounded up or had surrendered. Sibley directed his officers conducting the interrogations to determine guilt or innocence with the intent to hang all who were found guilty. General John Pope, Sibley's superior, had ordered Sibley to "exterminate them." Episcopal

Bishop Whipple reported that white settlers and the army were equally culpable as the Indians. Hundreds of Sioux Indians were charged with war crimes related to a general uprising in which large numbers of Indians, soldiers, and white settlers were killed. Three hundred and three Indians were found guilty by the military commission and sentenced to hang by Generals Pope and Sibley. President Lincoln intervened, reviewed all the evidence on each conviction, and allowed only thirty-nine to be hanged. The balance were given one- to three-year prison sentences by the military court.[4]

At the commencement of the Civil War, the U.S. Army's written rules of engagement dealt with little more than the shelter and feeding of prisoners of war. Both Union and Confederate armies were staffed primarily by civilians with little military training and even less experience—thus there were no established customs or standards of honor and decency regarding the treatment of noncombatants, prisoners of war, or Indians living in areas occupied by white settlers. In 1862 Secretary of War Edwin Stanton, on the recommendation of General of the Army Henry W. Halleck (who was a lawyer), appointed a panel comprised of four generals and law professor Francis Lieber to draft the army's first "laws of war" (entitled "Instructions for the Government of Armies of the United States in the Field"). Two of the panelists were lawyers, and one was a former instructor at West Point. Lieber was a Prussian immigrant who fought in the famous battles of Waterloo and Ligny. Lieber had two sons serving in the Union Army, and a third son died at Williamsburg fighting for the Confederates.

A comprehensive code was drafted, primarily by Lieber, approved by the panel and General Halleck, and adopted by President Lincoln. It was then promulgated by the War Department as "General Orders No. 100 for the ordinary operation of the army."[5] The "Lieber Code," as it was called, was considered so complete and necessary that it was also adopted in toto by the Confederate states.[6] During the Great Sioux War of 1876, General Orders No. 100 were embedded into and made binding on the armies commanded by Gen. George Crook, Gen. Alfred H. Terry, and the Seventh Cavalry Regiment commanded by Lt. Col. George Armstrong Custer, as well as President Grant and Generals Sherman and Sheridan.

General Orders No. 100 were found to be so practical and useful that

President Abraham Lincoln wanted a comprehensive set of rules governing the conduct of opposing armies regarding wounded and captured soldiers and the treatment of noncombatants. Courtesy Nebraska State Historical Society.

General of the Armies Henry W. Halleck. Courtesy U.S. Military Academy.

Professor Francis Lieber was a law professor at Columbia College who supervised the drafting of General Orders No. 100. Courtesy Columbia University Archives.

GENERAL ORDERS,  
No. 100. } WAR DEPARTMENT,  
ADJUTANT GENERAL'S OFFICE  
*Washington, April 24, 1863*

The following "Instructions for the Government of Armies of the United States in the Field," prepared by FRANCIS LIEBER, LL.D. and revised by a Board of Officers, of which Major General E. A. Hitchcock is president, having been approved by the President of the United States, he commands that they be published for the information of all concerned.

By ORDER OF THE SECRETARY OF WAR:  
E. D. TOWNSEND,  
*Assistant Adjutant General.*

Reprinted with permission of Stackpole Books.

they were later used by England, France, and Prussia. They formed the basis for the early Hague and Geneva conventions and were "the official guidance on the laws of war in all American conflicts until 1914."[7]

Much of the content of General Orders No. 100 was derived from the work of the brilliant seventeenth-century Dutch lawyer Hugo Grotius, author of the eternal text on humanity in war entitled *De Jure Belli ac Pacis* ("On the Law of War and Peace"). Grotius was not a futile idealist. He realized that wars are inevitable, but "his purpose was to strike the balance so that men might not believe that nothing is allowable or that everything is."[8] The principles of Grotius's theories, embodied in General Orders No. 100, were in effect when the 1868 Treaty of Fort Laramie was ratified by Congress and when General Sherman directed his armies to attack all Lakota and Cheyenne Indians who were off their reservations as of February 1, 1876. These attacks violated the due process clause of the Fifth Amendment and the 1868 Treaty of Fort Laramie, and they were conducted in ways that violated the requirements of General Orders No. 100. The following are examples in General Orders No. 100 that apply to the Little Big Horn battle in 1876 and the stern chases that followed over the next eighteen months.

Order No. 11 forbids cruelty and bad faith concerning "stipulations solemnly contracted" in time of peace. The 1868 Treaty of Fort Laramie allowed the Sioux the exclusive right to occupy and hunt buffalo north of the North Platte River and east of the summits of the Bighorn Mountains (where the Battle at the Little Big Horn River occurred) during the summer of 1876.[9] Order No. 37 recognizes the right of inhabitants to their private property and requires protection of persons, especially women. During the Great Sioux War the army destroyed the Indians' food and shelter, confiscated their horses, and left women and babies at the mercy of subzero weather without clothing, food, or shelter. Order No. 38 prohibits the seizure of private property, except for military necessity. The destruction of Indian food stores and shelter by the commands of Crook, Nelson Miles, and Ranald Mackenzie was not done out of military necessity. Order No. 42 acknowledges the law of nations and the doctrine that all men are equal. No other race of people in the United States (except Japanesse) has been forced by the U.S. Army in peacetime to reside and remain confined to a reservation against their will. Order No. 44 prohibits, under penalty of death, all wanton violence committed against persons in the invaded country, all destruction of property not commanded by the authorized officer, all robbery, pillage, or sacking, and all wounding, maiming, or killing of such inhabitants.[10] While Custer had no opportunity to rob, pillage, or sack the Indian encampment at the Little Big Horn as he did at Washita, Generals Crook, Miles, and Mackenzie, who finished out the balance of the 1876 campaign that extended into 1877, perpetrated egregious acts of wanton violence, pillage, and sacking against Cheyennes and Lakotas in the dead of winter. Order No. 68 provides that "modern wars are not internecine wars in which the killing of the enemy is the object. . . . Unnecessary or revengeful destruction of life is not lawful."[11]

Thus, in 1876 President Grant waged undeclared war on the Lakotas and Cheyennes. Not only was his act of war in violation of the Constitution,[12] but its purpose was to deprive the Sioux and Cheyennes of their lives, liberty, and property without any due process, by killing them or forcing them to retire from the hunting grounds guaranteed to them in the Treaty of 1868 and return to their reservation, where they were required to remain under threat of death and starvation.

Commenting on the violation of constitutional rights, American jurist Roscoe Pound noted, "Any considerable infringement of guaranteed individual or minority rights appears to involve much more than overriding a pronouncement of political ethics in a political instrument. It involves defiance of fundamental law; overthrow of established law upon which the maintenance of the general security rests."[13]

Unfortunately, in June of 1876, no legal counsel was available in the Sioux Indians' treaty lands located in southeastern Montana to enforce the due process clause of the Fifth Amendment, protect the Indians' treaty rights, and attempt to restrain President Grant and his army.[14]

During the nineteenth century, as America's frontier expanded westward to and beyond the Great Plains, its relationship with the various Indian nations and tribes was shaped by various written treaties. The Removal Act of 1830 made it legally permissible for the United States government to trade tracts of land with Indian tribes in order to effect their removal from areas that were settled or about to be settled in the near future.[15] Since treaties with the government played an integral part in the events leading up to the Sioux War of 1876 and the Battle at the Little Big Horn, information about the treaty process and how it was utilized to obtain land from Indians of the northern plains is not only useful, but essential.

A treaty is nothing more than a written agreement. As provided in Article VI of our Constitution, "all Treaties made . . . under the Authority of the United States, shall be the supreme Law of the Land." This means that a treaty with an Indian nation or tribe cannot be amended, countermanded, or ignored by the president of the United States or any General of the Army. In practice, a treaty is commonly thought of as a formal contract between sovereign entities. Prior to our Revolutionary War, many European nations entering the New World negotiated treaties with various Indian tribes, which they treated as sovereign states, covering such items as peace, friendship, and recognition of legal status.

For the U.S. government negotiating any issue with Indians, there were practical benefits in the use of treaties. A treaty could bind many Indians with the assent of a few. With its superior knowledge of the English language, the United States government could use its overwhelming population and its military prowess to do what it wanted.[16] While treaties could be reduced to writing, many Indians were unable to read.

Thus they were seldom adequately informed of the scope and meaning of the treaty. Attributing monetary value to land was a new concept. The written treaty might contain a consent to forcible removal, relinquishment of land, restrictions on movement, waiver of civil liberties, and acquiescence in the reservation system.

The Indians were at a disadvantage in negotiating treaties. They were left to negotiate for themselves, without the benefit of legal counsel and lacking experience and a linguistic understanding of issues and procedures. They signed treaties on the basis of oral representations that were translated and communicated by interpreters over days and months, and the interpreters were not always reliable or accurate. What the Indian signatory thought he was signing was based primarily on his individual recall of previous oral representations. Some of these American promises were false or inaccurate, conflicting, incomprehensible, illusory, and made in bad faith. The Indians rarely recognized the concessions that they made or the consequences of their own promises. Neither did the U.S. commissioners who negotiated the treaties for the United States. However, if a "bad bargain" for the United States was included in the terms of a treaty, the government would ignore or evade it because the Indians lacked the strength and methods to enforce it. In reality, treaty enforcement was the sole province of the United States government. Responsibility for enforcement also bounced back and forth among the president, the Interior Department (Indian Bureau), and the U.S. Army, causing bureaucratic and military confusion and tension among all parties. As the president might direct, a treaty could be enforced on a selective basis, i.e., strict enforcement, or as interpreted by the government, or not at all.

Treaties were used to establish tribal boundaries, cede land to the U.S. government, provide compensation and future indemnities for ceded land, and establish military alliances. Under normal procedures the treaty would be negotiated with and signed by a few Indians before it was submitted to the U.S. Senate for "ratification," binding the United States only when, if, and as approved by a two-thirds vote. As the United States expanded to the south, north, and west, the Indians were forced under military coercion to sign treaties ceding their land to the United States, calling for Indian removal to distant lands, forfeiting hunting and fishing rights, permitting passage through their lands, and agreeing to confinement on reservations. Reservations were often reserved out of larger tracts that were being ceded to the United States in the same treaty. The U.S. government developed devious tactics to negotiate the terms that they demanded. American negotiators would list everything they wanted without regard to the consequences to the Indians. Fairness and human rights were ignored, prior promises were voided, and conflicting promises about the same tract of land would be made to separate Indian nations.[17]

Not all treaties were the product of fraud, extortion, and coercion. In several instances treaty commissions staffed with righteous members who had humanitarian values negotiated in good faith, and certain treaties created advantages for both sides. However, if a treaty lacked short-term economic benefits to the U.S. government or its white settlers, it would be ignored, abrogated, or intentionally not enforced.

Before our Constitution was adopted, the Northwest Ordinance of 1787, enacted by the Continental Congress and reaffirmed with modifications by the new Congress in 1789, recognized good faith as an absolute standard involving governmental dealings with Indians. It stated:

> The utmost good faith shall always be observed towards the Indians; their lands and property shall never be taken from them without their consent; and in their property, rights, and liberty they never shall be invaded or disturbed, unless in just and lawful wars authorized by Congress; but laws founded in justice and humanity shall, from time to time, be made, for preventing wrongs being done to them, and for preserving peace and friendship with them.[18]

The basic human rights of freedom, equality, and due process of law guaranteed by our Constitution, as well as the Doctrine of Good Faith, applied to the 1868 Treaty of Fort Laramie and the Great Sioux War of 1876.

The Doctrine of Good Faith is essential to all treaties because a treaty can affect the lives of thousands or even millions of innocent and unprotected people. Good faith predates the common law of England and applies to the negotiation, the agreement itself, and the manner in which the treaty is performed. It involves both action and intention. It is based entirely upon honesty, which is required of all parties to a treaty, including not only the signatory parties but those who benefit or are affected by the agreement. Its antithesis is fraud and fraud's numerous relatives — dishonesty, infidelity, perfidy, mendacity, deception, extortion, undue influence, intimidation, bad faith, misrepresentation, false pretense, unfair advantage, greed, and cheating.

Common honor and decency require that good faith, actual and intended, must be present during the negotiation of a treaty. Each party must enter into treaty provisions with the intention of observing and carrying out its duties and responsibilities. Conversely, one may not enter into a treaty with the intention of ignoring or failing to comply with its provisions. One may not prevaricate or falsely represent the conditions upon which the agreement is negotiated. One may not withhold information that is material to the interests of the other party. One may not use threats, extortion, or false information to induce the other party to agree. If one party is able to read and the other is not, reasonable effort must be made to insure that the illiterate party understands all the terms and provisions of the treaty. One may not induce agreement through intoxication, intimidation, or false pretenses or stipulate provisions knowing that performance by the other party is or will be impossible. The United States may not use its size and strength, or its unique knowledge of the situation, to compel the other party to enter into an agreement on less than a voluntary basis.

When a treaty has been signed, each party must make reasonable efforts to carry out all its provisions and may not make less than a reasonable effort to comply, make false representations to excuse noncompliance, refuse to comply because the other party is incapable of enforcement, take secret or deceptive actions to avoid compliance, intentionally act in noncompliance, conspire with a third party to have the latter violate the treaty, or take action that interferes with compliance by the other party.

Thomas Jefferson and subsequent presidents played a significant role in formulating and carrying out the federal government's policy toward the Indians throughout the nineteenth century. The primary strategies utilized by the government to achieve expansion to the West were treaties and the use of military force. Commencing with Thomas Jefferson, through and including President Ulysses S. Grant, each president had to deal with issues and formulate policies involving Indians who occupied the land situated between the western boundaries of the original thirteen colonies and the Pacific Ocean—Indians who were at all times, and are presently, persons entitled to the protection of the Fifth Amendment to our Constitution. The government's primary strategy—a strategy that was conceived by Jefferson—was removal. Removal could be achieved through voluntary submission or by involuntary subjugation achieved through the use of military force.

President Jefferson's Indian policies commenced with the acquisition of the Louisiana Territory from France on May 2, 1803. In 1800 France had reacquired what we now call the "Louisiana Territory" from Spain, giving France control of New Orleans and the mouth of the Mississippi River. This caused Jefferson and the American government great concern because the American frontier had expanded west into the Cumberland, Tennessee, and Ohio river valleys, and American settlers were becoming increasingly dependent upon utilizing the Mississippi River to ship goods through the port of New Orleans. Jefferson's ideas for westward expansion of the republic included unfettered access to the Gulf of Mexico. The time was right for the United States to acquire the Louisiana Territory from France. The British navy was preventing France from conducting commerce with its overseas possessions, and Napoleon's treasury was short of funds. With the good help of two ministers, James Monroe and Robert Livingston, the United States was able to negotiate and consummate the purchase of Louisiana from France for fifteen million dollars plus interest.

At a cost of approximately three cents per acre, the Louisiana Purchase gave the United States a claim to govern 828,000 square miles of land, amounting to approximately 530 million acres. This doubled the size of the United States and opened the door to westward expansion, making manifest destiny a virtual reality. Included within Louisiana would be the entire states of Louisiana, Missouri, Arkansas, Iowa, North and South Dakota, Nebraska, and Oklahoma, together with most of the area comprised by Kansas, Colorado, Wyoming, Montana, and Minnesota.

The area covered by this "Treaty of Paris" had a population of approximately 146,000. Although the Louisiana Purchase doubled the area of the United States, it increased its population by only 3 percent.

Article III of the treaty governing this acquisition provides:

The inhabitants of the ceded territory shall be incorporated in the union of the United States, and admitted as soon as possible, according to the principles of the federal Constitution, to the enjoyment of all the rights, advantages and immunities of the citizens of the United States; and in the meantime they shall be maintained and protected in the free enjoyment of their liberty, property, and the religion which they profess.[19]

While it is commonly believed that the United States purchased title to the Louisiana Territory from France, such is not the case.[20] France had previously ceded whatever political control it possessed to Spain, and Spain had ceded (or quitclaimed) whatever interests it may have had back to France prior to the Louisiana Purchase.[21] Thus, France itself had no title to convey to the United States. Instead, France merely ceded political authority to govern the land, coupled with the power to tax. After purchasing the political power from France, the United States proceeded to acquire title to this same land from Indian tribes through treaties and voluntary cessions. Jefferson's motives and intentions in his dealings with the Indians can be summarized in his own words: "As to their fear, we presume that our strength and their weakness is now so visible that they must see that we have only to shut our hand to crush them, and that all our liberalities to them proceed from motives of pure humanity only."[22] Jefferson himself was not ignorant of the Constitution and good faith, but he knew how to step around them. His thoughts of "humanity" were not "pure," and its scope, in his hands, was severely limited.

William Henry Harrison served as U.S. commissioner plenipotentiary to all the Indian tribes north of the Ohio River, and he had responsibility for negotiations with the local tribes. Together with Secretary of War Henry Dearborn, Jefferson and Harrison indicated their intentions to treat the Indians with humanity and maintain a "benevolent" relationship with the Indians, except to the extent that it interfered with Jefferson's primary strategy—expansion.[23]

While Jefferson is remembered as the apostle of liberty and the evangelist of human rights, he had no intention of ever extending human rights to the Indians or of dealing with them on an honorable basis. His procedure for acquiring Indian lands was to run the Indians into debt and cut off their supplies, inducing them to pay their debts by ceding their land. Indian leaders were brought to the capital for negotiations and intimidated by parades of armed troops. Finally, they were threatened with war. Intimidation through the threat of war was initiated by white encroachment and atrocity toward Indians, followed by a bloody Indian retaliation, and military invasion by the army, which was concluded when a treaty in which the Indian lands were ceded to the United States was offered.[24]

Jefferson initiated the process of inducing the Indians east of the Mississippi to trade their land for land west of the Mississippi. He then expanded this procedure by encircling tribes east of the Mississippi after first acquiring the land along the *east* bank. He would then offer civilization and education to these eastern tribes in exchange for their lands. If they refused the assimilation or civilization offer, their only alternative would be forcible removal to land *west* of the Mississippi. This policy was aided and abetted by the constant threat of war if the Indians refused to cede their land and move west of the Mississippi.[25]

When Jefferson left office, the policy of forced removal to deprive the Indians of their ownership and possession of large tracts of land in the southeast part of the United States was quickly and firmly entrenched. James Monroe served as president from 1817 to 1825. He stated that forced removal would be revolting to humanity and utterly unjustifiable. This honorable doctrine from Monroe was not followed by subsequent presidents. John Quincy Adams succeeded Monroe and was unsuccessful in attempting to institute a new, less onerous removal policy. Andrew Jackson became president in 1829, bringing with him an attitude of "hatred, mistrust, and fear."[26] He referred to the Indians as savage, believing that they were barbaric and entitled to no good faith or trust. By the time Jackson became president, he had established himself as a great leader, with vision, energy, and a strong motivation to bring about manifest destiny. As a general he enjoyed great success in fighting—not only the Indians but against the British. He was strongwilled and self-righteous. However, he lacked one quality that permeated his relationship with the Indians. He had no honor.

Jackson was a strong advocate of forced removal. He used intimidation and force to negotiate whatever he wanted in treaties with various tribes. His attitude carried forward to the Cherokee removal during the term of his successor, Martin Van Buren. Historian Ronald Satz observed:

Perhaps the most brutal aspect of the internment of the Cherokees preceding their removal, however, were the acts of rape, bestiality, and murder committed by the "lawless rabble" and some soldiers who grossly exceeded their orders and the intentions of government officials in Washington.

One Georgia volunteer engaged in removing the Cherokees remarked years later, "I fought through the civil war and have seen men shot to pieces and slaughtered by thousands, but the Cherokee removal was the cruelest work I ever knew."[27]

The removal policies of Presidents Jefferson, Madison, Monroe, and Jackson and removal treaties enacted during the first half of the nineteenth century established a pattern that continued into the last half of the century. Pursuant to these treaties, Native tribes were forced against their will to abandon their homelands and, in some instances, their means of subsistence and travel to strange lands where they had few individual rights and had to attempt to subsist on government handouts. Some assimilated into white society while others remained in their tribal settings.

In late spring of 1851, Superintendent of Indian Affairs D. D. Mitchell, headquartered in St. Louis, assembled large delegations from the Sioux, Cheyenne, Arapaho, Crow, Assinaboine, Gros Ventre, Mandan, and Arikara nations in the vicinity of Fort Laramie (along the bank of the North Platte River in western Nebraska and eastern Wyoming) to promote a treaty that would bring peace among warring Plains tribes, acknowledge the right of the government to establish trails and military posts, and divide the northern plains into separate territories for each of the signatory Indian tribes. The signatory tribes would "abstain in future from all hostilities whatever against each other."

In addition to establishing peace among the warring Indian nations, each of the signatories recognized the right of the United States to build and maintain roads, military, and other posts within their respective territories. Luke Lea, the commissioner of Indian affairs, in his annual report dated November 27, 1851, stated: "The history of the Indian furnished abundant proof that he possesses all the elements essential to his elevation; all the powers, instincts and sympathies which appertain to his white brother; and which only need the proper development and direction to enable him to tread with equal step and dignity the walks of civilized life."[28]

The Great Smoke Treaty (the 1851 Treaty of Fort Laramie) had certain lasting effects, the most significant of which was the provision that gave, at the very least, an inchoate title to the Plains tribes involving all the land that was divided among them by the provisions of paragraph 5 of the treaty. However, the treaty was doomed from the start because to the U.S. government and its westbound settlers, it interfered with the expansion of the western frontier. It did, however, tone down some of the violence in the Great Plains until the Sand Creek massacre in 1864.[29]

The Great Smoke Treaty was followed by fifty-two treaties negotiated by Commissioner George W. Manypenny between March 1853 and November 1856, which were of three classes: (1) peace and friendship, (2) acquisition for settlement on permanent reservations, and (3) acquisition for settlement of individual Indians on separate allotments.[30] In a series of treaties, Manypenny obtained cessions of fifteen million acres from smaller tribes located along the lower reaches of the Missouri River, who were in turn allowed to keep about 1.3 million acres and live on much smaller reservations. The expansion of settlers into the Great Plains area was accelerated by the Kansas–Nebraska Act of May 30, 1854, which established two territorial governments but did not deprive the Indians of title to the lands that were apportioned to the various tribes under the Great Smoke.

The treaty that defined the relationship between our federal government and the Indians at the Little Big Horn was the 1868 Treaty of Fort Laramie.

Chapter Five

# The 1868 Treaty of Fort Laramie and President Grant's Conspiracy

*It is equally true that military posts among the Indians have frequently become centres of demoralization and destruction to the Indian tribes while the blunders and want of discretion of inexperienced officers in command have brought on long and expensive wars,*

—*Report of the "Doolittle Committee"*[1]

Custer's arrival at Fort Riley, Kansas, in 1866 ushered in the final decade of the dominance of the northern plains and the traditional way of life for Lakotas, Northern Cheyennes, and Arapahos. Twenty-five years later the roaming buffalo herds would all be gone, their vast grazing areas throughout the northern plains shattered into bits and pieces of land divided by Indian reservations, farmers, stock growers, railroads, burgeoning settlements, and barb wire, where the frozen bodies of more than 140 Lakota men, women, and children would lie moldering in a collective grave dug into a lonely and starkly beautiful plateau adjoining a dry ravine above Wounded Knee Creek in southwestern South Dakota.

The world was changing rapidly for those Lakotas and Cheyennes of the northern plains who would gather for a grand summer hunt at the Little Big Horn River in the summer of 1876. After the Civil War the volume of settlers moving west along the Overland and Oregon trails continued to increase. The U.S. Army was able to commit additional experienced officers and soldiers to maintain peace along the western frontier. The years 1865 through 1870 were filled with strife—Indians were raiding incoming settlers, and the army and state militias were retaliating. Meanwhile, Cheyennes and Lakotas watched the buffalo, the very means of their trade and survival, vanish as the Indians came under increasing control by the U.S. Army and the federal government.

Tensions between Cheyennes and whites exploded in November 1864 when soldiers of the New Mexico and Colorado militia, led by the diabolical and perverted Methodist minister Col. John M. Chivington, attacked the sleeping camp of Cheyenne peace chief Black Kettle at Sand Creek in southeast Colorado, massacring over 150 men, women, and children, some of whom were followers of Arapaho chief Little Raven. As a sign of their peaceful intentions, the Stars and Stripes, given to them by President Abraham Lincoln, flew over Black Kettle's camp. During the attack, the out-of-control militia indiscriminately killed defenseless women and children. Women were dismembered with sabres, babies' skulls were crushed, and several Indians were scalped. Some who attempted to flee were ridden down and killed like dogs. When the killing, butchery, and mutilation ended, Black Kettle's village was looted and then burned to the ground, and the Indians' pony herd was confiscated.[2] The massacre killed several Cheyenne leaders who favored peace and "both the Cheyennes and Arapahoes experienced familial and societal disruptions that have spanned generations."[3]

Over the next few years, the U.S. Army wrestled with continual raids and skirmishes across the northern plains as the Sioux, spurred on by Red Cloud, along with the Cheyennes and Arapahos, did what they could to resist the loss of their traditional hunting grounds. In January and February of 1865, Cheyennes and others, in retaliation for the Sand Creek Massacre, sacked and burned the small town of Julesburg, Colorado.[4] By 1866 the eastern division of the Union Pacific Railroad had reached Manhattan, Kansas, and in the same year Forts Reno, Philip Kearny, and C. F. Smith were established by the army along the Bozeman Trail in northeastern Wyoming and southeastern Montana.[5] On December 21, 1866, Lt. Col. William J. Fetterman of the Eighteenth Infantry Regiment, operating west of Fort Kearny in northeast Wyoming Territory, together with seventy-six enlisted men, two other officers, and two civilians, were killed in a raid by combined Cheyenne, Arapaho, and Sioux warriors.[6] Fetterman had an excellent combat record with the Union Army in the Civil War, but he and his men were decoyed into a well-planned ambush where all were destroyed.

Following the Fetterman fight in 1866, Gen. William T. Sherman, who was then commander of the army's Division of the Missouri, began advocating a racially motivated military solution to Gen. Ulysses

Grant, indicating that, "we must act with vindictive earnestness against the Sioux, even to their extermination, [of] men, women and children."[7] Accordingly, Sherman advocated attacking Indian camps in the dead of winter, where defenseless women and children could be killed. Following the Fetterman fight, in which only soldiers and warriors were involved, Sherman, who was then a lieutenant general commanding the Military Division of the Missouri, sent a letter to Brig. Gen. Philip St. George Cooke, ordering him to attack the Indians "with vindictive earnestness, until at least the Indians are killed for each white life lost," defining his genocidal strategy by ordering Cooke to "carry the war to the Indian camps, where the women and children are, and [you] should inflict such punishment that even Indians would discover they can be beaten with their own game." He further stated, "It is not necessary to find the very men who committed the acts, but destroy all of the same breed"[8]—that is blatant genocide and premeditated murder.

Two years earlier, on October 9, 1864, Sherman demonstrated his penchant for wanton violence and genocidal destruction of life when he wrote to (then General of the Army) Ulysses S. Grant for permission to destroy Atlanta and march thence to the sea stating, "Until we can repopulate Georgia, it is useless to occupy it, but the utter destruction of its roads, houses and people will cripple their military resources. . . . I can make the march and make Georgia howl!"[9] In 1867 Sherman told Secretary of War Edwin Stanton that, "if fifty Indians are allowed to remain between the Arkansas and the Platte [rivers] we will have to guard every stage station, every train, and all railroad working parties. In other words, fifty hostile Indians will checkmate 3,000 soldiers. Rather get them out as soon as possible, and it makes little difference whether they are coaxed out by Indian commissioners or killed."[10]

Sherman was rapidly becoming a disciple of genocide. In a letter dated December 20, 1866, to his brother, Senator John Sherman, General Sherman wrote, "The Sioux and Cheyennes are now so circumscribed that I suppose they must be exterminated, for they cannot and will not settle down, and our people will force us to do it."[11] Voicing opposition to annexation of Mexico, he said, "All I can say is that Mexico does not belong to our system. All its northern part is very barren and costly. Its southern part is very good tropical country, but not suited to our people or pursuits. Its inhabitants are a mixture of Indians, Negroes and Span-

On July 20, 1867, Congress created an Indian Peace Commission to make treaty arrangements, and select reservations with various tribes of the northern plains. The commission consisted of three army generals, Alfred W. Terry, William T. Sherman, and C. C. Augur; Commissioner of Indian Affairs N. G. Taylor; S. F. Tappan, chairman of the Senate Committee of Indian Affairs; and John B. Sanborn. Pictured above are Terry, Gen. William S. Harney, Sherman, an unknown Arapaho woman, Sanborn, Tappan, and Augur, near the site of the treaty conference. Courtesy of the Nelson-Atkins Museum of Art and the Hall Family Foundation.

ish, that can never be tortured into good citizens, and would have to be exterminated before the country could be made available to us."[12]

Native unrest generated congressional attention. On July 20, 1867, Congress created a Joint Peace Commission to negotiate peaceful solutions with the Indians. The commission included three generals—Sherman, Harney, and Terry—together with N. G. Taylor, commissioner of Indian affairs, and three civilian members. Sherman's participation in the peace commission is incongruous. While his duty as a peace commissioner required his utmost good faith to achieve peace through peaceful means, he had and always did advocate the use of his army to kill the Indians or forcibly remove them from the pathways of settlement. In its first report, dated January 7, 1868, the commission noted, "Have we [the United States] been uniformly unjust? We answer, unhesitatingly, yes."[13]

The peace commission negotiated a second Treaty of Fort Laramie with the "Sioux Nation of Indians," which was dated April 29, 1868,[14] and subsequently ratified by the United States Senate and proclaimed into law by President Johnson in February of 1869. This treaty resulted from extensive and extended negotiations between the parties. The government desperately needed commitments from the Lakotas that would enable the peaceful completion of the Union Pacific Railroad. The right of way and congressional land grants to the Union Pacific followed the valley of the North Platte River through the heart of the Lakotas' buffalo country. The government also wanted to move the Lakotas' reservations north, outside the state of Nebraska and into the Dakota Territory. This relocation resulted in a substantial reduction in the size of the Great Sioux Reservation and the area where the Lakotas hunted buffalo. In return, Red Cloud and his Lakota followers demanded that the government abandon Forts Reno, Phil Kearny, and C. F. Smith, which were situated on the Bozeman Trail (east of the Bighorn Mountains in eastern Wyoming and southeastern Montana), that they be permitted to hunt buffalo between the North Platte and Smoky Hill rivers (to the south), and that they have the right to exclusive occupancy and hunting on the land north of the North Platte River and east of the summits of the Bighorn Mountains. On its face the treaty represented a good faith effort to achieve lasting peace and equitable results for all the parties. It also gave a fresh start to peaceful relations among the various Indian tribes. Red Cloud and his followers signed the treaty in November 1868, more than two months after the Bozeman Trail forts were officially abandoned by the U.S. Army.[15] However, Sitting Bull and certain of his Hunkpapa followers, and Crazy Horse with other Lakotas, refused to sign. Later, in July of 1868, the peace commission met at Fort Rice (in what is now North Dakota) with approximately 1500 lodges of Lakotas, Nakotas, Dakotas, Gros Ventres, Cheyennes, and Arapahos to entice more Indians to sign this treaty. During the deliberations the famous Hunkpapa war leader Gall stated his forceful reasons why he distrusted the promises of the "Great Father":

Many of these men before me were at the [1851] treaty of Fort Laramie. The promises the "Great Father" made to us there were utterly false. He told us one thing and did another. He told us that the land set aside for

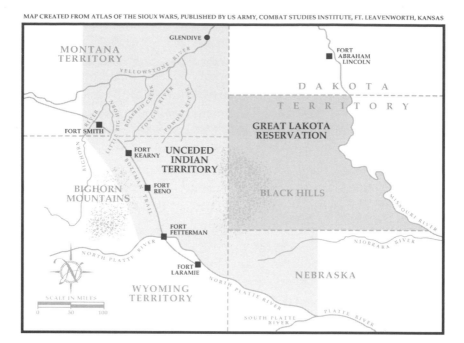

Map 2. Indian War Country—1868 Treaty Lands. Map copyright © Charles E. Wright.

us would not be invaded by white people, that we would be unmolested. Did he keep his compact? Before the treaty was a year old the white people built roads and bridges across our best hunting lands, without our consent and in the face of our protests. Did the "Great Father" stop his people from trespassing on our land? No![16]

The 1868 Treaty created two tracts of land (map 2) that were directly related to the Great Sioux War of 1876–1877, including the battles at Rosebud Creek and the Little Big Horn River. The first tract (described in article 2 of the treaty) was called the "Great Sioux Reservation" and spanned that portion of what is now the state of South Dakota west of the Missouri River, extending west to the eastern borders of the Montana Territory and what would become the Wyoming Territory on July 25, 1868. It included the Black Hills, located in western South Dakota. This reservation was set apart for the "absolute and undisturbed use and occupation of the Indians herein named." No one else, except officers, agents, or employees of the government "in discharge of duties enjoined by law"[17] would ever be permitted to pass over, settle upon, or reside on the reservation.

The second tract (described in article 16 of the treaty) was the Indians' "unceded Indian territory,"[18] described as "the country north of the North Platte River and east of the summits of the Bighorn Mountains." Its exclusive use and possession by the Sioux were clear: "No white person shall be permitted to settle upon or occupy any portion of the same; or without the consent of the Indians first had and obtained, to pass through the same."[19] There were no exceptions to this grant of exclusive use. In addition, this Article 16 required the United States to abandon Forts Reno, Phil Kearny, and Smith, which were located in the unceded Indian territory.

Confusion exists among historians and writers concerning the northern boundary of the unceded Indian territory. While the southern boundary is clearly the north bank of the North Platte River (the eastern boundary is immaterial) and the summits of the Bighorn Mountains (western boundary) are easily determined, there is no limitation to the northern extension of the boundary. The Little Big Horn Battlefield and the entire Yellowstone River basin east of the mouth of the Bighorn River are both north of the North Platte River and east of the summits of the Bighorn Mountains—and it is my contention that this entire area was part of the unceded Indian territory covered by Article 16 of the 1868 Treaty. In 1875 a congressional committee offered to purchase a portion of the "unceded Indian territory" of article 16 from the Sioux in which the northern boundary was defined as the Yellowstone River.[20] This contention was supported much later by the words of Supreme Court Justice Harry Blackmun, who observed, "In the winter of 1875–1876, many of the Sioux were hunting in the unceded territory north of the North Platte River, *reserved to them for that purpose in the Fort Laramie Treaty*" (emphasis supplied).[21] Indeed, the United States Supreme Court has held on more than one occasion that a treaty between the "United States and an Indian Tribe must be construed in the sense in which they [the treaty terms] would naturally be understood by the Indians," noting further that, "the United States, as the party with the presumptively superior negotiating skills and superior knowledge of the language in which the treaty is worded, has the responsibility to avoid taking advantage of the other side."[22] No one could seriously contend that the Sioux did not regard this area as part of their unceded hunting grounds because this is where sizeable buffalo herds were located—in both 1868 and 1876 and at all times intervening. This interpretation is in conformity with the army's actions. In August of 1868, Brig. Gen. Christopher C. Augur, commander of the Department of the Platte, notified all officers of the Indians' right to hunt in their ceded land without any interference from the army, unless depredations were involved.[23]

Thus, by the Treaty of 1868, the Sioux (and the Cheyennes with their permission) had (1) the unrestricted right to reside upon and occupy the Great Sioux Reservation in South Dakota (which included the Black Hills), and (2) the absolute unrestricted and exclusive right to travel upon, occupy, and hunt in the unceded Indian territory which included the land on the south side of the Yellowstone River in southeastern Montana, where the battles at Rosebud Creek and the Little Big Horn took place in June 1876. The unceded Indian territory was, in essence, a Sioux game preserve that was not available for settlement or trespass by white persons, including the U.S. Army. As further protection to the Sioux, Article 12 of the treaty also provided that no treaty for cession of any portion of the "reservation herein described which may be held in common" shall have any validity unless signed by three-fourths of all adult male Indians occupying or interested in the same.

Demonstrating his lack of good faith in failing to comply with the terms of the 1868 Treaty that he had helped to negotiate (which was the "supreme Law of the Land"), General Sherman wrote a letter to his brother John on September 28, 1868, declaring:

> All who cling to their old hunting grounds are hostile and will remain so til killed out. . . . From the nature of things we must take chances and clean out Indians as we encounter them.[24]
>
> The more we can kill this year, the less will have to be killed the next year, for the more I see of these Indians the more convinced I am that they will all have to be killed or be maintained as a species of paupers. Their attempts at civilization are simply ridiculous.[25]

These comments advocate premeditated murder, violations of the Fifth Amendment of the U.S. Constitution and Articles 2 and 16 of the 1868 Treaty of Fort Laramie. Congress ratified the 1868 Treaty of Fort Laramie on February 16, 1869. Eight days later (February 24), President

Andrew Johnson proclaimed the treaty, stating, "From this day forward all war between the parties to this agreement shall forever cease. *The Government of the United States desires peace, and its honor is hereby pledged to keep it.* The Indians desire peace, and they now pledge their honor to maintain it" (emphasis supplied).

Within two weeks Johnson was out of office, and Ulysses S. Grant was sworn in as the newly elected president. He openly supported the congressional peace policy that involved the appointment of representatives of various Christian denominations to serve as government agents on the Indians' reservations. Grant termed Indian extermination as "wicked" and advocated a policy of leniency.[26] When Grant became president, General Sherman took his position as General of the Armies. Sherman brought with him his racist addiction to unmitigated genocide. Notwithstanding his original intentions, the honor that was pledged by President Johnson was dishonored by President Grant and Generals Sherman and Sheridan in the subsequent decade.

By 1873 construction of the Northern Pacific Railroad extended west to Bismarck in Dakota Territory (now North Dakota). The Northern Pacific was sending survey parties ahead of construction into southeastern Montana along the Yellowstone and Musselshell rivers—the area that the Lakotas and Cheyennes considered prime buffalo-hunting grounds.[27] In 1871 a survey party worked between Fort Rice in North Dakota and Glendive Creek in Montana. Another survey operated out of Fort Ellis to a point near Pompey's Tower on the north bank of the Yellowstone River in unceded Indian territory. There were no attacks by Indians, but the surveyors were becoming apprehensive. Additional parties went out with a larger escort in 1872, and there were two significant encounters with the Indians. To complete the survey between Glendive Creek and Pompey's Tower in the summer of 1873, Custer and a force of 1,531 soldiers escorted 375 civilians and 2,300 horses and mules engaged in the task. In addition to protecting the survey party, the expedition turned into a festive hunting party with card playing, drinking, and chasing buffalo and other game with packs of dogs. The expedition was fiercely contested by the Sioux[28] who considered the survey excursions to be violations of the 1868 Treaty, since they occurred in their "unceded Indian territory," where trespass by any non-Indian person at any time for any purpose was prohibited.

In the meantime reports were circulating that gold could be found in the Black Hills—the heart of the Great Sioux Reservation.[29] Generals Sherman and Sheridan were bent upon using the army they commanded to remove the Lakotas and Cheyennes from their treaty lands to facilitate the construction of another transcontinental railroad and to provide land for settlement by the whites who would move into the area. A faltering national economy, experiencing a downturn in 1873–1874,[30] resulted in hundreds of unemployed workers and fortune hunters gathered south of Dakota Territory who were intent on moving north and finding gold in the Black Hills.

Until 1874 the U.S. Army prevented movement of white settlers into the Black Hills by enforcing the language in Article 2 of the 1868 Treaty. However, in 1874 Sheridan decided to establish a military post on the Sioux reservation. He gave Custer an order to take a contingent of 1,000 soldiers, 110 supply wagons, and 2,000 animals on an exploration expedition into the Black Hills.[31] This was another serious violation of Article 2 because the expedition had nothing to do with "duties enjoined by law," and Sheridan was not authorized to create duties or define the law. Any so-called "duties" would have to be specified in a law enacted by Congress or performed pursuant to a law or valid governmental regulation then in existence. None of these conditions were present. Engineers accompanied the expedition, and Custer provided exaggerated reports of the area, describing its suitability for settlement and indicating that engineers on the expedition had discovered gold. This information was rapidly disseminated to the public, and Sheridan helped promote the findings with his recommendation that the government move to regain the Black Hills from the Lakotas. With news of gold, prospectors and others flooded into the area despite the army's sporadic attempts to keep them out.[32] The influx continued well into 1875, when additional government officials were sent into the territory to continue the quest for gold and other minerals.

Although he had participated directly in the negotiation of the 1868 Treaty, Gen. Alfred W. Terry, a lawyer himself, saw nothing wrong with Custer's incursion. He stated, "From the earliest times the government has exercised the right of sending exploring parties of a military character into unceded territory, and this expedition is nothing more."[33] Terry's legal skills were nonexistent or had become rusty. The Black Hills were not "unceded territory." They were part of the Great Sioux Reservation, set aside and ceded to the Sioux in Article 2 for their use and occupancy forever. The treaty had been ratified by the Senate as part of its "peace process" and was signed into law by the president. As we shall soon observe, Terry had little skill in reading a map.

Public opinion and pressure mounted for the government to break the treaty and allow white settlement of the Black Hills. In 1875 Congress tried to take the high road by creating another commission with a mission to induce the Lakotas to sell or relinquish the Black Hills for a cash settlement. The secretary of the interior told the commissioners to remember that they were dealing with "an ignorant and almost helpless people" and that they must "secure the best interests of both parties so far as practicable."[34] The "Allison Commission" was named after William Boyd Allison, who was chairman of the Senate Committee of Indian Affairs from 1875 to 1881. The commission approached the Indians with a sell-or-starve ultimatum, offering them six million dollars for the Black Hills while, at the same time, demanding that the Sioux cede all their hunting rights in the previously unceded Indian territory. The Sioux countered with an offer to sell for seventy million dollars. An alternative government proposal to lease the Black Hills was unacceptable, and the negotiations broke down.[35] Commissioner of Indian Affairs Edward Smith refused to side with the Lakotas in the negotiations, and their support in Congress was waning.

Without waiting for Congress to take further action, President Grant got his hands dirty. In his inaugural 1869 address, Grant had described a new and humane approach toward the Indians: "Wars of extermination are demoralizing and wicked. Our superiority should make us lenient toward the Indian. . . . A system which looks to the extinction of a race is too horrible to adopt without entailing upon itself the wrath of all Christendom."[36] With this noble announcement Grant sought to establish a new peace commission that included representatives of the church. However, by 1875 his dark side had prevailed. He put aside the Constitution and the 1868 Treaty and succumbed to General Sherman's strategy based upon forcible removal and extermination. In matters dealing with the Indians in 1875 and thereafter, Grant, like Andrew Jackson and Thomas Jefferson, had no honor.

When the term "conspiracy" is linked to a president of the United States, it takes on a special significance. The full power of the executive

Ulysses S. Grant, president of the United States. Courtesy Nebraska State Historical Society.

General of the Armies William T. Sherman. Courtesy Nebraska State Historical Society.

Lt. Gen. Philip M. Sheridan, commander of the Division of Missouri. Courtesy Nebraska State Historical Society.

Maj. Gen. Alfred W. Terry, commander of the Department of Dakota. Courtesy Denver Public Library, Western History Collection (Z-3574).

branch is conferred on the office of the president by our Constitution—a Constitution that the president has sworn to "preserve, protect and defend." To conspire "is to join in a secret agreement to do a wrongful act."[37] Its four elements consist of an agreement, more than one conspirator, secrecy, and a wrongful act. The element of a wrongful act is by far the most important, particularly when the prime conspirator is the most powerful person in the nation and the wrongful act involves the intentional use of the U.S. Army to violate the Fifth Amendment to the Constitution and the terms of a solemn treaty enacted into law by Congress. The wrong in the wrongful act is magnified many times over when it is a secret action jointly undertaken with other constitutional officers of the government. The element of secrecy eliminated any oversight by Congress and the courts and concealed the wrong from the free press and public opinion. In this instance we are not dealing with subjective accusations in the heat of a hotly contested presidential election. Instead, we are confronting specific facts of an objective nature violating basic human rights of thousands of Indians. The Sioux and Cheyennes were persons entitled to life, liberty, and property under the Fifth Amendment, and their reservation and their hunting territories were specifically authorized and created in the 1868 Treaty.

While the Congressional peace commission was still in existence, Grant decided to subvert the law and utilize military force to remove the Lakotas and Cheyennes from the Black Hills and their unceded Indian territory. He succumbed to Sherman's views on the use of force as the most expedient and certain method of depriving the Indians of their land and their liberty to exist on it as hunters. Grant realized that the Indians lacked the ability to enforce the 1868 Treaty and gambled that no branch of the government, whether it be the courts or Congress, would exercise any restraint in regard to his intended actions. In October of 1875, Grant appointed former senator Zachariah Chandler to become secretary of the interior. The secretary of war was none other than Gen. William W. Belknap, who had served with Grant in the Union Army and was a strong advocate of a military solution to the Indian question.

In 1976 and 1991, Dr. John S. Gray, a medical doctor and physiology professor, published the first of two detailed books about Custer and the Battle at the Little Big Horn River in 1876. Gray described Grant's conspiracy, in which the president believed that "it would be advisable, however, to devise some smoke-screen to cloak such naked aggression from political opponents and the public. It would be imperative somehow to shift the onus to the Indians, especially the 'hostile' bands. This would demand a little ingenious conniving, inasmuch as the Sioux had chosen to remain so peaceful in the face of outrageous provocation."[38]

Grant proceeded to organize and place in motion a brutal and illegal military campaign. On November 3, 1875, he summoned Generals Sheridan and Crook to his office, together with Secretary of the Interior Zachariah Chandler and Secretary of War William W. Belknap, to formulate his plan. For reasons unknown, General of the Army William T. Sherman, the leading advocate of forcible removal, was not present. Grant, acting in bad faith, ordered Generals Sheridan and Crook to have their armies discontinue preventing miners and other settlers from trespassing onto the Great Sioux Reservation in the Black Hills, an order that was in specific violation of the Treaty of 1868. In addition, Sheridan's army was directed to initiate a punitive winter campaign in 1876 against those Lakotas and Cheyennes in their "unceded Indian territory" who failed to return and surrender at their agencies. Efforts were made to gain public approval by generating false information about Indian atrocities that would inflame the general public.

On November 4 the press announced that the army would no longer make any effort to keep settlers out of the Black Hills. In doing this, Grant was generating an influx of gold-seeking settlers to enhance his plan to (1) regain the Black Hills from the Lakotas and (2) use his army to subjugate the Lakotas and Cheyennes who were hunting in unceded Indian territory. E. C. Watkins, an Indian inspector with but two years' experience, released a report dated November 9, 1875, containing scurrilous comments about the Sioux who refused to cede back the Black Hills to the United States, calling them disrespectful of authority, plunderers, and murderers, and responsible for constantly stirring up warfare with other peaceful Indians in the area. His report was published six days *subsequent* to the clandestine meeting between Grant and his coconspirators on November 3. The Watkins report did not mention Grant's plan to reacquire the Black Hills. It merely characterized the Indians as terrorists who needed to be conquered and subdued.[39] Oddly, Sherman himself was left out of direct participation in the conspiratorial meeting of November 3. Perhaps President Grant, based upon his experiences with

General Sherman in the sacking of Atlanta during the Civil War, realized that Sherman was too intelligent to risk his career and reputation by attacking the Indians on their reservation or while hunting in their unceded Indian territory without the protection of an order from his commander in chief.

This is how Grant's conspiracy to take the Black Hills and the "unceded hunting territory" from the Sioux unfolded. In a letter dated November 9, 1875, General Sheridan wrote to Gen. Alfred H. Terry, who commanded the Department of Dakota, stating that while existing orders forbidding occupation of the Black Hills by miners would not be rescinded, there should be no further efforts by the U.S. Army to prevent the miners from entering the Black Hills. He ordered Terry to "quietly cause the troops in your department to assume such attitudes as will meet the views of the President in this respect" [secrecy and wrongful act]. Four days later Sheridan brought Sherman into the conspiracy by mailing to Sherman a copy of Sheridan's letter to Terry stating, "The enclosed copy of confidential letter to Terry will best explain the present status of the Black Hills. The whole thing has gone along about as I had expected." Acknowledging his awareness of the intentional violation of the 1868 Treaty, Sheridan cautioned his boss, "The Terry letter had best be kept confidential" [secrecy and more than one conspirator]. On November 20, 1875, Sherman added to the smoking-gun letters in his response to Sheridan, "Your letter of November 13 with enclosure was duly received, and would have been answered immediately. Only I know that the matter of the Black Hills was settled at all events for this year. In the Spring it may result in Collision and trouble." [Knowledge of intentional commission of wrongful act, and "count me in."] "But I think the Sioux Indians are all now so dependent on their rations, that they will have to do whatever they are required to do. My own idea of their Treaty is that the settlements may now be made all along the Western Boundary. And if some [incoming settlers] go over the Boundary into the Black Hills, I understand that the President and Interior Department will wink at it for the present"[40] [secrecy, wrongful act, agreement, and multiple parties]. Each of the four elements of a criminal conspiracy was abundantly present.

To initiate the wrongful action, the commissioner of Indian affairs (on December 6, 1875) directed the Indian agents on the Lakota reservations to notify the Lakotas and Cheyennes hunting in the unceded Indian territory that they must surrender and return to their agencies by January 31, 1876, or they would be treated as "hostile." Thus, Grant (without the knowledge or consent of Congress) violated the solemn provisions of an existing treaty (a treaty granted status as "the supreme Law of the Land" in Article VI of the Constitution) and engineered an undeclared war on the Indians of the northern plains who failed to surrender and return to their agencies by that date. The U.S. Army's actions against the Indians would generally follow a prescribed pattern of genocidal war, similar to Sherman's strategies in the Civil War, his actions against Indians in the southwest, and his written comments to President Grant, Secretary of War Stanton, and his brother, Senator John Sherman, on the use of force and extermination to solve the so-called "Indian problem." There would be indiscriminate and premeditated murder of noncombatants—including women and children. Shelter, horses, food, and other necessaries would be destroyed. The declaration of hostility authorized the army to treat all off-reservation Indians as hostile. For those Indians who were not killed, forcible removal to reservations selected by the government was the order of the day. Removal would include forfeiture of firearms and horses and confinement to the reservation (all of which constituted deprivation of the Indians' liberty and taking of their property, all without Fifth Amendment due process). While the number of Indians declared hostile was not large when compared with the population of the United States, it involved a large percentage of the Sioux and Northern Cheyenne populations and was nonetheless a declaration of war (against American persons protected by the Fifth Amendment) authored by President Grant without authorization by Congress. It proved to be a war of rapid attrition by an organized military against the Lakotas and Cheyennes, who, while hardy and resolute, lacked the resources, manpower, and military expertise to protect their treaty rights—all in violation of the Constitution and the 1868 Treaty of Fort Laramie, in a manner prohibited by General Orders No. 100.

For many of the Lakotas and Cheyennes, return to their agencies by January 31, 1876, was not possible due to the timing of the notice, the lack of sufficient communications, and the great distance to the reservation from their location in their unceded hunting territory.[41]

Edward L. Lazarus, in his book about Sioux litigation over their claim to the Black Hills, described Grant's disingenuous message to Congress:[42]

In his State of the Union message at the end of 1875, President Grant told the Congress and the country that in the next year it would be increasingly difficult to protect Sioux treaty rights and that the legislature would have "to adopt some measures to relieve the embarrassment" of the Black Hills predicament. Of course, Grant had already taken those measures. He had opened the hills and then set the stage for a military solution to the Sioux problem, putting to an end two decades of vacillation over what to do with the most powerful and vexing tribe still roaming the west.[43]

With General Sheridan at the helm of the Military Division of the Missouri, a brutal military solution was formulated and acted out, inflicting murder and remorseless hardship upon women, children, noncombatants, and innocent warriors of the Lakota, Cheyenne, and Arapaho nations—Indians who were all "persons" entitled to life, liberty, justice, and other rights under our Constitution. The policy also tested the honor and morality of the officers and enlisted men who were ordered to carry out brutal campaigns against isolated Indian villages during the extreme winter climate so prevalent on the northern plains.

Chapter Six

# The Great Sioux War Is Launched

*I expect to be in the field, in the summer, with the 7th, and think there will be lively work before us. I think the 7th Cavalry may have its greatest campaign ahead.*

—*Letter from Lt. Col. George A. Custer to his brother Tom, January, 1876*[1]

The commissioner of Indian affairs ordered all Lakotas to return to their agencies by January 31, 1876, or be treated as hostile. The order was turned over to Gen. William T. Sherman and his army for enforcement. Gen. Philip H. Sheridan commanded the Military Division of the Missouri, which included the Department of the Platte (commanded by Gen. George Crook) and the Department of Dakota (commanded by Gen. Alfred H. Terry). Anticipating that the U.S. Army's action against the Indians would occur on the Sioux treaty land in southeastern Montana, Sheridan ordered Crook to move his forces north out of Fort Fetterman in the direction of the Yellowstone River at the earliest possible date; he also ordered Terry to proceed west from Fort Abraham Lincoln in Dakota Territory along the north side of the Yellowstone River before turning south to attack the Indians, who would probably be located on one of the four principal watersheds flowing into the Yellowstone from the south. Crook commenced his movement north out of Fort Fetterman on the first of March, but it took Terry until the middle of May to assemble Custer and the entire Seventh Cavalry Regiment and start west from Fort Lincoln.[2]

Terry also had at his disposal troops that were stationed in western Montana under the command of Col. John Gibbon (called "No Hip Bone" by the Indians), who was directed to proceed north, then east from Fort Ellis in southwestern Montana along the north bank of the Yellowstone

River until he met Terry's command. It was left to Generals Crook and Terry to locate and attack those Indians who had not complied with the illegal order to return to their agencies. Sheridan believed that Crook's and Terry's commands were each of sufficient size and strength to overcome any force of Indians that they might encounter. Accordingly, his orders did not provide for any coordination between Crook and Terry. Each would operate on his own without knowledge of the Indians' strength and location and with no knowledge of where the other column was located or what it was doing.[3]

As commander of the Department of Dakota, General Terry would lead the "northern column" that would proceed west from Fort Abraham Lincoln in Dakota Territory (the timing was not coordinated with Crook's "southern column"), cross the Missouri River, and continue west on the north side of the Yellowstone River, all the while searching for the location of the Lakotas and Cheyennes who were hunting buffalo in southeastern Montana. Terry did not want to lead U.S. Army troops into combat with Indian camps, particularly when women and children were apt to be killed. He had devised a plan to have Custer and the Seventh Cavalry act as his strike force when the Lakotas and Cheyennes were located. Custer was anxious to lead another strike on an Indian encampment because it would afford him with an opportunity to attack and kill Indians, achieve a military victory, and enhance his reputation as a brave "Indian fighter." However, Custer was in trouble with President Grant over defamatory testimony about Grant's brother at a congressional hearing. While Custer was returning from congressional hearings to his regiment at Fort Lincoln, General Sherman ordered General Sheridan to detain him and "let the expedition proceed without him." Thus, on May 4, 1876, Custer was relieved of his command and was being held in Chicago when Terry and Sheridan came to his rescue, persuading Grant to allow Custer to be released from detention and accompany Terry and his northern column when it moved west out of Fort Lincoln on May 17, 1876.[4]

Fort Fetterman was located about forty miles due east of the present city of Casper, Wyoming, along the bank of the North Platte River. During February Gen. George Crook organized his "Big Horn Expedition,"[5] intending to move north from Fort Fetterman in the direction of the Powder and Tongue rivers, which run north out of Wyoming into the

Yellowstone River drainage in southeastern Montana. Crook's movement would be a violation of Article 16 of the 1868 Treaty—the very moment that he moved north from Fort Fetterman, he was trespassing into "unceded Indian territory." Since Sherman, Sheridan, and Crook were acting under orders from the president, only disobedience by General Crook or judicial oversight could have prevented Grant, Sherman, and Sheridan's violation of the 1868 Treaty enacted into law by Congress.

Crook used pack mules and mule-drawn wagons to carry food, grain, and ammunition.[6] Forty-five head of cattle on the hoof accompanied his expedition, which got underway in heavy snow on March 1, 1876. On the second night a small band of Lakotas ran off Crook's beef supply, leaving his expedition short on rations. On March 5 Crook initiated reconnaissance by sending out scouts and guides in search of the raiders. On March 16 his scouts located a trail leading to an Indian village of Lakotas and Northern Cheyennes,[7] which turned out to be a camp of 400 to 500 Indians containing one hundred lodges with approximately eighty-five warriors. Crook ordered an attack to be led by Col. Joseph J. Reynolds with 375 cavalry troopers. The objective was to locate and attack the Indians, kill or capture as many as possible, drive off the Indians' ponies, and confiscate their food supplies to replace Crook's stolen cattle.[8] Reynolds deployed his troopers into several units as they approached and surrounded the Indian village at nine o'clock on the morning of March 17. Despite the fact that it commenced in broad daylight, Reynolds' attack achieved a complete surprise. Cheyenne scouts had spotted the approach of Reynolds' battalion during daylight on the sixteenth. Ten young scouts were sent out for surveillance. The scouts' ponies were in bad condition, and they were unable to detect the soldiers in time to return to the camp and give adequate warning.[9]

Reynolds' charge began 200 yards from the camp. Women and children scattered as the warriors were driven out of the village. Reynolds maintained tactical control of his entire force throughout the battle. Although the capture of the pony herd was accomplished by mounted troopers, most of their fighting in and about the village was dismounted.

Casualties on each side were very light—the army lost four troops and six others were wounded, while three Indians were killed and one wounded.[10] Damage to the Indians amounted to the loss of all their shelter, ammunition, and food stores, 2,000 to 3,000 buffalo hides, as well as saddles and various other necessaries. Instead of saving the food and other provisions for use by Crook's expedition, Reynolds destroyed it all. Thus his attack, while it damaged the Indians' morale and left them in a state of potential starvation, was not successful in capturing or subjugating them or depriving them of all their horses. The Indian camp contained both Cheyenne and Oglala lodges.[11] Reynolds withdrew from the village at 1:00 p.m., having led what was later classified as a shoddy attack and a worse withdrawal.[12] Left behind were the remains of three dead soldiers and a seriously wounded trooper, who was still alive.[13] Wooden Leg, a Northern Cheyenne warrior, was part of the band of one hundred lodges attacked by Reynolds. Wooden Leg observed, "The Cheyennes were beaten away from the camp. From a distance we saw the destruction of our village. Our tepees were burned, with everything in them except what the soldiers may have taken. . . . The Cheyennes were rendered very poor. I had nothing left but the clothing I had on, with a soldier coat added."[14] The Cheyennes who escaped were not followed by the soldiers. Their warriors were able to recapture some of their ponies and bring them to their camp members for use in their escape.

When the battle was over, Crook's soldiers had slaughtered more than one hundred Indian ponies to provide meat for his troops. Officers under Reynolds' command as well as a newspaper reporter, Robert Strahorn of the *Rocky Mountain News*, and Crook's adjutant, Lt. John Bourke, leveled serious charges against Colonel Reynolds and his officers. After reviewing these accusations, Crook filed court-martial charges against Reynolds and Capt. Alexander Moore, charging Reynolds with abandoning the body of a wounded trooper, destroying the Indians' meat that was needed to feed soldiers, and allowing the Indians to recapture most of their ponies.[15]

The most significant aspect of the battle was the fact that Reynolds' force had been able to reach the Cheyenne and Lakota village without being detected. Despite the successful reconnaissance and the element of surprise, Reynolds' troops were not able to achieve any control over the Indians other than to destroy their stationary shelter and supplies. The Indians themselves easily escaped Reynolds' force of 375 fighting men. It should be noted that Reynolds' strike force was 49 percent greater than Custer's ultimate strike force of 210 troopers would be when it attempted three months later to attack an Indian encampment of 4,000 to 6,000

Indians containing approximately 1500 warriors on the Little Big Horn. In other words, Colonel Reynolds' strike force at Powder River had 3.5 troopers for each Indian warrior, whereas at Little Big Horn, Custer had only one trooper per 7.14 warriors.

Following the episode on Powder River, Crook returned to Fort Fetterman for reorganization and resupply. On May 29 he set out for a second time on a renewed "Bighorn and Yellowstone expedition." In his command were forty-seven officers and 1,002 men, accompanied by 103 six-mule wagons and 250 pack mules.[16] Crook dispatched guides Frank Grouard, Big Bat Pourier, and Louis Richard to recruit Crow scouts as guides for his next venture into southeastern Montana. On June 6 he took a wrong turn and reached a site along the south side of the Tongue River less than one mile from the Montana border. He pitched camp at this site to await the arrival of the Crow scouts. At 4:00 p.m. on June 9, Crook's camp was attacked from a distance of 600 yards by approximately 200 Northern Cheyennes led by Little Hawk. Crook immediately dispatched infantry and cavalry companies to secure the camp and protect his livestock. They exchanged fire with the Indians for approximately one hour before the Indians retired. Crook's casualties were two wounded, and the Indians suffered two wounded or killed warriors. The fighting was both mounted and dismounted. The encounter was of no particular significance other than to demonstrate to the U.S. troops that the Cheyennes were willing to attack and fight. On June 11 Crook proceeded to Goose Creek, which was not more than forty-five miles south of the main Indian encampment then located on the west bank of Rosebud Creek. Had Crook used long-range scouts (up to fifty miles), he might have been aware of the location and strength of the Indian encampment and devised a plan that would have placed him in proximity with Terry's forces coming from the north. However, Crook had no knowledge of Terry's movements or location, so there was nothing that he could do to coordinate.[17]

Following the Tongue River encounter, Crook returned twelve miles to the south, where he continued to await the much anticipated Crow and Shoshoni scouts. The Crow scouts arrived, 176 strong, on the afternoon of June 14, providing much comfort for General Crook. Shortly thereafter, they were joined by 86 Shoshoni warriors.[18] Since Indian scouts were not required to fight, it is not clear why 262 scouts were needed. Continuing north, Crook's expedition reached the north bank of Rosebud Creek on June 16. On the morning of the seventeenth, Crook's camp on the Rosebud was underway at 6:00 a.m., with his Crow scouts moving ahead and on his flanks.[19]

During the second week of June, at a point approximately fifty miles downstream on Rosebud Creek, Sitting Bull and his loyal Hunkpapas had staged a sun dance, one of the most strenuous and sacred of the Lakota spiritual rituals.[20] His arms pierced in one hundred places and bleeding profusely, Sitting Bull danced until he became unconscious. When he came to, he recounted a vision in which he "had observed, numerous as grasshoppers, soldiers and horses bearing down on an Indian village below. They came, men and animals both, upside down, their feet in the sky, their heads to the earth with hats falling off." Sitting Bull told his followers that the soldiers would die but that they (the Hunkpapas) should not "take their spoils."[21] All the soldiers would be killed and the Indians would win a great victory. Sitting Bull's vision, which was partially realized in the Battle at the Little Big Horn, galvanized the Indians' morale, consolidating their will to stand and fight. Within a week after the sun dance, Cheyenne and Lakota warriors discovered the approach of General Crook's expedition from the south.

Crook halted on Rosebud Creek at 8:00 a.m. on the seventeenth of June to rest his men and give the horses and mules a chance to graze (see map 3). At this time the main encampment of the Sioux and Cheyenne Indians was less than twenty miles northwest of Crook on the north bank of Reno Creek, at a point less than five miles from the Little Big Horn River. Cheyenne and Lakota warriors were moving to initiate a preemptive strike on Crook while he was at least one day's march southeast of their encampment.[22] Among the leaders of the attack were Crazy Horse, Gall, Rain in the Face, Little Horse, and Two Moon. Crook had dispatched scouts to hunt and scout ahead (north) of his column. About eleven miles out they encountered a large group of Cheyenne and Lakota warriors moving south toward Crook. Fleeing back to camp, the Crow scouts had sufficient time to alert Crook and his forces. The Indians' preemptive strike forestalled Crook's approaching scouts from sighting their encampment on Reno Creek.

The Rosebud battle commenced at 8:30 a.m. and lasted for more than seven hours. During the fight Crook exercised tactical control over his

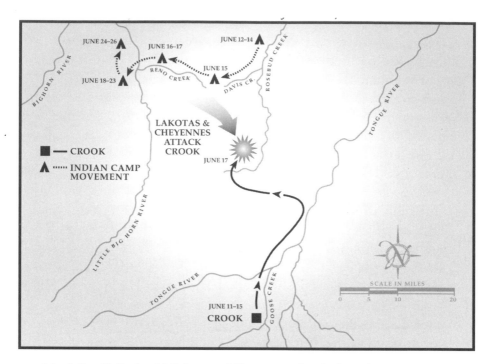

Map 3. Crook's Battle with Lakotas and Cheyennes at Rosebud Creek, June 17, 1876.
Map copyright © Charles E. Wright.

entire command, although impulsive action by Lieutenant Colonel Roy-
all endangered one small battalion. The Indians hit and ran, operating
without traditional military organization and tactics. Keeping his forces
together, Crook made several sound tactical moves, but his overall strategy was defense. He had successfully avoided an ambush. Crook sustained nine killed and twenty-one wounded[23] and lost sixteen horses.
Estimates for the Indians were twenty-six to thirty-six killed and six-
ty-three to eighty-six wounded.[24] Most of the army's fighting was done
while dismounted, and they expended an estimated 25,000 rounds of
ammunition.[25] Crook's Indian scouts fought bravely but had not ranged
far enough ahead to provide Crook with timely intelligence about the
size and location of the Indian encampment. In leading the battle, Crook
accepted advice from his junior officers and also listened to his scouts,
who cautioned him that they were being led up a canyon to the north
and west into an ambush. True or not (the scouts had seen nothing),

Crook determined not to continue north in search of the Indians' main camp, a decision that may well have determined the fate of Custer and his subsequent efforts at the Little Big Horn.

Following the battle Lakotas and Cheyennes believed that they had won a great victory. In addition to their dead and wounded, there had been significant expenditure of Indian ammunition. Offsetting this, the Indians gained experience, knowledge, and conviction—the U.S. Army was not invincible, and they now knew the location and strength of Crook's 1,000 troops. The army was pursuing them into and through their "unceded Indian territory."

After the battle Crook retired south to the Goose Creek area to re-plenish exhausted supplies and to obtain additional reinforcements and scouts to guide his intended movement north toward the Little Big Horn. Historian Neil Mangum has noted that "because of Crook's dilatory ac-tion after the battle, some critics have crucified the commander. He has often served as the scapegoat for the disaster that befell Custer eight days later on Little Bighorn."[26] However, Crook's decision to retire to Goose Creek made good sense. He was crossing rough ground more than 300 miles northwest of his base of supply, the Union Pacific terminal at Fort D. A. Russell near Cheyenne, Wyoming Territory. In the field for nineteen days, he needed to replace ammunition, resupply food for his men (and 262 scouts) and feed for his horses, obtain additional fighting strength, provide medical care for twenty-two wounded soldiers, and find new Indian scouts to lead him northward. His orders from General Sheridan said nothing about coordination with Terry, and neither Crook nor Ter-ry was aware of the other's location and direction of movement. But for the Rosebud battle Crook's ammunition would have been adequate, and he would not have had twenty-two wounded soldiers requiring medical care. Thus, he might well have continued moving northward toward the Little Big Horn and a chance meeting with Custer before Custer reached the Indians' grand encampment.

Chapter Seven
# June 21, 1876—The Setting

*I think my only plan will be to give Custer a secure base well up on the*
*Yellowstone to which he can retire at any time the Indians gather in too*
*great numbers for the small force he will have.*

—*Gen. Alfred H. Terry to his commanding officer, Gen. Philip Sheridan, on*
*February 21, 1876*

The fate awaiting Custer and his men would take place on the east side
of the Little Big Horn River in southeast Montana, approximately forty
miles north of the Montana-Wyoming border along the south side of the
Yellowstone River watershed. The Yellowstone flows north out of what
is now Yellowstone Park toward Fort Ellis in Montana Territory. There
it changes course and runs generally in a northeasterly direction until
it flows into the Missouri River near the Montana-Dakota border. The
Bighorn River flows north out of the Bighorn Mountains in northern
Wyoming for approximately fifty miles before its junction with the Little
Big Horn River near Hardin, Montana (see map 4).

The Yellowstone Basin is made up of four rivers (Bighorn, Rosebud
[Creek], Tongue, and Powder) and small creeks flowing into them, as well
as riparian valleys providing pastures of cool- and warm-season grasses
on which buffalo fed. By the middle of June, the warm-season grasses
were at their best stage of maturity for both buffalo and horses. The Indians' movements were governed by the location of the buffalo herds and
the availability of adequate grass and fresh water for their horses. This
area contained some of the last vestiges of the northern buffalo herd and
was utilized by Lakotas and Cheyennes as a traditional summer hunting
ground. Higher ground between the river valleys was rough and laced
with hills, dry and flowing creeks, coulees, gulches, and ravines, making

TERRY & GIBBON APPROACH FROM THE NORTH, CROOK APPROACHES FROM THE SOUTH

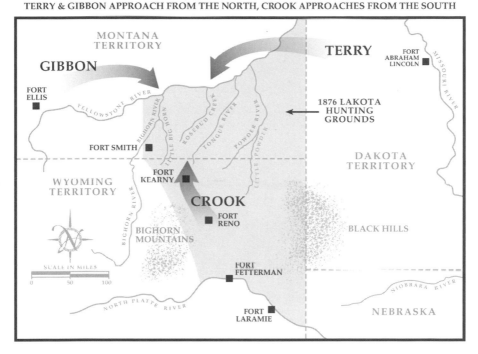

Map 4. Sheridan's Strategic Deployment. Map copyright © Charles E. Wright.

it slow and difficult for hauling supplies overland in wagons. On expeditions in the Yellowstone Basin, the army's supplies had to be hauled in wagons or on pack mules, while Indians carried their supplies in their rawhide parfleches and on the horse-drawn travois.

The army sent the steamship *Far West* to the upper reaches of the Yellowstone River, carrying grain, food, ammunition, and other supplies for General Terry's forces in his 1876 summer campaign. The *Far West* reached the mouth of the Powder River on June 8. Thereafter, it steamed up and down various sections of the Yellowstone, arriving at the mouth of Rosebud Creek on the morning of June 21, where it unloaded supplies for Terry's forthcoming campaign.

But where were the Indians and how strong were they? Neither the commanding officer of the Division of Missouri (Sheridan) nor the Department of Dakota (Terry) had accurate information about the location and size of the main Lakota and Cheyenne encampment, and Terry overlooked utilizing his numerous Crow and Arikara scouts to obtain this es-

Gen. George R. Crook, commander of the Department of the Platte. Courtesy Denver Public Library, Western History Collection (B-700).

Col. John Gibbon commanded four companies of cavalry and six companies of infantry. Denver Public Library, Western History Collection (B-548).

Col. Nelson A. Miles, with six or seven companies, joined the force of General Terry in August and continued attacking the Sioux and Cheyennes throughout the fall and winter of 1876–77. Courtesy Denver Public Library, Western History Collection (B-577).

sential intelligence. In fact, the 1876 spring-summer campaign had been launched while Sherman, Sheridan, Terry, and Custer harbored nothing but inconsistent and nonspecific guesses about the number of Indians and their location. Before Terry and his Dakota column headed west from Fort Lincoln on May 17, Sheridan told Terry that it was impossible for "any large number of Indians . . . [to keep] together as a hostile body for even a week."[1] In a May 27 letter to his maiden sister Fanchon, Terry confided that he hoped to find Indians gathered in force and willing to fight, but he had learned that they were scattered and feared that "I shall not be able to find them at all."[2] Three days later, Custer wrote to Libbie that it was "beyond a doubt that all stories about large bodies of Indians being here are the merest bosh."[3]

Gen. Alfred Terry attended law school at Yale and practiced law prior to the Civil War. A student of military history, he was given command of a Connecticut regiment in 1860. Soft spoken, introspective, and gentle, he was liked by his troops and by other officers. However, he had never commanded troops in the field against Indians. On May 23, 1876, his acting assistant surgeon, Dr. James M. DeWolf, overheard and recorded the following in his diary, "General Terry, I learn, wishes to try first to bring the Indians into the Reservations & if they wont [sic] come to fight them. He I believe is not in favor of the treatment they have received for some time past."[4] With his legal training Terry may also have been concerned about the legality of his mission and the consequences of his actions.

During spring of 1876, the "Montana column" of 400 mixed cavalry and infantry soldiers commanded by Col. John Gibbon was moving east along the north side of the Yellowstone, with orders to prevent the Lakotas and Cheyennes from moving north of the Yellowstone River and escaping into Canada. On May 17, Lt. James Bradley (attached to Gibbon's Montana column) observed a large Lakota village of 200 to 300 lodges on the Tongue River. Bradley reported this to Gibbon on the eighteenth, but Gibbon failed to notify General Terry, who was moving west through Dakota Territory with Custer and the Seventh Cavalry in tow, toward his rendezvous with Gibbon at Glendive on June 9.[5] On May 20 Gibbon's Crow scouts sighted a large body of "several hundred Sioux warriors" on the south side of the Yellowstone River, moving in the direction of the lower Rosebud. Gibbon sent a dispatch to Terry, making brief mention

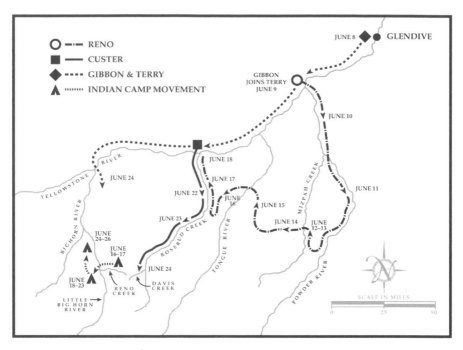

Map 5. Reno's Scout, Custer's Start, and the Indians' Movement.
Map copyright © Charles E. Wright.

of the Lakota camp on the Rosebud but failing to give Terry specific information about the number of Indians and the location of their camp.

On June 10 Terry ordered Maj. Marcus Reno, with six of the twelve companies (300 troopers) of the Seventh Cavalry Regiment, to scout upstream (south) from the mouth of the Powder River in search of the Indians (see map 5). Terry needed to know where they were located and the size of their fighting force. Reno's reconnaissance orders were very specific.[6] Terry directed him to proceed upstream to the mouth of the Little Powder River, then turn west, following certain small creeks until he reached the Tongue River. At this point Reno was ordered to turn north and descend the Tongue until he reached its junction with the Yellowstone.

Thus, Terry utilized half of his main strike force to conduct Reno's exhausting 238-mile reconnaissance.[7] This would, in turn, wear down 300 troopers and their horses and pack mules.[8] Interestingly, Terry failed to send his Crow scouts, the experienced half-breed Lakota scout Mitch Bouyer, or any of his reliable officers to conduct reconnaissance with smaller and less noticeable patrols. Had Reno been able to achieve visual contact with the Indians, they would most certainly have seen Reno's 300 troopers and their horses and thus have warning of the presence of Terry's Dakota column. Perhaps this is what Terry wanted.

By June 12, Reno was eighty miles upstream on the Powder River, having sighted no Indians. On this same date the Indian encampment (which was growing in size each day) was actually eighty miles to the southwest of Reno along the banks of Rosebud Creek, two watersheds to the west. On the twelfth Reno turned to the west, crossing Mizpah Creek, continuing until he reached the east bank of the Tongue River on June 15. Contrary to Terry's orders, Reno proceeded to cross the Tongue and continued west to Rosebud Creek, where he located the cold trail of the Indians who had passed there prior to June 7, moving upstream (south). On June 16 Reno followed the trail upstream along the Rosebud for several miles. Although he halted short of their village, he determined from examining the trail that the Indians had between 350 and 450 lodges and were continuing to move upstream on the Rosebud. By June 16 the Indians had actually moved upstream as far as Davis Creek, where they left the Rosebud drainage and turned to the west in the direction of the Little Big Horn River. At midday on June 16, Reno halted his upstream movement on the Rosebud at a point forty-five miles north and east of the Indians, who by then were camped on Reno Creek a few miles east of where it flowed into the Little Big Horn River. Without leaving any scouts to maintain surveillance, Reno reversed course and headed back downstream on Rosebud Creek (north and away from the Indian camp), arriving at the Yellowstone on June 18. Since General Terry was not present, Reno provided a brief report to Colonel Gibbon, anticipating a prompt and detailed debriefing by Terry thereafter. Terry was angry with Reno for continuing west to the Rosebud instead of returning downstream on the Tongue as ordered. On June 19 Reno provided Terry with a cryptic written report, indicating that he would provide more detailed information to Terry in person on the morning of June 20.[9] Reno tried to report directly to Terry, who was upset and refused to talk with him—strange behavior for a mission commander who was in desperate need of intelligence about the enemy forces with whom he was about to do battle.

Reno's fresh and more accurate information forced Terry to change his pedantic plans. The Lakotas and Cheyennes were not north of the Yellowstone, nor were they on the Tongue or Powder Rivers. Instead of sending his attack force upstream along the Tongue River as Terry had originally planned, Reno's information required Terry to move his force one and two watersheds west to Rosebud Creek and the Little Big Horn. The information that Reno provided to Terry increased the likelihood of a close-range encounter with the main Indian encampment.

By June 18 the Indians had crossed to the west bank of the Little Big Horn, where they remained for six days. On June 24 they moved downstream on the west side of the Little Big Horn to the encampment site where they were located on June 25 when the battle occurred.

It should be noted that if Reno had followed Terry's orders and turned north when he reached the Tongue River, he would have discovered no useful information. Reno's actions saved Terry from engaging in a fruitless snipe hunt along the Tongue River, many miles from the Indians who were two watersheds to the west on the Little Big Horn. One is left to ponder whether Terry was quietly but intentionally trying to avoid a direct confrontation with the Indian encampment.

On June 17, at a time when Reno's battalion was returning from its reconnaissance in force to the mouth of Rosebud Creek, elements of the Indian encampment, including large numbers of Cheyennes, were engaged in heavy fighting with the forces of Gen. George Crook on upper Rosebud Creek. Prior to the Rosebud battle Crook's column (with 1,000 officers and enlisted men, 300 mules, eighty-five miners and packers, and 260 Indian scouts) was headed north down Rosebud Creek.[10] The Rosebud battle was just twenty-two miles southeast of the main Indian encampment then located on the north side of Reno Creek. The battle on June 17 was significant in that it terminated the northerly movement of Crook's southern column. Had Crook continued north and encountered Custer, Crook would have outranked Custer and had authority to assert tactical command of the entire operation. The combined Crook and Custer strike force would have been increased to more than 1,600 soldiers, including an additional fifteen companies from the Second and Third Cavalry Regiments.[11]

On June 21, Terry, Gibbon, and Custer were on the Yellowstone at the mouth of the Bighorn River. They were not aware of Crook's location and vice versa. The Indians, having stopped Crook's northern advance, seemed unaware that Terry was at the mouth of Rosebud Creek. Reno's reconnaissance, as slow and cumbersome as it was, did provide Terry with the general location of the Indian encampment so that he could begin formulating some semblance of a plan to bring his forces into contact with the Indians. It is obvious that Terry, in preparing his plan, intended to have Custer lead and initiate the first contact. On February 21, when he obtained Custer's orders to report to Fort Lincoln in May, Terry had advised General Sheridan of his plans for Custer: "I think my only plan will be to give Custer a secure base well up on the Yellowstone to which he can retire at any time the Indians gather in too great numbers for the small force he will have."[12] This prophetic plan turned out to be a naive and misguided grasp of how Custer would respond when he was turned loose with command of an independent tactical combat unit. Before Terry's northern column departed from Fort Lincoln, it was clear that Terry had no intention himself of leading a cavalry unit in combat with Plains Indians, and thus he never did.

Terry's forces would be pursuing a highly mobile enemy whose whereabouts changed on a daily basis. Terry had a finite number of fighting men and might be outnumbered. His overall strategic objective was to locate and subjugate these Indians, forcing them back to their reservations. His strategy, the basis for any tactical planning, required that he place as many troops as possible in close contact with the Indians in circumstances under which he could terminate their summer hunt and force them (by negotiation or military aggression) to return to their reservations. Surprise and rapid confrontation were essential. Correct tactical maneuvers were mandatory for success.

Terry met with Custer, Maj. Jim Brisbin, and Gibbon aboard the river boat *Far West* at the mouth of the Rosebud on the evening of June 21. Reno was not invited.[13] Terry knew that the Indians were not on the Powder or the Tongue Rivers and that within the past twenty days several hundred (or perhaps thousands of) Indians had been located forty to fifty miles upstream on Rosebud Creek in the vicinity of Greenleaf Creek. He had no knowledge of Crook's fight at the Rosebud or that Crook was then located on Goose Creek some ninety-five miles south-southeast of the mouth of the Bighorn River.

Terry needed a plan, but without detailed knowledge of the location, strength, and direction of movement of the Lakotas and Cheyennes, the plan could not be specific. Dividing his command, he decided to send Custer and the Seventh Cavalry upstream on the Rosebud and to order Gibbon with his Montana column upstream on the Bighorn. Terry divided his strength to such an extent that he violated cardinal military tactical rules requiring (1) that as many troops as possible should be brought into the engagement at the decisive point, and (2) that, without definite numerical superiority, it is extremely dangerous to use widely separated columns in attempting to envelop the enemy, both on the battlefield and in the theater of operations—tactically or strategically. Terry had no idea when or where the decisive point would be. As fate would have it, Sheridan sent a prophetic letter (written early in June but delivered after the battle) directing Terry "not to split his command, as he had information that at least five thousand warriors were assembled."[14]

Terry's plan directed Custer to take 60 percent of Terry's total force more than seventy miles upstream on Rosebud Creek, placing Custer away from Terry's tactical control, with no directions to exchange information or bring about a coordinated and concentrated attack on the Indians. Terry permitted Custer to dictate the terms of his deployment, i.e., no Gatling guns, no infantry, and no additional support from the Second Cavalry.[15] Terry was intentionally abdicating his duty to command the combined forces of the Dakota and Montana columns in the anticipated battle with an undetermined but large number of well-armed Lakotas and Cheyennes. Between the time that Reno returned on June 18 and Custer's departure on June 22, Terry failed to send out small reconnaissance patrols in an effort to verify the strength and location of the Indians and keep them under surveillance. A disaster was brewing.

The Indians at the Little Big Horn encampment on June 21 numbered 4,000 to 10,000, the warriors 1,000 to 2,000, their lodges 900 to 2,500, and their ponies 5,000 to 12,000. Indians, soldiers, historians, and archaeologists have, with great effort and sincerity, arrived at divergent numbers in their efforts to analyze and report. To create an accurate analysis of the battle, it is not necessary to use precise numbers for the Indians' total population, their warrior count, or their pony herds, and in any event precise numbers are not available.[16]

The Indians were breaking no law. Article 16 of the 1868 Treaty approved by President Andrew Johnson had granted them the right to be where they were, hunting in unceded Indian territory. They were posing no threat to existing white settlements; in fact, there were virtually no white settlements in the area because white settlement was prohibited in the Treaty of 1868. The Indians were hunting buffalo to keep from starving. They not only needed summer food but had to prepare dried meat for the coming winter when fresh food sources would not be available. Their means of transportation were limited to the horse, the dog, and walking.

Certain elements favored the Indians. They were defending their entire encampment, their treaty rights, and their liberty. They were trained warriors who knew the territory, and their warriors outnumbered Terry's soldiers. As Maj. Marcus Reno observed, they could either fight for their freedom as long as possible or try to "make the best of a loser's hand."

While Indians were trained to fight individually, they had no formalized military training, medical treatment, tactics, order of battle, command, or other military structure. No Indian had the power to order another into battle. They had no means to replace their battle casualties other than internal tribal reproduction. They had no long-term strategic plan other than continuing to exist as hunter-gatherers by utilizing buffalo as their primary source of food.

With respect to the Seventh Cavalry, it was supported by the population and resources of the United States. The white population of the United States outnumbered the Lakotas by more than four thousand to one. The Seventh Cavalry was a military organization with a chain of command, up-to-date weaponry, strategy, tactics, and the ability to use maps and charts. Compared to the Indians, it had a virtually unlimited reserve of manpower, food, horses, mules, feed, and weaponry. The *wasicu* could manufacture their own metal, guns, ammunition, shelter, containers, clothing, nonperishable foods, feed, grain, sugar, flour, and medical supplies. They were equipped with the latest armaments, including breech-loading carbines with rifled barrels, copper and brass cartridges, pistols, and even a crude form of machine gun known as the Gatling gun.

By June 21, 1876, the strategy of the Lakotas and Cheyennes boiled down to one simple element—survival. Survival required daily rations of adequate food, a commodity not readily available on their reservations.[17] The Lakotas and Cheyennes preferred to provide their own food by continuing to hunt the buffalo in their "unceded Indian territory." This survival-based strategy governed the Indians' tactics in their battles with the U.S. Army. Pitched battles were avoided unless they outnumbered the army. They carefully avoided exposure to short-range fire from infantry or dismounted cavalry. They continually attempted to lead mounted cavalry into an ambush where they could surround and trap the troopers in crossfire. However, they traveled in entire villages, with all their belongings and families moving and camping together. When they went into camp, they were more vulnerable because they seemed never to post night sentries and outposts to provide warning of an enemy attack. Because of their lax attitude in failing to protect their camps after sundown, Indian survival strategy in their unceded Indian territory was doomed to failure—it was simply a matter of time.

This was the situation that existed on June 21, 1876, as General Terry met with Custer and Gibbon to plan for their first encounter with the Indians.

## Chapter Eight
# June 22—Terry's Plan—Custer Moves Out

*Porter, there is a large camp of Indians ahead, and we are going to have a great killing.*

—*Lt. Col. George A. Custer to Regimental Surgeon Harry R. Porter, 10 a.m., June 25, 1876*[1]

Custer and his regiment got underway shortly after noon on June 22. Before leaving, Custer set a trap for himself when he fired off his own press report to the *New York Herald* committing himself and his regiment to an all-out attack on the Indians whenever, wherever, and under whatever conditions he could find them. He told the press that he would locate the Indian trail where Reno had abandoned it and "follow the Indians as long and as far as horse flesh and human endurance could carry his command."[2]

What Custer meant in setting these standards for his effort is illustrated in a comment by Lt. James H. Bradley, who was part of Colonel Gibbon's column that would travel up the Bighorn River with General Terry: "It is understood that if Custer arrives first he is at liberty to attack at once if he deems prudent. We have little hope of being in at the death, as Custer will undoubtedly exert himself to the utmost to get there first and win all the laurels for himself and his regiment."[3] Obviously "laurels" meant the indiscriminate killing of Indians. Based upon this comment, Custer was premeditating murder and his intended attack on the Indians' encampment was clearly an act of genocide, in that he intended to kill Lakota and Cheyenne Indians, causing serious bodily and mental harm to members of the group, deliberately inflicting on these Lakotas and Cheyennes "conditions of life calculated to bring about its [the group's] physical destruction in whole or in part."[4]

Further intentions are revealed in a letter Custer wrote to Libbie on the same date, shortly before departing: "Think of the valuable time lost! I am now going to take up the trail where the scouting party [Reno's] turned back. I fear that their failure to follow up the Indians has imperiled our plans, but I feel hopeful for accomplishing great results."[5] We do not know what was meant by "our plans" and "great results," but Custer's subsequent statements and actions indicate that they included instantaneous attack by the troopers he commanded and the killing of Indians. During the early morning hours of June 25, before Custer's battalion broke camp, Custer approached Dr. Henry R. Porter and told him, "Porter, there is a large camp of Indians ahead, and we are going to have a great killing."[6] These are personal indications of Custer's intent to commit premeditated murder and, thus, his overall genocidal objective. From this point until he reached Medicine Tail Coulee on June 25, all his actions point toward attacking the Indians whenever and wherever he could find them with the strategic objective of achieving a great military victory—and much killing.

Additional intent may be gleaned from a letter sent by Boston Custer (Custer's younger brother, serving as a "guide" on the quartermaster's rolls) to their mother dated June 21, 1876, on the eve of their departure:

> Armstrong [Custer] takes the whole command, and starts up the Sweet Briar [Rosebud] on an Indian trail with the full hope and belief of overhauling them—which I think he probably will, with a little hard riding. They will be much entertained. I hope to catch one or two Indian ponies with a buffalo robe for Nev, but he must not be disappointed if I don't. Judging by the number of lodges counted by scouts who saw the trail, there are something like 800 Indians and probably more. But, be the number great or small, I hope I can truthfully say when I get back, that one or more were sent to the happy hunting grounds.[7]

Boston Custer's lust for genocide eventually got him in trouble. One of the primary objectives of the mission, in the eyes of Boston Custer, was the killing of Indians. The success of the mission would be evaluated on the basis of the number of Indians killed. Like the dream of Don Quixote, Custer's dream of killing and conquering the Lakota and Cheyenne Indians was impossible—it was also outrageous.

Lt. Col. George A. Custer, senior officer present at the Battle of Little Big Horn. Courtesy Denver Public Library, Western History Collection (B-696).

Maj. Marcus A. Reno, second in command of the Seventh Cavalry Regiment. Courtesy Denver Public Library, Western History Collection (B-545).

Capt. Frederick Benteen, third in command of the Seventh Cavalry Regiment. Courtesy Denver Public Library, Western History Collection (B-302).

Dr. Henry R. Porter, acting assistant surgeon of the Seventh Cavalry Regiment at Little Big Horn. Courtesy Denver Public Library, Western History Collection (B-607).

After rattling around writing his letters on the morning of June 22, Custer got underway shortly after noon. Before Custer departed, Terry, acting through his adjutant, Capt. E. W. Smith, gave Custer these written instructions:

Camp at Mouth of Rosebud River, Montana Territory
June 22d, 1876.
Lieutenant Colonel Custer, 7th Cavalry

Colonel:
The Brigadier-General Commanding directs that, as soon as your regiment can be made ready for the march, you will proceed up the Rosebud in pursuit of the Indians whose trail was discovered by Major Reno a few days since. It is, of course, impossible to give you any definite instructions in regard to this movement, and were it not impossible to do so the Department Commander [General Terry] places too much confidence in your zeal, energy, and ability to wish to impose upon you precise orders which might hamper your action when nearly in contact with the enemy.

He will, however, indicate to you his own views of what your action should be, and he desires that you should conform to them unless you shall see sufficient reasons for departing from them. He thinks that you should proceed up the Rosebud until you ascertain definitely the direction in which the trail above spoken of leads. Should it be found (as it appears almost certain that it will be found) to turn towards the Little Horn, he thinks that you should still proceed southward, perhaps as far as the headwaters of the Tongue, and then turn towards the Little Horn, feeling constantly, however, to your left, so as to preclude the possibility of the escape of the Indians to the south or southeast by passing around your left flank.

[It is desired that you conform as nearly as possible to those instructions and that you do not depart from them unless you shall see absolute necessity for doing so.][8]

The column of Colonel Gibbon is now in motion for the mouth of the Big Horn. As soon as it reaches that point it will cross the Yellowstone and move up at least as far as the forks of the Big and Little Horns. Of course its future movements must be controlled by circumstances as they arise, but it is hoped that the Indians, if upon the Little Horn, may be so nearly inclosed by two columns that their escape will be impossible.

The Department Commander desires that on your way up the Rosebud you should thoroughly examine the upper part of Tullock's Creek, and that you should endeavor to send a scout through to Colonel Gibbon's column, with information of the result of your examination. The lower part of the creek will be examined by a detachment from Colonel Gibbon's command.

The supply steamer will be pushed up the Big Horn as far as the forks if the river is found to be navigable for that distance, and the Department Commander, who will accompany the column of Colonel Gibbon, desires you to report to him there not later than the expiration of the time for which your troops are rationed, unless in the meantime you receive further orders.

Very respectfully, your obedient servant,
E. W. Smith,
Captain 18th Infantry,
Acting Assistant Adjutant General.[9]

The order is perhaps most significant for what it did not say. It failed to describe any strategic objective other than pursuit of the Indians whose trail was discovered by Major Reno the prior week. There were no directives as to what Custer and his column should or might do. Specifically, the order *does not* direct Custer to attack or kill Indians. Was Custer to pursue and observe, show force and parley, or attack and attempt to subjugate? It is apparent that Terry wanted it memorialized in writing that he at no time ordered Custer to attack the Indians. If Custer did initiate an attack, it was not pursuant to Terry's orders.

Without an expressed strategic objective, it is difficult for a tactical commander in the field to assess his responsibility with respect to the quantity of effort that is required. In other words, was he to attack immediately and fight to the last man, or should the commander follow the time-honored doctrine of calculated risk?

There was no requirement that Custer keep Terry informed about the Indians' strength and disposition or when and where he intended to fight, nor were there any indications as to how Terry might deploy Gibbon's column. Similarly, there was no plan for any possible coordination between the two columns, particularly with respect to time and location. This could have been accomplished through the use of messengers after Custer's departure on June 22. Everything in the entire order, except the direction to "proceed up the Rosebud," was a series of precatory and nonspecific suggestions. In the course of presenting suggestions to Custer, the order stated, "[Terry] desires that you should conform to them unless you shall see sufficient reason for departing from them."

In essence, Terry pointed Custer south toward the Indians and cut him loose to act on his own, with no effort on Terry's part to maintain tactical or strategic control over Custer unless and until, at some indeterminate location and time, Custer's column might accidentally reunite with Terry. Terry relied entirely on Custer's military judgment and his reputation for aggressive offensive tactics to make contact and achieve subjugation of the Indians, while Terry remained distant from Custer, avoiding control and permitting matters to run their course pursuant to Custer's own judgment. The interpreter Fred Gerard overheard Terry remark shortly after Custer's departure from Terry, "Custer is happy now, off with a roving command of fifteen days. I told him if he found the Indians not to do as Reno did, but if he thought he could whip them to do so."[10] This is not what Terry expressed in his written order to Custer.

Terry's actions in dividing his command were questioned by Maj. Jim Brisbin ("Grasshopper"), who was serving as second in command of Gibbon's Montana column. Grasshopper told Terry that Terry himself should lead Custer's column and that Custer's column was undermanned. Terry in turn offered to send Brisbin and two companies from the Montana column along with Custer. Brisbin replied that he did not want to serve in any circumstances under Custer's command but that he would be pleased to go if Terry would assume the command. Disregarding the junior officer's advice and admonition, Terry told Brisbin to offer additional troops from the Montana battalion to Custer. Brisbin presented the offer to Custer, and Custer declined, indicating that he preferred to have the Seventh Cavalry fight as a separate unit, and in any event additional troops were not necessary for his purposes.[11] Why did Terry merely offer additional troops to Custer rather than ordering him to take them? Why did he fail to maintain command?

After departing from Terry, the Seventh Cavalry proceeded twelve miles up the Rosebud and went into evening camp at 4:00 p.m. on June

22. Custer held an officers' call at sunset, at which he indicated that there would be no further bugle calls, that the regiment would be awakened at 3:00 a.m. and would move out at 5:00 a.m. each day. First Lieutenant Edward S. Godfrey, writing subsequent to the battle, indicated that Custer told his officers at their evening officers' call on June 22 that, "there might be enough young men from the agencies visiting their hostile friends to make a total of 1,500 . . . that there would not be an opposing force of more than 1,500." Godfrey also reported a similar conversation between himself and the interpreter-scout, Mitch Bouyer, immediately after officers' call in which Godfrey repeated the estimate of 1500. Bouyer replied that "we are going to have a damned big fight."[12] After officers' call some officers noted that Custer was not as aggressive and confident as usual. He appeared depressed, and his scouts were pessimistic.[13] Whether he fully realized it or not, Custer was actually on his own and had been given both oral and written ability to formulate his strategy and all his tactical planning. Since he commanded only 600 troopers, his estimate of 1500 warriors at officers' call indicated that he was well aware that he could be outnumbered by as much as seven to one. Lieutenant Godfrey, who commanded Company K, noted that Custer's attitude and general demeanor before his regimental officers was unusual:

> This "talk" of his, as we called it, was considered at the time as something extraordinary for General Custer, for it was not his habit to unbosom himself to his officers. In it he showed a lack of self-confidence, a reliance on somebody else; there was an indefinable something that was not Custer. His manner and tone, usually brusque and aggressive, or somewhat rasping, was on this occasion conciliating and subdued. There was something akin to an appeal, as if depressed, that made a deep impression on all present. We compared watches to get the official time, and separated to attend to our various duties. Lieutenants McIntosh, Wallace and myself walked to our bivouac, for some distance in silence, when Wallace remarked: "Godfrey, I believe General Custer is going to be killed," "Why, Wallace," I replied, "what makes you think so?" "Because," said he, "I have never heard Custer talk in that way before."[14]

Custer's subsequent actions may indicate some awareness that he was overmatched and out-manned. They could also possibly indicate the presence of insecurity or outright fear.

Between the end of the Civil War and June 21, 1876, Custer had never commanded troops in a pitched battle with Plains Indians whose strength of force was greater than his own. Headed toward a new experience, under no oversight by a superior officer, and with no prospect of support from nearby army forces, he had exclusive command of an independent tactical combat unit with orders directing him to pursue Indians and act in his own discretion. The army handbook outlining the duties of a commanding officer discusses the concept of "capacity to command":

> 649. The capacity to command is peculiar and exceptional. There is something pertaining to the assumption of *exclusive command*, that either brings out the weakness or strength of the officer for the position . . . yet in the storm of war when human life is at stake, and results immense with their importance, depend upon his skill and judgment, they often only serve to prove how incompetent he is for a Commanding Officer.[15]

On June 25, 1876, Custer's competence can be defined by his actions as commanding officer of his regiment and the results that occurred at the Custer Battlefield.

# Chapter Nine
## Lack of Intelligence and Inadequate Planning

*Long Hair wants to tell you that tonight you shall go without sleep. You are to go ahead, you are to try to locate the Sioux camp.*

—*Custer's orders to his Arikara scouts at 9 p.m. on June 24*

As ordered, the Seventh Cavalry moved out in broad daylight at 5:00 a.m. on June 23 with two color-bearers up front with Custer. The regiment traveled upstream along Rosebud Creek, crossing it several times in the process. Rosebud Creek was nothing more than a small creek at that time, approximately three inches deep and three to four feet wide.[1] Five miles out of camp they struck the cold Indian trail that Reno had discovered nine days earlier. Indian trails were well marked because the Indians used the travois, supported by slender lodgepole trunks, to carry the bulk of their belongings. The large ends of the trunk were dragged across the ground, and the small ends were attached to both sides of the working pony. In the damp, soft, sandy river-bottom soil the dragging trunks left marks that (together with hoof prints and manure) were easily sighted and followed. The trail led to an Indian campsite, which by then was nearly one month old.

On the twenty-third, the Seventh Cavalry traveled upstream on the Rosebud for thirty-three miles and went into camp at 4:30 p.m. The pack train did not arrive until sundown, lagging more than three hours behind the cavalry.

Custer desperately needed to know where the Indians were and, given stale intelligence that he was outnumbered by at least two to one, how many warriors he would have to face. It would have been possible to launch small reconnaissance patrols on the evenings of both June 22 and June 23. A small patrol could travel at night in an effort to remain hidden. The trail was clearly marked with travois lines, hoof prints, and horse droppings. "Near an enemy daily reconnoissances [sic] are made to observe the ground in front, and to discover whether the advanced guards of the enemy have been increased or put in motion, or any other sign of his preparation for march or action."[2] Custer failed to reconnoiter. Was this failure deliberate?

During the morning of the twenty-fourth, the regiment continued to follow the Indian trail up Rosebud Creek. They were forty-eight miles east of the Indian encampment, which by then had moved west to the west bank of the Little Big Horn three miles downstream (north) from the mouth of Reno Creek. At 6:30 a.m. Custer halted at the old Hunkpapa sun dance camp where Sitting Bull had his famous vision about "soldiers falling into camp." Proceeding upstream, they stopped again at 1:00 p.m. near a deserted campsite that had been abandoned on June 12. As Custer continued his march, additional and more recent campsites were sighted, indicating that the Indians were within forty miles. While halted, Custer received and pondered reports from Indian scouts who were searching a few miles ahead and on each flank. The regiment resumed marching upstream at 5:00 p.m., sighting additional trails. It halted in the twilight at approximately 9:00 p.m. near the mouth of Davis Creek on the west bank of the Rosebud.[3] Full darkness was approaching.

At this halt Custer received word from his scouts that the Indians' trail had turned to the west at the mouth of Davis Creek, heading toward the Little Big Horn River. Terry's order to Custer had specifically suggested that if the Indian trail turned toward the Little Big Horn (as Terry predicted it would), Custer should continue to proceed south along the Rosebud until he reached the headwaters of the Tongue River to "preclude" escaping Indians from passing to the south of his column. Instead of heeding Terry's "wise counsel," Custer turned to the west and followed the Indians' trail toward the Little Big Horn.[4]

It is difficult to criticize Custer for turning west to follow the obvious trail of the Indians toward the Little Big Horn. If he had continued south up the Rosebud as Terry suggested, he would have moved fifty miles farther away from the warm trail and risked losing contact—increasing the possibility that the Indians would elude him entirely. Critics have condemned Custer for "disobeying" Terry's suggestion.[5] They are incorrect in saying that Custer disobeyed. The language in Terry's order was wholly precatory and enabled Custer to use his own best judgment with respect to whatever action he decided to take. There was no plan to coordinate with Gibbon. The only reason that Custer should have continued on a fool's chase to the south would have been to avoid or delay contact with the Indians until the arrival of Gibbon's plodding forces from the north. If this was what Terry intended, he could have easily included details for coordination in his written order to Custer.[6] Since the force commanded by Terry was never able to make direct contact with the Indians for the balance of the year, it is not unreasonable to speculate that Terry was intentionally evading contact.

On June 24 the sun set at 7:53 p.m.; it became too dark to read at 8:31 p.m.; full darkness occurred at 9:22 p.m.; faint light appeared in the east at 2:44 a.m.; and sunrise occurred at 4:13 a.m. the following morning.[7] Custer held an officers' call at 9:30 p.m., while he was still at the junction of Davis Creek and the Rosebud. He told his officers of his plan to move the regiment west from the Rosebud at 11:00 p.m., heading toward the Little Big Horn. They would go into hiding during daylight on the twenty-fifth and mount a surprise attack on the Indians at dawn of the twenty-sixth.[8] A plan indeed, but Custer did not realize that he was more than thirty-five miles east from the actual location of the encampment. He did not know exactly where the Indians were located or how long it would take to reach them, and he had never seen the Little Big Horn River or the high bluffs along its east bank.

Shortly after 9:00 p.m. on the evening of the twenty-fourth, Red Star and four other Arikara scouts reported to Custer for orders. Their interpreter, Frederick Gerard, relayed these instructions from Custer, "Long Hair wants to tell you that tonight you shall go without sleep. You are to go ahead, you are to try to locate the Sioux camp. You are to do your best to find this camp. Travel all night, when day comes if you have not found the Sioux camp, keep on going until noon. If your search is useless by this time you are to come back to camp."[9] This is exactly what a competent field commander should have done at that instant, but Custer was a day or two too late—his Seventh Cavalry Regiment was too far west of the Indians' encampment to stage an undetected dawn attack on June 25.

Six Arikara scouts were then sent out with the white scout, "Lonesome" Charlie Reynolds, four of the six Crow scouts, and the interpreter, Frederick Gerard. The Crow scouts were to guide them, but Lt.

Charles Varnum was in charge. Being "in charge" meant that Varnum was responsible to insure that Custer's order was carried out. The Arikara scouts soon stopped for a smoke and were told by the Crow guides that the scouting party was going to a high mountain from which they could see a long distance. Further on they stopped for another smoke and were told that they were near a lookout point (commonly referred to as the "Crow's Nest") that was about twelve miles east of the Little Big Horn River.

Before dawn the Crow scouts climbed up to the Crow's Nest, followed by Red Star. The rest of the scouting party halted nearby. The search that was ordered by Custer ended before dawn on the morning of June 25 without providing Custer with meaningful evidence of the Indians' location. Either Varnum was not aware of Custer's orders or he chose to disregard them—this scouting party traveled no farther than the Crow's Nest, fifteen miles distant from the Indian encampment. The exhausted Varnum dropped to the ground and slept until dawn. Custer had ordered the scouts to search throughout the night and continue searching the following day (June 25) until they located the Indian camp. They failed to carry out this most important task as Custer had ordered.

It was not that Custer lacked knowledge about the necessity of reconnaissance. Fourteen years earlier (in May 1862), he had been stationed near the Chickahominy River with the Union army as it was moving toward Richmond, Virginia. As the army moved forward, Custer gained valuable experience about the necessity of sending small scouting patrols ahead of the army. Gen. George B. ("Little Mac") McClellan and his advancing army needed maps and information about where and how to cross the muddy, swampy Chickahominy, which stood in his path. In both the Mexican and Civil Wars, it was customary for engineer officers to gather intelligence and prepare maps for the tactical commanders. In broad daylight Custer accompanied Brig. Gen. John G. Barnard past the Union sentries to the banks of the Chickahominy. They could see across the river and there were no Confederates in sight. General Barnard ordered Custer into the river. Custer stripped off his jacket and jumped in the water, holding his pistol above his head. Alone, he proceeded to wade across the river and was soon into water up to his neck.[10] Reaching the opposite bank while the astounded General Barnard watched, Custer proceeded to conduct a daylight scout, during which he located a Confederate picket post and discovered a location on the river that afforded a suitable place for McClellan's army to cross and capture the picket. Custer waded back across the river unnoticed and provided this valuable information to General Barnard. Barnard eventually relayed this intelligence to General McClellan, who was so pleased with Custer's display of bravery and initiative that he asked him to serve on his staff.[11]

This is exactly the type of bravery and resourcefulness that would have been required of a reconnaissance patrol to locate and maintain undetected surveillance of the Indian encampment on the Little Big Horn. Custer could certainly have done it himself, but it would have been foolish for the commanding officer to expose himself to such risks when he was needed to plan and lead the regiment in the anticipated battle. There were at least two or three intelligent and trustworthy officers who had sufficient bravery and resourcefulness to conduct the scouting that was so essential. The scout Mitch Bouyer would also have been a likely candidate, as would certain of the six Crow scouts. Custer should have sent out one or more scouting parties no later than June 23 to follow the travois tracks until the Indian encampment was located. The search initiated after dark on June 24 was too little and too late—and it turned out to be incomplete, and thus ineffective.

Custer's regiment was now within one day's ride of the Indians' encampment located on the west bank of the Little Big Horn River. His scouts and their officer in charge, Lt. Charles Varnum, instead of following the Indians' clearly visible trail, were holed up at the base of an elevated observation point fifteen miles distant from the Indian encampment, having a few smokes and taking a nap until the morning sun illuminated the distant horizon.

# Chapter Ten
# June 25—Custer Deploys for Battle

*I guess we'll get through with them in one day.*

—*George A. Custer*[1]

In the 11 p.m. darkness of June 24, Custer moved west from his halt at Rosebud Creek, following Davis Creek westward toward the Little Big Horn. He halted at 3:15 a.m. the next day near the divide between the Rosebud and Little Big Horn watersheds, about five miles northeast of the Crow's Nest. There he made camp, giving his men and horses a much-needed rest. The Crow's Nest was a lookout point on a high ridge located about eleven miles east of the Little Big Horn River and fifteen miles southeast of the Lakota and Cheyenne encampment.

Between 8 and 10 a.m. on June 25, Custer was confronted with several incidents that caused him to revise his plan for a surprise attack at dawn on the twenty-sixth. Shortly before 9 a.m. he received a note from Lt. Charles Varnum at the Crow's Nest, indicating that his scouts could see an Indian encampment. Custer immediately rode to the Crow's Nest. Due to the ninety-foot hills on the east bank of the Little Big Horn River and the changing atmospheric conditions, Custer's own view failed to convince him that they had located the Indian encampment.

Varnum then informed Custer about two early-morning encounters with unidentified Indians in the vicinity of the Crow's Nest and the unsuccessful efforts, using gunfire, to kill or capture them. Thereafter, at 11:30 a.m., through the interpreter, Frederick Gerard, Arikara scout Bloody Knife told Custer that he would find enough Sioux to keep him fighting for two or three days. "I guess we'll get through with them in one day," Custer replied. However, these Crow scouts did convince Custer that if he crossed the divide between the Rosebud and the Little Big Horn in daylight, his regiment would be detected by Indians who were at the encampment. Custer then received a report about Sgt. William A. Curtis of F Company, who that morning had taken a small squad out on the back trail to recover a box of hardtack that had fallen from a mule pack on the evening of the twenty-fourth. Curtis's squad had opened fire on a small group of Indians who were attempting to loot the hardtack. The Indians fled from the scene unharmed.[2]

Upon learning about the hardtack incident, Custer abandoned his plan to hide out on June 25 and conduct a surprise attack at dawn the next day. Shortly before noon on the twenty-fifth, when the regiment and pack train were near the divide, he told his officers that the regiment would proceed without delay to initiate an afternoon attack on the Indians, whose village he had not yet located. This was the extent of Custer's plan for battle on June 25. Most historians indicate that Custer's decision to abandon his plan for a surprise attack on the twenty-sixth and proceed with a frontal attack on the afternoon of the twenty-fifth was based on the two sightings of Indians near the Crow's Nest and the hardtack incident where Sergeant Curtis's squad fired at Indian looters.[3] While Custer cannot be blamed for making this decision with the limited intelligence at his disposal, it should be noted that these incidents were each more than fifteen miles southeast of the encampment and were out of the sight and hearing of the Indians at the encampment. In actuality, neither incident precipitated a warning to the encampment, but Custer's subsequent daylight attack did. Custer's decision to attack on the afternoon of June 25 was based on a hunch rather than real-time intelligence—intelligence that could have been obtained with a more vigorous scouting effort, coupled with ongoing surveillance.

Tulloch's Creek (Fork)[4] flows into the Bighorn River about three miles south of the junction of the Bighorn and the Yellowstone River. General Terry's column crossed Tulloch's Creek on June 24 as it headed south toward the mouth of the Little Big Horn River. The headwaters of Tulloch's Creek that Custer was ordered to scout were seventeen to thirty miles northwest of Custer's trail along Rosebud Creek, were twenty to thirty miles north of Custer's movement to the west along Reno Creek, and were never less than twenty miles northeast of Custer's battalion as it moved north along the east side of the Little Big Horn. In any event, Custer had ignored Terry's request that he scout the upper reaches of

Tulloch's Creek.[5] Custer had been directed, after completing the scout, to send the scout George Herendeen back to Terry with information concerning the situation at Tulloch's Creek. Custer's failure to scout Tulloch's Creek was of no particular consequence other than the fact that Herendeen could also have informed Terry that Custer was not continuing south along the Rosebud but was instead cutting across the divide, heading west on Reno Creek, following the Indians' warm trail into the Little Big Horn Valley. Had Terry known of this, there is little that he could have done to change things, other than to engage Gibbon's column in a forced march to expedite its arrival at the Little Big Horn.

Pursuant to Custer's new plan, the regiment moved west at 11:45 a.m., crossing the divide between Rosebud Creek and the Little Big Horn. It halted shortly after noon when Custer reached the headwaters of Reno Creek. During this halt Custer proceeded to designate three separate battalions from the eleven companies not involved with the pack train. The first, consisting of Companies A, G, and M (approximately 130 troopers), was assigned to Maj. Marcus Reno. A second, consisting of Companies D, H, and K (approximately 130 troopers), was assigned to Capt. Frederick Benteen. Custer retained Companies C, E, F, I, and L (210 troopers) under his direct command. Company B, under Capt. Thomas McDougall, remained in the rear, in charge of the 175 mules in the pack train. Additional troopers from the other eleven companies had been detailed to assist and protect the pack train, bringing the count for McDougall and the pack train to approximately 130.[6] The exact numbers for each battalion, including the pack train, are not available. The most certain and significant numbers are the 600 troopers in the entire Seventh Cavalry Regiment and the 210 troopers who remained in Companies C, E, F, I, and L under Custer's direct control when they were annihilated at Custer Battlefield. This would leave 390 for allocation to the battalions of Benteen, Reno, and the pack train, which fought as one unit after they joined together at approximately 5:00 p.m. on June 25.

Reno Creek is a small, spring-fed stream running west from the divide between the Little Big Horn River and Rosebud Creek.[7] It flows west into the Little Big Horn at a point approximately 3.5 miles upstream (southeast) from the Indian encampment and 4.4 miles west of an abandoned Sans Arc campsite on which there was a tepee ("Lone Tepee") that contained the corpse of an unidentified Indian.

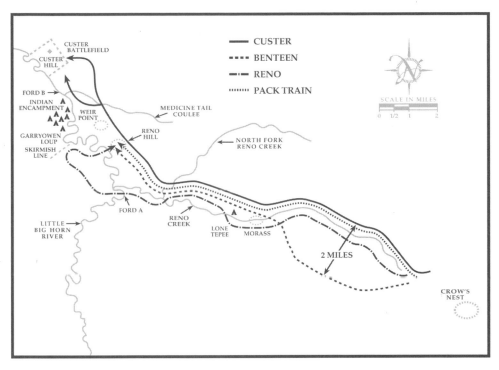

Map 6. Custer's Deployment of Seventh Cavalry Regiment, June 25, 1876.
Map copyright © Charles E. Wright.

Custer's overall strategic objective was to utilize his regiment to attack the Lakotas and Cheyennes where he found them, to achieve a military victory, and to force them back to their distant reservations in Nebraska and Dakota Territory. In his only prior pitched battle with Plains Indians, at the Washita River in 1868, Custer's attack force outnumbered Black Kettle's entire camp by three to one and outnumbered the warriors in the camp by seven to one. Now, as he approached the Little Big Horn, his regiment was moving to attack an Indian encampment where fighting warriors outnumbered the 600 troopers in the Seventh Cavalry Regiment by at least two and one-half to one. The encampment was too large for him to surround. By attacking in daylight he would not achieve surprise, and it would be virtually impossible for his 600 troopers to take even a small percentage of the Indians prisoner, even if Custer were able to subdue them militarily. There was no Ben Clark to advise him about how to maneuver if he suddenly became surrounded, and there was no

General Sheridan to help him break out if he should blunder into a trap. His scouts had not followed the trail and located the Indians' camp as directed. Since he had no knowledge of the size and location of the encampment, he had no specific target in his sights.

Custer pressed on, spoiling for a fight, undermanned, with no plan for his intended attack.

### Benteen's Scout

Custer had previously assigned a battalion comprised of Companies D, H, and K to Captain Benteen, who was the third-ranking officer of the regiment. Less than a mile after crossing the divide, Custer gave oral orders directly to Benteen that he was to take his battalion and proceed to the left, approximately forty-five degrees from the intended path of the regiment and scout for Indians. Benteen was to attack ("pitch into") any Indians he encountered (without any limitation as to their size or direction of movement) and notify Custer immediately if he encountered any Indians. He was also told to utilize an advance party of one officer and approximately six men to scout ahead of his battalion and to move rapidly.[8] Custer's orders made no sense to Benteen, who testified:

> That is the way I would like to have it, that is the way I understood it. I understood it as rather a senseless order. We were on the main trail of the Indians. There were plenty of them on that trail. We had passed through immense villages the preceding days and it was scarcely worthwhile hunting up any more. We knew there were eight or ten thousand Indians on the trail we were on. . . . As it was I was certainly too far to cooperate when he wanted.[9]

Long after the battle, Pvt. Charles Windolph recalled the exchange between Benteen and Custer. Benteen had said, "Hadn't we better keep the regiment together, General? If this is as big a camp as they say, we'll need every man we have." Custer replied, "You have your orders."[10]

Custer's orders to Benteen were arcane, cryptic, and inadequate. There was no restriction on how far Benteen might roam to his left or right, nor as to which direction he might take if he sighted any Indians. If he "pitched into" a band of Indians, there were no limitations to his commitment to combat. If he became overwhelmed, he was left to his own fate. Benteen was placed out of sight and effective control of Custer and Reno. There were no instructions for Benteen's subsequent return to the regiment, nor was there information about whatever plan Custer may have had for Benteen to coordinate with the regiment at a subsequent time and location. Custer's fitness to command the regiment and his subsequent actions during the battle can be both defined and evaluated by his deployment of Benteen's battalion at this time and location.

At the point where Benteen commenced his scout, the entire regiment was thirteen miles southeast of the Indian encampment. Benteen turned left and marched off immediately (at 12:12 p.m.). After he had traveled about one mile, he received a messenger from Custer ordering him to continue his scout farther out to a second line of bluffs if nothing was seen at the first. This created greater separation from Custer. After an additional mile a second messenger ordered Benteen to continue his scout in that direction, past a third line of bluffs and down into a valley on the other side—more separation.

Benteen's scouting mission fragmented the 600-man regiment. The 175-mule pack train guarded by 130 troopers was already lagging in the rear, out of sight and control, and it would continue to drop farther behind as the day progressed. Before deploying Benteen there were 470 troopers remaining under Custer's direct command. After Benteen's deployment there remained eight companies, containing 340 troopers (56 percent of the regiment's strength) under Custer's direct command.

Respected and respectable historians have given Custer a free pass on Benteen's scout.[11] They justify the order on the basis of (1) Custer's need for reconnaissance and (2) the need to prevent the Indians from escaping the area. There can be no doubt that Custer needed reconnaissance desperately. However, this could not have been his reason for ordering Benteen away from the Indian trail. A moving reconnaissance by three companies of mounted cavalry in broad daylight would be more likely to be detected by Indians well before their observation by Benteen's battalion. Such a scout would only have served to warn the Indians in Benteen's path of Custer's approach, enhancing their ability to escape or organize a counterattack. The proper method of conducting a scout for the information he and his own battalion required would have been to send out one or more small scouting parties between dusk on June 23 and dawn on June 24 to follow the plainly marked Indian trail with stealth and

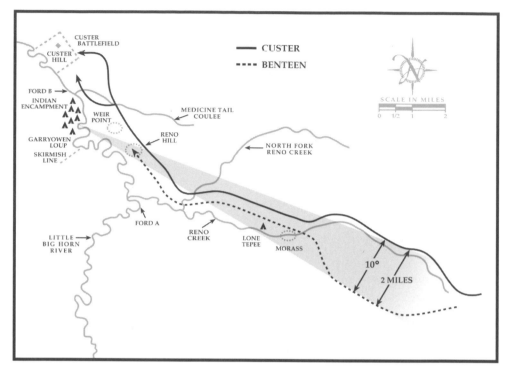

Map 7. Benteen's Scout to the left—follows Custer's Track, June 25, 1876, 12:15 p.m.
Map copyright © Charles E. Wright.

caution until they were able to locate the encampment and determine its size. In addition to his troopers, Custer had immediate access to more than forty Indian scouts. Use of small Indian scouting parties would not have weakened Custer's strike force and would have enabled him to retain tactical control of Benteen's battalion. A small scouting party was less likely to be seen by the Indians, and one or two scouts would have been sufficient to bring Custer the information he required.

Custer's scouts needed to contribute something to the efforts of the regiment. They were not well led, ineffective at scouting, and ultimately unable to drive off the Lakotas' and Cheyennes' ponies. Thus, they were not providing Custer with any real-time intelligence or assistance in crippling the Indians' mobility.

Custer was no longer using Benteen's battalion and its 130 troopers. They were out of his sight, hearing, and control. When Custer came in sight of the Indians' encampment, he did not know where Benteen was located or what he was doing. With his own puny battalion of 200 troopers, he would need all of Benteen's 130 troopers in order to stage any kind of offensive maneuver against the Sioux and Cheyenne warriors on the other bank of the Little Big Horn. Custer should have listened to Benteen when he cautioned him not to split the regiment.

The futility of Benteen's scout to prevent Indians from escaping from their encampment is demonstrated on map 7. If the Indians were fleeing from their encampment, Benteen's scout would have covered only 2.8 percent (10 degrees of 360 degrees) of the Indians' potential escape routes from the encampment. The area where Benteen conducted his scout was more than six miles east of the Little Big Horn River—whereas the Indian encampment was on the west bank of the river. In addition, after Benteen's deployment Custer's regiment continued to the northwest in the general direction of the Indian encampment in such a manner that he was directly in line between Benteen's battalion and the encampment. If escaping Indians crossed back to the east side of the Little Big Horn, Custer himself would have intercepted them before they reached the area of Benteen's search. Escaping Indians walking up the south bank of Reno Creek after Benteen completed his search and returned to Custer's trail would also have eluded detection. Finally, Benteen's battalion lacked sufficient numbers to have prevented the escape of 4,500 to 7,500 Indians and their many horses. Benteen's biographer noted, "Why would he send a battalion to the east bank to block the escape of warriors camping on the west bank?"[12]

Benteen's scout began at approximately 12:15 p.m. on June 25, covered slightly more than seven miles, and ended when his battalion returned to Custer's trail a short distance east of a morass on Reno Creek at approximately 2:30 p.m.[13] Benteen's single-phase reconnaissance revealed only that for 135 minutes his entire battalion was not in the position to see the presence of any Indians over an area two miles wide and three miles long, which stands directly to the southeast of the route that was currently being traveled by Custer as he proceeded west down Reno Creek and then northwest in the direction of the Indian encampment. Neither Benteen nor any of his troopers sighted any Indians. When he completed his scout as ordered, Benteen was on Reno Creek more than two miles behind Custer. He did not know where Custer and Reno were presently located (nor did Reno know Benteen's whereabouts). Benteen's only alternative was to follow Custer's trail. His battalion had just completed a strenuous seven-mile ride that amounted to nothing more than a "fool's chase," and both his men and their mounts needed to replenish their water. Benteen's battalion consumed approximately twenty minutes in taking water from Reno Creek, then rode west along Custer's trail to the Lone Tepee, arriving there at approximately 3:15 p.m. Although messengers subsequently sent to Benteen by Custer made contact with Benteen's battalion, it would never again come under Custer's tactical control.[14]

After Benteen's deployment the combined Custer and Reno battalions, eight companies in number (containing 340 troopers), proceeded downstream (west) along both sides of Reno Creek for about seven miles. Various Indian scouts, under the leadership of Lieutenants Charles Varnum and Luther Hare, were a short distance ahead of Custer. The scouts wandered at will in various places, and some who were traveling ahead of Custer climbed to the top of chalk buttes located a short distance north of the Lone Tepee, where they could observe Custer's approach. They spotted twenty to forty Sans Arc Lakotas fleeing downstream from the Lone Tepee, well ahead of Custer and Reno's advancing battalions. Arikara scouts rode down to the Lone Tepee, cut it open with a knife, and discovered an Indian corpse. They began to whoop and holler, but no one took the trouble to gallop back and inform Custer about the fleeing Indians. When Custer arrived a few minutes later, they provided him with this information, and he berated them, through their interpreter Gerard, for not chasing the Indians. Hare and Varnum provided scant leadership and little direction over the scouts, and Custer exercised little control over the situation. Men and scouts had shouted, discharged firearms, and set fire to the Lone Tepee, any of which actions could serve to alert the fleeing Indians and hasten further warnings of Custer's presence to the Indian encampment.

### Reno's Charge in the Valley

Custer then ordered Reno's battalion to cross over to the north bank of Reno Creek (ahead of Custer's five companies) in pursuit of the fleeing Sans Arcs (see map 6). As Reno rode through the Lone Tepee campsite, cooking fires were still smoldering, complete with cooking utensils in place. The Lone Tepee was seven miles southeast of the Indian encampment. At this point Custer paid no attention to stealth and security as he

Spotted Elk, also known as Big Foot, a leader of the Minneconjou. Although not active-ly involved in the Great Sioux War, he later became involved with the Ghost Dance and was murdered by the army at Wounded Knee. His picture as a frozen corpse serves as an icon of Wounded Knee. Courtesy Nebraska State Historical Society.

One Bull served as a guard for his uncle, Sitting Bull, and was active in the fighting at Little Big Horn. Courtesy Nebraska State Historical Society.

Red Horse, a Miniconjou Lakota, was an active fighter at Little Big Horn, later created drawings of the battle. Courtesy Denver Public Library, Western History Collection (B-484).

Flying By survived the Battle of Little Big Horn and surrendered at Fort Robinson, where he remained until Crazy Horse was killed. He then fled to Canada, where he lived for three years, after which he returned to the United States and enlisted as an Indian scout. Courtesy Denver Public Library, Western History Collection (B-497).

Sitting Bull, the venerable and respected chief of the Hunkpapa Lakotas, was the senior Indian present at the Battle of Little Big Horn. Courtesy Denver Public Library, Western History Collection (B-122).

Crow King, a Hunkpapa war chief, was heavily involved in the fighting at Little Big Horn. Courtesy Denver Public Library, Western History Collection (B-179).

Gall, a prominent Hunkpapa warrior at Little Big Horn, had both praise and criticism from fellow warriors. Courtesy Denver Public Library, Western History Collection (B-86).

Rain in the Face, a Hunkpapa Lakota, was one-time prisoner of the army at Fort Abraham Lincoln, escaped and was involved in the fighting at Rosebud and Little Big Horn. Courtesy Denver Public Library, Western History Collection (B-149).

Spotted Eagle, a Sans Arc Lakota chief, fought at Little Big Horn and later fled to Canada with Sitting Bull. Courtesy Nebraska State Historical Society.

Spotted Tail, a Brulé chief. Courtesy Denver Public Library, Western History Collection (B-201).

John Grass, a Blackfeet Lakota, was not involved in the fighting at Little Big Horn but later served as a tribal judge at the Standing Rock agency. Courtesy Denver Public Library, Western History Collection (B-896).

Hollow Horn Bear, a Brulé Lakota, was active in the Fetterman massacre and at Little Big Horn. Courtesy Nebraska State Historical Society.

followed Reno downstream.

Reno moved downstream at a trot,[15] the Sans Arcs well ahead of him. Custer dispatched Lt. William W. Cooke and Capt. Myles Keogh with a message directing Reno to "take as rapid a gait as you think prudent and charge the village afterwards, and you will be supported by the whole outfit."[16] At this point neither Custer nor Reno knew the location of the Indian encampment, nor did they know whether the encampment actually existed.[17] Reno's troopers crossed to the south side of Reno Creek and proceeded downstream until they reached and forded the Little Big Horn River. Implicit in the order to charge was authorization to commence firing.

By ordering Reno's battalion to pursue the fleeing Sans Arc, Custer had deployed another 22 percent of his strike force to chase what turned out to be 1 percent of the Indians whom he was attempting to surround and subjugate. Custer was left with only 210 troopers, one-third of his original strike force of 600.

It should be noted at this juncture that Custer was no longer attempting to conceal his presence from the Indians. He ordered Reno to attack but made no effort to keep up with him. When Custer reached the Little Big Horn and after Reno launched his "attack" along the west bank, Custer made no effort to follow Reno. Did Custer realize that he was heavily outnumbered? Was he deliberately trying to cause the Indians to flee before he arrived on the scene?

After watering their horses at the ford, Reno's troopers crossed to the west side of the Little Big Horn and rode downstream (northwest) in a "column of fours." His battalion was less than four miles upstream (southeast) from the Indian encampment. After a half-mile, Reno deployed his three companies in a line moving toward the encampment, following the west bank of the Little Big Horn River, the line itself being perpendicular to the river.[18] Reno's battalion commenced firing, which further alerted the Indian encampment located two and a half to three miles downstream. Reno led his charge with a drawn revolver. He sent two separate messengers to Custer to report that large numbers of warriors were appearing in a ravine 800 yards in front of him and that the Indians intended to stand and fight. Custer forgot or reneged on the support that he had promised. As Reno moved two miles downstream, the south end of the Indian village came into view. According to John Gray's detailed chronological sequence,[19] Reno initiated his charge at 3:03 p.m.; he halted in the face of large numbers of Indians and a possible ambush at 3:18 p.m.[20] This halt ended Reno's offensive maneuver. His battalion was in a defensive mode for the balance of the battle. Reno's battalion then dismounted and deployed in a skirmish line (perpendicular to the river) with Company M on the left (west), Company A in the center, and Company G on the right (east), extending east to a patch of timber located on the west bank of the Little Big Horn. Consistent with army tactical regulations, when Reno's battalion dismounted, 25 percent of his troopers were removed from the skirmish line to hold the horses in the rear. Since the fighting troopers were out in the open with scant cover, they had to lie flat on the ground and fire their carbines from a prone position. A short immobile line is not a good defensive formation. The Indians promptly flanked Reno's line on its left and surrounded it from behind. To keep from being flanked on two sides, Reno found it necessary to rotate his left flank some ninety degrees to the left so that the line then ran parallel to the river. Shortly thereafter, Reno called all three companies back into timber along the west bank, where he attempted to fight off increasing numbers of surrounding warriors for approximately twenty minutes.

Although Reno's battalion had taken few losses at this point, he was being overwhelmed by superior numbers and had good reason to believe that he was in an indefensible position. The Indians could fire into the timber from above, infiltrate the timber at will, and start grass fires to drive him out from his cover. Meanwhile, Reno's finite supply of ammunition was being depleted. At 3:53 p.m. (Gray's time) Reno initiated and led a raggedy retreat for approximately one mile to the southeast, parallel to the river, where he was able to ford the Little Big Horn and scramble eighty feet up steep hills on the east bank. There he located some high ground where he immediately established a defensive perimeter. This area is now called the "Reno-Benteen Battlefield." By this time it was 4:10 p.m. More than thirty officers and men serving under Reno were killed, and eleven were wounded during their fight and retreat from the valley.[21] Retreating troopers could not outrun the Indian ponies and were extremely vulnerable while in flight. Their carbines were of little use, some of their revolvers were empty, and it was difficult to sit on a galloping gelding and fire at moving targets to the rear. Fleeing troopers were jerked off their horses by hand, struck with war clubs, or shot at point-blank range.[22]

Reno was joined by Benteen and his three unbloodied companies at 4:20 p.m. The pack train with 130 additional troopers arrived from the south at 5:20 p.m. By 4:18 p.m. elements of Custer's battalion were engaged in heavy firing at the mouth of Medicine Tail Coulee. Custer's battalion was three miles north of Reno's battalion. Neither Reno nor Custer knew where the other was located, nor was Reno aware of the situation confronting Custer. Reno had deployed the ninety or so troopers remaining in his battalion in a circular defense perimeter. Reno's position was augmented by the arrival of Benteen, the pack train, and 260 additional troopers. The horses and pack mules were led to a slight depression and placed in the center of the defense perimeter in a circular arrangement surrounding an open-air field hospital manned by Dr. H. R. Porter.

Custer, moving north on the east bank, was informed by his chief guide, Mitch Bouyer,[23] of Reno's retreat.[24] However, he did not know where Reno, Benteen, or the pack train were then located. Similarly, neither Reno nor Capt. Thomas McDougall with the pack train knew where Custer was located or what he was doing. They realized that they could, if they were so inclined, locate him by following his trail, which headed north along the east bank of the river. The Indians had followed Reno from the river to his defense perimeter and surrounded him on all sides, although they had not blocked off the trail taken by Benteen and the pack train that led to Reno's defense perimeter from the south.

By the time Benteen arrived, Reno's men had expended part of their ammunition. Reno exclaimed, "For God's sake, Benteen, halt your command and help me. I've lost half my men."[25] Benteen, Capt. Thomas Weir, and other officers were concerned about the status and location of Custer. Reno needed to replenish his ammunition and, as the senior officer present, had responsibility for his wounded and the pack train. At 5:05 Captain Weir (of Benteen's battalion) on his own headed north in the direction of the gunfire, followed by Company D. At 5:23 Benteen followed Weir with Companies H, K, and M. Reno was left with the wounded and the pack train. The Arikara scouts abandoned Reno and took off for home at 5:30. At 5:40 Reno set out after Benteen, with Companies A, B, G, and the wounded, followed by the pack train. Their movement to the northwest was brief. Heavy Indian fire in the vicinity of

Weir Point caused all to return to the Reno-Benteen Battlefield by 6:10. The last to return were Lieutenants Edward Godfrey and Luther Hare with Company K, serving as rear guard for the retreat. After returning to the original defense site, Reno and Benteen reorganized their defensive perimeter, where they held out until the Indians abandoned their attack late in the afternoon of June 26.

Following the battle Reno was subjected to criticism by the correspondent Frederick Whittaker, by public comments from Custer's widow, Libbie, and by certain army officers. A few present-day writers are also not kindly disposed.[26] Critics have asserted that Reno should have stood fast in the valley and fought to the last man. This was an unrealistic expectation. Reno's mission was impossible from the beginning—over 1,000 warriors in the encampment had been alerted to Reno's approach in sufficient time to launch a powerful preemptive counterstrike, halting Reno's battalion several hundred yards short of the encampment. Indians riding toward Reno from the encampment were beyond the range of the cavalry revolvers, and the troopers' only long-range weapons were their single-shot carbines (which required both hands to reload). It was necessary to halt, dismount, and deploy into a skirmish line in order to return fire and reload the clumsy carbines. His skirmish line was less than 300 yards in length and was soon flanked on its left and thereafter surrounded on its north, west, and south sides. Reno's troopers faced a serious dilemma. If they continued a mounted charge, they could not reload; but when they dismounted and formed a skirmish line, where they had two hands to reload, they lost their mobility. In addition, Indians were firing into the timber from the east where Reno's horses were held. Reno lacked sufficient men to keep the Indians from infiltrating the timber. His men were consuming their carbine ammunition. With only 130 troopers, Reno and his battalion would have been destroyed in short order by the greater number of warriors.[27] The reckless and needless sacrifice of 130 troopers (22 percent of the regiment's fighting strength) would have seriously compromised the strategic objective of the entire campaign, as well as the safety of the pack train and Benteen's battalion.

A second and somewhat similar complaint is that Reno failed to continue his charge to the Lakota and Cheyenne encampment as ordered by Custer; if Reno had charged on, the argument goes, Custer would have been able to pull off a successful flank attack and subdue the Indians.[28] This accusation is based upon a false premise; Custer never ordered Reno to charge the Indian encampment. When Custer gave Reno his orders, Custer did not even know whether the grand encampment existed, let alone where it was located.[29] Armed only with single-shot carbines and six-shot pistols, and with no weapons for hand-to-hand combat, Reno's troopers would have had to gallop with empty guns through several hundred warriors directly in their path in order to reach the Indian encampment. If any of Reno's troopers had reached the encampment alive, they would have been easy targets and quickly dispatched. In the meantime Reno's wounded troopers would have been abandoned.[30]

Reno has also been criticized for running away from the timber stand at the head of his battalion, leading a retreat that was ragged and disorganized, neglecting to establish a rear guard, and losing thirty troopers.[31] This criticism can be made only by those who do not understand a battle condition in extremis (at the point of death). Within the space of a few moments, Reno was surrounded and outnumbered by a margin of eight to one, in a position that could not be held for any length of time, a position caused by Custer's impulsive order (without benefit of reconnaissance) to pursue and "pitch in." Reno had to find a correct path to the good ground and hope that enough troopers would survive to establish a defensible perimeter. The retreat was over unknown ground. Reno knew only that there were bluffs along the east bank of the river leading to higher ground where he would be able to find Custer's trail. Who better than Reno to lead the breakout, the breakaway, the scramble up the bluffs, and to select the location for his defense? There was no time for indecision when his battalion reached the top of the bluffs. A rear guard in the valley would have been wasted and would have been easily surrounded and wiped out by Indians at the river bank. Where could it have been placed to ward off the encircling Indians? How many troopers would be required to prevent the rear guard from being surrounded, engulfed, or bypassed? Although thirty troopers were lost, one hundred lived to fight again. Reno made a rapid decision that resulted in a successful retreat. The fact that it was ragged and disorderly is immaterial. It was the only possible maneuver for survival—and it worked. Clausewitz had this to say about a retreat, "When a dangerous position has to be abandoned, time is often wasted on trivial formalities thereby compounding the danger. In such a case, everything depends on getting away as quickly as possible."[32]

Commanders in the field are often called upon to make decisions that will result in death to some soldiers and the survival of others. In his later years Benteen intimated to certain officers that he was disgusted with Reno, who had broached to him, after dark on the evening of the twenty-fifth, the subject of retreating from the perimeter defense area under cover of darkness, abandoning the wounded soldiers who were being protected in the center. Benteen had little business broaching this topic as he did, well after the death of Reno. It was Benteen himself who, on the afternoon of the twenty-fifth, pulled away from Reno's defense perimeter with three companies—H, K, and M—following Captain Weir and Company D north in the direction of gunfire. In doing so, he abandoned Reno, who remained with Companies A, B, and G, to tend to the wounded and protect the pack train. When the pack train arrived, Reno proceeded to load up the wounded[33] and follow down the trail after Weir and Benteen until all were turned back by heavy Indian fire. In any event, Reno had remained with his wounded, and Benteen was the one who had abandoned to their fate the same wounded troopers who were the subject of his later criticism of Reno. After reviewing the Custer Battlefield in 1877, General Sheridan approved of Reno's conduct and specifically mentioned the fact that Reno had to protect his wounded troopers and did not know where Custer was located.[34]

After sending Reno to chase the fleeing Sans Arcs, Custer with his five companies (at a slower pace) followed one mile behind, moving west along the north bank of Reno Creek until they reached its junction with the north fork of Reno Creek. Arriving after Reno (at 2:45 p.m.), Custer watered his horses and turned north, moving downstream along the east bank of the Little Big Horn. Since Custer's turn to the north on the east side of the river at 3:00 p.m. determined the fate of his five companies, a review of the situation at this time and place is in order.

At the start of his turn to the north, Custer continued to lack the necessary intelligence about his enemy and the topography of the area he was approaching. He controlled only one-third of his original strike force. The element of surprise was eliminated by Reno's firing in the valley, and Indians in the encampment were on the alert. If Custer had any plan at all, he had not told Reno and Benteen, nor had he informed the commander of his pack train. There was no real-time intelligence, no co-ordination of his battalions, and no effective plan or effort to separate Indians at the encampment from their horses. Custer was operating under cryptic and ambiguous orders from Terry that fell short of defining his overall strategic objective and made no provision for the coordination of their separate movements.

Custer proceeded north along the high ground in the direction of Weir Point, galloping on level ground and trotting when going up and down a hill. At certain locations the bluffs were broken by small and large ravines, coulees, washes, draws, gulches, and gullies that descended downhill (west) toward the Little Big Horn. Mitch Bouyer and four Crow scouts were able to station themselves ahead of Custer on Weir Point (one of the highest points of ground on the bluffs bordering the east bank of the river), which was located two and three-quarter miles downstream from the mouth of the north fork of Reno Creek and approximately one and one-third miles southeast of the mouth of Medicine Tail Coulee. From Weir Point Custer may have seen Reno's charge down the valley along the west bank and portions of the Indian encampment ahead of Reno on the west bank opposite Medicine Tail Coulee.

Custer's need for concentration of force at the point of attack and his tactical control of the four components of his regiment involve a discussion of distance, relative location, and relative movement. While the Indian encampment contained hundreds of highly mobile warriors, the encampment itself remained stationary prior to and throughout the battle. Using John Gray's time-study analysis,[35] which is based upon accepted scientific principles (often called "dead reckoning") related to location, time, motion, direction and distance, it is possible to determine with a reasonable degree of accuracy the relative motion, location, and distances among Custer, Reno, Benteen, the pack train, and the Indian encampment during the one hour and fifteen minutes preceding the final battle on Custer Battlefield.

Custer's overall strategic objective required him to attack and kill or subdue the Lakotas and Cheyennes at the encampment. In order to attack the Indians, he had to be moving toward them. Maps 8 through 11 (based on Gray's data) provide a graphic illustration of the movements of Custer in relation to Reno's and Benteen's companies while Custer moved

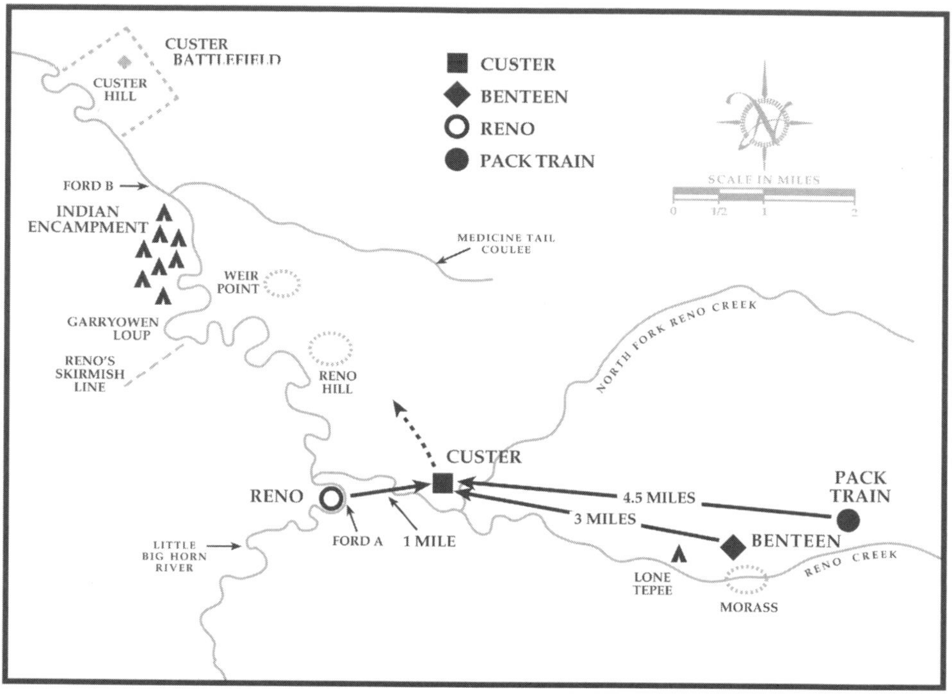

Map 8. Custer's Separation from Reno, Benteen, and Pack Train at 3:00 p.m.
Map copyright © Charles E. Wright.

toward, then away from, the Indian encampment and as he quickly abandoned his attack and increased his distance from the pack train and his other two battalions.

Custer's relative locations from Reno, Benteen, and the pack train at 3:00, 3:15, 3:50, and 4:15 p.m. are shown in maps 8, 9, 10, and 11, respectively. The most important items to note are the change in relative locations and the distances of Custer from Reno, Benteen, and the Indian encampment from 3:00 p.m. (map 8) until 4:15 p.m. (map 11).

**3:00 p.m.** Custer and his five companies have crossed the north fork of Reno Creek and turned north on the bluffs situated along the east bank of the Little Big Horn. He is moving at a trot (uphill) and a lope (level and downhill) in the direction of the Indian encampment, which is four miles to the northwest on the west bank. Reno is one mile to the west of Custer, commencing his charge downstream along the opposite side of the river. Benteen is three miles east of Custer on the north bank

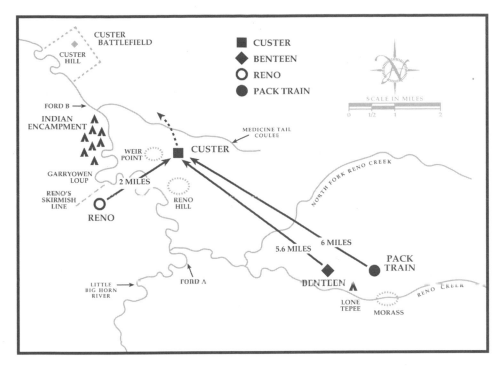

Map 9. Custer's Separation from Reno, Benteen, and Pack Train at 3:15 p.m.
Map copyright © Charles E. Wright.

of the middle fork of Reno Creek. The pack train is four and a half miles east of Custer and one and a half miles behind Benteen. Benteen and the pack train are both headed west, moving at a slower rate than Custer. From this point on, Custer will never again speak with Benteen or Reno.

As Custer heads northwest along the east bank, he can see Reno down in the valley engaged with Indians riding out from the encampment, while Reno can observe Custer moving away (northwest) from him along the bluffs on the east bank. It is also possible that Custer has sighted portions of the encampment as he passed by Reno Hill. This will be the last visual contact between Custer and Reno.

**3:15 p.m.** (map 9) Custer, moving northwest, reaches Weir Point, from which he is able to see a substantial portion of the Indian encampment. Custer is two miles northeast of Reno, who is fighting at his skirmish line on the west bank. Custer has increased his distance from Benteen (who has just crossed to the north side of Reno Creek near the Lone

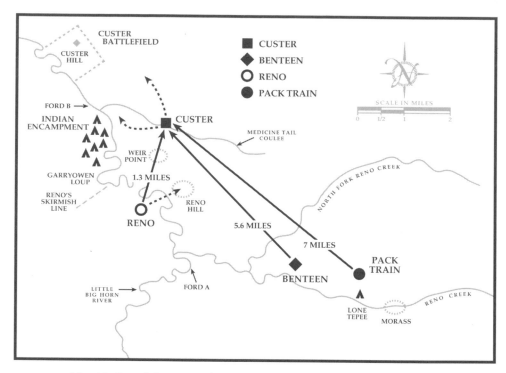

Map 10. Custer's Separation from Reno, Benteen, and Pack Train at 3:50 p.m.
Map copyright © Charles E. Wright.

Tepee) to 5.6 miles. The pack train is now six miles southeast of Custer, moving at its top speed of approximately three miles per hour. Custer's movement is parallel to both the river and the Indian encampment.

**3:50 p.m.** (give or take five minutes). (Map 10) Custer continues moving northwest, maintaining an interval of 5.6 miles from Benteen (who is following Custer's trail) and seven miles from the pack train, which cannot keep up with Benteen. Reno has moved into the timber shortly prior to his retreat and is 1.3 miles southwest of Custer. Some elements of Custer's battalion (the "left wing") move northwesterly toward the mouth of Medicine Tail Coulee. Custer's remaining troopers (the "right wing") veer north, *away* from the encampment, toward the high ground on Nye-Cartwright Ridge. Custer has sent two messengers to Benteen, ordering him to join him and bring along the pack train.

**4:10–4:20 p.m.** Custer's left wing commences engagement with the Indians, firing into their encampment from the east bank of the river. His

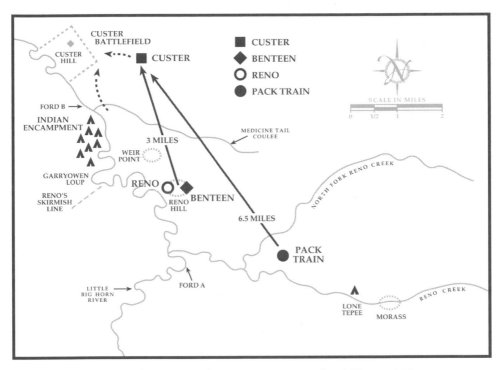

Map 11. Custer's Separation from Reno, Benteen, and Pack Train at 4:15 p.m.
Map copyright © Charles E. Wright.

left wing promptly breaks off its attack, and then both the left and right wings move north and west toward a rendezvous near the east corner of the Custer Battlefield. This movement was *away* from the Indian encampment (Custer's strategic objective) and left Custer's battalion three miles north of Reno (who had retreated to "Reno Hill") and Benteen, who had joined up with Reno at 4:20. The pack train was one hour and three miles behind Benteen. Parts of Custer's battalion would eventually reach Custer Hill—four miles north of Reno and Benteen. Custer's orders have divided his regiment into four weakened components, three of which are out of his sight and beyond his control. This is the situation as the final battle commences at or about 4:46 p.m. near the eastern corner of Custer Battlefield.

The only surviving witnesses to Custer's maneuvers between Reno Creek and Medicine Tail Coulee were the two messengers dispatched to summon Benteen and the pack train (Sgt. Daniel Kanipe and trumpeter

John Martin), the four Crow scouts accompanying Custer, and various Indian survivors of the battle who provided subsequent oral accounts. The most important aspect of Custer's movement is not the route he took but the fact that his direction and momentum created greater separation from Reno and Benteen, eliminating any possibility of concentrating his forces at the point of attack. It also brought the 210 troopers in Custer's battalion to the doorstep of the encampment where 1,500 battle-tested warriors were awaiting his arrival and willing to fight to protect their people.

Walter Camp, a civil engineer and retired railroad employee, interviewed Custer's two messengers and the four Crow scouts, who were with Custer until the main battle commenced. Sergeant Kanipe, the first messenger, told Camp of the first vantage point (Weir Point), from which it was possible for Custer to see Reno and his battalion charging down the valley and also view part of the encampment.[36] After sighting the encampment, Custer conferred with some of his officers and directed his brother Tom to send Kanipe with a message ordering Capt. Thomas McDougall "to bring the pack train straight across to high ground—if packs get loose don't stop to fix them, cut them off."[37] If Kanipe could locate Benteen, he was to tell him to come as soon as possible. There were reasons for bringing up the packs, particularly if food and ammunition were needed. However, the packs were more than one hour to the rear, vulnerable to attack, and slow afoot. Custer was about to need mobility in the worst way. If his pack train was present, his battalion would lose its mobility, and subsequent tactical movements would be very difficult to execute.

Kanipe headed back along Custer's old trail, encountering Benteen west of a swampy area called the "morass." Benteen had watered his horses and was moving his battalion west, down Reno Creek toward the Little Big Horn.[38] He informed Kanipe that the pack train was about two miles back, and Kanipe continued east, following the back trail. Kanipe told Benteen, "They want you up there as quick as you can get there—they have struck a big Indian camp."[39] When Kanipe reached the pack train, he led it north, following Custer's trail, by which time Benteen had arrived at Reno Hill and joined up with Reno's battalion.

At this point Custer, by his actions and orders to Kanipe, was indicating his desire to regroup the regiment. He did not know the location of either the pack train or Benteen, nor did he know whether either of them was engaged in combat or was even within supporting distance. He had not given either of them any instructions about rejoining the regiment or being at a certain place at a given time.

As Custer's troopers sighted the encampment, excitement broke out, the horses became gassy, and Custer shouted, "Boys, hold your horses, there are plenty of them down there for us all."[40] This comment indicated that Custer and his excited troopers were intent upon killing Indians. Custer halted for approximately ten minutes at Weir Point and examined the Indian encampment through field glasses. Historian Robert Utley summarized the situation: "For the first time, Custer had reliable knowledge of enemy location, enemy strength, and the battle terrain. The village was much larger than expected, but this probably did not daunt him."[41]

Custer and his troopers saw children and dogs at play, but no warriors. Some officers thought that the warriors were out hunting. Custer told his battalion that they would cross to the west bank of the Little Big Horn and capture the village. This brought wild cheering from the men. Then Custer moved out smartly to the north, following Cedar Coulee toward its junction with Medicine Tail Coulee.

After traveling about one-half mile, Adjutant W. W. Cooke gave trumpeter John Martin a written message to Benteen, stating, "Benteen, Come on, Big Village, Be quick, Bring packs. P.S. Bring pacs. W. W. Cooke." The phrase "Be quick, Bring packs" makes no sense because the pack train with its sore-back mules was incapable of moving quickly and was at least two hours distant from Custer and a mile behind Benteen. For Benteen to backtrack to the pack train would have delayed his battalion for more than two hours, during which time Custer and his battalion would be wiped out.

As Martin continued down the back trail, he encountered Custer's brother Boston, who had deserted the pack train and was galloping to rejoin his brother—a fateful decision on his part. Martin rode to the top of a ridge overlooking the east bank, from which he could see Indians swarming and charging toward the ford ("Ford B") at Medicine Tail Coulee. Some warriors were waving buffalo robes to spook the cavalry horses. Looking back to the north he could see Custer headed north, away from Ford B. Martin continued south down the trail at a rapid gait and eventually delivered his written message to Benteen, who was moving west down Reno Creek, following Custer's trail. Martin told Benteen that Custer was three miles to the north and was under attack. Martin then joined up with Benteen's battalion and was with them when they reached Reno.[42]

In a subsequent interview with Camp, Martin stated that when he stopped to look back from Weir Point, he could see Custer and his battalion on a flat. Custer's men were "falling back" and were being fired on by the Indians. After the battle Martin showed Benteen where he had departed from Custer with the message, and Benteen estimated that the distance was 600 yards from Ford B.

Curley, one of the four Crow scouts with Mitch Bouyer, was the best oriented and most articulate of the group.[43] Bouyer and the scouts had stationed themselves on a high, rocky bluff (which could have been Weir Point), from which they could observe the Indian encampment and watch Reno charge down the valley. When Custer approached their vantage point, they joined up with his battalion, which proceeded to move north, parallel to Cedar Coulee toward its junction with Medicine Tail Coulee.

According to various Indian accounts, three of the Crow scouts—Hairy Moccasin, Goes-Ahead, and White-Man-Runs-Him—departed from the battle in the vicinity of Weir Point. Thereafter Curley also departed as the Indians began their attack from across the river at the mouth of Medicine Tail Coulee. When Curley left, Bouyer had been wounded in the leg and was physically unable to leave. Bouyer told Curley that he (Bouyer) was going to die.

By the time Custer's men opened fire on the Indian encampment in the vicinity of Medicine Tail Coulee (4:18 p.m.), only 210 (35 percent) of the 600 soldiers of the Seventh Cavalry were under Custer's control. The remaining 390 (inclusive of those killed that day) were with the battalions of Reno and Benteen, which were pinned down under fire more than four miles distant or were engaged in escorting the 175-mule pack train, which would not arrive at the Reno-Benteen defense area for another hour. At this point, Custer had little ability to summon the rest of the battalion for help or to communicate with them about his current situation. He had built a trap for himself by declining the additional cavalry and infantry support offered by General Terry and by committing himself to an all-out attack regardless of the circumstances. His 210 soldiers were mounted on jaded horses and were facing an attack by 1,500 well-armed Lakota and Cheyenne warriors, some of whom had recently attacked Reno, Benteen, and the pack train, and who had successfully fought 1,000 troops of Gen. George Crook to a standstill for eight hours on June 17. Custer had no ability to go on the offensive, but if he retreated he would lose face.

The fate of Custer and his five companies would play out on Custer Battlefield.

## Chapter Eleven

# The Little Big Horn Battlefield

*Our people were roaming through the country that had been given them before the coming of the whites. The country was good; there was rich grass for the ponies, and sweet water; the fields glowed with prairie flowers of yellow and red and blue; there were buffaloes in the valleys and Indian turnips on the hills for the digging. We were rich in provisions, and no man had a right to put out his hand and tell us that we should not roam.*

—Beautiful White Cow, wife of Hunkpapa warrior Spotted Horn Bull[1]

Map 12 is an aerial photograph taken in the 1980s, overlaid with the names of the critical points of the battle between Custer's Seventh Cavalry Regiment and the Lakota and Cheyenne Indians in the vicinity of their grand encampment on the west bank of the Little Big Horn River.

The "Little Big Horn Battlefield" is a generic term covering an area of more than 23,000 acres extending north from the mouth of Reno Creek to the ground, situated 1,000 yards north and west of Last Stand Hill, where various units of the regiment fought at different times between noon until dusk on June 25, 1876. Within the Little Big Horn Battlefield are two smaller areas of concentrated fighting: "Custer Battlefield" (approximately 640 acres) and "Reno-Benteen Battlefield" (160 acres). They are separated by more than three miles. Custer Battlefield and Reno-Benteen Battlefield are administered today by the National Park Service under the title "Little Bighorn Battlefield National Monument."

Map 12 reveals the relative locations of Custer Battlefield and Reno-Benteen Battlefield. Custer Battlefield is basically one square mile, situated so that its four corners run roughly on a north-south and east-west axis, with its southwestern boundary line following the meandering path

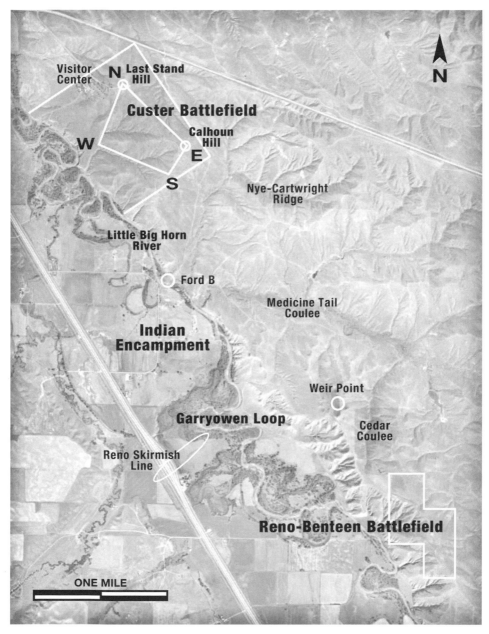

Map 12. Aerial Map of Little Big Horn Battlefield. Map by Darrel Stevens, map copyright © Charles E. Wright.

of the Little Big Horn River. While Custer's remains were later removed to West Point, Custer Battlefield is the area where the troopers in Custer's battalion were killed on June 25, 1876, and where white marble headstones mark the location of their remains. Reno-Benteen Battlefield is where the pack train and the six companies commanded by Major Reno and Captain Benteen fought off the Indians until the Indians withdrew late in the afternoon of June 26.

The west bank of the Little Big Horn River, flowing northwest from the mouth of Reno Creek, comprises a relatively level riparian segment running from southeast to northwest for more than ten miles. This segment of the river is shown in map 12 running parallel to the path of interstate highway I-90. Along the west bank the river meanders back and forth with numerous bends, curves, and oxbows so that the overall length of the river is more than twice the linear distance that it travels. In places its banks are lined with willows and other woody shrubs, together with several stands of cottonwood trees. One particular salient on the river, called the "Garryowen Loop," extends several hundred yards to the west of the principal thread of the river. Nestled into the north of Garryowen Loop was the southernmost component of the Indian encampment, the Hunkpapa circle. Located downstream (north), parallel to the river on its west bank, were five additional Lakota circles occupied by the Blackfeet, Minneconjou, Brulé, Oglala, Sans Arc, and (at the north end) the Cheyenne circle. The Cheyenne circle was a short distance directly south of the ford (Ford B) at the confluence of Medicine Tail Coulee and Deep Coulee. The river valley along the west bank was subject to seasonal flooding. Directly north of Ford B on the east bank is a level plateau of approximately 200 acres (the "flat") extending northward to the southwest line of Custer Battlefield.

Within the encampment there were 1,000 to 2,000 warriors capable of fighting the Seventh Cavalry. Many of these warriors had participated in the battle with General Crook at Rosebud Creek on June 17, which gave them further confidence in their ability to fight the invading wasicu soldiers.

On the morning of June 25, the Indians in the encampment were calm and relaxed. Many had danced well into the night, and some of the warriors were sleeping late. There does not seem to be any reliable information that any of the Indians in the encampment anticipated additional combat with the army following the June 17 battle with Crook.[2] Their intelligence told them that Crook had retired from the Rosebud battlefield and headed south, in the direction of Fort Fetterman. Similarly, while the Indians had sighted Gibbon's Montana column at various locations north of the Yellowstone River in April, May, and early June, they were not anticipating an attack from the north. More significantly, none of the contacts between elements of the Seventh Cavalry Regiment and small groups of Indians near the Crow's Nest during the early morning hours of June 25 had actually warned any Indians at the encampment of Custer's approach.

Portions of the encampment were alerted when Reno began firing at Ford A in the valley. A wild scramble ensued at the south end of the camp as women and children sought to pack and run, while some of the warriors set about retrieving their ponies and putting on war paint and battle dress in preparation for another big fight with the U.S. Army. Despite the general alert that flowed through the camp from south to north as Reno approached, no one seemed aware of Custer's presence along the east bank until he was sighted by turnip gatherers and horse herders in the vicinity of Weir Point.[3] Minneconjou warrior Lights had little advance warning.[4] Brulé Hollow Horn Bear did not learn of Custer's presence until "shortly after" the fight with Reno.[5] Julia Face, an Oglala, did not see the soldiers until they were as near to the camp as they ever got.[6] Pretty White Buffalo (wife of Spotted Horn Bull), a Hunkpapa, spoke of cavalry bullets rattling through their tepees and fearful women and children who at first believed that "the Great Father had sent all his men for the destruction of the Sioux." Speaking of the location of the encampment, she stated, "Our camp was not pitched anticipating a battle. The warriors would not have picked such a place for a fight with white men, open to attack from both ends and from the west side."[7] She also indicated that on the evening of June 24, there was nothing but merrymaking; they were not anticipating a fight. In the opinion of Pretty White Buffalo, the encampment on the west bank was vulnerable from the south, west, and north—but Custer chose to approach and attack from the east. He was definitely not in a position to prevent any or all of the Indians from escaping if they chose to run rather than fight.

Kate Big Head ("Antelope") was a sister of Cheyenne brothers White Bull and White Moon. On the morning of June 25, she visited the Minneconjou circle and then bathed in the river while watching men, women, and children playing and fishing along the west bank. Some Lakotas were already beginning to dismantle their lodges for an anticipated move north in the direction of Yellowstone River. Two young Lakota boys suddenly ran into camp, warning that soldiers were coming from the southeast.[8] Black Elk, the Oglala memorialized by John Niehardt, was then a thirteen-year-old horse herder. After dawn he and other youthful companions went back to camp for breakfast. After breakfast he had returned to the river to swim when he heard cries warning of the approaching soldiers.[9]

Oglala warrior Low Dog was asleep in his lodge at noon when the approach of the soldiers awakened him. He stated that Indians from camp were chasing lost horses on the east bank when they were spotted by white scouts, who tried to kill them. One of the horse chasers outran the wasicu horsemen and brought the warning to the encampment.[10] White Bull, a Minneconjou, was herding horses that morning. He had loosened the picket ropes on his family's horses and drove them to breaks by the river. After watering the horses, he herded them north to good grass and returned back to his lodge around 8:00 a.m. for breakfast. After breakfast he took his Winchester rifle and cartridge belts and returned to the horses. Shortly before midday watering, White Bull heard someone shouting an alarm. He climbed a nearby hill and saw soldiers approaching from the south. He jumped on one of his horses and brought the remainder back to camp.[11]

An excellent explanation concerning the three groups of Indians who were sighted by Custer's scouts and troopers in the vicinity of the Crow's Nest on the morning of June 25 is provided in an interview with a summer roamer from the Red Cloud Agency named Black Bear, taken by the amateur historian Walter Camp on July 18, 1911.[12] Black Bear, an Oglala, left the Red Cloud Agency in northwest Nebraska with a party of six men and one woman, searching for horses that had been stolen by other Indians en route to join Crazy Horse and Sitting Bull on the summer hunt. Black Bear's party recovered their horses and temporarily joined the encampment at the Little Big Horn. On the morning of the twenty-fifth, they departed from the encampment and were returning to the Red Cloud Agency when they ran across three Cheyennes, who told them they had been following soldiers all the way from Powder River.

The Cheyennes had stumbled onto the dropped hardtack box, were fired upon while they were opening it, fled, and subsequently followed the Seventh Cavalry toward the Little Big Horn. According to Black Bear, his party continued back to the agency, and the three Cheyennes who had opened the box of hardtack did not return to the encampment in time to warn of Custer's presence. Black Bear also learned of an old Indian man and boy, hunting lost horses, who had sighted the soldiers in the morning. The boy was killed by the soldiers while the old man warned the village. The time of this warning is not known. In addition, an Indian who had killed a buffalo on the east bank was startled by the arrival of the soldiers and ran off, returning to the camp after the battle.

The element of surprise was essential to the success of Custer's mission because, with his small battalion of 210 troopers, it was impossible for him to contain or subjugate even a small portion of the Lakotas and Cheyennes who were located in the encampment. The key aspect of the surprise element was the requirement that Custer's attack force deprive the Indians of their mobility by separating them from their ponies at the instant of attack. This happened at Washita, where Custer achieved total surprise, separated the victims from their ponies, and held his casualties to a minimum. Since tribal groups pastured their ponies in separate herds, gaining control of the ponies would have required precise timing and swift action to prevent them from being recovered by their warriors and herders.

Thus, while Custer had good reason to think that he had been discovered and the encampment warned, this was not the case. He continued to have the element of surprise in his pocket—at least until his men fired at and burned the Lone Tepee, or possibly until Reno commenced his charge up the valley, or perhaps even until he appeared, coming out of the east in the vicinity of Weir Point. While Custer, acting upon reliable reports from Sgt. William Curtis and his Crow and Arikara scouts, believed that surprise was lost, it was in fact intact until sometime after noon on June 25. His best evidence was merely conjecture because he had neglected to locate the Indians' encampment and maintain it under surveillance. He had acted on instinct or a hunch, rather than real-time intelligence. With factual information Custer might have been able to keep his regiment hidden during daylight on June 25 and attempt to achieve a surprise attack in the early morning light of the following day.

Surprise remained a possibility, but it is mere speculation as to whether it could have been maintained until dawn on June 26.

One additional fact of a subjective nature deserves consideration. What standard of effort was called for with respect to Custer and his battalion? This was not covered in Sheridan's orders to Terry or Terry's orders to Custer. Was it necessary to attack and fight to the last trooper? Were parley or retreat viable options? Did Custer have any duty to weigh his chances and consider the lives of his men? What were the stakes? Surely, national security was not involved. The purpose of the entire mission was to deprive the Lakotas and Cheyennes of their freedom, killing as many as necessary to remove them from the vast areas of semi-arid plains in their unceded Indian territory in order that the Northern Pacific Railroad could be built and the area claimed by wasicu settlers.

The Indians at Custer Battlefield possessed between 354 and 414 rifles, of which 198 to 232 were Henry or Winchester repeating rifles.[13] After the battle Sgt. Charles Windolph stated that at least half the Indian warriors fought without firearms and that 25 to 30 percent had repeating rifles.[14] Windolph's numbers are consistent with the number of Indian rifles that were determined from subsequent archaeological surveys. In addition to their guns, the Indians fought with arrows, lances, war clubs, and knives. They were living as they had for hundreds of years—a mobile society on the arid high plains, seeking out and hunting their primary source of food, the buffalo. There was no immediate threat to civilians or to peace and quiet in the unceded Indian territory of southeastern Montana. There were no recent raids, thefts, or attacks on military or civilian populations in the area. Article 16 of the 1868 Treaty of Fort Laramie allowed them to hunt in their unceded Indian territory and prohibited white settlement or trespass.

The overwhelming number of warriors gave the Indians a sizeable temporary military advantage. However, since they had no outside source of supply and no permanent supply base, they had to move constantly in search of grass and game. Geographically, because there was little food for them to the south or west, they could move only to the north and east. Just about any type of military encounter would end their hunt and force them to move. In locating adequate food in areas outside the Yellowstone basin, they would need to divide into smaller groups—making them more vulnerable to the U.S. Army, whose mission was to subdue them and force them to live on reservations. Because of the difficulties they faced in providing a bare-bones subsistence for themselves, their numbers would be difficult to sustain. Under these circumstances their strategy of freedom to survive as traders and hunter-gatherers was doomed. They could either submit now or fight.

Chapter Twelve
# Custer's Final Battle: The Evidence and Battle Tactics

*It's the hell-served-for-breakfast that's hard.*
—*Robert W. Service, "The Quitter"*[1]

When Lt. Col. George A. Custer's battalion reached Custer Battlefield, he had real-time knowledge that he was vastly outnumbered. By his own orders he had created a separation of three miles from the battalions of Maj. Marcus Reno, Capt. Frederick Benteen, and the pack train, which contained two-thirds of Custer's fighting force. He was under a counter-attack by Lakota and Cheyenne warriors, who were about to surround his five companies on all sides. He was nearly one mile away from the river and the essential water for his men and horses. His only access to ammunition was the 124 rounds of carbine and pistol cartridges that each trooper carried on himself or his horse. Reno and Benteen were not riding to assist. Custer was not aware of Gen. George Crook's forces to the south and had no plans for cooperation with or assistance from Gen. Alfred H. Terry's forces approaching from the north. The precious moments in which he could retreat or run for his life were about to expire. With a strength of force deficiency of at least one to seven and an overall strategic objective of attack and subjugation, Custer's chances for success were gone and his opportunity for survival was in serious doubt—his life expectancy was, as they say, in extremis.

The Indians were familiar with the topography of the battlefield, but neither Custer nor any of his battalion had ever been there. Half the warriors had firearms and one-fourth of them had repeating rifles, while Custer's troopers had only their single-shot carbines and .45-caliber revolvers. All of Custer's Arikara and Crow scouts had departed. The Lakotas and Cheyennes had many routes available if they needed to escape from their river bank encampment, while Custer, for a few fleeting seconds before he was surrounded, might have been able to flee southward on the bluffs along the east bank to rejoin Reno and Benteen. The Lakota and Cheyenne leaders—Crazy Horse, Gall, Lame Whiteman, Two Moon, and White Bull—each had considerable experience in plains warfare, while Custer's last pitched battle with Indians had taken place at Washita in 1868, where Custer's troopers outnumbered Black Kettle's surprised warriors by seven and a half to one. Numbers two and three in Custer's chain of command were pinned down and fighting for their lives out of Custer's sight and were three miles distant.

The terms "left wing" and "right wing" create confusion. They have been used by historians to refer to separate parts of Custer's battalion. Some historians contend that Custer's battalion had no wings. Whether or not Custer's battalion had "wings" is immaterial. The terminology, however, can assist in describing the movements of the separate components of the five companies under Custer's direct control as they converged near the east corner of Custer Battlefield.

As Custer approached the Indian encampment from the southeast, he sent a portion of his battalion ("left wing") downhill along the banks of Medicine Tail Coulee to a point called Ford B (see map 12), where the coulee reached the east bank of the Little Big Horn. This was opposite the northern end of the Indians' encampment on the west bank. We cannot be certain which companies or how many troops were detailed for this mission, but reliable scholars, including the archaeologists Douglas D. Scott and Peter Bleed,[2] suggest that Custer's left wing, consisting of Companies E and F commanded by Capt. George Yates, conducted this maneuver. The left wing fired shots directly into the encampment, with the Indians returning fire from across the Little Big Horn and immediately counterattacking as they crossed to the east bank of the Little Big Horn upstream and downstream from the left wing.[3]

A 1994 archaeological study conducted outside the boundaries of Custer Battlefield found a small number of army cartridge cases and battle artifacts on the east bank in the vicinity of Medicine Tail Ford (Ford B), where the Crow scout Curley had observed the left wing approach and open fire.[4] As the Indians returned fire, Custer's left wing proceeded downstream following flat ground between the river and the bluffs, and then turned north to higher ground along the west side of Deep Coulee in the direction of Calhoun Hill. There it would join the right wing, consisting of Companies C, I, and L.

While the left wing was stirring up a hornets' nest in the river valley, the right wing, on higher ground, moved northeast about two-thirds of a mile toward Luce and Nye-Cartwright ridges, where they discharged two or more volleys from their carbines. These movements by the right wing were *away* from the Indian encampment that Custer supposedly intended to attack and subdue.

The volleys along Nye-Cartwright and Luce ridges were corroborated by several amateur archaeologists. Between 1928 and 1971 Joseph A. Blummer (a local rancher), R. G. Cartwright (a schoolteacher from South Dakota), and Col. Elwood L. Nye (an army veterinarian), individually and collectively reported finding more than 260 expended 1873 Springfield cartridge cases along Nye-Cartwright Ridge, establishing that some part of Custer's battalion passed through this area en route to Custer Battlefield.[5] These cartridge cases extended in a line approximately 500 yards in length along Nye-Cartwright Ridge. In 1943 Edward S. Luce, then the battlefield superintendent, discovered approximately 150 expended carbine cases on a smaller ridge (Luce Ridge), located southeast of Nye-Cartwright.[6] No human remains or Indian cartridges have been located in the vicinity of either ridge, notwithstanding the fact that several hundred army rounds were fired in this vicinity.[7]

There is no indication that the right wing was being fired upon by the Indians or that they were firing at the Indians. The volley firing was within hearing distance of the Indians in the encampment. This movement to the northeast increased the right wing's distance from the left wing and from Custer's overall objective (the encampment), while it decreased Custer's opportunity to regroup his battalion or reunite with Reno and Benteen. Custer's movement away from the Indian encampment terminated his attempt at attack, placing him on the defensive when the Indians commenced their counterattack. Learned and persuasive historians contend to this day that Custer firmly believed that the Indians would flee when they discovered his presence.[8] This turns out to be irrelevant because instead of taking flight, the Indians mounted an all-out counterattack directly at Custer's five companies.

Questions arise over the left wing firing across the river into the Indian camp—and the right wing intentionally separating itself two-thirds of a mile to the northeast of the left wing, where it discharged volleys from the Luce and Nye-Cartwright ridges. What was Custer trying to accomplish? Was he fending off attacking Indians or sending a signal to Benteen to come to his aid? Or was he hoping to induce the Indians to take flight? From Custer's position on the east side of the Little Big Horn, the Lakotas and Cheyennes in their encampment on the west bank were free to flee in three directions—north, west, or south. If these Indians decided to flee, as they had in past encounters, Custer was powerless to stop them, and his strategic objective (attack and subjugate) would be impossible to achieve. If the Indians fled, what would Custer tell General Sheridan? What would his readers in the *New York Herald* think of him? The right-wing volleys accomplished nothing but a slight consumption of their limited ammunition and an indication of Custer's presence to all within earshot. One conclusion seems to fit the circumstances. Custer admitted at officers' call on June 22 that he was badly outnumbered. His prior deployments had reduced his immediate attack force to 210 troopers. The current Indian counterattack eliminated his own ability to attack, surround, or subjugate the Indians. If Custer was in touch with reality, he was aware by this time that he was unable to subdue the encampment. Without an attack he had no chance of success, and his only option was to cause the Indians to take flight—then regroup and pursue them when conditions were more favorable. Other conclusions can be reached, but they provide no justification for his movement of three of his five companies away from the Indian encampment and the volleys that he fired. Unless the Indians took flight, no maneuver he might make (other than immediate flight) would help him or his battalion—and his strategic objective was no longer possible.

Map 13, an aerial photo prepared by Douglas D. Scott,[9] shows the locations of the white marble burial markers (indicated by white dots) in relation to the various waypoints on Custer Battlefield. The boundary of Custer Battlefield is outlined in white. The black lines and writing (inserted by the author) demonstrate the arrangement and location of the marble burial markers, indicating where Custer's troopers were killed as they fled from the attacking Indians. Significant numbers of U.S. Army and Indian cartridges have been discovered on and around the marble headstones clustered at the top of Calhoun Hill,[10] providing good reason to believe that both wings of Custer's battalion reunited in this vicinity.

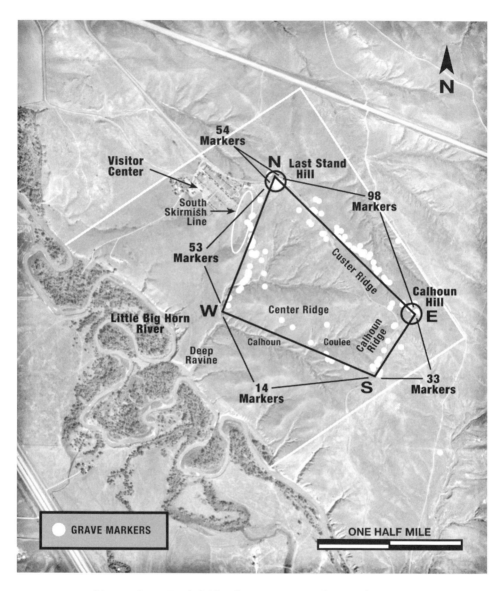

Map 13. Custer Battlefield and Waypoints. Map by Darrel Stevens,
map copyright © Charles E. Wright.

John S. Gray's time-motion study indicates that the left and right wings reunited at 4:46 p.m. and that one or both groups were then under attack.[11]

To reconstruct what happened next, primary reliance upon archaeological studies conducted by the National Park Service at Custer Battlefield following the grass fire of 1983 is crucial.[12] Geodetically accurate aerial photos (maps 13–19) show the boundaries of Custer Battlefield in which various ravines, hills, and ridges associated with the battle are located and labeled. The white dots mark the marble headstones of fallen troopers. Under the supervision of Douglas D. Scott, metal detectors were utilized to locate the Indian and U.S. Army cartridges and bullets found on Custer Battlefield. The location of each item was documented on a computerized grid of the battlefield, and each bullet and empty cartridge case was identified by size and caliber, thus identifying it as either "Indian" or "army."[13] Thus there is an accurate picture of the marble headstones in relation to each other and in relation to where the Indian and army cartridges have been located and identified in these archaeological studies.

Of special significance are the locations of the empty Indian and army cartridge cases. The various types of firearms used by the Indians differed from the .45-caliber Springfield carbines and the .45-caliber Colt pistols used by Custer's Seventh Cavalry. All bullets and cartridges recovered on the battlefield were examined and identified by the firearms and tool marks identification procedures of the Criminalistics Laboratory operated by the Nebraska State Patrol.[14] Examination enabled the laboratory to identify all cartridge cases and bullets as either army or Indian and eliminate extraneous items that were neither. After identification each cartridge case was located on the grid of Custer Battlefield utilizing the computer-assisted mapping program called Fastdraft.[15]

Unsworn statements from Indians and other participants who observed the battle have been used to supplement the archaeological evidence. While most of the Indian testimony is hearsay, similar testimony gathered from multiple witnesses, if consistent, can be utilized to corroborate and thus provide a measure of credibility to other hearsay statements about specific locations, time, and details of the battle.

A third category of evidence consists of certain reasonable and readily verifiable facts about which historians and readers are justified in tak-

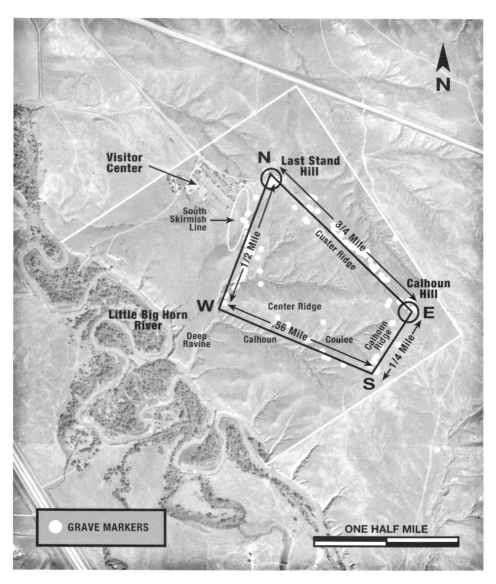

Map 14. Custer Battlefield—Combat Zone. Map by Darrel Stevens, map copyright ©
Charles E. Wright.

ing actual notice. These include facts that are either generally known or are capable of determination through sources whose accuracy cannot reasonably be questioned. For example, the reader may take actual notice of the U.S. Army regulations prevailing in the nineteenth century, as well as the geographical locations of rivers and battlefields in southeastern Montana.

Finally, the manuscript may indulge in certain presumptions when the existence of the presumed fact is more probable than its nonexistence. For example, in order to continue firing, it was necessary, and thus standard procedure, for each warrior and trooper to eject the empty cartridge case from each rifle or carbine immediately after it was fired. Thus, it may be presumed that the location of a rifle cartridge case indicates the location of an Indian warrior as he fired upon a trooper—or vice versa. However, an empty case from a revolver (which could fire up to six rounds before reloading) would merely mark the location where it was ejected from the pistol rather than where it was fired—a fact that has little relevance to our reconstruction. In examining the photographs of the battlefield, consideration is given not only to *where* the headstones and cartridge cases are located but where they were *not found*.

Map 14 is a skeletal drawing of the "combat zone," that portion of Custer Battlefield in which Custer's troopers were killed.[16] The lines provide an indication of the location and the approximate pattern of the distribution of the headstones within Custer Battlefield.

The most significant information provided by the archaeology studies is validation of the location of the dead troopers immediately following the battle. Records of the battlefield indicate that the 252 white marble headstones were placed on Custer Battlefield by the army in 1890. Since there were no more than 210 troopers killed on this battlefield, there are at least forty-two duplicate or "spurious" markers that do not mark authentic death sites.[17] The archaeologists attribute some of the excess markers to the phenomenon that occurred when, in certain instances, two markers were placed where there was but a single body. Comparing photographs taken at different times, the archaeologists noted minor instances where markers had been moved. Nonetheless, they conclude that results of "the archaeological testing program demonstrate that the distribution of markers on the field conveys a relatively accurate impression of where a soldier fell on June 25 . . . 1876."[18] Similarly, there is no reason to believe that the Indians would deliberately move any or all bodies of dead troopers any great distance from where they fell to the ground.

For our purposes in assessing what happened to the Seventh Cavalry, individual death sites mean very little, but the grouping and location in relation to each other is a significant determinative factor as to what happened. On map 13 the actual location of each headstone marker on Custer Battlefield is indicated by a small white dot that has been superimposed onto an aerial photograph of the battlefield. Names of significant battle points and specific topographical features associated with the fighting have been inserted. Looking at the entire spectrum of the markers, the "combat zone" (see map 14) consists of a series of four unequal connected lines (outlined in white), which form the shape of a trapezoid, whose four corners are labeled S, E, N, and W (corresponding with south, east, north, and west of the true compass), thus producing four segments titled:

| "S-E" | ¼ mile in length | extending from south end of Calhoun Ridge to Calhoun Hill |
| "E-N" | ¾ mile in length | extending northwesterly from Calhoun Hill to Last Stand Hill |
| "N-W" | ½ mile in length | extending south from Last Stand Hill to junction of Deep Ravine and Calhoun Coulee |
| "W-S" | .56 mile in length | extending southeasterly from junction of Deep Ravine and Calhoun Coulee to south end of Calhoun Ridge |

Since archaeological studies (and most historians) indicate that Custer's troops entered Custer Battlefield at or near Calhoun Hill, it is used as the reference point to determine the movement of Custer's troopers for the balance of the battle. There are thirty-three white dots extending from the south end of Calhoun Ridge (S) to Calhoun Hill (E), with twelve of these markers clustered around Calhoun Hill and the remaining twenty-one extending south to the southern end of Calhoun Ridge. It is not known whether the movement on Calhoun Ridge was from north to south, or vice versa, or both, but this makes little difference.

There are ninety-eight markers in the segment from Calhoun Hill (E) to Last Stand Hill (N). Since Calhoun Hill was the entry point to Custer Battlefield, the movement went from east to north, in a northwesterly direction. A substantial number of troopers were killed in this movement.

There are fifty-four markers in a tight cluster around Last Stand Hill (N). Along the line from Last Stand Hill to the junction of Deep Ravine and Calhoun Coulee (W), there are an additional fifty-three markers. Neither eyewitness accounts nor archeological evidence can explain the movement of troops from Last Stand Hill (N) down the South Skirmish Line to the head wall of Deep Ravine (W). While the issue is more or less irrelevant, there does not appear to be a conclusive explanation for this maneuver. Similarly, it is not known whether the fighting at the South Skirmish Line and at the head of Deep Ravine occurred prior to, simultaneous with, or subsequent to combat at Last Stand Hill. There does not appear to be any connection between them other than the irregular but discernable line extending from Deep Ravine through the South Skirmish Line to Last Stand Hill. This could have been a dash to safety, an attempt to seek better cover, or a feint to lure the Indians away from Custer at Last Stand Hill. Of these three, the scramble to escape may be the most probable. The accounts by Indian survivors Respects Nothing and Moses Flying Hawk indicate that the troopers moved on foot to Deep Ravine from Last Stand Hill and that many troops were killed by hand weapons.[19]

Finally, in the segment extending .56 of a mile in a rough line between Deep Ravine (W) and the south end of Calhoun Ridge (S), there are fourteen widely spaced markers. It is uncertain whether these markers represent some form of organized movement, whether they consisted entirely of stragglers or those intending to escape, or whether they were part of the group of forty-two spurious markers that do not represent any fallen troopers on the battlefield.

At this point it is important to note that the circumference of the entire trapezoid (the "combat zone") is more than two miles in length and within the first three legs, S-E, E-N, and N-W, there is a linear distance of more than one and a half miles. In addition, the movements from S to E and from E to N are away from the Indian encampment and away from the Reno-Benteen Battlefield. These movements, while taking numerous casualties along the way, establish conclusively that Custer was no longer on the offensive. With his deficiency in relative strength, and with his options to achieve surprise and drive off the Indians' ponies no longer available, Custer lacked any ability (for several additional reasons as well) to attack the Indians. Contrary to the opinions of various writers,[20] Custer was on the defensive whether he knew it or not. Similarly, from the instant that Custer's troopers fired on the encampment from the east bank, the Indians attacked Custer and remained on the offensive until Custer and his entire battalion of five companies had been killed. It is not difficult to discern whether one is on defense or offense. The concept of defense is parrying a blow, its characteristic feature is awaiting an attack, its object is preservation, and its essence is to stand fast.[21]

Since defense is based on standing fast, it generally occurs at one or more locations and requires some type of tactical formation or deployment. The formation must meet certain requirements to be effective. It should provide some internal concealment and shelter from direct fire, allow all flanks and sides protection from being enfiladed, and permit the defenders to view enemy movements. It requires an unobstructed line for retreat and should, in general, provide more advantages for the defenders than their enemy.[22]

In establishing a defensive position, the simplest formation is a straight line, which is easy to establish and provides adequate opportunities for observation. However, if the line is too short, it is easy to flank and enfilade, and without depth it may be easy to penetrate. A line is not a satisfactory defensive formation for cavalry because the troopers have to dismount and locate cover for the protection of their horses, thereby depriving themselves of instant mobility.

A square formation requires greater numbers than Custer's 210 troopers and is vulnerable to enfilade fire from each of its four corners. A triangle formation has similar deficiencies.

The circle, which requires a greater number of troops to be effective, is flexible and can be modified to fit existing terrain. It is the best formation of the four, is easy to form, need not have a precise shape, permits a 360-degree perimeter defense, and works best if it can completely surround a high point with the defenders facing outward. While the circle can be penetrated and surrounded, it is never enfiladed at the corners because it has none. This formation enabled Reno, Benteen, and the troopers with the pack train at the Reno-Benteen Battlefield to survive after they were surrounded.

The very worst formation from a defensive standpoint is a formless and exposed cluster of dismounted troopers armed with single-shot carbines and revolvers, exposed to fire from all sides, crowded closely together with no defined field of fire, surrounded by angry and mobile warriors who are taking no prisoners and from whom there is no hope of escape. The defensive cluster rewards "flock shooting" because if your enemy misses one trooper, he stands a chance of hitting another nearby. While in a cluster, each trooper is faced with a restricted area in which he cannot fire because of the likelihood of killing or wounding fellow troopers. It is a situation such as this where tactical maneuvers and sound leadership determine the outcome of a battle. The location of gravestones on the battlefield indicates that the cluster situation existed at Calhoun Hill and Custer Hill, and probably at the head of Deep Ravine. The cluster phenomena could be due to several causes. Troopers on the defensive could have been driven or compressed into a cluster by heavy fire from all sides—they might have been forced into a cluster through panic and fear (inducing loss of hope and irrational behavior).

Drawing upon the information developed in the archaeological studies of 1984 and 1985, additional conclusions about the battle can be made. Maps 13 and 15 through 19 were prepared by Douglas Scott. The Custer Battlefield labels and the lines connecting the marble headstones have been added. Maps 15 and 17 show, respectively, the location of the Indian and army cartridge cases, and map 19 is a combination of both Indian and army cases, all in relation to the marble headstones. The *Archaeological Perspectives* study indicates the likelihood of an organized "south defensive area" along line N-W, extending from Last Stand Hill to Deep Ravine.[23]

The location of the Indian cartridge cases (black diamonds) on map 15 indicates where the Indians fired at Custer's troopers. These black diamonds indicate (1) that the Indians surrounded the troopers on all sides as they fired into the "combat zone," and (2) that much of the Indians' firing was at ranges greater than 200 yards. There is a significant cluster of marble headstones and Indian cases surrounding Calhoun Hill. However, there are very few cases at Last Stand Hill, where fifty-four headstones are located, suggesting that most of the troopers at Last Stand and the north end of Custer Ridge were either killed with arrows and bows or through their own suicidal action.

Map 16 shows the location of the Indian bullets (black triangles) in

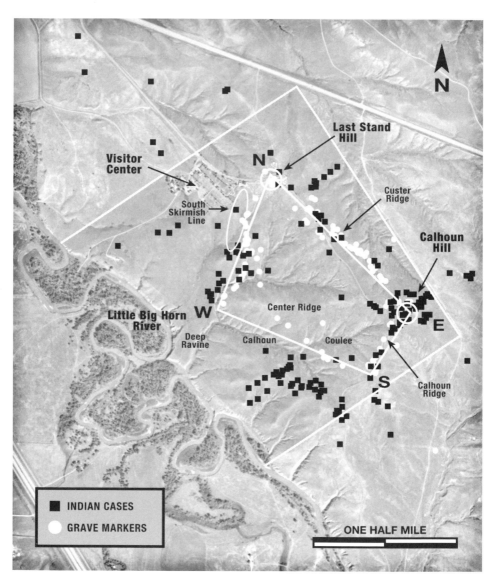

Map 15. Custer Battlefield—Indian Cartridge Cases. Map by Darrel Stevens, map copyright © Charles E. Wright.

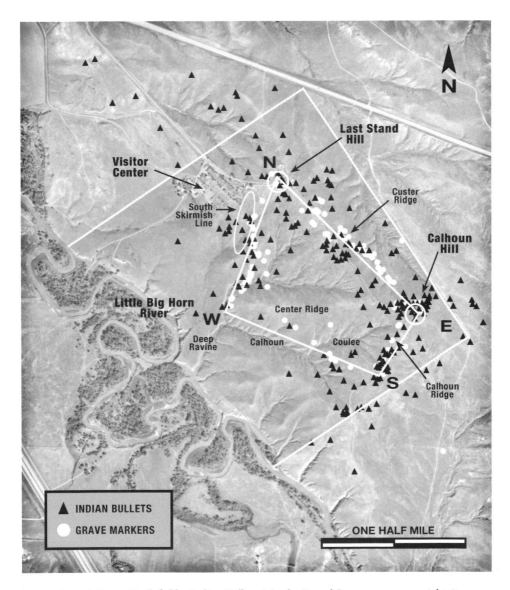

Map 16. Custer Battlefield—Indian Bullets. Map by Darrel Stevens, map copyright © Charles E. Wright.

relation to the headstones. Similar to the Indian cartridge cases, there were few bullets at Last Stand Hill and many at Calhoun Hill and the South Skirmish Line. The absence of Indian bullets at Last Stand Hill corroborates the conclusion that troopers in that area were either killed with hand weapons or died at their own hands. This map may create more questions than it solves because it is difficult to trace the bullets from the numerous Indian cases fired from a considerable distance south and west of Calhoun Ridge.

Map 17 shows the location of the army cartridges (black squares), which consist entirely of spent cases from the Springfield .45-carbine. (The location of the Colt revolver cartridges is not significant because a trooper could fire up to six shots before reloading.) Most army cases are also outside the combat zone, with a relatively heavy concentration on top of Calhoun Hill, south of line W-S and north of Last Stand Hill. The number of army cartridges outside the combat zone also indicates that Custer's troopers were surrounded on all sides and compressed toward the center. The cases south of line W-S indicate army movement away from the lower ground on the east bank of the river toward line S-E and Calhoun Hill. They also indicate that troopers traveled several hundred yards to the north of Last Stand Hill before returning to the clusters at Last Stand Hill and Deep Ravine. North of Last Stand Hill there is also a possibility that some or all of the carbine cases were fired by Indians using carbines recovered from fallen troopers. There is a surprising lack of army cases in the center of the combat zone. Army cases are distributed about equally in the northern and southern zones.

Since most of the army cartridges are from the 1873 Springfield, a carbine that is difficult to reload while mounted, the sheer number of carbine cartridges indicates that much of the fighting by Custer's men was done while dismounted.

Map 18 shows the army bullets (black stars) in relation to the headstones. As with the Indian bullets, the army bullets are much more difficult to analyze than the empty shell casings. This is to be expected because we are not able to determine in each instance the point from which the bullet was fired. There is a greater number of bullets than cartridges, which creates additional confusion. However, it is safe to conclude that most of the troopers' shots were fired from their Springfield carbines, that Custer's troopers fired more rounds than the Indians, and that due

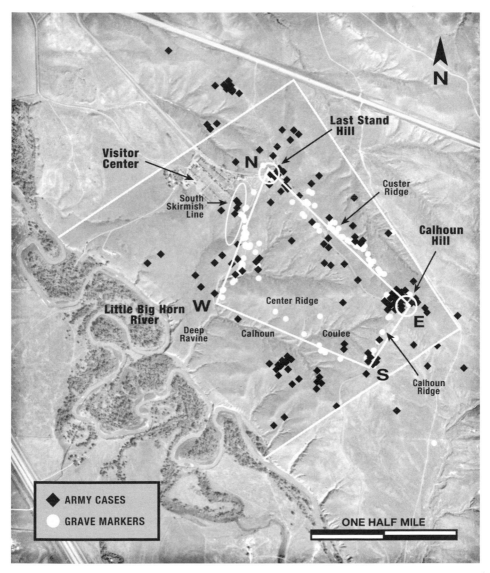

Map 17. Custer Battlefield—Army Cartridge Cases. Map by Darrel Stevens,
map copyright © Charles E. Wright.

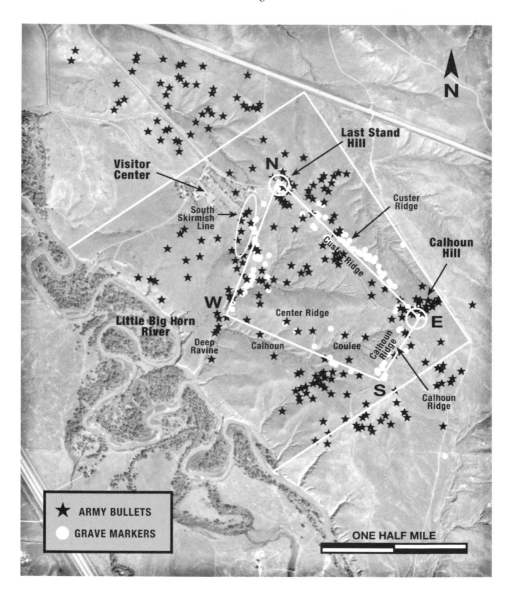

Map 18. Custer Battlefield—Army Bullets. Map by Darrel Stevens,
map copyright © Charles E. Wright.

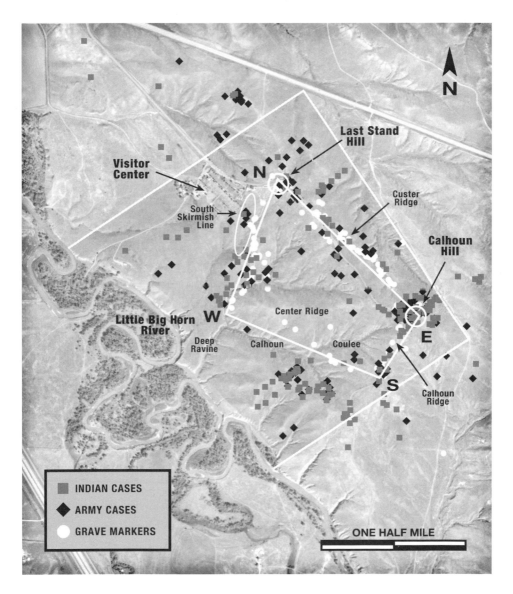

Map 19. Custer Battlefield—Indian and Army Cartridge Cases. Map by Darrel Stevens, map copyright © Charles E. Wright.

to the difficulty of reloading while mounted, most of the troopers' shots were fired while dismounted. This may account for the heavy casualties between Calhoun Hill and Last Stand Hill. It is difficult to explain the large quantity of bullets south of Calhoun Ridge and in the area 400 to 1,000 yards west and north of Last Stand Hill. While the location of the bullets is worth consideration, its relevance to the events occurring during the battle is not overly significant.

There are virtually no army bullets or cases or Indian cases on the east side of the south half of Custer Ridge, creating a rebuttable presumption that most of the troopers in this segment were killed with hand weapons while fleeing northward on foot.

Map 19 shows the location of both Indian (black diamonds) and army (black squares) cartridge cases and demonstrates conclusively that Indian attacks on Custer's men came from outside the combat zone. The Indians completely surrounded the 210 troopers, leaving no route for escape. All that the troopers could do was to stand fast and continue to fight until they were either killed or the Indians withdrew. Mysteriously, there are few Indian cases at Last Stand Hill where army cases and headstones are plentiful.

There are several army carbine cases located north of the battlefield boundary line connecting the west and north corners, which are approximately one-fourth of a mile north of the northern-most headstone, creating a presumption that these shots were fired by Indians from carbines taken from dead troopers earlier in the battle. Scott's study found numerous army bullets vertically impacted in the ground in the area of troop positions, indicating that Indians utilized captured army weapons to dispatch downed or wounded troopers while standing over them.[24] In the alternative, some of these bullets could be the result of suicide among despairing troopers.

The location of the marble stones indicates that no traditional defensive maneuvers were taken by Custer's battalion. This was corroborated by Captain Benteen, who viewed the Custer Battlefield on July 27. "There was no line formed, there was no line on the battlefield. You can take a handful of corn and scatter it over the floor and make just such lines, there were none."[25] Once Custer's troopers were dismounted and their horses driven off, they were easily surrounded, and there was no hope of escape. At Last Stand Hill, soldiers were clustered together in a tight group, using (dead and live) cavalry mounts as shields. Warriors moved up from the gully below and initiated a final charge. No prisoners were taken, and the wounded were either shot, clubbed, or filled with arrows. According to Gray's time-motion study, Custer's men were all killed over a time period of thirty-nine minutes.[26]

In the end, 210 troopers were killed at the Custer Battlefield while forty-eight were killed with Reno and Benteen. These 257 casualties amounted to more than one-fourth of all U.S. Army casualties in Indian battles west of the Mississippi.[27] The Indians were able to accomplish these results through long- and short-range rifle fire, direct and indirect fire from their bows and arrows, followed by close-hand combat, and ending, in many instances, with blunt-force trauma administered primarily with stone-headed war clubs.[28] Several Indians testified that they witnessed individuals and group-administered suicide among the troopers.[29] The archaeological study could neither confirm nor dispute this testimony because the available osteological remains included no complete skulls.

By any standards, the number of Indian warriors killed was considerably lower than the death loss in the Seventh Cavalry.[30] Perhaps as few as fifteen or as many as forty-five warriors died during the entire battle, most of whom were killed on Custer Battlefield. Richard G. Hardorff has devoted an entire book to the subject, citing numerous informants among Indian survivors and providing a tabulation from more than forty interviews indicating Indian death losses as low as fourteen and as high as 136.[31] Since most of the death lists were compiled more than twenty years subsequent to the battle, their weight and credibility are somewhat suspect. However, Hardorff eliminated the two high and low responses and arrived at a median range of thirty to forty, which was the figure attributed to 53 percent of his responses. Thus it would appear that Indian losses were inversely related to the numerical superiority of the Indian warriors. The ratio of warrior to trooper losses (1 to 6.4) is not significantly different from the numerical superiority of their warriors (7.5 to 1). There may be no correlation, but it is difficult to explain why Indian casualties would be so low in relation to the cavalry death loss, particularly when the cavalry was on the defense and the Indians were on the offense.

Although the issues of when and where Custer was killed are of secondary importance, it is nonetheless worthwhile to determine, if possible, whether Custer survived until the final moments at Custer Hill, or whether the vast and disorganized linear movements and inept performance of his battalion resulted from his inability to function due to death or injury. There is no indication of any offensive maneuvering by Custer's five companies. The linear distance from Calhoun Ridge to the South Skirmish Line is two-thirds of a mile. Troopers who were fighting in the vicinity of Calhoun Hill could scarcely communicate or receive tactical orders from the vicinity of the Keogh area, Last Stand Hill, or the South Skirmish Line. Not one Indian who was subsequently interviewed professed the ability to recognize Custer on sight prior to or during the battle. Since Custer's corpse was located at Last Stand Hill and positively identified by Seventh Cavalry survivors on June 26, there is at least a rebuttable presumption that this is where Custer died, and that he was alive and well until he reached this area. In addition, none of the Indian testimony indicated that any of the army corpses were moved after the battle, and no reasons have been advanced as to why there would have been any significant movement. Accordingly, it would not be unreasonable for us to proceed on the basis that Custer was alive and functioning as the commanding officer of the battalion until he was killed in the vicinity of Last Stand Hill. On the other hand, due primarily to a total lack of tactical maneuvers and the seeming inability of Custer's troopers to mount any effective defense, it would not be unreasonable to consider the possibility that Custer was killed or mortally wounded at the river shortly after the battle commenced and that his surviving troopers moved north (with Custer in tow) and then west in irregular and leaderless fashion as they were slaughtered along the way.[32]

It should be noted that, as Custer's battalion moved north of Weir Point and along Nye-Cartwright Ridge toward Calhoun Hill, they were moving farther from the river with its much-needed water and increasing the distance from any assistance they might hope to receive from Reno and Benteen.

Were other options available to Custer? The most obvious option would have been to turn tail (at Weir Point or when the Indians began their charge across the river) and retreat in the direction of Reno and Benteen. While this might also have failed, the odds of survival were better because, at the time Custer first sighted the Indian village from Weir Point, there were not sufficient numbers of warriors to block a retreat by

Custer to the south toward the Reno-Benteen defense area. According to John Gray, Reno reached his defense perimeter following his retreat from the valley at 4:10 p.m.[33] Near that time or shortly thereafter, Custer's left wing reached Ford B at the mouth of Medicine Tail Coulee (two and a half miles northwest of Reno and Benteen) and was firing at the Indian encampment on the west side of the river. Custer himself, if he was with his right wing, reached Luce Ridge by 4:20 and was in a position to see Indians ascending from Medicine Tail Coulee to attack him. This was the decisive time as far as his final opportunity to retreat. Had Custer chosen to retreat toward Reno, his arrival would have coincided with Benteen's arrival, if Gray's time-motion study is accurate. The presence of Custer and his five companies at the Reno-Benteen defense perimeter would have enhanced the defensive capabilities of the entire Seventh Cavalry Regiment and thus increased their chances for survival.

As the battle wound down and the gunfire subsided, groups of Indians converged on Custer Hill. Troopers not yet dead were dispatched, and warriors, women, and children proceeded to loot the corpses for guns, ammunition, and anything of interest or value. Clothing was removed, several corpses were mutilated, and the warriors at the Custer Battlefield returned to the Reno-Benteen Battlefield to harass the tired and thirsty troopers of Reno and Benteen with long-distance firing.[34] Custer would not have to explain his defeat to General Sheridan and the readers of the *New York Herald*.

Fear, despair, savagery, death, waste, pain, arrogance, stupidity, incompetence, bravery—and in the end, futility—they all were present, and none alone does justice to the battle. The Lakotas and Cheyennes won—but they lost. Custer's battalion was annihilated, but in losing it had scored a great political victory for President Ulysses Grant and his policy of forceful relocation of Indian nations to designated reservations. The men of the Seventh Cavalry and all the Lakotas, Cheyennes, and the few Arapahos in the encampment were the victims of a severely flawed government strategy and a battle that should never have been.

Modern-day Lakota historian William T. Marshall, III, noted in an article entitled "A Battle Won and a War Lost":

> Indeed. The twenty-twenty hindsight of time has revealed that this, of all battles, in the eventual fifty-year struggle to repel Euramerican encroachment and invasion of the Plains was the turning point, but

not because it was a Lakota victory. I believe that the planners of that summer's campaign against the Lakotas were expecting nothing short of a decisive army victory, to break the Lakotas' will and ability to resist militarily and force them onto reservations. Although the Greasy Grass was a loss for the United States Army, it still turned out to be that turning point and became a rallying cry for many Euramericans on the same level as the Alamo. And the eventual intended result was that the Lakotas were forced onto reservations.[35]

Meanwhile, where was General Sherman—and what was General Sheridan doing back in Chicago, beyond direct oversight of Generals Crook and Terry and not aware of what Custer was doing?

The sad plight of Custer's troopers is aptly described in the following stanza by Robert W. Service:

When you're lost in the Wild, and you're scared as a child,
And Death looks you bang in the eye,
And you're sore as a boil, it's according to Hoyle
To cock your revolver and . . . die.
But the Code of a Man says: 'Fight all you can,'
And self-dissolution is barred.
In hunger and woe, oh, it's easy to blow . . .
It's the hell-served-for-breakfast that's hard.[36]

Chapter Thirteen
# Aftermath of Battle

*We have killed their leader. Let them go.*

—*Sitting Bull*

According to Gray's time-motion study, Maj. Marcus Reno and Capt. Frederick Benteen reassembled the remnants of their seven companies and the pack train at approximately 6:30 p.m. on June 25 in the general area where Reno had originally established a defensive perimeter following his retreat from the valley. After the aborted attempt to rejoin Custer and the reassembly, the survivors in Reno's command consisted of 339 enlisted men, fourteen officers, and an assortment of nonmilitary personnel that included packers and teamsters. Among the group were thirteen wounded troopers.[1] The area had certain advantages for defense. It had proximity to ravines leading down to the river, there was a good view in all directions, and there was a slight depression in the center that afforded a certain level of protection for the horses, mules, and wounded troopers. Reno at times shared certain command responsibilities with Benteen, and the two of them promptly deployed their troops, on a company-by-company basis, in a circular perimeter providing observation and firing capability in all directions.

The Reno-Benteen Battlefield consists of an irregularly shaped area of 162 acres encompassing Reno Hill, Benteen Hill, a knoll located north of these hills, and the south half of Sharpshooter's Ridge to the north. It is approximately four miles south of Last Stand Hill on the Custer Battlefield where Custer's body was found (see map 12). K Company was stationed at the north end of Reno's oblong defensive perimeter; D, G, and A Companies were stationed along the east side; H Company occupied a series of trenches forming a tail to the perimeter at its south end; and B and M Companies shared responsibility along the western edge.

Fighting at Reno-Benteen Battlefield halted at sunset on June 25. Most of the companies used this respite to rest, dig in, and improve their defensive perimeter. The area was vulnerable to long-range firing from Sharpshooter's Ridge, and surrounding draws and gullies could be utilized by Indians to achieve short-range positions without being detected. While they had access to food and plenty of ammunition from the pack train, the troopers and their horses and mules were suffering from a terrible thirst.

Captain Benteen testified at Major Reno's court of inquiry[2] that the Indians resumed firing at the Reno-Benteen Battlefield about 3:30 a.m. on June 26. As fighting resumed, the Indians' primary tactics were desultory long-distance fire and the occasional massed charge against perceived weak points in the perimeter.[3] Later in the morning of the twenty-sixth, troopers organized a water party. With the protection of screening fire, heroic troopers were able to reach the river with canteens, buckets, and kettles with which they were able to provide minimal relief for the thirsty troopers.[4] Reno described the water shortage: "Our casualties continued to mount and now our water ran out. Thirst in the intense heat became intolerable. I ordered the men to use no more tobacco. Some of them ate grass and roots without relief. Some tried to excite the glands by putting pebbles in their mouths. Some tried eating hard bread, but it was impossible to swallow. Dr. Porter advised me that some of the wounded would die unless they were given water."[5] Numerous Congressional Medals of Honor were awarded to the water carriers.

During the morning Benteen led a charge that caused the Indians to retreat along the south perimeter, and Reno led a similar charge on the north. By noon Indian firing began to recede, and during the early evening of June 26, Reno's men could see Indians moving their camp southward along the west bank of the Little Big Horn River.

According to the Hunkpapa warrior Crow King, Sitting Bull called a halt to the fighting at Reno-Benteen Battlefield, telling his warriors, "This is not my doings, nor these men's. They are fighting because they were commanded to fight. We have killed their leader. Let them go. I shall call on the great spirit to witness what I say. We did not want to fight. Long Hair sent us word that he was coming to fight us, and we had decided to defend ourselves and our wives and children."[6] By the evening of June 26, Reno's contingent had seven additional killed and forty-one wounded.

Reno watched the Indians break camp and move out late in the afternoon. They moved in a single line about three miles in length and half a mile wide, densely packed with the entire village of Indians and their horses. On the evening of June 26, four missing soldiers of Reno's original battalion who had been hiding in the timber in the river valley, returned to camp. By the morning of June 27, all the remaining Indians at the encampment were gone, and the battle was over. As senior officer present at Little Big Horn Battlefield, Reno prepared a letter to be delivered to Gen. Alfred H. Terry, indicating that he had been involved in a terrific engagement, that the Indians had moved south in the direction of the Bighorn Mountains, that he was in a crippled condition and could not pursue them, that he had not seen or heard from Custer, and that he had many wounded soldiers on his hands and could not therefore move.[7] He needed help. Altogether, he had fifty-nine wounded soldiers who had to be moved by hand or mule litter back to the steamship *Far West* located at the mouth of the Little Big Horn. Terry and his column would soon arrive.

By 11:00 a.m. on June 27, Reno learned the fate of Custer's battalion. The twenty-seventh was a miserable day for the surviving troopers of the Seventh Cavalry. They provided what information they could to Terry, identified survivors, made lists of the killed and wounded, shot wounded animals, removed carcasses, and rounded up stray mules and horses. They cared for the wounded as best they could and made stretchers to carry them back to the steamship. "Flies and stench made the evening nauseating."[8] On June 28 the surviving troopers went to Custer Battlefield and buried 210 soldiers, many of whom could not be identified because of decomposition and mutilation.

Reno had this to say in summing up his feelings at the end of the fight:

> But after the fight was over, after we had suffered a humiliating defeat, after we had buried our dead and placed our wounded on board the *Far West* to be taken to Bismark, the 7th Cavalry that headed back to Fort Lincoln looked very different. We were totally exhausted both in mind and body. We were so filthy that we could be smelled before we could be seen or heard. We dreaded the prospects of explaining to

troopers, family, and friends what had happened to us. We found it hard to accept the failure in spite of the fact that we knew in our hearts that we had done our very best. We knew that we had been defeated by a superior force of well-armed, well-disciplined, well-generaled, and extremely determined warriors who had made up their minds to fight to the death to defend their lands, their wives, and their children. We knew what had happened, but we wondered if anyone else would understand.[9]

On of June 28, Capt. Edward Ball of the Second Cavalry followed the Indian trail out of the encampment and determined that, after going upstream for a short distance, the Indians had divided into two groups, one of which turned to the east and the other toward the Bighorn Mountains. Terry's column, with all the wounded on their litters, reached the mouth of the Little Big Horn at 2:00 a.m. on June 30, and the *Far West* proceeded downstream, carrying the wounded to Fort Abraham Lincoln.

Terry then attempted to locate Gen. George Crook. Three privates from the Seventh Infantry Regiment were able to travel south through Indian territory, locate Crook, and return with his reply. Sheridan collected additional troops from other areas of the frontier and sent them by railroad to join Terry's depleted command. On July 18 the secretary of the interior authorized the U.S. Army to assume control of all Indian agencies in Sioux country. However, in the meantime, the Lakotas were able to replenish part of their ammunition expenditures. A census taken at the Red Cloud and Rosebud agencies indicated that only half the Oglalas and Brulés (together with other Lakotas and Cheyennes) were present.

Reno had this to say about Custer in the letter that he wrote to his son Ross some years later:

> I always had great admiration for Custer and I believe we all made the same mistake; we underestimated the strength and temperament of the Indians. I know Custer made the best decisions based on the information he had and on his interpretation of that information. It was the information he did not have that spelled disaster, the number in their village, their determination and maybe most of all their decision

to take us on in a pitched battle rather than flee or fight a hit-and-run battle as we expected.[10]

Reno got it right—but his critics did not.

While Custer and his regiment had been soundly defeated, their attack on the Lakotas' and Cheyennes' encampment had halted and prematurely terminated the Indians' great summer hunt, causing the grand encampment to disintegrate into smaller tribal and familial groups. Some groups continued to hunt, while others commenced the long easterly trek toward their agencies and reservations in Nebraska and the Dakota Territory. The Indians were fully aware that the U.S. Army was persistent and that it would be used to force them to vacate their "unceded Indian territory" where the remaining buffalo were located.

It is tempting to wonder what might have happened if Reno, Benteen, and the pack train had reunited with Custer before he reached Custer Battlefield. Would the regiment have been able to defend itself—establish a defensive perimeter—and survive until Terry's forces reached them? If not, what would have become of the regiment and the pack train? Would the Indians have fled—or would they have attacked Terry and Gibbon? Since the answers are at best only guesswork and involve numerous unverifiable presumptions, they are best left to unwritten speculation.

## Chapter Fourteen

# Standards for Evaluation of Custer

*No force should ever be detached from the main body unless the need is definite and urgent.*

—*Carl von Clausewitz*[1]

Nineteenth-century military regulations and common tactical doctrines come to life when they are applied to specific battles and particular tactical incidents. They are both relevant and essential when assessing Lt. Col. George A. Custer's performance at the Little Big Horn. Evaluation of Custer requires a description of his duties as commanding officer of the Seventh Cavalry and his responsibilities while leading them in battle. These responsibilities included advance preparation, planning, deployment, and maneuvering during actual combat.

Preparations for battle require the gathering of intelligence, training, provisions for logistical and medical support, and inspection of the readiness of soldiers and their weapons. Intelligence includes finding the location and determining the strength of the enemy, knowledge of the terrain where the fighting will occur, and recognition of the existing strengths or weaknesses in the enemy's disposition. Planning must focus on the strategic objective by utilizing the intelligence that is acquired through reconnaissance. It must provide for deployment of forces consistent with regulations, military custom, and the acquired intelligence. Economy of force, coordination of maneuvers, and a means of communication during battle are essential. The plan must be communicated to the officers and troops. A method and avenue for retreat should be considered. The timing of deployment must coincide with the plan and must be understood by the officers and soldiers. While maneuvers during battle should be consistent with the plan, there must also be sufficient flexibility and adequate internal communication to respond to unforeseen events and countermaneuvers by the enemy.[2]

Custer's express orders from Gen. Alfred H. Terry were to pursue the Indians. Custer's letters and actions shortly before the battle indicated that his own strategy was to attack, kill, and conquer. His strategy was consistent with the strategic objectives of Sherman's 1876 campaign—attack (kill if necessary or expedient), contain, subjugate, and confine all Lakotas and Cheyennes within the boundaries of their reservations.

Custer's duties in commanding his regiment were outlined in the regulations and customs of service that were published and in use throughout the entire time of Custer's U.S. Army experience. In 1863 the army promulgated revisions to its 1861 regulations, which were approved by the president, with the admonishment of the secretary of war that, "from and after the date hereof, they shall be strictly observed as the sole and standing authority upon the matter therein contained. . . . Nothing contrary to the tenor of these regulations will be enjoined in any part of the forces of the United States by any commander whatsoever."[3]

With respect to reconnaissance, these regulations provided:

RECONNOISSANCES

656. Near an enemy, daily reconnoissances are made to observe the ground in front, and to discover whether the advance guards of the enemy have been increased or put in motion, or any other sign of his preparation for march or action.

658. Reconnoitering parties observe the following precautions: to leave small posts, or sentinels at intervals, to transmit intelligence to the advanced posts of the army, unless the return is to be by a different route; to march with caution, to avoid fighting; and see, if possible, without being seen.

The regulations also contained paragraph 678, concerning strength of force, communication, and mutual support:

678. The force is divided into as many columns as circumstances permit, without weakening any one too much. They ought to preserve

their communications, and be within supporting distance of each other. The commander of each column ought to know the strength and direction of the others.[4]

In addition to the army regulations, there were substantial written instructions on intelligence and reconnaissance by recognized and experienced army officers to guide tactical commanders in the field. During each of his four years at West Point, Custer received instruction on rifle and light-infantry tactics from Lt. Col. W. J. Hardee and studied a treatise authored by Dennis Hart Mahan.[5] Among the rules to which Custer was exposed in class were:

Cavalry is seldom called on to use firearms.[6]

The *defensive* qualities of cavalry lie in the *offensive*. A body of cavalry which waits to receive a charge of cavalry, or is exposed to a fire of infantry . . . must either retire, or be destroyed (emphasis supplied).[7]

Attack **against** infantry. So long as infantry maintains its position firmly, particularly if the ground is at all unfavorable to the movements of cavalry, the chances are against a successful attack by the latter.[8]

There are no more important duties, which an officer may be called upon to perform, than those of collecting and arraying the information upon which either the general or daily operation of a campaign must be based.[9]

To supply these deficiencies of maps, an examination of the ground must be made by the eye, and verbal information be gained, on all the points connected with the operation over this ground. This examination and collection of facts is termed reconnaissance.[10]

The main duties of a patrol are to find the enemy if in the neighborhood; gain a good idea of his position and strength; to make out his movements; and to bring in an accurate account of his distance from the out-posts of their own force.[11]

In 1865 August V. Kautz, Captain, U.S. Cavalry, a brigadier general and brevet major general of volunteers, and an 1852 graduate of West Point, published *Customs of Service for Officers of the Army as Derived from Law and Regulations and Practised in the United States Army, Being a Hand Book of Military Administration for Officers of the Line, Showing the Specific Duties of Each Grade from the Lowest to the Highest, Enabling Officers Promoted to a New Grade to Know What They Have To Do, and How to Do It.*[12]

Most of this volume's 804 paragraphs would apply to Custer's responsibilities as commanding officer of the Seventh Cavalry on June 21 through June 25, 1876. Regarding the use of reconnaissance patrols, "the principal object in sending out patrols is usually to ascertain the position and strength of the enemy, and to find out his intended movements; also to ascertain the distance he is from the lines, and what is the character of the intermediate country "[13]; and on the use of cavalry for attack, "Cavalry and Artillery are both helpless under a well directed Infantry fire at long range. The introduction of repeating arms has also diminished the efficiency of Cavalry in an attack; for long before it has passed over the usual charging distance, it is thrown into irremediable confusion by the rapidity with which Infantry can fire, when armed with long-range repeating arms."[14] Concerning division of force, "the division of the main force into two or more parts, co-operating from diverse points against the same enemy, should be avoided if possible, unless each force is considered either equal to or capable of holding the enemy in check."[15] On the use of cavalry for defense, "having availed itself of the rapid movement of the horses to seize a strategic point, . . . the Cavalry may dismount and hold it like intrenched Infantry; for pure Cavalry cannot hold positions on the defensive—it must either fight to win or run away"[16]; and concerning the necessity of adequate reconnaissance, "however complete in every respect an Army may be, it can do nothing well unless certain and positive knowledge of the enemy's strength, location, and condition can be obtained. Hence it is of the first importance that this knowledge should be obtained at any cost."[17]

In 1860 and 1861 Custer was taught military tactics from a treatise authored by a noted French militarist, Baron Antoine Henri de Jomini, entitled *The Art of War*.[18] On the necessity of reconnaissance, Jomini held that, "A general should neglect no means of gaining information of the enemy's movements and, for this purpose, should make use of reconnaissances, spies, bodies of light troops commanded by capable officers, signals, and questioning deserters and prisoners."[19]

Reconnaissance and proper deployment of a fighting unit were not new. They were recognized, understood, and mandatory in 1876 at the

Little Big Horn. Reconnaissance was also considered and commented on by other noted militarists whose work was available to American officers prior to the Civil War. No militarist is better known and more often quoted on the subject of military strategy and battlefield tactics than Carl von Clausewitz, the son of a retired Prussian officer, whose first exposure to war was as a thirteen-year-old infantry ensign in 1793. While it was not translated into English until 1874, his work is so logical and articulate that it was studied and utilized by most of the great militarists in the nineteenth and twentieth centuries. Clausewitz defines "intelligence in war" as "every sort of information about the enemy and his country—the basis, in short, of our own plans and operations."[20] To march boldly into an encounter with an armed enemy while lacking both intelligence and a plan was unthinkable. Clausewitz was a firm believer in the mandate of massing of forces at the decisive point. In his words, "the best strategy is always *to be very strong*, first in general, and then at the decisive point. Apart from the effort needed to create military strength, which does not always emanate from the general, there is no higher and simpler law of strategy than that of *keeping one's forces concentrated.* No force should ever be detached from the main body unless the need is definite and urgent."[21]

These rules would apply not only to the division of the Seventh Cavalry at the Little Big Horn, but to the division of the entire northern force by Gen. Alfred Terry at the Yellowstone River. In other words, Terry actually divided his command without any express plan to coordinate the divided components when and if they encountered a large force of Indians. The division of forces by both Terry and Custer involved "widely separated columns."

Clausewitz was also a stickler for utilizing the element of surprise: "The subject of the previous chapter—the universal desire for relative numerical superiority—leads to another desire, which is consequently no less universal: that *to take the enemy by surprise.* This desire is more or less basic to all operations, for without it superiority at the decisive point is hardly conceivable."[22] Clausewitz's thinking paralleled that of Kautz concerning the relative strength of cavalry, infantry, and artillery, and the best uses of cavalry. To him, cavalry was effective only by way of individual combat, was totally incapable of defense, but was preeminent in attack where movement and mobility were important. To him cavalry was the weakest agent of destruction.

Finally, Clausewitz believed in the use of historical examples, which, he said, "clarify everything and also provide the best kind of proof in the empirical sciences. This is particularly true in the art of war."[23] Historical examples can be utilized to explain an idea, to show the application of an idea, to support a statement, and finally, to make it possible to deduce a doctrine.[24]

Another noted militarist whose work had been available for centuries prior to the Little Big Horn was Sun Tzu, who lived some 500 years before Jesus and was referred to at various times as "Master Sun" (pronounced "soon") or "Master Sun Wu"; he is currently referred to as "Sun Tzu." His treatise, *The Art of War*, has been studied for centuries and was more recently translated by John Minford.[25] It is referred to as "one of China's key proverbial texts." It is based primarily on logic tied to an exceptional manner of precise articulation. Sun Tzu held that if you outnumbered your enemy ten to one you should surround him; at five to one you should attack; at two to one you should split him in half; and if equally matched you could fight it out.

Concerning underestimation of the enemy, Sun Tzu states:

When a general
  Misjudges his enemy
  And sends a lesser force
  Against a larger one,
  A weaker contingent
  Against a stronger one;
  When he fails to pick
  A good vanguard,
  The outcome is
  Rout.[26]

The following four examples explain the necessity for reconnaissance and its utilization to overcome a numerical disadvantage and develop a successful tactical plan to achieve a strategic objective. First, the story of *Ghost Soldiers*[27] provides an excellent example of how persistent and undetected visual reconnaissance enabled a small force of 120 Army Rangers to attack a Japanese prison camp, kill all the Japanese military guards, and save the lives of 500 American and British prisoners of war. Late in 1944 U.S. intelligence learned that the Japanese War Ministry in Tokyo had ordered the extermination of all Allied prisoners of war in the face of advancing Allied armies. The orders were to "annihilate them all, and not to leave any traces."[28] Gen. Douglas MacArthur and 200,000 troops landed on the Philippine island of Luzon on January 9, 1945, moving in the direction of Manila. In the path of advance of the American Sixth Army was a small prison camp located near the town of Cabanatuan, situated approximately sixty miles north of Manila. The prisoners were underfed, overworked, and had suffered a 60-percent death loss. Gen. Walter Krueger commanded the American Sixth Army that was advancing toward Manila. Krueger sent a Ranger company of 120, commanded by Lt. Col. Henry Mucci, behind Japanese lines and ahead of his army in an effort to rescue the helpless prisoners before they were massacred by the Japanese. Mucci's rangers had to walk thirty miles to reach the camp, and after the rescue the rescued prisoners were faced with the same thirty-mile walkout. Since they were behind enemy lines, radio silence had to be observed. Mucci's strategic objective was to rescue all the prisoners and remove them to the American lines. He needed information about the layout of the prison camp, where the Japanese soldiers were quartered, their strength, and the location of pillboxes and guardhouses surrounding the camp. He had to determine the location of every fence, the size of the gate, the best routes of ingress and egress, the number of prisoners, and their location. The area surrounding the camp was flat for at least one and a half miles on all sides, being surrounded by level rice fields. Tactically, Mucci had to mount a surprise attack after surrounding the entire camp, and it was necessary that he neutralize all Japanese resistance with massed fire. Utilizing brilliant and detailed intelligence provided by his recon scouts, Mucci and his 120 gung-ho Rangers were successful in wiping out all the Japanese guards, rescuing 500 prisoners, and returning them to the American lines. Two Rangers were killed in the fighting, and two prisoners perished by reason of poor health. Approximately 1,000 Japanese troops were killed during the raid.[29]

This incident serves to illustrate the necessity of reconnaissance, the ability to achieve it under adverse circumstances without being detected, and the requirement of a carefully drafted plan that relates to the strategic objective. The American Rangers were concentrated at the point of attack by surrounding the prison camp, and the element of surprise was preserved. Without the excellent and thorough reconnaissance conducted prior to the raid, Mucci and his Rangers would not have been able to overcome a force five times greater than their number.

The Battle of Midway in June 1942 provides excellent examples of the importance of (1) timely and accurate intelligence and (2) the necessity of the basic tactical rule requiring concentration of force at the decisive time and place, economy of force, surprise, and thorough reconnaissance.

In February 1942, the U.S. Navy's Combat Intelligence Unit broke the Japanese naval code. Shortly after May 15, Admiral Nimitz concluded that the Japanese were planning a major strike to conquer Midway Island on June 5.[30] The primary Japanese strike force contained four aircraft carriers. The mission of the carrier strike force was to protect the landing of troops on Midway and also to ambush and destroy three of the remaining U.S. carriers that would be sent out from Pearl Harbor to challenge the invasion. The Japanese had a separate invasion force (to land on Midway) plus a separate "northern" force to attack the Aleutian Islands. Thus, the Japanese carrier strike force had a dual mission (support of invasion and destruction of U.S. carriers); the "invasion force" was to capture Midway while the "northern" force would be off attacking the Aleutians.

Adm. Isoroku Yamamoto, Japan's senior naval officer, believed that he would achieve complete surprise and anticipated no opposition confronting his invasion force.[31] Shortly before departure, Admiral Yamamoto speculated about what might happen if American carriers suddenly showed up at an unexpected place while his carriers were in the process of attacking Midway.[32]

The U.S. Pacific fleet had only three carriers available to oppose the Japanese attack. One of them, the crippled *Yorktown*, was undergoing hasty repairs at Pearl Harbor. Fleet Adm. Chester W. Nimitz concentrated his three carriers (task forces 16 and 17) into one carrier force and was able to accurately predict the route that would be followed by the Japanese carrier strike force as it approached Midway. The Japanese surface fleet outnumbered the US Fleet by approximately three to one, and their carrier-based aircraft outnumbered the U.S. by 325 to 233. Nimitz stationed his carriers north-northeast of Midway Island a sufficient distance from the expected path of the Japanese carrier force to be beyond their air-search reconnaissance. The Americans were also short on intelligence and would need to conduct vigorous aerial reconnaissance in order to prevail.

The Japanese, who were the attackers, utilized perfunctory and inadequate reconnaissance. By dawn on June 4, the Japanese launched their first air strike at Midway without having completed any reconnaissance. Like Custer, they did not know the strength or location of their enemy. The Japanese had merely launched a "single phase," or single-shot aerial reconnaissance operation. Anything occurring before or after the operation would remain undiscovered. This is exactly the same situation that existed with respect to Captain Benteen's scout to the left. Benteen's scout was a one-shot operation involving a relatively short period of time, and anything that was not sighted on the first attempt would remain undiscovered.

Sixty years after Midway, Japanese aviator Mitsuo Fuchida, who had led the first strike on Pearl Harbor, wrote: "The fundamental cause of this failure, again, lay in the Japanese Navy's overemphasis on attack, which resulted in inadequate attention to search and reconnaissance."[33] However, the Americans' visual reconnaissance by carrier-based aircraft and land-based planes flying out of Midway encountered many difficulties. Inexperienced pilots had difficulty identifying surface ships as friend or foe ("IFF")—mistaking one kind of ship for another—as well as plotting their location, course, and speed. When U.S. attack planes were launched without the accurate location of the Japanese ships, they often out-flew their fuel capacity and had to ditch out of sight of their carriers.[34]

Concerning the element of surprise, Fuchida also noted: "The absence of surprise sharply reduced the effectiveness of our attack."[35] Like the Indian warriors who counterattacked Custer at the Indian encampment, pilots from the American carrier group were eventually able to mount a surprise dive bomber attack on the Japanese carrier strike force while Japanese planes were attacking Midway or returning from an attack. In the course of the next twenty-four hours, the Americans were able to sink all four Japanese carriers, thereby achieving the primary mission of the navy, which was to defend Midway and sink the Japanese carriers.[36] Midway is a good example of what happens when reconnaissance is either incomplete or ineffective.

The Japanese were unable to preserve the element of surprise, and the efforts of their three task forces were not oriented around their strategic objective. The separation of the three Japanese task forces at Midway was similar to the situation that confronted Custer when he first spotted the Indian encampment and realized that Benteen's and Reno's battalions were out of his sight and control. He had created a remote control problem, and he was then confronted with a rapidly developing and changing tactical situation.

At Midway the losses of the United States consisted of 307 men, 147 aircraft, one large carrier, and one destroyer. The Japanese lost 2,500 seamen and aviators, 332 aircraft, four large carriers, and one heavy cruiser. With fewer ships and aircraft, the Americans prevailed over the Japanese because the Japanese had failed in their reconnaissance and lacked economy of force, while the Americans were able to preserve the element of surprise and concentrate their carrier-based aircraft at the decisive point. The doctrines of reconnaissance, economy of force, and surprise are timeless. However, in addition to these basic doctrines, good luck, individual incidents, and exceptional courage and effort by individual carrier pilots and squadron leaders, some of whom defied orders from superiors and used their own judgment in conducting sorties against enemy targets,[37] determined the outcome of this historic battle. The American reconnaissance pilots seemed to have little training or awareness about the necessity of determining the location, course, and speed of the enemy ships nor any ability to identify a ship as friend or foe—or whether it was a carrier, battleship, cruiser, or tanker. Each of these factors emphasizes the necessity of training and the value of prior experience—issues that were also significant in the performance of the Seventh Cavalry Regiment at Little Big Horn.[38]

Sgt. Fred H. Salter was a recon scout assigned to the U.S. Ninety-first Cavalry Reconnaissance Squadron, which was active in North Africa, Sicily, and Italy during World War II. Salter saw his duties and responsibilities evolve into a regular routine, in which he would be sent alone and afoot on nightly reconnaissance patrols directly in front of German entrenchments that stood in the path of the Allied advance in North Africa and Italy. He was able, time after time, to conduct successful one-man scouting patrols in close proximity to and in the front of the German army, providing his officers with the information they needed to defend and attack along the North African and Italian fronts.[39] His main objective was to "gather information, learn where the enemy planned to establish a line of defense, then locate their weak points." It was "far better to lose a few men in finding out where the enemy intended to make their stand, than to lose the main fighting force. . . . Recon units were to an advancing army what scouts were to a company of infantry moving forward into battle."[40] In the Italian campaign Salter was able to go out alone on nightly reconnaissance patrols, wade across the Rapido River on foot, determine whether the Germans were massing a defensive position or preparing for a counterattack, and return before daylight. Salter needed knowledge about the wilderness, common sense, and a great deal of luck. He learned to use darkness to his advantage, to be patient, to never move without studying the land, and to memorize the terrain before he started. He picked out alternate routes, never crossed an open area, and psyched himself into thinking like the Germans and believing that he was part of the environment. Custer had more than forty Crow and Arikara scouts at his disposal, and he had none of them perform as a "recon scout."

Salter's actions demonstrate that it is possible for one or two men to accomplish effective reconnaissance at night, bring themselves into close contact with the enemy, conduct an accurate visual observation, and return unharmed to their source. While there would have been difficulties in conducting a patrol to make a visual observation of the Indian encampment prior to June 25, there were many conditions present at that time that would have made it a viable possibility. Unoccupied high bluffs along the east side of the river covered the approach from being detected by the Indians in the river valley. The ground approaching the east bank of the Little Big Horn from the east was rough and broken with hills, gullies, and ravines, which offered opportunities to approach the edge of the bluffs unseen. The Indians did not station sentries, mounted videttes, or lookout posts around their camp at night. During the evening of June 24, the Indians were busily engaged in social affairs involving interactions among the various tribal circles (including dancing, celebrating, and storytelling), which occupied their attention far into the night. Campfires in the tribal circles illuminated the encampment and its occupants. The weather was clear, and there were no significant obstacles to a clear path of vision once the reconnaissance patrol or a single scout reached the edge of the bluffs.

The previous three examples of reconnaissance all took place during World War II, nearly seventy years after the Battle at the Little Big Horn. However, as previously noted, the U.S. Army regulations and customs in effect in 1876 contained precise instructions and definite requirements for visual reconnaissance in the field.

Prior to the Little Big Horn, the story of Capt. Robert E. Lee is a good example of effective reconnaissance. Congress declared war against Mexico on May 13, 1846. Many of the young U.S. Army officers would become leading generals for both sides in the Civil War. On March 9, 1847, Gen. Winfield Scott landed a sizeable invasion force at Vera Cruz on the east coast of Mexico and captured it on March 27.[41] His overall strategic objective was to achieve peace with Mexico by conquering it. To do this he needed to capture Mexico City. Scott needed to move rapidly west from coastal Vera Cruz in order to reach the central highland areas, where there was less malaria. The natural route to Mexico City from Vera Cruz was to follow the National Highway, which ran in a northwesterly direction near the town of Cerro Gordo. The Mexican army was commanded by Gen. Antonio López de Santa Anna, who had defeated the Texans at the Alamo in March 1836. Santa Anna set his primary defense parallel to the National Highway near Cerro Gordo, placing his artillery batteries on a hillside south of the highway, where he intended to shell Scott's forces as they moved westward.

A short distance north of the highway and not more than 2,200 yards east of Cerro Gordo was a 1,000-foot hill called "El Telegrafo." El Telegrafo dominated a pass along the National Highway through which Scott would have to move his army. Santa Anna's defense was strong and well organized; with his artillery set to fire on the highway, he would exact heavy casualties from Scott's advancing army. Santa Anna anticipated a direct frontal attack and paid little attention to his left flank which, consisting of rough, high ground, was thought to be virtually impassible.[42] General Scott always required thorough reconnaissance preparations. The U.S. Army customarily used engineer officers to conduct field reconnaissance. First Lt. Pierre G. T. Beauregard (who later achieved great fame as a Confederate general in the Civil War) conducted the initial scout around Santa Anna's left flank. Scott then ordered young Capt. Robert E. Lee to conduct another scout. Lee walked out alone and undetected past the end of Beauregard's scout until he was actually located in a mountainous area in the rear of Santa Anna's forces. Scott studied Lee's reports for three days. Lee had located a trail that enabled Scott to launch a surprise attack on Santa Anna that carried the day. Using this trail around the left flank of Santa Anna, Scott was able to haul in small artillery pieces and mount a surprise attack. Scott captured Cerro Gordo after a brief but fierce fight, defeating and putting to rout some 12,000 to 18,000 Mexican troops.[43]

While on this reconnaissance, Lee utilized some of the same tactics that were used by Fred Salter when he was out on individual patrols. Alone, Lee traveled slowly up ravines north of Rio del Plan, and as he traveled, he found a path over which Scott's troops, while undetected, would be able to construct a road, which would place them in position to attack Santa Anna from the rear of his left flank.[44] Both Scott and Lee, as well as all of Scott's army, appeared to recognize at this early date how essential it is to have accurate visual reconnaissance before tactical maneuvers were planned for any assault on defended enemy positions.[45]

This example demonstrates that twenty-eight years before the Battle at the Little Big Horn, American commanders in the field recognized the need for reconnaissance and were utilizing their best officers to seek out and provide this essential information prior to developing plans for attack. The successful reconnaissance conducted by Beauregard and Lee enabled Scott's army to achieve a smashing success with only light casualties, allowing the American army to continue its advance toward Mexico City. The use of reconnaissance, despite the delays that it occasioned in commencing the attack, proved highly profitable to Scott throughout the war with Mexico. While Scott was generally familiar with the strength of Santa Anna's forces, he needed to find ways in which to surprise him, confront the Mexican forces with unexpected crises, and cause them to either flee or surrender. This incident also demonstrates that, not only were tactical commanders in the field aware of reconnaissance, but they knew how to use it effectively. On Scott's part he used the man whom he described as his best officer to gather intelligence for his army. There is no reason why adequate intelligence, obtained through covert reconnaissance, would not have provided positive results for the U.S. Army in its attempt to fight the Plains Indians. In order to take proper advantage of the element of surprise, Custer absolutely needed to know the location of the Indians and their strength. If information concerning the topographical surroundings and terrain had been available, and if this information had indicated situations where the Indians were at a disadvantage, Custer would have been able to incorporate it into his tactical plans.

## Chapter Fifteen

# Factors Affecting Custer's Performance

*Mounted fire action is the least effective use of cavalry, and it may be well to repeat that it should never be used when either shock action or dismounted fire is practicable.*

—*Arthur L. Wagner*[1]

In addition to reconnaissance, planning, utilization of time-tested tactics, and sound strategy, the performance of Custer's cavalry troopers was affected by the horses they rode, the mules that carried their supplies, and the firearms they used. While the horse and the mule provided mobility and supplies for the Seventh Cavalry, each created significant limitations on its performance.

The horses had no armor and were susceptible to injury from Indian firearms and arrows, particularly at close range. The horses' daily feed ration required twenty pounds of mixed grain and/or hay per horse to maintain a proper energy level, together with fifteen to twenty gallons of water. Heat was also a limiting factor in the horses' performance. A horse has three times the surface area of a human being, while it has nine times the body mass to cool. Heat is generated by the horse's muscles and is also absorbed through the horse's coat. The horse expels excess heat from its body through evaporation of sweat and perspiration, created by heated blood circulating in the surface blood vessels, where it forces perspiration from the skin. As the body temperature increases, blood flow rises to the skin to stimulate the sweat. While this is an efficient way to rid the body of unwanted heat, it depletes the horse's body of water and electrolytes.

In the situation faced by the Seventh Cavalry, and particularly that of the mules and horses within the Reno-Benteen defense perimeter, no water was available for twenty-four to thirty-six hours under hot, dry, and stressful conditions. This caused each horse and mule to become significantly dehydrated. Horses were conditioned to carry a load averaging 250 pounds and trained to obey simple commands transmitted through the reins, headstall, and bit. Extended cavalry campaigns required large numbers of wagon or pack mules to transport grain for the horses—as well as for the mules themselves.

Army regulations provided specific and detailed rules for the care and maintenance of horses, together with stiff penalties for failure to comply. The officer who drafted many of these rules had this to say about a trooper's mount: "The horses must, therefore, be nursed with great care, in order that they endure the utmost fatigue when emergencies demand it."[2] Regulation No. 1193 prescribes, in some detail, the treatment and care of horses while on the march. Among other things, it states that reveille should not be sounded before daylight to allow the horses to rest from midnight to dawn, the average march should be fifteen to twenty miles per day, and the habitual gait was at a walk. Until the horses were in good condition, ten or fifteen miles a day was sufficient, and there should be a halt of five to ten minutes' duration at the end of every hour to adjust the equipment and tighten the cinch. During these brief stops horses should be permitted to graze. There should be a halt of twenty to forty-five minutes at noon. On extended march men were required to dismount and lead for twenty to forty minutes every second or third hour, and horses should always be led over steep ground, particularly downhill, to ease the strain on their backs. At water call company commanders dismounted their troops, and the horses were unbitted while watering. If one horse was watered, all were to be watered. Lounging in the saddle was prohibited because it chafed the horse's back. The penalty for failing to sit squarely on the horse would be to dismount and lead.[3]

Lest it appear that these regulations are lighthearted and informal, the order promulgating these tactics states: "To ensure uniformity, all exercises, evolutions, and ceremonies not embraced in these tactics are prohibited, and those therein prescribed will be strictly observed."

A wagon mule needed special training if it was to be converted into a pack mule and vice versa. The mules comprising the pack train for Custer and his Seventh Cavalry at the Little Big Horn were wagon mules that had not been trained to carry packs. Custer's wagon mules were packed by teamsters and troopers instead of trained mule packers. Thus, Custer's wagon mules balked at their packs and wasted a considerable amount of time each day before the Seventh Cavalry Regiment could resume its march. An unbalanced or improperly loaded pack would cause a mule's back to become "sored." Their hides were galled, and their muscles were gored. A "sore-backed" mule balked at loading and movement. Placing a pack saddle with a load of 200 to 300 pounds on the open sores of a mule was a pitiful and painful process that became worse on each successive day. At the Little Big Horn, Custer was traveling over rugged ground and fording streams and rivers. He believed that using pack mules would enable his regiment to move at a faster pace. While Custer sought greater speed by converting the wagon mules to pack mules, he actually sacrificed speed and created tactical problems because his wagon mules, with their improperly loaded packs, became so sore that they refused to move out at the rate of the regiment. Thus, they lagged behind the mounted regiment as much as three hours as it proceeded toward its encounter with the Indians.

Elwood L. Nye (for whom "Nye-Cartwright Ridge" is named), a lieutenant colonel of the veterinary corps, reviewed the entire Little Big Horn encounter in 1941:

> A good cavalry leader will conserve the strength of his animals to the greatest possible extent in order that they may reach the field of action in the most effective condition the situation will permit. In other words he must arrive as cavalry, and not as infantry.
>
> What of Custer in this respect? The whole story of his military life shows a brutal disregard of the well-being of his men and animals. There can be no doubt that this contributed, in part, to his tragic end beside the "Greasy Grass."[4]

John G. Bourke, an officer serving with Gen. George Crook, had this to say about Custer's pack train: "Behind them one could see the other pack-train [of Custer], a string of mules, of all sizes, each led by one soldier and beaten and driven along by another—attendants often rivaling animals in dumbness—and it was hard to repress a smile except by reflection that this was the motive power of a column supposed to be in pursuit of savages."[5]

Problems with his pack mules caused Custer to assign one entire company (Company B), together with six or seven troopers from each of the other eleven companies, in an effort to expedite movement of the pack train. This removed 22 percent of his fighting strength from participation in the battle.

Throughout the entire Little Big Horn battle, mounted fire by Reno's battalion in the valley, while charging the encampment and while retreating to the high ground on the east bank, was totally ineffective. Mounted fire by Custer's battalion into the Indians' encampment, and thereafter while fleeing from the Indians at Custer Battlefield, was equally futile. Noted U.S. Army tactician Gen. Arthur L. Wagner wrote, "Mounted fire action is the least effective use of cavalry, and it may be well to repeat that it should never be used when either shock action or dismounted fire is practicable."[6] The movement of Custer's horses (and the troopers mounted on their backs) created problems with accurate marksmanship. The use of one hand to control the horse created problems with reloading, aiming, and firing. Because of this, every trooper who was engaged in fighting Indians at Little Big Horn had to do most of his fighting dismounted. Dismounting to fight created additional problems. The procedure for fighting dismounted required three riders to hand their reins to a fourth,[7] who then had to lead all four horses to a protected area away from the fighting and hold them in the rear until they were needed. This removed 25 percent of the troopers from the firing line, and four "gassy" geldings were often more than one trooper could control. Meanwhile, the held horses were vulnerable to enemy fire or being captured or driven off. In a dismounted state Custer's troopers, having lost mobility, were vulnerable to being surrounded and injured or killed. Thus, it was imperative that Custer form his five companies into an organized defensive formation from which they could fight dismounted, retain possession of their horses, and mass sufficient firepower to keep the Indians at a safe distance.

The only positive aspect that the horse provided at Little Big Horn was mobility. They were able to transport troopers into proximity with the Indian encampment—they might also have given Custer the ability to flee in the face of overwhelming numbers—but this opportunity vanished when Custer's battalion was surrounded.

Having left their sabres on the steamship *Far West*, Custer's troopers had only two weapons to fight Indians—the .45-caliber Springfield 1873 carbine and the .45-caliber Colt revolver. Both of these firearms were inadequate to mount a long-range attack on the Indian encampment. Neither was adequate to defend Custer's troopers from attack by superior numbers of Indians. The carbine carried but a single round in its firing chamber. It was forty-one inches in length with a barrel of twenty-two inches and a weight of seven pounds. Its barrel was rifled so that the bullet made one complete turn before exiting the muzzle.

The bullet was made of molten lead alloyed with 2.5 to 5 percent tin. Tin is lighter and harder than lead, but it creates a molten alloy that will cast a better-shaped bullet when poured into a mold. The bullet contains a hollow base (rear end) that must expand when fired to create a gas seal that will propel the bullet and prevent unburned black-powder residue from fouling the firing chamber and the rifling in the barrel. Since the gas seal was not perfect, a certain amount of powder residue would find its way into the firing chamber and rifling. If the rifling was fouled, the bullet would not spin—thus it would tumble during flight and lose its accuracy and trajectory within 150 yards. If the firing chamber was fouled, the extractor mechanism would jam or fail, rendering the carbine inoperable. The carbine could become fouled with gunpowder residue when as few as five rounds were fired.[8] There is some indication that 4–6 percent of the Seventh Cavalry carbines suffered extraction failure. Efforts were made to coat the carbine bullets with a lubricant that would soften this fouling—but they were not always effective. On a clear day when the winds were calm, firing the black-powder cartridge produced a dense cloud of white smoke, pinpointing the location of a trooper.

A trooper firing his guns while mounted faced two problems of a disabling nature—marksmanship and reloading. Marksmanship was impaired by ballistics (the science of the motion of the bullet when it is fired) and the movement of the trooper's horse. The instant a bullet left the carbine muzzle, it was spinning rapidly clockwise, falling with the pull of gravity, traveling forward at a speed of 1,150 feet per second (f.p.s.), and deflecting sideways by the movement of air across its trajectory. The cavalry exchanged shots with Indians at ranges varying from twenty to six hundred yards and beyond. The velocity of the bullet declined as it left the muzzle of the carbine; by the time it had traveled 200 yards its velocity was reduced to 913 f.p.s., and at 400 yards it was

757 f.p.s. The slower the bullet's velocity, the more it dropped during each 100 yards of distance. Remember that a trooper shooting at a target 400 yards distant had to elevate his aim nine feet four inches in order to hit his target.[9] This difficulty was compounded many times over when the trooper was firing from a moving horse at a moving target.

In the battle at Rosebud Creek, which occurred on June 17, 1876, infantrymen and troopers under the command of Gen. George Crook fired in excess of 25,000 rounds, and the most reliable indication of Indians killed was the report of General Crook that the bodies of thirteen Indians were found shortly after the battle.[10] Many of these 25,000 rounds were fired at ranges substantially less than 500 yards. It should be noted that dismounted Indians were cautious about exposing themselves to gunfire. They used distance, movement, and available ground cover for maximum protection.

Another reason for poor marksmanship was lack of training. Historian Thomas R. Buecker observed that training at Fort Robinson in 1875 was minimal:

> The infantry men shot at targets 72 x 22 inches in size, placed at 200 yards, with their long range .45/70-caliber rifles, that had replaced the earlier, .50-caliber models. The cavalrymen used .45/55 carbines and shot at wider targets 150 yards away. With limited allowances of ammunition allotted for target practice, each soldier fired a miserly ten rounds per month, alternating three shots one week and two the next. A typical consolidated report of target practice recorded that in September 1875 the Camp Robinson garrison fired a total of 1,570 shots. Only 652, 42%, hit the target board.[11]

One of the reasons that the army selected the single-shot Springfield carbine for use by the frontier cavalry was to conserve ammunition—cartridges were heavy to transport, and they cost money. Prior to the Little Big Horn, the penny-wise and pound-poor U.S. Army paid little heed to marksmanship. It prescribed a mere twenty rounds as an annual allotment for target practice. Col. Philip M. Shockley writes, "The finer points of rifle marksmanship were not taught. Firing at moving targets was unheard of."[12]

The aiming process for the carbine involved a small, stationary front sight, called a "blade" (shaped in the manner of an inverted exclamation point) at the end of the barrel and an adjustable open *v*, called a "leaf," at the rear sight (nearest to the shooter), on which a trooper could make vertical but not horizontal adjustments to compensate for range to the target and wind drift. The trooper would peer with one eye through the open *v* of the rear sight and align the front sight on the target, establishing his "line of sight." Troopers were instructed to hold the seven-pound carbine to their right shoulder with their right hand while using the left hand on the reins to control the horse. Whatever accuracy the carbine possessed was disrupted by the motion of the horse, which moved the trooper and the front sight of the carbine with the result that there was little accuracy beyond fifty yards.

The impact of the horse's movement upon mounted marksmanship can be demonstrated by the following mathematical calculations. A movement of one-quarter inch at the front sight caused a deviation of the bullet of 6.6 feet at 150 yards, 15.6 feet at 350 yards, and 22.2 feet at 500 yards. A movement of one-half inch at the front sight caused deviations of 13.2 feet, 31.2 feet, and 44.1 feet at these same ranges. To place this in perspective, if one aimed at the head of a man who was six feet six inches tall and 150 yards ahead and the front sight dipped one-quarter inch when the carbine fired, the bullet would hit *below* the feet of the intended target.

Managing the seven-pound carbine with one hand was awkward. Its hammer had to be cocked with the thumb before it would fire. With its 150 pounds of recoil, it jarred a trooper each time it was fired. In short, except at point-blank range, carbine fire by a mounted trooper was ineffective.

The mounted trooper's horizontal angle of fire while in motion was also severely limited by his ability to rotate his shoulders on the axis of his spine. One can readily determine that if the carbine is held firmly to the right shoulder, with one foot in the stirrup on each side of the horse, it is not possible to rotate the spine and shoulders much farther than 90 degrees to either side in attempting to fire at a target in the rear. A mounted warrior pursuing from the rear could close on a trooper with less risk of being shot with the carbine. The trooper would have a few extra degrees on each side to aim and fire his revolver, which had only a 7½-inch barrel and did not need to be pressed to the shoulder before firing.

A key element of a trooper's fighting ability that has been virtually ignored by writers, including those who were experienced troopers, is the fact that it was extremely difficult for a mounted trooper to reload a carbine while charging or moving at a rapid gait. The trooper needed one hand to hold the reins with which he controlled his mount. The carbine loaded and fired but a single shot. It contained no magazine for mechanical reloading. Once the single round had been fired, it required one hand to hold onto the carbine and use of the other hand to open its trap-door breech. In order to open the trap-door breech and keep it open, the muzzle of the carbine had to be pointed below horizontal. The trap-door breech was opened by moving it forward with a rapid motion that had the effect of extracting the spent copper cartridge case from its chamber. Opening required the use of one hand to hold the carbine while the other hand opened the trap door. In some instances the extractor failed. When this happened, the trooper had to use either a short ramrod or a knife to attempt manual extraction of the cartridge case. In each instance two hands were required. Unless and until the spent case was extracted, the carbine could not be reloaded. Assuming that the extraction was accomplished by opening the trap-door mechanism (a metal breech block attached to the receiver at its forward end), the trooper would then have to use his free hand to grasp a live cartridge and place it manually in the open breech of the carbine. He would then close the trap-door mechanism and cock the hammer on the carbine. It was then ready to fire one more shot.

This process took a significant amount of time and was virtually impossible to accomplish from the back of a moving cavalry mount unless the mount was so well trained that a trooper could control it with his legs, dropping his reins on the pommel of his saddle or the neck of his charging mount, enabling the use of both hands to reload. A high percentage of Seventh Cavalry troopers and their mounts were green riders. Their horses became gassy and uncontrollable when the entire battalion charged, particularly when firing commenced. At these times and under these conditions, reloading was virtually impossible. If a trooper attempted to stop and reload, he would be left behind, presenting an isolated, stationary target for any nearby Indian who happened to spot him in this condition. Thus, when a trooper's carbine was discharged, his sole remaining active weapon was his six-shot pistol.

The 1873 model Colt .45 pistol was carried by each trooper in a holster attached to a belt on his right side. The pistol was withdrawn from its holster by the right hand and transferred to the left hand for firing.[13] It was a single-action revolver, meaning that it was necessary to cock the hammer with the thumb before pulling the trigger to fire. The cocking of the hammer rotated a revolving cylinder containing six chambers, positioning a new chamber with a live round in line with the inside of the barrel for firing. Troopers were instructed to keep fire low, to never cock the pistol until the time came for firing, and to aim directly over the horse's head so that the trooper would be afforded protection by being partially covered by the horse.

It was also difficult to aim and fire the revolver. While the revolver could be an effective offensive as well as defensive weapon at ranges of up to thirty yards, its accuracy, particularly from the back of a moving horse, declined rapidly at ranges beyond ten yards. Troopers were given target practice on stationary targets at distances of ten, twenty, thirty, forty, and fifty paces.[14] Beyond that distance, revolvers were virtually worthless.

If the trooper's target was stationary, his accuracy would be increased in direct proportion to his proximity to the target. However, the nearer he was to his target, the more vulnerable he became to enemy fire. If he was able to surprise his adversary, particularly when the adversary was not armed, his prospects for accurate fire were increased. Nonetheless, despite what Tom Mix and John Wayne demonstrated on the silver screen, there was little likelihood of accurate fire, even at close range, from the back of a galloping cavalry mount. The aiming process with a pistol was accomplished more by intuition and direction than by actual utilization of the front and rear stationary sights with which the revolver was equipped.

Reloading the Colt revolver was equally as difficult as the carbine. The revolving cylinder that held the cartridges had six chambers. The cylinder was not detachable from the revolver. Once six rounds were fired, the cylinder had to be reloaded. The reloading process was virtually impossible without the use of both hands. Army instructions on reloading of the cavalry pistol all envisioned the horse standing quietly. In this position the trooper freed up both hands by resting his reins on the pommel of his saddle. The cylinder of the revolver would then be rotated around its stationary center pin, bringing each chamber in line with a spring-loaded ejector rod that would be pushed with a finger to dislodge the spent cases, one at a time. It was necessary to manually grasp and discard each spent case from the revolver. (The ejector rod did not expel the empty case  it merely dislodged it from its chamber.) Then live cartridges (six of them) could be reloaded, one at a time, using one hand to hold the pistol and the other hand to grab and stuff each live cartridge into its empty chamber. If a trooper's revolver became empty during the course of a charge against the enemy, he could either shift over to his single-shot carbine or continue the charge without any offensive capacity other than the momentum of his horse. In the middle of combat with an armed enemy, it was suicidal to stop the mount and pause for the sixty to ninety seconds that would be consumed in reloading the revolver. Thus, after its six rounds were expended, the revolver was no longer a weapon for a mounted and moving trooper.

By this time it should be apparent that a charging cavalry troop lacked sufficient sustained firepower to engage an armed enemy for more than a brief twenty to thirty seconds, after which the troop, individually and collectively, had no means of fighting or defending until its revolvers and carbines were reloaded. This is what happened to Major Reno and his troops during their fight in the valley.

As early as 1865 at the end of the Civil War, limitations on the use of cavalry and the dire need for repeating rifles were common knowledge. Brig. Gen. August Kautz wrote of this future problem in *Customs of Service*. With respect to a "commanding officer," Kautz states:

702. Recent improvements in arms and equipments have made it necessary that the greater portion of our Cavalry should be armed with repeating carbines and metallic percussion cartridges. The sabre may be dispensed with altogether, or if forming part of the equipment, should be strapped to the saddle. Such a force is almost as formidable as Infantry, and its principal use is to surprise and capture strategical points, and hold them until they can be occupied by the Infantry; they act as skirmishers or flankers to the army when advancing, or retreating. They go into action generally dismounted, and their horses are used only as a means of transportation. Such Cavalry is of special value in a wooded or broken country, where the horses may be covered, and the character of the troops thus concealed from the enemy.[15]

At the Little Big Horn the Seventh Cavalry lacked adequate weapons to mount a long-range attack on the Indian encampment. Neither could they defend themselves from attack by the superior number of Indians. Unless they were able to surround the Indian encampment and fire their carbines while dismounted, there was little that they could do to contain and subdue a large village of Indians. Since each trooper carried only one hundred rounds of carbine ammunition, the action would be of relatively short duration.

Chapter Sixteen
# Evaluation of Custer and the Seventh Cavalry
# at Little Big Horn

*I went over it carefully with a view to determine in my own mind how
the fight was fought. I arrived at the conclusion then, as I have now, that
it was a rout, a panic, till the last man was killed.*

—*Captain Benteen*

Setting aside consideration of the impact of Custer's lifelong recklessness
and disregard for rules and regulations, there are other more systematic
means for assessing the reasons why Lt. Col. George A. Custer and over
200 men died that day. The staff at the U.S. Naval War College developed
the formula O2S4MEC as a system for analyzing battles.[1] While the formula was designed primarily to analyze combat by warships and aircraft
on the high seas, and the Battle at the Little Big Horn involved only a
small force of United States Cavalry in land warfare utilizing mounted
and dismounted firing against a greater number of Indian warriors, the
War College formula employs standardized terminology that permits an
organized analysis of the decisive factors that determined the result at
the Little Big Horn. In the formula the two *O*'s stand for *objective* and
*offensive*, the four *S*'s stand for *superiority at point of contact, surprise,
security*, and *simplicity*, while *M* stands for *movement and mobility*, *E*
stands for *economy of force*, and *C* stands for *cooperation* (which involves
unity of command).

The strategic *objective* of President Ulysses Grant was to wrest possession of the northern plains from the Lakotas and Cheyennes and disarm
and remove them to designated reservations where they were required to
remain. The strategy to achieve this objective was conceived and executed by Generals Sherman and Sheridan by initiating surprise attacks on

Indian encampments with cavalry and infantry, using whatever force was necessary to subjugate and induce those who survived to return to and remain on their reservations. Custer's personal objective was to achieve a decisive and conspicuous military victory over the Cheyennes and Lakotas whenever and wherever he could find them.[2] There was considerable overlap in each objective. The extent of genocide was left up to the tactical field commander. Thus Custer's *objective* (military victory) was to be achieved by attacking, killing, and military conquest. The objective of Grant, Sherman, and Sheridan did not require attack and killing if (and only if) subjugation and return to the reservation could be accomplished by starvation, intimidation, and conquest on the battlefields. However, with General William T. Sherman as commanding general, the actions of the U.S. Army were certain to involve genocide and premeditated murder because, as he had stated in 1868, "the more we can kill this year, the less will have to be killed next year."[3] At Little Big Horn unless Custer had a tactical plan that would enable him to achieve a military victory over an enemy that greatly outnumbered his own attack force, his objective was impossible. Possible tactical maneuvers involving the element of surprise, driving off the Indians' ponies to strip them of their mobility, or some unspecified benefit to be gained from topographical circumstances (or a combination of the three) were necessary for him to achieve any kind of military victory. The Indians' massive counterattack, launched from their encampment, terminated Custer's movement toward their encampment, ending any possibility for him to achieve his objective.

*Offense* was essential to Custer's objective, but he lacked the strength and sufficient information about his enemy (intelligence) to attack and remain on the offensive. As a result, his attack terminated shortly after his left wing commenced firing at the Indians' encampment from the opposite bank of the Little Big Horn River. Custer was on the defensive from the moment the Indians returned fire at Medicine Tail Coulee until his battalion of five companies was annihilated.

Custer lacked any *superiority at point of contact*. The deployment of Captain Benteen's battalion on a fool's chase, his order directing Major Reno's battalion to charge down the valley on the east bank after the small band of fleeing Sans Arcs, and his use of significant numbers of troopers to operate the pack train decimated his strike force. He had declined the use of additional cavalry and infantry companies offered by General

Terry. Two-thirds of his effective strike force was out of sight and beyond his ability to direct or control when the Indians launched their all-out counterattack from their encampment on the west bank.

*Surprise* was a key element in the success or failure of the Japanese effort to invade Midway. It enabled Lt. Col. Henry Mucci's special forces to wipe out the entire Japanese contingent at Cabanatuan prison where his rescuing force was outnumbered by eight to one. Surprise was the essential element in Custer's need to neutralize the Indians' numerical superiority. Custer had to mount a surprise attack, close immediately with the Indians, and drive off their ponies to deprive them of their mobility—mobility to either flee or counterattack. Some historians assert that Custer anticipated that the Indians would cut and run when confronted by his cavalry since this had been their behavior on certain prior occasions. However, this is inconsistent with Custer's actions commencing at noon on June 25. Mistakenly believing that the Indian encampment was aware of his presence, he ordered an all-out attack by Major Reno's battalion from a distance in excess of two miles, during daylight hours, abandoning his plan for a surprise attack at dawn on June 26. This gave the Indians the time that they needed to retrieve their grazing ponies and be in a state of readiness for Reno's charge and Custer's mid-afternoon walk-on approach to their camp from the east bank of the river. Had the Indians intended to take flight, Custer's attack in broad daylight gave them earlier warning than a surprise attack at dawn, creating a better opportunity for them to escape. The Indians not only stood and fought aggressively to defend their encampment, but they had rounded up their war ponies and proceeded without delay to counterattack, surround, and annihilate Custer's five companies.

*Security* is closely related to surprise. Custer's efforts to avoid detection were careless and ineffective. His battalion traveled mostly in daylight when they could be sighted at a distance. Their dust was visible for miles. Troopers and moving animals were noisy and unrestrained on the march. They opened fire on small groups of Indians without permission. Early on the morning of June 25, cooking fires and trumpet calls were allowed. Shortly thereafter Sgt. William Curtis and a small squad left camp and fired at stray Indians without permission. Custer authorized Reno's battalion to commence firing well before Custer had sighted the encampment. Custer's left wing attacked the encampment, firing into it in broad

daylight from across the river, giving the Indians sufficient time to counterattack and maneuver to prevent any of Custer's men from crossing the
Little Big Horn. It would almost appear that Custer attempted to assist
the Indians in discovering his presence.

*Simplicity* was an important element in any plan that Custer may have
had because he had little advance intelligence with which to determine
the Indians' location and their relative strength. When the Indians commenced their counterattack at Medicine Tail Coulee, Custer lacked any
ability to communicate with his other three battalions, which contained
two-thirds of his fighting men. Since there was no reconnaissance, there
was no surveillance to provide information regarding the Indians' location and state of readiness. No one has ever provided a credible description of any plan that Custer might have had, other than his announcement on June 24 that he would hide during the twenty-fifth and mount a
surprise attack at dawn on the twenty-sixth. When he changed his plan
on the morning of the twenty-fifth and announced that he would attack during daylight on that day, no details were either discussed with
or communicated to any of the officers or scouts with the battalions of
Reno, Benteen, or the pack train. From the time the regiment crossed
the divide between Rosebud Creek and Little Big Horn River, Custer's
orders and actions were nothing but a series of impulsive, inconsistent,
and inexplicable reactions to a series of minor incidents that came to his
attention. The maneuvers of Custer's battalion when the Indians charged
out from their village, crossing the river to surround and attack him,
indicate nothing but ragged and leaderless scrambling on the part of the
poor, exhausted troopers, who were in a position to see that they were
not only overwhelmed by vastly superior numbers but surrounded with
no hope of escape.

As for *movement and mobility*, Benteen's scout to the left was a movement away from Custer's objective and away from the obvious direction
taken by the numerous Indian trails that Custer was following. The slow
pace of the pack train and the exhaustion of the horses severely reduced
mobility. Similarly, after Reno's attack failed, Custer himself was not in a
position to initiate an offensive operation or prevent the Indians from escaping because, through his own impulsive ordering of Reno's premature
firing in the valley, he had sacrificed the element of surprise and lacked
sufficient strength in numbers to fight his way across the Little Big Horn

River and attempt to separate the Indians from their horses. After firing across the river from Medicine Tail Coulee, Custer's movements were *away* from an attack on the encampment and *away* from the only path of retreat that he had at the time. His troopers had to dismount in order to reload and generate return fire. In dismounting, they discarded their mobility (horses)—permanently.

When Custer approached the Little Big Horn moving west toward the Indians' encampment, he had a regiment of 600 officers and armed troopers directly under his control. When Custer and his five companies (C, E, F, I, and L) approached Calhoun Hill and Custer Battlefield, he had only 210 troopers with which to attack and subdue more than 1,500 armed warriors and more than 4,000 noncombatants. The other 390 troopers were either managing the pack train, searching empty pastures four miles to the rear, or forming a defensive perimeter three miles to the southeast. Thus, 390 of his 600 troopers were not available to participate in Custer's intended attack on the Indian encampment. Each of these three separations was due to intentional orders issued by Custer, pursuant to which Custer was unable to reassemble his regiment when he initiated a tentative, clumsy, and ill-timed daylight attack at the mouth of Medicine Tail Coulee. Custer had weakened his overall fighting ability to the extent that his primary strike force was too small to attack and succeed. Concerning the doctrine of *economy of force*, Clausewitz stated, "If a segment of one's force is located where it is not sufficiently busy with the enemy, or if troops are on the march—that is, idle—while the enemy is fighting, then these forces are being managed uneconomically. In this sense they are being wasted, which is even worse than using them inappropriately."[4] The army's field manual states that, "Economy of Force involves the discriminating employment and distribution of forces. Commanders never leave any element without a purpose. When the time comes to execute, all elements should have tasks to perform."[5]

The final criterion for evaluating Custer, *cooperation*, required a unity of command and a coordinated effort by all twelve companies. This, in turn, requires an overall tactical plan that must be known and understood by all units engaged in or supporting the operation. The plan must be such that if separate units are deployed, their movement will be capable of coordination with the remaining units, and they must be cautioned about and authorized to react to unforeseen contingencies as they arise. Since Custer obviously had no radio communication, he needed to make other arrangements to communicate, not only with his regiment, but with Terry at predesignated intervals so that Terry could maintain control in a manner that would be most beneficial to the success of his operation. Because Custer had deployed the battalions of Reno and Benteen without a comprehensive plan, in such manner that he was unable to regain control of two-thirds of his attack force, there was no coordinated effort to either attack or defend when Custer finally sighted the encampment.

For reasons that will perhaps never be established, Custer's remaining 210 troopers were unable to mount any significant defense when the Indians attacked from their encampment. This is established by the linear arrangement and clusters of the marble grave markers and the distribution of the spent cartridge cases and bullets recovered from the battlefield. This conclusion is also supported by the sworn testimony of Captain Benteen at the Reno Court of Inquiry:

> I went over it carefully with a view to determine in my own mind how the fight was fought. I arrived at the conclusion then, as I have now, that it was a rout, a panic, till the last man was killed. That there was no line formed, there was no line on the battlefield. You can take a handful of corn and scatter it over the floor and make just such lines, there were none. The only approach to a line was . . . 5 or 6 horses at equal distances like skirmishers. Ahead of those 5 or 6 horses there were 5 or 6 men at about the same distances, showing that the horses were killed and the riders jumped off and were all heading to get where General Custer was. That was the only approach to a line on the field. There were more than 20 killed there to the right. There were 4 or 5 at one place all within the space of 20 or 30 yards. That was the condition all over the field and in the [gorge].[6]

In a formal report to U.S. General of the Army William T. Sherman dated November 25, 1876, Custer's sponsor, protector, and mentor, Lt. Gen. Philip Sheridan (commanding officer of the Military Division of the Missouri) noted, "Had the Seventh Cavalry been kept together, it is my belief it would have been able to handle the Indians on the Little Big Horn, and under any circumstances it could have at least defended itself;

but, separated as it was into three distinct detachments, the Indians had largely the advantage, in addition to their overwhelming numbers."[7]

In addition to the direct reference to splitting Custer's command, Sheridan's comments imply, for obvious reasons, that Custer's battalion was utterly unable to defend itself. While this is a direct reflection on the fact that Custer was badly outnumbered, even a battalion as small as Custer's 210 troopers, had they been properly led, should at the very least have been able to form up and mount a credible defense for a short period of time.

During the twentieth century various army officers have conducted studies and provided evaluations of Custer and his regiment. In a 1934 article Col. Timothy Coughlan criticized Custer for failing to provide support for Reno as he had promised, stating, "Good faith is as necessary a requirement in the senior as the junior." He was also critical of Custer for Benteen's scout, failure to keep subordinate officers informed, and dividing his command, noting, "He will be ever remembered as the dashing, daring and courageous Custer, who died a hero with his men, but as far as his observance of tactics or strategy at the battle of the Little Big Horn is concerned, the book is closed."[8]

During the twentieth century military strategists and tacticians coined the term "victory disease" to describe common strategic and tactical errors that lead to inadequate performance by officers commanding operations in the field. During the 1960s the U.S. Army developed a "U.S. Army Training and Doctrine Command," located at its Combat Studies Institute in Fort Leavenworth, Kansas. In a study published by the institute entitled "Understanding the Victory Disease, from the Little Big Horn to Mogadishu and Beyond," Maj. Timothy Karcher and Lt. Col. Thomas T. Smith singled out Custer and the Battle of the Little Big Horn as one of their two prime examples, noting, "Few finer historical examples of the victory disease exist than the Battle of the Little Big Horn."[9] The three basic symptoms of the victory disease are arrogance, complacency, and the habit of using established patterns to solve a military problem. The victory disease will bring defeat to a previously victorious nation or military.[10]

Custer's arrogance was exhibited on many occasions. Prior to the battle at the Washita River in 1868, he boasted that all of the Indians in the country could not whip his Seventh Cavalry. On June 21 and 22, in parting from General Terry, Custer boasted to Col. John Gibbon that he would not save any Indians for him. He also informed his scout and interpreter, Mitch Bouyer, that the Seventh Cavalry could whip any Indians that it met.[11] In Custer's case the element of complacency was directly related to his arrogance. He misunderstood Indian culture; he and the U.S. Army repeatedly ignored warnings about the size of the Indian gathering; and Custer failed to take even rudimentary steps to obtain knowledge of its size and location.[12] He was out of touch with reality regarding the ability of his troopers to fight with firearms while mounted. Custer fell into the trap of utilizing established patterns when he divided his regiment prior to his principal attack. Historians claim that Custer was certain that the Indians would flee when he confronted them. If this is accurate, then how did Custer plan to surround 4,000 to 7,000 Indians with his small battalion of 210 trail-weary troopers when he determined to attack them in broad daylight—from the opposite side of the river?

Neil C. Mangum, a respected historian with long service at the Little Big Horn Battlefield, had this observation of Custer's performance, "Custer fought the Battle of the Little Big Horn as if he was a line officer, rather than a regimental commander."[13]

In describing military misfortunes and their causes, current analysts recognize three basic kinds of failure: (1) failure to learn, (2) failure to anticipate, and (3) failure to adapt.[14] To this I would add, failure to think. At the Little Big Horn, Custer had failed to learn the absolute need for reconnaissance and planning, did not anticipate that he might be attacked by superior numbers of Indians, and thus was wholly unable to adapt to the situation when he found himself with only one-third of his fighting force available at the point of attack, facing more than 1,000 armed and angry warriors intent upon killing all the troopers in his battalion.

To summarize the evaluation, there are certain issues about which there are no definitive answers. After sighting the Indian encampment from Weir Point, why did Custer move away from the encampment (north and west) if he intended to attack it? Why did he not make a stand and attempt a defensive perimeter at Calhoun Hill? Was suicide prevalent at the end? Did alcohol and intoxication impair the performance of any officers or enlisted men? Did any elements of Custer's battalion ever reach the east bank of the Little Big Horn? While the answers might be of interest to all, none of these issues seem determinative of the causes of Custer's defeat.

Custer formulated his strategic objective—attack and military victo-

ry—without any real-time intelligence about his adversary and their location. His objective was bound to fail unless his strategy was achievable
and his tactics adequate. To carry out his strategy (attack and military
victory), he was committed to defeat 1,000 to 1,500 warriors with his 210
troopers at the point of attack. He proceeded to execute his ambitious
strategy with no tactical plan of attack and little possibility of coordinat-
ing with his other 340 troopers. Heavily outnumbered, lacking knowledge of his enemy and the terrain, riding jaded mounts, armed with inadequate weapons, and without a tactical plan, there was nothing left for
Custer and his battalion but failure and death. The predicament facing
Custer and his battalion when they fired their weapons across the Little
Big Horn River at and into the Indian encampment on the west bank was
entirely of Custer's own doing and in accordance with the objective he
had set for himself and his regiment. Custer was the senior officer present. The problems facing each component of the Seventh Cavalry were
all the result of his errors of commission—and omission. He entered into
a pitched battle that turned into a rout because he was unable to formulate adequate tactics to achieve his objective. Because of this, Custer and
his battalion were defeated—and paid for that defeat with their lives.

In summary, Custer acquired a reputation at the Washita massacre
as an "Indian fighter" and was sought out by Generals Sherman, Sheridan, and Terry to lead a genocidal military attack on those Sioux and
Cheyennes who did not return to their reservations by January 31, 1876.
Custer was most anxious to lead this attack in order to achieve personal
notoriety through a military victory in which there would be a "great
killing" of these Indians. He was given tactical command of the Seventh
Cavalry Regiment and ordered to pursue a large group of Lakotas and
Cheyennes—numbering anywhere from 4,000 to 10,000—who were
hunting game south of the Yellowstone River in southeastern Montana.
Custer disdained the use of the additional infantry and cavalry companies, plus automatic weapons, offered by General Terry, and set forth
from the mouth of Rosebud Creek on June 21, 1876, with orders that allowed him, at his discretion, to pursue and attack any Indians whenever
and wherever he might find them.

As Custer marched south and west in search of the Lakotas and Cheyennes, he made scant use of the forty-five Arikara and Crow scouts at his
disposal. He sent no reconnaissance patrols to follow the fresh Indian
trails in order to determine the Indians' strength and location. Before he

learned their location and strength, he had split his 600-man regiment into three battalions, after assigning 130 men to manage a lengthy pack train that was unable to keep up with the regiment. He then detailed two battalions, totaling 260 men, on useless missions that separated them from Custer's support and control, without any plan for his anticipated attack on the Indian village. This left Custer with only 210 troopers (approximately one-third of his original strike force of 600) with which to locate the Indians' encampment, surround and attack it, have his great killing, subdue all the Indians, and force them to return to their reservations. Custer's men and horses were tired, and the troopers were armed only with single-shot carbines and six-shot revolvers for which they each carried a limited supply of ammunition.

While Custer had predicted a great battle to the American public, he approached the Indians' grand encampment at a walk and fired into it from across the Little Big Horn River. These actions suggest that he was merely attempting to cause the Indians to flee from their encampment. The Indians crossed him up and attacked his 210-member battalion en masse, surrounding and killing him and each of his troopers in short order. Custer's dead troopers were strung out along a four-sided trapezoid for a distance exceeding two miles—having mounted no effective defense and having utterly failed to attack and subdue any of the targeted Lakota and Cheyenne Indians.

The error in Custer's belief that his Seventh Cavalry Regiment could whip "any Indians that it met" is summed up by the director of the Army's Combat Studies Institute: "In both the nineteenth and twentieth centuries, technologically and organizationally sophisticated forces have come to grief at the hands of supposedly backward foes—a lesson often forgotten by soldiers of many nations."[15]

The location of the Indians' cartridge cases and (to a lesser extent) their bullets provide a dynamic panorama of the battle, demonstrating how and where Custer's battalion was destroyed. The Indians' grand tactic was to flank Custer's troopers—and they continued to flank them until the entire combat zone was surrounded. Once they were surrounded, Custer's troopers had to fight dismounted. With no mobility and no avenue for retreat they were soon overwhelmed by superior numbers, and in the end the Indians were able to kill the remaining troops with arrows and hand-held weapons.

In a rare expression of humility combined with candor, Custer once admitted that his conduct as a cadet at West Point had little to recommend it "unless as an example to be carefully avoided."[16] The same could be said for his conduct as commanding officer of the Seventh Cavalry Regiment at the Little Big Horn.

General Philip Sheridan grew up in Somerset, Ohio, with a lifelong friend, Henry C. Greiner. During a visit to Somerset in June of 1881, Sheridan confided in Greiner:

> Poor Custer, he was the embodiment of gallantry. If there was any poetry or romance in war he could develop it. But I was always fearful that he would catch it if allowed a separate command. Yes, I told him he would get it some time, and I told others so. It was not much of a surprise to me when I heard of the disaster, but it was a great blow, as he served me so gallantly in the Shenandoah Valley. He always needed someone to restrain him; he was too impetuous, without deliberation, he thought himself invincible and having a charmed life. When I think of the many brave fellows who went down with him that day, it is sickening.[17]

Chapter Seventeen
# The Impact of Custer's Defeat on the Cheyenne and Lakota Indians

*But they [General Crook's relief force] did not reach us in time, as the excessive cold had forced the Cheyennes to withdraw from our immediate front, eleven of their little babies having frozen to death in their mothers' arms the first night and three others the second night after the fight.*

—Recorded by Capt. John G. Bourke following the Dull Knife Fight, November 25, 1876[1]

On June 25, 1876, Lakotas and Cheyennes were gathered at their grand encampment on the Little Big Horn for one reason—to hunt buffalo for the food and hides that were essential for their survival. They intended to provide for themselves rather than submit to confinement on their agencies and reservations, where they would exist as mere supplicants awaiting uncertain and insufficient food rations from the government. They were occupying their 1868 Treaty lands, were committing no crime, and were "persons" entitled to life, liberty, and property under the Fifth Amendment of the U.S. Constitution. Thus, they had no legal obligation to obey the directive from the commissioner of Indian affairs to return to their reservations. Similarly, and due to these same legal restraints, President Grant lacked any authority to order the Lakotas and Cheyennes to be conquered and forcibly removed from their treaty lands to designated reservations against their will.

The Indians' annihilation of Custer and his five companies at Little Big Horn turned Congress and public opinion against them. America's crack cavalry regiment had been shot up and humiliated—and General of the Army William T. Sherman, who advocated extermination of the Indians, was hell-bent on waging genocidal war on all Sioux and Cheyenne men, women, and children who failed to obey—and shifting the blame to lower-ranking officers.

Following Little Big Horn, the Indians terminated their hunt, broke camp, and separated into smaller groups. Many began to work their way back to reservations and agencies in Dakota Territory and Nebraska, intending to utilize the meat from their summer hunt to feed themselves during the coming fall and winter. Others, notably Lakota followers of Crazy Horse and Sitting Bull, and lesser numbers of Northern Cheyennes, elected to remain in eastern Montana and western Dakota Territory, continuing to hunt and live in their treaty lands, where white men were prohibited from trespassing. General Sheridan, who commanded the Division of the Missouri, ordered Generals George Crook and Alfred Terry to continue in all-out pursuit of those Sioux and Cheyennes who remained at large. This meant indiscriminate killing, destruction of shelter, plunder of food, and confiscation of ponies and firearms—and ultimately (for those who were not killed by the army) surrender, loss of their Fifth Amendment liberty, and removal to designated reservations.

After Little Big Horn, Crook and Terry replenished and augmented their separate commands. Col. Nelson Miles and his Fifth Infantry Regiment were sent to reinforce Terry. Col. Wesley Merritt, with additional cavalry, reported to Crook. Terry and Crook, having joined briefly on Rosebud Creek, split up on August 26, 1876. Terry sent Col. John Gibbon back west to Fort Shaw and ordered Colonel Miles and his regiment to establish a cantonment (temporary quarters for his troops) at the mouth of the Tongue River. Terry then retired from the Great Sioux War to Fort Abraham Lincoln in northern Dakota Territory with the balance of his forces, having successfully avoided being present in any incident where his troops located and attacked Indian villages.

### Battle of Slim Buttes—September 9, 1876

On August 26 Crook moved northeast from the Powder River with his reorganized Bighorn and Yellowstone Expedition provisioned with light rations for a fifteen-day campaign. His force consisted of 1,500 cavalry troopers and 450 foot soldiers, together with 285 white and Indian scouts and 240 pack mules. Cold and continual rain coupled with insufficient rations made this "one of the most grueling marches in military history."[2]

While it is reasonable and proper to take pity on Crook and his soldiers for their suffering due to adverse weather and light rations, it should be kept in mind that the Lakotas and Cheyennes being pursued by Crook—men, women, and children—had to endure these same conditions, and there was no friendly government settlement in the Black Hills where they could find shelter or replenish their food.

By September 5, Crook had reached the Heart River in Dakota Territory and was desperately short of food. On the seventh he sent Capt. Anson Mills with 150 troopers and a pack train south toward Custer City in the southern Black Hills for provisions. At mid-afternoon on the eighth, Mills' scouts discovered a small Minneconjou village of 250, containing 100 warriors, located in Dakota Territory less than one mile east of the northeast corner of Wyoming Territory. Prepared for an attack, Mills' forces concealed themselves in a nearby ravine until 2 a.m. Historian Jerome Greene described their dawn attack as follows:

> Mills proceeded to carry out the classic military tactic of the Indian Wars period, an ancient design resurrected in response to the unconventional nature of warfare with the Plains Indians—the attack at dawn. This tactic, though never formally stated, was in part an extension of the annihilation philosophy fostered by Generals Sherman, Sheridan, and Ulysses S. Grant during the Civil War. On the plains the maneuver of surprise and destruction, augmented philosophically by the "total-war" concept, worked best against elusive tribesmen who seldom stood and fought. The most successful assaults occurred at daybreak, with three or more columns of soldiers striking a sleeping camp simultaneously. Against such disconcerting thrusts defense was futile, and warriors rushed from their lodges only to be cut down in the charge. Tragically, large numbers of women and children often died in the confusion of the dawn strike. Once sacked, the village with its supplies was burned, and the ponies were killed. Tribesmen subjected to the tactic of surprise at dawn experienced psychological shock and abjectly surrendered. Humanistically speaking, the tactic was immoral, but for an army charged with subjugating the Sioux and other dissident Plains tribes, it was justified for the simple reason that it worked.[3]

In addition to immorality, the attack was also constitutionally outrageous. The Indians' camp contained tons of dried meat, 6,500 buffalo robes and skins, arms, and ammunition that were essential for survival.[4]

They were left without shelter. While "confusion" may have caused some of the killing of women and children, most of it must be attributed to intentional shots fired by attacking soldiers. Thus, in actuality, it was intentional murder.

Speaking from the Indians' perspective, Minneconjou chief Red Horse indicated that his camp of forty-eight lodges was surprised early in the morning, when it was still dark and misting. The women took their children to rocks in the higher ground. Red Horse was returning his camp to their reservation to surrender when Mills attacked. The attack provided temporary food for Crook's soldiers and nothing but misery and hatred for the Minneconjous. Those who fled were "almost helpless, and in a destitute condition."[5] How could this attack be "justified" when Red Horse and his followers were voluntarily returning to their reservation with their food and buffalo robes?

Crazy Horse and large numbers of Lakotas were in the vicinity of Slim Buttes, and they continued to skirmish with Crook's entire expedition during the afternoon of September 9. Crook continued southward on the tenth and arrived in Custer City on September 23.

While Crook was occupied with Crazy Horse and his Lakota followers in the Black Hills and Terry had retired from the field, Col. Nelson Miles had established a cantonment at the mouth of the Tongue River, where he initiated and continued relentless pressure on Sitting Bull and a sizeable group of Hunkpapas and other non-treaty Indians who were searching for scattered herds of buffalo between the Yellowstone and the Missouri rivers in eastern Montana—a land known for fierce winter blizzards and subzero temperatures.

### Spring Creek and Cedar Creek, October–December 1876

Miles' Tongue River cantonment was garrisoned by the Fifth Infantry Regiment. Another cantonment was established at Glendive (also on the Yellowstone River) about 120 miles to the northeast. The Glendive cantonment was garrisoned by eight companies of infantry that were used to escort wagon trains carrying supplies to the Tongue. On October 11 a supply train out of Glendive was attacked and turned back by Sitting Bull's warriors. The supply train turned back, reorganized, and set out again on the fourteenth. It was attacked by 400 to 500 warriors, who were repelled by Miles' well-organized infantry. On the sixteenth Sitting Bull sent a note challenging the troops for trespassing over his hunting grounds but seeking peace—along with some food.

Discussions resumed on October 17 near Cedar Creek. Colonel Miles himself was now involved, and 600 warriors were present. While Sitting Bull declined to yield, several other chiefs appeared ready to surrender. When the discussions failed, Miles moved quickly to flank the hoard of warriors. Heavy firing commenced, and the Indians were driven off. After skirmishing off and on through the twenty-fourth, the Indians were being defeated at every turn, and the infantry was able to capture and deprive the Indians of their essential winter supplies. Parley resumed on the twenty-fifth without an agreement. Miles insisted on unconditional surrender, cessation of hunting, and relinquishment of ponies and firearms. Without the consent of Sitting Bull, 600 lodges of Minneconjous and Sans Arcs agreed to surrender at their agency. Sitting Bull's influence over his followers was rapidly eroding.

### Col. Nelson Miles—Tongue River and Fort Peck—November and December 1876

Meanwhile, Colonel Miles retired to his Tongue River cantonment to refit and take on supplies. On November 6 he launched a new campaign in the direction of the Fort Peck Agency, located to the northwest on the banks of the Missouri River. The Montana winter was out in all its fury. Miles and his men and horses were facing daily blizzards and subzero temperatures with little or no shelter. The Missouri River was completely frozen over while running a significant current below the ice. At this time there remained Cheyennes on the Bighorn River, Crazy Horse's Oglala followers to the south in Wyoming, and Sitting Bull's band of Hunkpapas (which had shrunk to less than one hundred lodges) in the vicinity of Fort Peck, located on the Missouri River about seventy miles north-northwest of Glendive. Elements of Miles' party went on to Fort Buford, located sixty-five miles east of Fort Peck, and Miles, with another contingent, reached the Tongue River cantonment on December 13, thus ending the Fort Peck expedition.

Three companies of the Fifth Infantry under Lt. Frank D. Baldwin continued to pursue Sitting Bull and his followers for more than nine days in bitterly cold weather that reached minus forty-two degrees. They walked from Fort Peck over 100 miles to the east and south, returning with frostbitten fingers, toes, and limbs. His soldiers had "driven the Indians out of their winter camp at the most inclement season of the year. The suffering of the troops, although great, could in no way be compared to that of the Indians, including that of women and children."[6] On December 18, back in the field, floundering in the snow, Baldwin's men found and sacked an Indian camp with 122 lodges, destroying all their meat, buffalo robes, and other provisions.

### Dull Knife Battle—November 25, 1876

Meanwhile, General Crook reached Camp Robinson in northwestern Nebraska on October 24, 1876. He proceeded to organize a new Powder River expedition early in November to pursue bands of Lakotas and Cheyennes who were off their reservations hunting buffalo in northeastern Wyoming. This was "unceded Indian territory," where they had specific treaty rights to exclusive occupancy and to hunt. Crook's expedition was assembled at Fort Fetterman by November 4 and consisted of 2,200 fighting men. The cavalry regiments were commanded by Col. Ranald McKenzie, and the infantry companies were commanded by Col. Richard I. Dodge.[7] They were assisted by a large contingent of Cheyenne, Sioux, and Arapaho scouts.[8] The temperature dropped to thirteen below zero on November 13, and the expedition moved out from Fort Fetterman, heading north on the fifteenth. On November 20, Crook's scouts captured and brought in a Cheyenne boy who told him that Crazy Horse was located in the area. Crook also learned that there was a large Cheyenne village nearby, which his scouts were able to locate on November 23. Two hundred Cheyenne lodges were encamped on the Red Fork of the Powder River fifteen miles distant from Crook's camp. His scouts verified the location of the camp, together with its pony herd and tepees. The Cheyennes had detected Crook's approach, and many rank-and-file tribe members wanted to flee. However, on November 24, Chief Last Bull, who headed the Cheyenne Kit Fox warrior society, demanded that they stand and fight. That evening they commenced a war dance and were still dancing on the morning of November 25, when Colonel Mackenzie ordered a cavalry charge to commence one mile from the camp. Although this gave the Indians some warning, they were not prepared to fight or defend. The attack, under the tactical control of Mackenzie, caused the Indians to flee to the west and north. The Cheyennes removed their women and children from the village while Mackenzie's forces captured 700 to 750 ponies. The attack was made by 1,100 troops, and they were opposed by a total of 400 to 500 warriors.[9] Mackenzie's odds were better than two to one. Mackenzie suffered seven killed and twenty-six wounded, while the Indians had sixteen to thirty-eight killed and sixty-five wounded. Eleven Cheyenne babies froze to death in the minus-thirty-degree temperatures that evening.[10] When the shooting stopped, Dull Knife called out to Crook's Indian scouts to "go home," and other Cheyennes called out, "You have killed and hurt a heap of our people . . . and you may as well stay now and kill the rest of us."[11] The army was sparing no one, trooper or Indian, in its efforts to clear free-roaming Indians from their treaty lands.

All 200 of the Indians' lodges were destroyed, and large quantities of food, ammunition, supplies, tepees, and all sorts of camping gear were confiscated or destroyed, along with 750 to 1,000 ponies. The battle impaired the Cheyennes' will to resist and impressed upon them the inevitability of an army triumph. Many women and children were killed or wounded. They were out in the cold with winter coming on, their morale was shattered, and there were few alternatives other than to surrender. The army's strategy of genocide and starvation in the dead of winter was making it impossible for the Sioux Indians to occupy their unceded Indian territory. General Crook, with a touch of humanity, did not continue to pursue the Cheyennes, stating that, "the loss of life to both sides would not be worth it."

The Cheyennes had selected Red Fork Canyon as a sheltered place to spend the winter of 1876–1877. In this conflict they seemed to do everything wrong. They should have fled. The army had amazing luck with its reconnaissance. Risking their lives and clinging to their Fifth Amendment liberty, the Cheyennes had spurned surrender overtures and paid for it in misery and death.

Cheyenne warrior Beaver Heart stated that following the battle there was much suffering by wounded warriors, and women and children were freezing to death. He indicated that some children were warmed back to life by cradling them in the stomachs of recently butchered horses.[12] Historian John D. McDermott noted, "When the troops completely destroyed the Cheyenne village they rid the Cheyennes not only of their shelter, food, and clothing, but the means of replacing them by capturing their horses, ammunition, tools and implements. They had no homes, no means of subsistence, and no prospects."[13]

Either in ignorance or in flagrant disregard of the suffering that his illegal orders were inflicting on the disconsolate Lakotas and Cheyennes who were attempting to avoid starvation during the winter of 1876–1877, General Sherman wrote to Sheridan, "Please convey to Generals Crook and Mackenzie my congratulations, and assure them that we appreciate highly the services of our brave officers and men who are now fighting savages in the most inhospitable regions of our continent. I hope their efforts this winter will result in perfect success and that our troops will hereafter be spared the necessity of these hard winter campaigns."[14] Sherman was praising Crook and Mackenzie for his own flagrant violations of the Fifth Amendment, the 1868 Treaty of Fort Laramie, and General Orders No. 100.

### Crazy Horse, December 1876–May 1877

Colonel Miles continued to pursue Crazy Horse and Sitting Bull's bands in the unceded Indian territory of southeastern Montana. He was beginning to employ a new tactic—marching after the Indians with infantry when there was heavy snow covering the ground. When the infantry could locate the Indians and achieve close proximity, they were much more effective fighters than the cavalry. Miles moved out on December 29 with seven companies of infantry, totaling 436 officers and men, heading south up the Tongue River toward the winter camps of Crazy Horse. The Indians abandoned their camps in the path of the advancing infantry. On the evening of January 7, a young warrior and seven Cheyenne women and children, relatives of a tribal leader, were captured. On the eighth the Indians fought to regain the prisoners, sending 600 warriors against Miles' forces. The fight took place in a canyon located on a spur of the Wolf Mountain Range. There was ice and snow to depths ranging from twelve to thirty-six inches. Fighting conditions were bad. Facing 600 warriors, the army had three men killed and eight wounded. There were fifteen Indians killed and an unknown number wounded. This battle led to the surrender of Crazy Horse and his followers in various increments. The surrender negotiations were initiated by Miles on February 1, 1877, followed by conferences on February 19 and March 18, which resulted in the surrender of 300 Indians led by Two Moons, Little Chief, and Hump, and ultimately to the surrender of 2,000 more led by Crazy Horse, Little Hawk, and others at the Red Cloud and Spotted Tail agencies in May.[15] Cheyenne leader Little Chief responded to Miles' surrender demands, "We are weak, compared with you and your forces; we are out of ammunition; we cannot make a rifle, a round of ammunition, or a knife; in fact we are at the mercy of those who are taking possession of our country; your terms are harsh and cruel, but we are going to accept them and place ourselves at your mercy."[16]

Miles was persistent and knew what he was doing. In addition, his overall strategic objective appeared to be to force the Indians to surrender, rather than to kill them. Using infantry in the dead of winter, he was able to locate the Indians' camps well in advance and, if he did not bring them to battle, he drove them from their villages with a concomitant loss of food, ponies, and shelter. One is left to ponder whether Miles, had he been in charge of the Seventh Cavalry, would have attempted to parley with Sitting Bull before launching an attack at the Little Big Horn on June 25, 1876.

**Lame Deer—May 7, 1877**

While Crazy Horse was surrendering at Camp Robinson, Sitting Bull, with 135 Lakota lodges, was moving north toward the Canadian border following the White Mud River in northern Montana. On May 7, 1877, Miles was pursuing the final remnants of a small band of Minneconjous led by Lame Deer. He had five companies of cavalry and five of infantry and was opposed by 250 Indians. Miles believed in reconnaissance. Long-range scouting by Johnny Bruguier and Sioux warrior Hump had located Lame Deer's camp along a small tributary of Rosebud Creek. Miles moved out at midnight on the sixth of May and rode twenty miles, reaching Lame Deer's camp at 4:00 a.m., undetected and achieving complete surprise. The Indians fled on sight.

Miles' surprise attack was well planned. He communicated with his officers. His deployment was purposeful and organized. He made sound tactical maneuvers when he reached the camp and had little difficulty in outmaneuvering the Indians. He had persuaded them to surrender, but the truce atmosphere was destroyed by a shot from an Indian scout. This resulted in a running battle with warriors attempting to protect their families.[17] The fighting that took place was mostly dismounted. The army suffered four killed and seven wounded, while the Indians had fourteen killed, including Chiefs Lame Deer and Iron Star. The Indians lost their entire camp and 600 horses. It was an inevitable defeat and demonstrated the futility of further resistance. These were the last remnants of the free-roaming Indians of the high plains. However, Sitting Bull remained in Canada until 1881.

### The Removal of Standing Bear and the Poncas

*The Indians possess the inherent right of expatriation, as well as the more fortunate white race, and have the inalienable right to life, liberty and the pursuit of happiness.*[18]

In April of 1877, shortly before Crazy Horse surrendered at Camp Robinson, Indian Commissioner John Q. Smith[19] ordered a small tribe of 700 Ponca Indians to move from their 93,000-acre reservation along the Niobrara River in Dakota Territory to a new and undesignated reservation in the unknown Indian territory that is now the state of Oklahoma. When the Ponca refused to move, Secretary of the Interior Carl Schurz directed the army to remove them. The army broke into their homes, put their household goods into wagons, and proceeded to force their removal to a new and unwanted homeland. In 1879 Ponca chief Standing Bear and twenty-nine followers (eight men and twenty-one women and children) fled the Indian territory and walked back to Nebraska in the dead of winter.[20] When they arrived Gen. George Crook was ordered to arrest and hold them in detention at Fort Omaha pending their return to Indian territory. With substantial assistance from General Crook and newspaper editor Thomas Henry Tibbles, Standing Bear (who was represented by Andrew Jackson Poppleton, general counsel for the Union Pacific Railroad, and Omaha lawyer John Lee Webster) sought and obtained relief from the United States District Court in Nebraska. That court held that Standing Bear and his followers were "persons" entitled to be released from the custody of General Crook (upholding their Fifth Amendment due process rights, without specific reference to the Con-

Standing Bear, a chief of the Ponca tribe, left the Ponca reservation in Indian territory with twenty-nine followers, without permission, and walked back to Nebraska in January 1879. Courtesy Nebraska State Historical Society.

Andrew Jackson Poppleton, legal counsel for Standing Bear. Courtesy Nebraska State Historical Society.

Susette La Flesche, daughter of Omaha chief Iron Eye, who assisted Standing Bear and his lawyers. Courtesy Nebraska State Historical Society.

Carl Schurz, U.S. secretary of the interior, ordered Gen. George Crook to arrest Standing Bear and the other Poncas and return them to Indian territory against their will. Courtesy Nebraska State Historical Society.

Black Kettle, a Southern Cheyenne peace chief whose village was attacked by Col. John M. Chivington at the infamous massacre at Sand Creek. He was later killed by Seventh Cavalry troops under Custer at the Washita massacre. Courtesy Denver Public Library, Western History Collection (X-32364).

Dull Knife (seated), also known as Morning Star, a Northern Cheyenne chief whose village was destroyed by the army on November 25, 1876, and Little Wolf (standing). Dull Knife later led a group of Northern Cheyenne in a breakaway from their reservation in Indian territory. His followers were imprisoned in an army barracks, after which they escaped and were killed or captured. Courtesy Nebraska State Historical Society.

Little Wolf, a Northern Cheyenne chief who was also involved in the breakaway from Indian territory. Little Wolf separated from Dull Knife's followers, and his group settled permanently in southeastern Montana, directly east of the Little Big Horn Battlefield. Courtesy Nebraska State Historical Society.

stitution) and that "Indians possess the inherent right of expatriation, as well as the more fortunate white race, and have the inalienable right to "life, liberty and the pursuit of happiness." Thus, the government had no "rightful authority" to remove the Poncas to Indian territory against their will.[21] From a legal standpoint, President Grant and his army officers Sherman, Sheridan, Terry, and Custer had no more right to remove the Lakotas and Cheyennes from the Wyoming and Montana territories than the government had to remove Standing Bear to Indian territory—none whatever.[22] In his annual report dated November 1, 1880, Secretary of the Interior Carl Schurz told Congress that he very much regretted the forced removal of both the Poncas and the Northern Cheyennes, calling it a "mistaken policy which I have found good cause to very much regret."[23]

### Cheyenne Outbreak—Camp Robinson, 1879

The famous interpreter William Garnett thought that "the Cheyennes were the most reckless, uncalculating, uncompromising and obstinate fighters of any of the northern Indians."[24] A majority of the Southern Cheyenne tribe lived on their reservation in Indian territory (now Oklahoma) and did not fight at the Little Big Horn. The Northern Cheyennes who fought in the outbreak at Camp Robinson were led by Dull Knife. In 1874 Indian Commissioner Edward Smith had ordered the Northern Cheyennes to be transferred to Indian territory in order to separate them from the "potentially troublesome Sioux."[25] They had not been removed by the summer of 1876 when they departed the Red Cloud Agency in northwest Nebraska to participate in the summer hunt on the unceded Indian territory along the Yellowstone River in southeastern Montana. In the spring of 1877, the Northern Cheyennes were corralled and marched south to Indian territory. Many believed that they had the right to return if they remained dissatisfied. They disliked Indian territory, became restless, and on September 9, under the leadership of chiefs Dull Knife and Little Wolf, 350 Cheyennes, including ninety warriors, fled their reservation without permission and headed north toward their former homeland.

Treated as hostile fugitives, they were pursued by the army but never subdued or captured. Along the way they burned, pillaged, and were alleged to have killed several white settlers in western Kansas. When they reached the North Platte River in western Nebraska, they split into two groups. Dull Knife led one group north toward the Red Cloud Agency in northwest Nebraska while Little Wolf led his followers northwest toward the Powder River country in southeastern Montana. Dull Knife's band began to scatter as they neared the Pine Ridge area, where Camp Robinson, the Red Cloud Agency, Camp Sheridan, and the nearby Spotted Tail Agency were located. These two agencies were stations where the government distributed treaty allotments to the Lakotas, Cheyennes, and Arapahos. The Oglalas and Brulés at the Red Cloud and Spotted Tail agencies were becoming restless and agitated. The army wanted to prevent Dull Knife's Cheyennes from rejoining them, which would add fuel to the fire. Additional troops were ordered in.

Late in October the elusive Northern Cheyennes began arriving at the Pine Ridge area in small groups. Dull Knife and his band were discovered by two companies of cavalry on October 21, and on October 26 they were disarmed and taken to Camp Robinson.[26] Dull Knife and his followers were ordered back to Indian territory but refused to go. They were adamant in defending their liberty. Their continued refusals resulted in confinement to a barracks in Camp Robinson. There were no means at hand for these Cheyennes to resist the illegality of their detention. After the evening meal on January 4, 1879, they were subjected to additional outrageous physical and mental agony through the withholding of all food and water. The imprisoned Cheyennes were desperate, and historian George Bird Grinnell noted, "During these days of starvation some of them acted like a lot of drunken people. A young man would say, 'I want to jump out now and be killed.' Then the others would hold him and not let him do it. Others used to stand up and make speeches, saying, 'We might as well be killed outside as starve here in this house.'"[27] During darkness on the evening of January 9, in bitterly cold weather, the 130 remaining Cheyenne prisoners, including Dull Knife, succeeded in breaking out with a few hidden weapons. They were desperately fighting for their constitutional rights of life and liberty. Several were killed and more were wounded, and the army initiated a vigorous pursuit. During the next day twenty-seven Cheyennes were ridden down and killed while thirty-five were recaptured. On January 12 about forty-five were surrounded in a stronghold along Soldier Creek, from which thirty-two escaped on the evening of the thirteenth. They were determined not to return to Indian territory. The Cheyennes exhibited exceptional stamina, bravery, and agility in their ability to remain alive and avoid capture in the dead of winter. The remaining thirty-two fugitives were discovered and surrounded on January 22. They were subjected to intense fire from all sides and then ordered to surrender by Capt. Henry W. Wessels, Jr.[28] In the end twenty-three were killed, and the remaining nine Cheyennes, including six seriously wounded, were taken prisoner.

Little Wolf's band made it to Montana Territory, where they were allowed to remain. The fifty-five ultimate survivors of Dull Knife's band were eventually allowed to join Little Wolf in Montana. Wild Hog and twenty others were sent to Kansas to be tried for the depredations that occurred during the fall of 1878. These prosecutions were ultimately dismissed, and the Indians were returned to Indian territory. In 1883 any Cheyennes who remained dissatisfied with Indian territory were granted part of their liberty and allowed to return to southeastern Montana. Finally, in 1884, the Northern Cheyennes were given their own reservation directly to the east of the Crow Reservation and the Little Bighorn Battlefield National Monument, where they had been driven out by the U.S. Army in the summer of 1876.[29] Dull Knife eventually rejoined his friends and relatives in Montana, where he lived out the balance of his life, having succeeded, like the Ponca chief Standing Bear, in avoiding an unwanted return "to the heat."[30]

The defeat of Custer at the Little Big Horn produced loss of life and property for the Lakota and Cheyenne combatants and their families. They no longer had their liberty to continue their mobile existence, living off the buffalo and other wild game over vast, arid areas of the northern plains. The loss of their food source and the overwhelming power of the U.S. Army forever changed their nomadic culture, forcing them to rely on new and different methods of subsistence and to attempt to survive new perils brought on by refined flour and sugar (obesity and diabetes), alcohol (alcoholism), and germs (small pox, measles, dysentery, cholera, and gonorrhea) introduced from Europe and Asia.

From the standpoint of legality, President Grant had no authority to declare war on the Lakotas and Cheyennes without a declaration by Congress. The attack by Captain Mills and General Crook at Slim Buttes took place on the Great Sioux Reservation created by the treaty of April 29,

1868, where the army was forbidden to trespass. Similarly, the battles at Rosebud Creek, Muddy Creek, Wolf Mountain, and Powder River took place in southeastern Montana in the unceded Indian territory, where the army was also forbidden to trespass. The indiscriminate killing of women, children, and other noncombatants, the sacking and burning of entire villages, imprisonment without food and water, the confiscation of food and other supplies, including firearms and ponies, were all genocidal acts prohibited by General Orders No. 100—egregious violations of the United States' own "laws of war," as well as the traditional rules of honor, decency, good faith, and the Indians' Fifth Amendment life, liberty, and property rights.

While the Indians were entitled to liberty and freedom under the Fifth Amendment of the Constitution and well-defined rights under the 1868 Treaty and our laws of war, neither Congress nor President Grant had any interest in their future, and they had virtually no access to the federal courts. Without the ability to enforce them in court or militarily, these rights were little more than words printed on scraps of paper—words that many of them could neither read or comprehend.

### Crook and His Sense of Honor and Decency

When General Crook organized his Powder River expedition at Fort Fetterman in November of 1876, he had recruited fifty-seven Lakota and ten Cheyenne scouts to be part of the expedition, along with a sizable number of Pawnee and Arapaho scouts. In recruiting the Sioux and Arapaho scouts, Crook gave his personal assurances that, while the warriors were out on the expedition, their families would be fed and sheltered and that the scouts would be "properly armed and mounted."[31] However, Crook could not speak for General Sheridan, who ordered that the scouts' families who remained on the reservation must surrender all of their firearms and ponies. Pursuant to this order, 290 ponies and seventy-five guns were confiscated at the Red Cloud Agency, and the horses were given to Pawnee scouts or sold at sale barns in Cheyenne and Sidney. While Crook was a tough and skillful fighter against the Indians, he would not lie to them. Accordingly, while powerless to countermand Sheridan's order, he was furious.[32] Not all the frontier generals agreed with Sherman's policies of extermination and conquest.

Historian John D. McDermott believes that "Crook possessed two qualities found in the great ones: patience and persistence." McDermott's exhaustive research discovered Crook's address to the 1884 class at West Point:

> The savage is hemmed in by civilization, and he sees that the inevitable must be faced. He is more ready to abandon his old habits and accept civilization, than civilization is to accept him. With all his faults, and he has many, the American Indian is not half so black as he has been painted. He is cruel in war, treacherous at times, and not overly clean, but so were our forefathers. His nature, however, is responsible to a treatment which assures him that it is based upon justice, truth, honesty and common sense; it is not impossible that with a fair and square system of dealing with him, the American Indian would make a better citizen than many who neglect the duties and abuse the privileges of that proud title.[33]

Crook gave these additional words of wisdom to the cadet class of May 1886:

> Make them no promises which you cannot fulfill; make no statements you cannot verify. When difficulties arise, as they occasionally will, endeavor to be so well informed of the circumstances of the case that your action may be powerful and convincing. . . . Let the Indian see that you administer one law for both the white-skinned and the red-skinned; that you do this without regard for praise or censure, and you will gain his confidence because you have shown yourself worthy of it. The rest will be easy. Don't expect too much at once, and don't lose courage or patience on account of backsliding. He should be encouraged to work and to save. The man who works and saves is fast leaving savagery behind him.[34]

Similarly, General John Pope criticized the government's policy of starving Indians who were removed to reservations and the burden it cast on the conscience of officers and men of the army charged with enforcing it. Pope said, "It is with painful reluctance that the military forces take the field against the Indians who only leave their reservations because they are starved there, and who must hunt food for themselves and their families, or see them perish with hunger."[35]

The relationship between the Lakotas on their reservations and the government in Washington continued to fester for decades. On December 19, 1890, ten days before troopers of the Seventh Cavalry Regiment killed more than 150 Lakotas at the infamous massacre at Wounded Knee Creek in southwest South Dakota, Gen. Nelson A. Miles telegraphed a blunt message to the commanding General of the Army John Schofield regarding the pending tension over the emerging "Ghost Dance" movement among the ill-fed Hunkpapas and Minneconjou Lakotas on their reservations:

> The difficult Indian problem cannot be solved permanently at this end of the line. It requires the fulfillment of Congress of the treaty obligations that the Indians were entreated and coerced into signing. They signed away a valuable portion of their reservation, and it is now occupied by white people, for which they have received nothing.
>
> They understood that ample provision would be made for their support; instead, their supplies have been reduced, and much of the time they have been living on half and two-thirds rations. Their crops, as well as the crops of the white people, for two years have been almost total failures.
>
> The dissatisfaction is wide spread, especially among the Sioux, while the Cheyennes have been on the verge of starvation, and were forced to commit depredations to sustain life. These facts are beyond question, and the evidence is positive and sustained by thousands of witnesses.[36]

It is unfortunate that Sherman, rather than Crook or Miles, had the ability to create government policy and then use the army he commanded to enforce it on the Indians. The ideas presented to the corps of cadets by Crook and to the war department by General Miles would have achieved better and more humane results.

Chapter Eighteen
# Epilogue

*A military order, however unconstitutional, is not apt to last longer than the military emergency. Even during that period a succeeding commander may revoke it all. But once a judicial opinion rationalizes such an order to show that it conforms to the Constitution, or rather rationalizes the Constitution to show that the Constitution sanctions such an order, the Court for all time has validated the principle of racial discrimination in transplanting American citizens. The principle then lies about like a loaded weapon ready for the hand of any authority that can bring forward a plausible claim of an urgent need. Every repetition imbeds that principle more deeply in our law and thinking and expands it to new purposes. All who observe the work of courts are familiar with what Judge Cardozo described as "the tendency of a principle to expand itself to the limit of its logic."*

—*Associate Justice Robert Jackson, dissenting in* Korematsu v. United States, *323 U.S. 214, 1944*

Nothing is more precious to Americans than their lives, nothing is more cherished than their liberty, and nothing will be defended with more vigor than their homelands. So it was with the Lakotas and Cheyennes who were removed from their unceded Indian territory and their Great Sioux Reservation by the order of President Grant to General Sherman and the U.S. Army to make internecine war against them. As a result they were killed indiscriminately, deprived of their liberty to live and hunt on their treaty lands, and their food, firearms, shelter, ponies, and other properties were confiscated or destroyed by the U.S. Army—all without a fair trial before an impartial judge. Primary responsibility for enforcement of the Indians' Fifth Amendment due process rights rested with the president, the army he commanded, his cabinet, and his Department of Justice. Acknowledging reality, the record shows that during the 1870s the American Indians' civil rights were continually violated with impunity by the president and the army. Post–Revolutionary War history shows that American presidents and the executive branch have paid little attention to Indians' rights and tended to ignore or distort even their basic Fifth Amendment due process rights.

When the president and his executive department were the perpetrators of major due process violations, or when the president (who is sworn to support the Constitution) ignored or failed to act on violations by others, there was little that the Lakotas and Cheyennes could do to protect their lives, liberty, and property from the attacks perpetrated by the U.S. Army in the Great Sioux War. While nineteenth century Indians were not recognized as citizens by the Supreme Court,[1] the Fourteenth Amendment made citizens of all persons "born . . . in the United States" and subject to the jurisdiction of the United States. Even so, President Grant's violation of the Indians' due process rights did not depend upon their status as "citizens" because their Fifth Amendment rights protect all "persons" regardless of their citizenship.

The arguments of Supreme Court Justice Robert H. Jackson in his dissenting opinion condemning the forcible relocation and internment of American citizens of Japanese descent following Pearl Harbor are instructive: the Lakota and Cheyenne Indians involved in the Great Sioux War were born on U.S. soil, of Lakota and Cheyenne parents who were also born in the United States. These Indians were citizens of the U.S. by nativity, and they were being attacked by the army because they refused to vacate their treaty lands and submit to forcible and permanent relocation on reservations where they chose not to live—attitudes and actions directly associated with liberty—actions not commonly a crime. The actions of the Sioux and Cheyenne Indians consisted merely in being present in territories of the United States where they had been granted the exclusive right of occupancy by a valid and existing treaty, near where many of them were born, lived, and survived by hunting, gathering, and trading. Their offense to the United States existed only in that they were born of different racial stock. If any fundamental assumption underlies our system of laws and justice, it is that guilt is personal and not inheritable. Even if all the parents of these Lakotas and Cheyennes had been convicted of raiding or trespass, the Constitution forbids the parents' penalties to be visited upon their children. President Grant's declaration of war against the Lakotas and Cheyennes who refused to vacate their treaty lands was an attempt to make otherwise innocent and lawful occupancy of these treaty lands a crime merely because the Lakotas and Cheyennes were descendants of parents as to whom they had no choice and because they belonged to a race from which there was no way to resign.

At certain times Congress did become involved and did, in many instances, attempt to strengthen and clarify Lakota and Cheyenne due process rights and provide compensation for prior takings. Unfortunately, looking backward toward the federal courts, much of the responsibility for the historic trampling of American Indian due process rights involving their liberty and the land they occupied can first be attributed to the racism of Chief Justice John Marshall and the decisions of the United States Supreme Court.

### The Nineteenth-Century Supreme Court—Title by Conquest

Racism has been characterized as a four-step process. First, it stresses real or imaginary differences between the racist and the victim. Next, subjective values are assigned to the differences in a manner detrimental to the victim. Third, the differences are treated as absolute; and fourth, they are used to justify dishonorable and unjust treatment of the victim by the racist.[2]

In 1823 Chief Justice John Marshall invented and described the United States' imperial doctrine of "title by conquest."[3] Paraphrasing Marshall's theory, the United States was once governed by Britain, and Britain, in turn, acquired title to its British colonies through conquest. When the United States won the Revolutionary War, it automatically acquired all title to the land acquired by the prior British conquest comprising the British colonies, including lands then occupied by Indians. Britain's title, and thus the title acquired by the United States, was absolute. This "title by conquest is acquired and maintained by force." Commencing the first step in the racism process, the chief justice noted the imaginary and inaccurate differences in the Indians. "But the tribes of Indians inhabiting this country were fierce savages, whose occupation was war, and whose subsistence was drawn chiefly from the forest." Thus, the second step—

Chief Justice John Marshall authored the opinion in *Johnson v. M'Intosh* in 1823. Collection
of the Supreme Court of the United States.

Chief Justice Edward Douglas White
authored the opinion in *Lone Wolf v. Hitchcock*
in 1903. Collection of the Supreme
Court of the United States.

assignment of subjective values. Marshall continued, "To leave them in
possession of *their country* was to leave the country a wilderness" (emphasis supplied). Here, the third step—the differences are absolute. "To
govern them as a distinct people was impossible."[4] Then, according to
the false, irrational, and irrelevant thought processes of Justice Marshall
(fourth step), the validity of U.S. title to the land that Britain acquired
by conquest has never been questioned, and "it has been exercised uniformly over territory in possession of the Indians. The existence of this
power must negate the existence of any right which may conflict with,
and control it."[5]

In his opinion the chief justice wrote:

[T]he United States . . . have *unequivocally* acceded to that great and
broad rule by which its civilized inhabitants now hold this country.
They hold, and assert in themselves, the title by which it was acquired.

Associate Justice Harry Blackmun authored the opinion in *United States v. Sioux Nation of Indians* in 1980. Collection of the Supreme Court of the United States.

U.S. District Judge Elmer Scipio Dundy presided in the trial of Ponca chief Standing Bear in Omaha on May 1, 1879. Courtesy Nebraska State Historical Society.

They maintain, as all others have maintained, that discovery gave an exclusive right to extinguish the Indian title of occupancy, either by purchase or by conquest; and gave also a right to such a degree of sovereignty, as the circumstances of the people would allow them to exercise. *The power now possessed by the government of the United States to grant lands, resided, while we were colonies, in the crown or its grantees. The validity of the titles given by either has never been questioned in our courts. It has been exercised uniformly over territory in possession of the Indians.* The existence of this power must negative the existence of any right which may conflict with and control it.[6]

The opinion, and Marshall's attempt to justify it, ignores the Northwest Ordinance of 1787, reaffirmed with slight modification by the U.S. Congress in 1789, which contains unequivocal language that "the utmost good faith shall always be observed towards the Indians; their lands and property shall never be taken from them without their consent; and in their property, rights and liberty they shall never be invaded or disturbed, unless in just and lawful wars authorized by Congress; but laws founded in justice and humanity, shall from time to time be made for preventing wrongs being done to them, and for preserving peace and friendship with them."[7]

Thus, this doctrine of title by conquest, founded upon racism and fallacy, was and continued to be maintained by force, resulting in unjust and dishonorable treatment of the Indians—and constituting a direct conflict with their constitutional rights to liberty and property. The title-by-conquest doctrine has spawned subsequent judicial errors based upon further racial discrimination, making it virtually impossible for the Indians to protect their equal protection and due process rights, as well as their rights under solemn treaties with the United States—treaties that have constitutional status as the "supreme law of the land."[8]

Noted legal scholar Stuart Banner recently provided an articulate and cogent critique of Chief Justice Marshall's opinion creating the doctrine of "title by discovery," in which Banner states that it is "flat wrong," describing the chief justice's opinion as a "wildly inaccurate account of colonial land acquisition." He also accuses Marshall of mistakenly, or in bad faith, substituting the term "conquest" for the term "discovery," stating, "As a factual matter, of course, the country had *not* been acquired and held under any such principle. If anyone was guilty of 'converting the discovery of an inhabited country into conquest,' it was John Marshall in *Johnson v. M'Intosh*, not the British colonists or their government."[9]

### Indian Pupilage

> *The history of Indians and the Bill of Rights is a story of continuity and change. . . . It is a continuing history that must be constantly told and retold.*[10]

"Pupilage" is not something that crawled out of a cocoon. It is a word used by Chief Justice Marshall in 1831[11] to classify the relationship of Cherokee Indians to the United States, a relationship that "resembles that of a ward" (the Indian) "to his guardian" (the United States). No one can say precisely what Marshall meant, but we do know that he used the word intentionally. Cherokee Indians did not voluntarily assume the status of wardship, and in the context of the opinion in *Cherokee Nation v. State of Georgia*, "pupilage" is intended to confer a status of inferiority upon Cherokees and the Cherokee Nation because of race. In 1944 Justice Robert Jackson warned that once a judicial opinion validates a racially discriminative action, it has "for all time validated the principle of racial discrimination. . . . The principle then lies about like a loaded weapon ready for the hand of any authority that can bring forward a plausible claim of an urgent need. . . . All who observe the work of courts are familiar with what Judge Cardozo described as 'the tendency of a principle to expand itself to the limit of its logic.'"[12]

### Pupilage and Judicial Perpetuation of Indian Discrimination

Following the *Cherokee Nation* case,[13] instead of being treated with extra care, honor, and due process, the Cherokees, the wards of the United States who existed in a state of "pupilage," were brutally removed by the U.S. Army to Indian territory in one of the darkest moments of the American republic.[14] Expanding the evil of racism, in 1884 the U.S. Supreme Court denied a Winnebago Indian named John Elk the right to register and vote, finding that Elk was not a citizen, even though he was born in the United States and resided in the city of Omaha.[15]

Adding injury to insult, in 1903 Chief Justice Edward White, who is said to have been a member of the Ku Klux Klan, wrote an opinion stating, "Plenary authority over the tribal relations of the Indians has been exercised by Congress from the beginning, and the power has always been deemed a political one, not subject to be controlled by the judicial department of the government."[16] A plenary power is such that it is complete in every respect, absolute and unqualified. One of the main purposes of our judicial branch and our federal court system is to check and balance the executive branch and Congress and to enforce the rights of minority citizens and persons who are protected by our Fifth Amendment or are interested parties directly affected by the various treaties between the Indian nations and the United States. It was not the Constitution but the imperious and irrational opinion of Chief Justice White that bestowed Congress with plenary power to amend or abdicate Indians' treaty rights—the Constitution has never granted Congress the right to exercise plenary power without due process proceedings.

In 1980 the U.S. Supreme Court, in an opinion by Associate Justice Harry Blackmun, did affirm an award by the U.S. Court of Claims to the Sioux Nation of Indians in the amount of $17.1 million, together with interest from 1877, for the illegal taking of the Black Hills through a treaty of questionable validity.[17]

And in 2009 the U.S. Court of Appeals for the District of Columbia entered a multibillion-dollar judgment resulting from an accounting of Indian trust funds received and held by the government for the benefit of more than 300,000 Indian beneficiaries.[18]

The battles at Rosebud Creek and Little Big Horn in 1876 took place in unceded Indian territory situated in the Wyoming and Montana territories, where federal courts were distant or non-existent, leaving the Lakotas and Cheyennes with four choices when Crook's and Terry's forces entered their treaty lands. They could fight, run, surrender, or attempt to negotiate. In any event, without court intervention they were destined to lose their liberty and their property—and many lives as well. Without the assistance of the federal court system to enforce their due process and treaty rights, the Indians have been deprived of many of their constitutional rights and most of their land.

General John Pope, in 1865, while serving as commander of the Department of Missouri, indicated that senior army officers disliked their orders requiring the army to keep starving Indians on their reservations:

> It is revolting to any humane man to see such things done, and far more so to be required to be the active party to commit violence upon forlorn Indians, who, under pressure of such necessity, only do what any man would do under the circumstances. I desire to say with all emphasis, what every army officer on the frontier will corroborate, that there is no class of men in this country who are so disinclined to war with the Indians as the army stationed among them.[19]

Continuing his attack on the government's Indian policies, General Pope wrote in 1878:

> To the Army officer a state of peace with Indians is, of all things, the most desirable, and no man in all the country east or west would do more to avert an Indian war. To him war with Indians means far more than to anyone else except the actual victim. He sees its beginning in injustice and wrong to the Indian, which he has not the power to prevent; he sees the Indian gradually reach a condition of starvation impossible of longer endurance and thus forced to take what he can get to

save himself from dying of hunger, and cannot help sympathizing with him for doing so; but because he does so the officer is ordered to use force against him. . . . If successful, it is a massacre of Indians; if unsuccessful, it is worthlessness or imbecility, and these judgments confront the Army in every newspaper and in public speeches in Congress and elsewhere—judgments passed by men who are absolutely ignorant of the subject at all, or by those who, knowing better, misrepresent for a purpose.[20]

There simply had to be a better way to facilitate the construction of the transcontinental railroads and accommodate the settlement of the Great Plains and the treaty lands that were occupied by Indians without utilizing the U.S. Army to attack and subjugate them, using the cruel and inhumane concept of total war against outnumbered and defenseless Indian villages, all in violation of their lives and liberty protected by the Fifth Amendment. There was then, and there is today, plenty of land to accommodate the needs of both Indians and non-Indians. As time played out in the nineteenth century, Indians continually wound up with less land and of the poorest quality. If the value of their land increased, methods were devised by the government and private citizens to further displace them—again and again.

On April 15, 2013, our nation was shocked by two explosions that occurred during the annual Boston marathon, killing and severely injuring more than 100 participants. The attack was without warning, unprovoked, and obviously intended by the perpetrators to kill and wound nearby runners and spectators who were not only innocent but vulnerable to death and injury. While the motive may never be entirely determined, the result was not only death and pain but worldwide terror accompanied by immense sorrow and misery. This event is similar to the surprise attacks on the Indian villages at Sand Creek, the Washita River, Wounded Knee, and during the Great Sioux War. Each incident was intentional and involved instruments of war intended to murder and injure innocent and vulnerable victims, thereby creating terror and misery. However, there is one significant difference. The Boston attack was not planned or perpetrated by any civilized organization or rational human being, while the surprise attacks on the Indian villages were each planned and carried out by President Grant and senior officers of the United States Army, notably Generals William T. Sherman and Philip

H. Sheridan, two of the most successful and experienced Union officers of the Civil War, each of whom had taken an oath requiring them to support the Constitution. The sorrow, terror, and misery endured by the families and friends of the Boston marathon victims is in many respects similar to the terror and misery endured by the Indian victims and survivors of the surprise attacks on their villages at Washita and during the Great Sioux War.

The use of the U.S. Army in time of peace to expedite economic and political gain by violating the constitutional rights of persons who are militarily and politically unable to defend themselves is not—and must not be—the American way. It is important to all citizens, and all persons within our boundaries, that we become and remain aware of the history of our government and its relationship with the Indians who lived here for centuries before 1492. The "right to life, liberty, and the pursuit of happiness" are not just idle words contained in the Northwest Ordinance and the Declaration of Independence—they are the essence of our very existence and must be guarded and preserved by the vigilance and determination of all Americans.

One cannot help but feel a sense of remorse for the troopers of the Seventh Cavalry Regiment who died on June 25, 1876, believing that their cause was just and doing what they could to accomplish an objective that, for reasons previously outlined, was impossible and legally and morally outrageous. Much of the post-battle carnage that followed in the process of conquering the remaining Sioux and Cheyennes might well have been avoided if some effort had been made to parley rather than fight—if Grant had made a good faith effort to settle issues with the Indians in a fair and legal manner instead of allowing Sherman to serve on the Indian Peace Commission while he deceived the Lakotas and Cheyennes and pursued his cruel genocidal solution. Unfortunately, Sherman and his co-conspirator Sheridan preferred extermination and total war, and their enforcer, Lt. Colonel Custer, in order to enhance his self-image and corrupt quest for glory, was hell-bent on attacking and killing Indians. The marble headstones of the Seventh Cavalry troopers and the striking Native memorial recently constructed at the Custer Battlefield create a sad but forceful monument to the bitter fight between the U.S. Army and the Indians of the northern plains—and a reminder that liberty and justice do not always come easily.

The word "liberty" is not only embedded in the Fifth Amendment due process clause ("life, liberty and property"), it is the lynchpin of our Pledge of Allegiance ("with liberty and justice for all"), used by all Americans to define their country ("sweet land of liberty") in the widely sung and highly popular hymn "America" ("My Country, 'Tis of Thee"), and since 1776 or thereabouts, the nation's icon has been a 2,000-pound bell made of tin and cooper, on which is inscribed the biblical tribute to independence and liberty, "Proclaim LIBERTY throughout all the Land unto all the Inhabitants thereof. Lev. XXV X."

While writing this epilogue, it suddenly occurred to me that my own life commenced during 1932 in the small town of Scottsbluff, Nebraska, which was created in 1899, twenty-three years after Custer's battle. In 1900 my grandfather Vandenburg built a six-chair barbershop on Broadway, my great-grandfather Wright filed a homestead of 160 acres located at the northeast corner of town, and my grandfather Wright was instrumental in litigation involving the construction of irrigation canals distributing large quantities of water from the North Platte River to irrigate thousands of acres of fertile farmland. In December 1941, I was nine years of age and a student in Miss Lucille Barnett's fourth grade class in the brand new Longfellow Grade School, built by employees of the WPA with federal funds. Each morning my class would stand and recite the Lord's Prayer. Then we would extend our right hand and pledge allegiance to Old Glory, "and to the Republic for Which it Stands—one Nation, indivisible, with liberty and justice for all." After this we sang in unison while Miss Barnett played on her piano "Off We Go, Into the Wild Blue Yonder," "Over Hill Over Dale We have Hit the Dusty Trail," "Anchors Aweigh," "From the Halls of Montezuma," and perhaps "Over There." All of these lots, acres, canals, and Longfellow Grade School were situated on the north side of the North Platte River and were part of the Sioux Nation of Indians' "unceded Indian territory," where "no white persons shall be permitted to settle upon or occupy any portion of the same." Thus, I was born, raised, and had all the benefits of living in this wonderful town located in what its early occupants called "America's Valley of the Nile" on land that rightfully belonged to the Sioux Nation of Indians. Oh yes, our patriotism ran high—still does. But it is tragic that our history lessons did not tell us about due process and the rights of the Plains Indians to the very lands where we were born and raised. God bless 'em—they were our first peoples!

# NOTES

**Foreword**

1. See Colin Woodard, *The Republic of Pirates: Being the True and Surprising Story of the Caribbean Pirates and the Man Who Brought Them Down* (New York: Harcourt Brace, 2008); Jon Latimer, *Buccaneers of the Caribbean: How Piracy Forged an Empire* (Cambridge, MA: Harvard University Press, 2009); Robert Ritchie, *Captain Kidd and the War against Pirates* (Cambridge, MA: Harvard University Press, 1989).
2. See generally, Jennifer K. Elsea and Richard F. Grimmett, *Declarations of War and Authorizations for the Use of Military Force: Historical Background and Legal Implications*, Congressional Research Service, RL31133, March 17, 2011, www.crs.gov.
3. W. A. Graham, *The Custer Myth: A Source Book of Custeriana* (Harrisburg, PA: Stackpole, 1953).
4. Joan Nabseth Stevenson, *Deliverance from the Little Big Horn: Doctor Henry Porter and Custer's Seventh Cavalry* (Norman: University of Oklahoma Press, 2012).
5. Larry McMurtry, *Custer* (New York: Simon & Schuster, 2012).

**Acknowledgments**

1. Power, *Problem from Hell*.

**Introduction**

1. Bradley, *Lidice: Sacrificial Village*, 72–127.
2. Hartigan, *Military Rules*, 15–26.
3. The glossary following the text defines the terms "genocide," "war crimes," "wanton," "internecine war," "attempted crime," "murder," "extermination," "massacre," "person," "citizen," "due process," "military necessity," "total

war," as well as the Lieber Code, the United Nations Convention on the Prevention and Punishment of the Crime of Genocide, and Resolution 1674 adopted by the United Nations Security Council on April 28, 2006.

4. Articles 2 and 3 of the Convention on Prevention and Punishment of the Crime of Genocide.
5. Lemkin, *Totally Unofficial*, xi–xv.
6. Power, *Problem from Hell*, 26–29.
7. Lemkin, *Totally Unofficial*, 112–80.
8. Bourke, *On the Border with Crook*, vi.
9. Winthrop, *Military Law and Precedents*, 876.
10. Act of Congress, July 2, 1862.
11. U.S. Constitution, Fifth Amendment.
12. Article 9, Articles of War, approved by Congress April 10, 1806.
13. *Manual for Courts-Martial*, Art. 90, para. 14c.(2)(a)(i), page IV-19.
14. Sides, *Blood and Terror*, 85–88, 96.
15. Heizer, *Destruction of California Indians*, 243–48; Secrest, *Great Spirit Died*, 23–35.
16. Beck, *First Sioux War*, 52–62.
17. Ibid., 92.
18. Ibid., 108.
19. Greene, *Washita*, 1–5; Hoig, *Sand Creek Massacre*, 152–57.
20. Kelman, *Misplaced Massacre*, 22–25.
21. Ibid., 175–76.
22. Wert, *Custer*, 272.
23. Fifer, *Montana Battlefields*, 30–39.
24. Bennett, *Death, Too*, 107–33.
25. Hutton, *Phil Sheridan*, 222.
26. Ibid., 222–26.

## Chapter 1

1. Monaghan, *Custer*, 4.
2. Wert, *Custer*, 17.
3. Robbins, *Last in Their Class*, 185, n11, taken from "Custer as a Boy," *New York Times*, July 29, 1876.
4. Information about Custer's formative years taken from Monaghan, *Custer*, 4–9; and Wert, *Custer*, 18–23.
5. Robbins, *Last in Their Class*, 187.
6. See *Official Register of the Officers and Cadets of the U.S. Military Academy*,

for the years 1858–1861, inclusive. For each year the register provides the cadet's name, age at admission, "order of merit" (standing) for each class, and the cadet's demerit record for the year and the preceding six months. On separate pages are shown the curriculum for each cadet class, names of instructors, and the textbooks utilized for each course of study.

7. Hardee, *Hardee's Rifle and Light Infantry Tactics*. With respect to the Great Sioux War, "tactics" refers to the arrangement and maneuvering of the Indian forces and Custer's troopers before, during, and after the Battle at the Little Big Horn.

8. Dennis Hart Mahan, *Advanced Guard, Outpost, and Detachment Service of Troops, with the Essential Principles of Strategy and Grand Tactics*, was used widely by officers in both armies during the Civil War.

9. de Jomini, *Art of War*.

10. *Official Register*.

11. Robbins, *Last in Their Class*, ix; Custer's quote is paraphrased by Evan S. Connell in *Son of the Morning Star*, 108.

12. Robbins, *Last in Their Class*, 193.

13. Ibid., 184.

14. Connell, *Son of the Morning Star*, 107–8; *Official Register*.

15. Robbins, *Last in Their Class*, 188 et seq.

16. Wert, *Custer*, 44.

17. Merington, *Custer Story*, 48–49.

18. Monaghan, *Custer*, 61; Wert, *Custer*, 46.

19. Dates and details on Custer's frequent promotions obtained from pages 837–38 of the *Biographical Register of the Officers and Graduates of the U.S. Military Academy*.

20. Wert, *Custer*, 51 et seq.

21. Merington, *Custer Story*, 69.

22. A detailed synopsis of Custer's promotions and battlefield involvement will be found in the *Biographical Register of the Officers and Graduates*, 837–39.

23. "Thus a captain may also be a colonel by brevet, but unless he has been specially assigned to duty according to his brevet rank, and is serving at the time under that assignment, he cannot claim any right of command pertaining to such rank." Winthrop, *Military Law and Precedents*, 756.

24. Smythe, *Guerrilla Warrior*, 125.

25. Longacre, *Cavalry at Gettysburg*, 200–53.

26. *Biographical Register of Officers and Graduates*, 837–39.

27. Utley, *Cavalier in Buckskin*, 29.

28. Dustin, *Custer Tragedy*, 16.

29. Merington, *Custer Story*, 159.

30. Utley, *Cavalier in Buckskin*, 35.

31. Connell, *Son of the Morning Star*, 113.

32. Wert, *Custer*, 121–22.

33. A detailed account of Custer's involvement at Trevilian Station is provided in Wert, *Custer*, 162–65.

34. Coffman, *Old Army*, 219.

35. *Biographical Register of Officers and Graduates*, 837, 839.

36. Wert, *Custer*, 243.

37. Reno, *Reno and Apsaalooka*, 77.

38. Ibid., 85.

39. DuMont, *Custer Battle Guns*, 25.

40. Shockley, *Trap-Door Springfield*, 6.

41. Waite and Ernst, *Trap-Door Springfield*, 18.

42. Reno, *Reno and Apsaalooka*, 101–2.

43. Ibid., 125.

44. Conversation with noted historian John McDermott, who filed an evidentiary affidavit in support of Reno in these proceedings. See Reno, *Reno and Apsaalooka*, 273–303.

## Chapter 2

1. Dippie, *Nomad*, from an article written by Custer that was published in the *Sportsmen's Journal*.

2. Chandler, *Of Garryowen in Glory*, 2. It is interesting to note that "wrongs" were committed by "whites," but "atrocities" were committed by "Indians."

3. Utley, *Frontier Regulars*, 13–14.

4. Hirshson, *White Tecumseh*, 3–7.

5. Coffman, *Old Army*, 371–75.

6. Utley, *Frontier Regulars*, 19, 21–22.

7. Kautz, *1865 Customs of Service*, 275, para. 529.

8. Monaghan, *Custer*, 281.

9. Coffman, *Old Army*, 347.

10. McDermott, *Crook's 1876 Campaigns*, 80; see Custer's letter to *New York Herald*, dated June 22, 1876, in John Gray, *Centennial Campaign*, 146.

11. Utley, *Frontier Regulars*, 86–87; Rickey, *Forty Miles*, 88–115.

12. Coffman, *Old Army*, 171.

13. Rickey, *Forty Miles*, 122, 124.

14. Wert, *Custer*, 233–34; letter to Jenny Barnitz, dated May 11, 1867 in Utley, *Life in Custer's Cavalry*, 52; Utley, *Cavalier in Buckskin*, 50.

15. Graham, *Custer Myth*, 157.

16. Carroll, *Benteen-Goldin Letters*, 266–67; John Gray, *Centennial Campaign*, 153.

17. Monaghan, *Custer*, 282–83.

18. Wert, *Custer*, 248; Utley, *Cavalier in Buckskin*, 107–8.

19. Monaghan, *Custer*, 283; see also Brian W. Dippie, "Custer the Indian Fighter," 109.

20. Utley, *Life in Custer's Cavalry*, 50.

21. Ibid., letter from Albert to Jennie, 51–52.

22. The mathematics are quite simple. A properly conditioned and packed mule could carry a pack weighing 275 pounds. See Bourke, *On the Border*, 153–54. The mule, without grass, required twenty pounds of grain each day. Thus, the poor beast could carry only sufficient feed to satisfy his own needs for less than two weeks. See *Cavalry School*, vol. 2, part 3, para. 99–100, pp. 115–16 relative to field rations for horses and mules.

23. Wyman, *Wild Horse*, 115; William Carter, *U.S. Cavalry Horse*, 160.

24. Nichols, *Reno Court of Inquiry*, 387, testimony of Sgt. F. A. Culbertson, A Company, Seventh Cavalry Regiment.

25. Chalfant, *Hancock's War*, 75.

26. Ibid., 171, 190.

27. Monaghan, *Custer*, 289.

28. Dippie, *Nomad*, 11.

29. Ibid., 121n15.

30. Ibid.

31. Lewis, *Sherman*, 572–73.

32. Monaghan, *Custer*, 289 et seq.

33. Chalfant, *Hancock's War*, 312.

34. Merington, *Custer Story*, 204, reciting Custer's notes of that date.

35. Utley, *Life in Custer's Cavalry*, 44, 161, letter of Albert Barnitz. Barnitz is also quoted in Connell, *Son of the Morning Star*, 150.

36. Connell, *Son of the Morning Star*, 49; Frost, *Court-Martial*, 35.

37. Monaghan, *Custer*, 296.

38. Frost, *Court-Martial*, 151–55, testimony of Lt. Thomas W. Custer.

39. Wert, *Custer*, 258, quoting from Elizabeth Custer, *Tenting on the Plains*, 581–82.

40. Utley, *Cavalier in Buckskin*, 51.

41. Ibid., 48, 51.

42. Ibid., map on p. 48.

43. Johnson and Allan, *Dispatch to Custer*, 30.

44. Utley, *Cavalier in Buckskin*, 52.

45. Monaghan, *Custer*, 297.

46. Utley, *Cavalier in Buckskin*, 53.

47. Wert, *Custer*, 262–63; Frost, *Court-Martial*, 99–100, 245-46; 1863 Articles of War.

48. Kautz, *1865 Customs of Service*, 230–31.

49. Frost, *Court-Martial*, 254. The letter of November 18 from Sheridan to Custer is part of Frost's personal collection.

50. George Custer, *My Life*, 143.

51. Wert, *Custer*, 267–68.

52. Monaghan, *Custer*, 306.

53. Greene, *Washita*, 94.

54. Chalfant, *Hancock's War*, 465.

55. Greene, *Washita*, 72, 227n20.

56. Ibid., 71.

57. Ibid., 72.

58. Ibid., 107.

59. Statement of Magpie, a sixteen-year-old Cheyenne who was present in Black Kettle's village when Custer attacked; recorded on September 19, 1930, by Charles Brill at the site of the battle, reproduced in Hardorff, *Washita Memories*, 302–9. Narratives of scout Ben Clark reported in ibid., 202–36.

60. Hoig, *Battle of the Washita*, 94, 126–27.

61. Greene, *Washita*, 102n12, indicates that there were approximately 6,000 other Indians in the vicinity of Black Kettle's camp.

62. Michael Mooney, *Army Magazine*.

63. Greene, *Washita*, 136–37. The exact number killed and wounded and the breakdown between warriors, women, and children remains in doubt today. Estimates of killed range from 104 warriors (Custer) to 13 (George Bent) and 13 women and children (Bent) to 75 (Ben Clark). The author estimates that the ratio of 1 to 1, killed to wounded, is reasonable.

64. Hardorff, *Washita Memories*, 131, report of 1st Lt. Edward S. Godfrey.

65. Ibid., 143, report of Edward S. Godfrey.

66. Hoig, *Battle of Washita*, 154.

67. Hardorff, *Washita Memories*, 153–54, eyewitness account of 2nd Lt. M. Gibson.

68. *In re Yamashita*, 327 U.S. 1 (1946).

69. Hardorff, *Washita Memories*, 174–77, letter of Frederick Benteen to William J. DeGresse, dated December 22, 1868.

70. Ibid., 209–10, 226, report of the scout Ben Clark in an interview given to the *New York Sun* on May 14, 1899.

71. Greene, *Washita*, 187–88.

72. Wert, *Custer*, 277.

73. Greene, *Washita*, 187–88, 260n9–11; Utley, *Cavalier in Buckskin*, 75–76.

74. Hoig, *Washita*, 184–95.

75. Utley, *Cavalier in Buckskin*, 103.

76. Monaghan, *Custer*, 351.

77. Ibid., 243.

78. Stewart, *Custer's Luck*, 58, extract from the personal memoirs of General Stanley.

79. John Gray, *Centennial Campaign*, 100–101.

80. American Articles of War, Art. 41, enacted as of June 22, 1874, provides, "Any officer who, by any means whatsoever occasions false alarms in camp, garrison or quarters shall suffer death, or such other punishment as a court martial shall direct." See also Winthrop, *Military Law and Precedents* 2: 987.

## Chapter 3

1. George Custer, *My Life*, 22.

2. White, "Winning of the West," 321.

3. Grinnell, *Cheyenne Indians*, 1.

4. 1868 Treaty of Fort Laramie, Art. 2, 15 Stat. 635.

5. White, "Winning of the West," 321.

6. George Hyde, *Red Cloud's Folk*, 3–5.

7. Information on map 1 was obtained from the "Map of Sioux Migrations, 1680–1820," in Hanson, *Northwest Nebraska's Indian People*, 26, 30, 32; it was supplemented by information contained in White, "Winning of the West," 319–43.

8. White, "Winning of the West," 184.

9. Ibid., 321–28.

10. Hassrick, *Sioux*, 68.

11. Joseph Marshall, *Lakota Way*, 9.

12. Hassrick, *Sioux*, 32–54.

13. Powell, *Sweet Medicine*, 19–23.

14. Berthrong, *Southern Cheyennes*, 9.

15. Hanson, *Northwest Nebraska's Indian People*; Berthrong, *Southern Cheyennes*, 14; Powell, *Sweet Medicine*, 25–27; George Hyde, *Indians of the High Plains*, 143–44.

16. Grinnell, *Cheyenne Indians*, 253; Powell, *Sweet Medicine*, 28.

17. Grinnell, *Fighting Cheyennes*, 218–20; Greene, *Washita*, 26–27.
18. Stands in Timber and Liberty, *Cheyenne Memories*, 59.
19. Berthrong, *Southern Cheyennes*, 41–43.
20. Hassrick, *Sioux*, 33.
21. White, "Winning of the West," 329.
22. Bogy, *1866 Report*, 4.
23. Isenberg, *Destruction of the Bison*, 20; source attributed to James Mooney, *Aboriginal Population*, 13; see Bray, "Teton Sioux," 165–88, which provides more conservative numbers on the Lakota population.
24. McDermott, *Guide to the Indian Wars*, 68–70.
25. Bray, *Northern Nation*.
26. Beck, *Inkpaduta*, 135–39.
27. Utley, *Lance and Shield*, 26 et seq.
28. Bray, *Northern Nation*; see also Bray, *Crazy Horse*, 68, 152.
29. Powers, *Killing of Crazy Horse*, 17; Hassrick, *Sioux*, 7.
30. Dee Brown, *Fetterman Massacre*, 177–83; Shannon Smith, *Give Me Eighty Men*, 105.
31. Olson, *Red Cloud*, 218–22.
32. Irving, *Captain Bonneville*, 164–65. Crow Country includes the area where the Little Big Horn River flows into the Bighorn River.
33. McDermott, "Custer," 98n17.
34. Chandler, *Of Garryowen in Glory*, 45–46.
35. Statutes at Large, Treaties and Proclamations of the United States of America from December 1863 to December 1865, Act admitting Montana Territory, 38th Congress, 1st Sess., Ch. 95, Sec. 17, pp. 91–92.

## Chapter 4

1. Declaration of Independence, in Congress, July 4, 1776. While this declaration does not have the status of a United States law, it was utilized by the Continental Congress to initiate the successful revolution from England and served as a guideline for defining the people's civil rights and liberty contained in the Fifth and Fourteenth Amendments to the U.S. Constitution.
2. Fifth Amendment, U.S. Constitution.
3. *Olmstead v. United States*, 277 U.S. 438, 485 (1928), VanDevelder, *Savages and Scoundrels*.
4. Chaky, *Terrible Justice*, 136–41.
5. U.S. War Department, *1863 Laws of War*.
6. Morris, "Laws of War," 9–13.

7. Ibid.

8. Edwards, *Hugo Grotius*, 199.

9. 1868 Treaty of Fort Laramie, Article 16, provided that this land "shall be held and considered unceded Indian territory . . . and no white person shall be permitted to settle upon . . . or without the consent of the Indians first had and obtained, to pass through the same."

10. In the war with Mexico (1847), Maj. Gen. Winfield Scott (also a lawyer) was ordered to pillage Mexican farms and villages to provide support for his troops. Disobeying the order, Scott directed his army to pay reasonable prices for all provisions taken from the Mexican citizens and drew up a martial conduct order that helped win over the Mexican population to his side.

11. U.S. War Department, *1863 Laws of War*.

12. U.S. Constitution, Article I, Section 8. Only Congress has the power "to declare war."

13. Pound, *Development of Constitutional Guarantees*, v.

14. Guice, *Rocky Mountain Bench*.

15. U.S. Statutes at Large, 4:411–12, May 28, 1830.

16. Prucha, *American Indian Treaties*, 6.

17. Wallace, *Jefferson and the Indians*, 295–96.

18. Lucy Cohen, *Legal Conscience*, 242; Northwest Ordinance, July 13, 1787.

19. After being proclaimed by President Jefferson, the treaty was first published on the front page of the *National Intelligencer* on November 2, 1803. The original document is owned by Walter Scott, Jr., and is displayed at the Joslyn Art Museum in Omaha, Nebraska.

20. Cohen, *Legal Conscience*, 280.

21. See Mapp, *Elusive West*.

22. Drinnon, *Facing West*, 89. The quote is from a letter by Jefferson to Indiana Governor William Henry Harrison, February 27, 1803.

23. Owens, *Mr. Jefferson's Hammer*, 58–68.

24. Wallace, *Jefferson and the Indians*, 19–20; Owens, *Mr. Jefferson's Hammer*, 65, 76, 79, 81, 89–91.

25. Wallace, *Jefferson and the Indians*, 225; Owens, *Mr. Jefferson's Hammer*.

26. Remini, *Andrew Jackson*, 15.

27. Satz, *American Indian Policy*, 101, see 117n9.

28. House Executive Document No. 2, 32nd Congress, 1st Sess., serial 636, pp. 273–74, reported in Prucha, *Indian Policy*, 85.

29. Anne Hyde, *Empires, Nations and Families*, 416–21.

30. Senate Executive Document No. 5, 34th Congress, 3rd Sess., serial 875, pp. 571–75, reported in Prucha, *Indian Policy*, 89–91.

## Chapter 5

1. Senate Report No. 156, 39th Congress, 2d Sess., serial 1279, pp. 3–10, report of the Joint Special Committee of Congress (the "Doolittle Committee"), dated January 26, 1867.
2. Cox-Paul, "Chivington," 132.
3. Greene and Scott, *Finding Sand Creek*, 22.
4. McDermott, *Circle of Fire*, 18–19, 33–34; McDermott, *Red Cloud's War*.
5. See Greene, "Hayfield Fight."
6. Dee Brown, *Fetterman Massacre*, 13 et seq.; Shannon Smith, *Give Me Eighty Men*, 85; John Monnett, *Hundred Soldiers*, 124–33.
7. Axelrod, *Chronicle*, 203.
8. McDermott, *Red Cloud's War*, 275–76, letter from Sherman to Cooke.
9. Lewis, *Sherman*, 429.
10. Killoren, *Come Blackrobe*, 297.
11. Thorndike, *Sherman Letters*, 287.
12. Ibid., 285–86.
13. House Executive Document No. 97, 40th Congress, 2d Sess., serial 1337, pp. 15–22, report of the Indian Peace Commission, January 7, 1868.
14. Kappler, *Indian Affairs*, 2: 998–1003.
15. McDermott, *Red Cloud's War*, 524–25.
16. Crawford, *Exploits of Ben Arnold*, 170.
17. Kappler, *Indian Affairs*; 1868 Treaty of Fort Laramie, art. 2.
18. The term "unceded Indian territory" means first, that it is Sioux "Indian territory," and second, that it has not been ceded by the Sioux to anyone else.
19. Kappler, *Indian Affairs*, 2: 998–1003; 1868 Treaty of Fort Laramie, art. 16.
20. Ostler, *Lakotas and Black Hills*, 63n9.
21. *United States v. Sioux Nation of Indians*, 448 U.S. 371, 379, 100 S.Ct. 2716 (1980) (emphasis supplied).
22. *Washington v. Fishing Vessel Ass'n*, 443 U.S. 658 (1979); *Jones v. Meehan*, 175 U.S. 1 (1899).
23. McDermott, *Red Cloud's War*, 499, citing Department of the Platte Circular to Commanding Officers, August 29, 1868.
24. Thorndike, *Sherman Letters*, 321.
25. Kennedy, *On the Plains*, 146n2. Kennedy writes that this final paragraph was omitted from the Sherman letter of September 23, 1868, that Rachel Sherman Thorndike (William T. Sherman's daughter) published in *The Sherman Letters*.

26. Bunting, *Ulysses S. Grant*, 119–20.

27. Mark Brown, *Plainsmen of the Yellowstone*, 196–200.

28. Hedren, *Fort Laramie*, 8–10.

29. McDermott, *Gold Rush*, 5.

30. See Lubetkin, *Jay Cooke's Gamble*.

31. McDermott, *Gold Rush*, 8–14.

32. Ibid., 12–13.

33. Lazarus, *Black Hills/White Justice*, 74.

34. Ibid., 80; Hutton, *Phil Sheridan*, 297–99.

35. Unrefuted evidence presented to the U.S. Court of Claims, *Sioux Nation of Indians v. United States*, 601 F.2d 1157, 1164 (1979); McDermott, *Gold Rush*, 20–22.

36. Quote taken from Bunting, *Ulysses S. Grant*, 119–20.

37. *Webster's New World Collegiate Dictionary*, 247.

38. John Gray, *Centennial Campaign*, 24; see also John Gray, *Custer's Last Campaign*; LaVelle, "Rescuing Paha Sapa," 46n29; *United States v. Sioux Nation of Indians*, 448 U.S. 371, 379; Hutton, *Phil Sheridan*, 298–300.

39. House Executive Document No. 184, report of E. C. Watkins dated November 9, 1875, entitled "Military Expedition against the Sioux Indians," 8–9.

40. *United States v. Sioux Nation*, 207 Ct. Cl. 234 (1975), exhibit in Appendix C of reply brief of Sioux Nation in Court of Claims No. 148-78, at p. 60.

41. Crawford, *Exploits of Ben Arnold*, 239.

42. Lazarus, *Black Hills/White Justice*, 85. Arthur Lazarus, Jr., served as legal counsel for the Sioux Tribe for a period of twenty-three years as it pursued Sioux claims against the United States over the loss of the Black Hills. His son, Edward L. Lazarus, a graduate of Yale Law School, served as law clerk for Supreme Court Justice Harry Blackmun, who wrote the majority opinion for the Supreme Court in the 1980 case of *United States v. Sioux Nation of Indians*, 448 U.S. 371 (1980), which affirmed an award of seventeen million dollars of additional compensation and interest to the Sioux Tribe for the taking of the Black Hills. As of this date the Sioux Indians have spurned and rejected the award, claiming that the proper remedy is to return the "Great Sioux Reservation" to the Sioux Nation of Indians.

43. Lazarus, *Black Hills/White Justice*, 85.

## Chapter 6

1. Merington, *Custer Story*, 277.

2. John Gray, *Custer's Last Campaign*, 125; John Gray, *Centennial Campaign*, 90.

3. Mangum, *Battle of the Rosebud*, 20, 97; Utley, *Frontier Regulars*, 251; McDermott, *Crook's 1876 Campaigns*, 46; Robinson, *General Crook*, 166, 179.

4. Wert, *Custer*, 324n24.

5. Robinson, *Diaries of Bourke*, 164.

6. Vaughn, *Reynolds Campaign*, 29–42. See also McDermott, *Crook's 1876 Campaigns*, 13–17.

7. Robinson, *Diaries of Bourke*, 255; McDermott, *Crook's 1876 Campaigns*, 14.

8. Vaughn, *Reynolds Campaign*, 61.

9. Ibid., 130–31.

10. McDermott, *Crook's 1876 Campaigns*, 14.

11. Vaughn, *Reynolds Campaign*, 97; Marquis, *Wooden Leg*, 164–67.

12. John Gray, *Centennial Campaign*, 56.

13. McDermott, *Crook's 1876 Campaigns*, 15.

14. Greene, *Lakota and Cheyenne*, 7–8; Marquis, *Wooden Leg*, 167–68.

15. John Gray, *Centennial Campaign*, 57; Bourke, *On the Border*, 261–62.

16. McDermott, *Crook's 1876 Campaigns*, 24.

17. See Mangum, *Battle of the Rosebud*, 20, regarding the time and distance involved in transmitting a telegram via Fort Fetterman to General Terry via Fort Abraham Lincoln.

18. McDermott, *Crook's 1876 Campaigns*, 27.

19. Ibid., 31; Mangum, *Battle of the Rosebud*, 51–52.

20. Bray, *Crazy Horse*, 310–13; McLaughlin, *My Friend*, 30–32.

21. Utley, *Lance and Shield*, 138.

22. McDermott, *Crook's 1876 Campaigns*, 31.

23. Ibid., 43–44, Crook's report to Sheridan, dated June 19, 1876.

24. Mangum, *Battle of the Rosebud*, 87–88n24, 166–67.

25. Shockley, *Trap-Door Springfield*, 18.

26. Mangum, *Battle of the Rosebud*, 97.

## Chapter 7

1. Barnett, *Touched by Fire*, 283, citing Sheridan to Terry, May 16, 1876.

2. Ibid., 283.

3. Elizabeth Custer, *Boots and Saddles*, 268.

4. Darling, *Sad and Terrible Blunder*, 77, quoting directly from the diary of Dr. DeWolf; Knight, *Following the Indian Wars*. This may account for Terry's reluctance to lead the attack against the Indians.

5. John Gray, *Centennial Campaign*, 80–81.

6. John Gray, *Custer's Last Campaign*, 183.

7. Reno, *Reno and Apsaalooka*, 140.

8. John Gray, *Centennial Campaign*, 136–37.

9. Darling, *Sad and Terrible Blunder*, 48–56.

10. Mangum, *Battle of the Rosebud*, 46.

11. Vaughn, *With Crook*, 8.

12. Reno, *Reno and Apsaalooka*, 128. Material in quotes taken from a letter written by Major Reno to his son Ross following his dishonorable discharge from the army.

13. It should be noted that while Terry chose not to include Reno (who was Custer's number two) at the meeting, Reno had obtained Terry's only reliable intelligence concerning the Indians' strength and location.

14. Graham, *Custer Myth*, 243; letter dated July 4, 1876, from Lieutenant Varnum to his parents.

15. Evidence concerning Custer's refusal to take Gatling guns and part of Gibbon's Second Cavalry with him is all hearsay and definitely not "pig iron under water." However, it was mentioned by various officers after the battle. See ibid., 147, entitled "General Godfrey's narrative"; Utley, *Cavalier in Buckskin*, 176; Dustin, *Custer Tragedy*, 94.

16. See Michno, *Lakota Noon*, 3–20; Utley, *Cavalier in Buckskin*, 179; John Gray, *Centennial Campaign*, 153–54, 346–57.

17. Carroll, *General Custer*, 14; report of James S. Hastings, United States Indian agent, Red Cloud Agency, Nebraska, dated April 3, 1876.

## Chapter 8

1. Walker, *Henry R. Porter*, 55.

2. John Gray, *Centennial Campaign*, 146.

3. Ibid., 146.

4. From the definition of "genocide" in Convention on Prevention and Punishment of the Crime of Genocide, adopted by the General Assembly of the United Nations on December 9, 1948.

5. Elizabeth Custer, *Boots and Saddles*, 275.

6. Walker, *Henry R. Porter*, 55.

7. Merington, *Custer Story*, 306.

8. To avoid criticism from General Sheridan and the press over the wide discretion given to Custer, Terry may have inserted this paragraph in the order after Custer's death. See Darling, *Sad and Terrible Blunder*, 67.

9. Godfrey, "Custer's Last Battle," 273–75.

10. Stewart, *Custer's Luck*, 253n61; Holley, *Once Their Home*, 262. Various spellings of "Gerard" exist, including "Girard."

11. Darling, *Sad and Terrible Blunder*, 1–3; Connell, *Son of the Morning Star*, 256–57.
12. Godfrey, "Custer's Last Battle," 276–77; Graham, *Custer Myth*, 134–35; John Gray, *Custer's Last Campaign*, 208.
13. Dustin, *Custer Tragedy*, 94; Stewart, *Custer's Luck*, 254.
14. Godfrey, *Custer's Last Campaign*, 35.
15. Kautz, *1865 Customs of Service*, 317 (emphasis supplied).

**Chapter 9**

1. McClernand, *On Time for Disaster*, 165; report of Lieutenant Wallace.
2. Revised U.S. Army Regulations, para. 656.
3. John Gray, *Centennial Campaign*, 162.
4. Ibid., 164.
5. Brininstool, *Troopers with Custer*, 11–13; Dustin, *Custer Tragedy*, 103.
6. See John Gray, *Custer's Last Campaign*, 220–21, which also provides good reasons for Custer's conduct in taking the direct route west following the Indians' obvious trail.
7. Ibid., 225.
8. Ibid., 224–26.
9. Libby, *Arikara Narrative*, 86, attributed to the Arikara scout Red Star.
10. Monaghan, *Custer*, 78.
11. Wert, *Custer*, 53.

**Chapter 10**

1. Graham, *Custer Myth*, 136, General Godfrey's narrative.
2. Utley, *Cavalier in Buckskin*, 181; John Gray, *Centennial Campaign*, 170; Godfrey, *Custer's Last Campaign*, 43.
3. Godfrey, *Custer's Last Campaign*, 43–44; John Gray, *Centennial Campaign*, 169–71; Utley, *Cavalier in Buckskin*, 181–82.
4. See map 5.
5. Darling, *Sad and Terrible Blunder*, 149.
6. John Gray, *Centennial Campaign*, 172, 178; Wert, *Custer*, 342; Nichols, *Reno Court of Inquiry*, 403; Scott, Fox et al., *Archaeological Perspectives*, 49–50.
7. See map 5.
8. Nichols, *Reno Court of Inquiry*, 431–32.
9. Ibid.
10. Darling, *Benteen's Scout*, 4.
11. John Gray, *Custer's Last Campaign*, 258–61; Utley, *Frontier Regulars*, 258; Darling, *Benteen's Scout*, xv; Utley, *Cavalier in Buckskin*, 197–98.

12. Ladenheim, *Custer's Thorn*, 167.

13. John Gray, *Custer's Last Campaign*, 251.

14. Ibid., 251, table 5.

15. Utley, *Cavalier in Buckskin*, 183.

16. Nichols, *Reno Court of Inquiry*, 561; testimony of Reno.

17. Darling, *Final Hours*, 9.

18. Nichols, *Reno Court of Inquiry*, 216; testimony of Capt. Myles Moylan, 19; testimony of 1st Lt. George D. Wallace.

19. John Gray, *Centennial Campaign*, 272–73.

20. Ibid., 318.

21. Ibid., 278, 294.

22. Marquis, *Wooden Leg*, 221, 223–24.

23. Bouyer, the son of a French trapper and a Santee Sioux mother, was fluent in Native languages and served as an interpreter, chief guide, and scout for Custer at Little Big Horn, where he was killed. John Gray, *Custer's Last Campaign*, 373–75.

24. Utley, *Cavalier in Buckskin*, 187; Hammer, *Custer in '76*, 166, 172. Bouyer saw the retreat and told Custer and Curley.

25. Andrist, *Long Death*, 283; Hammer, *Custer in '76*, 101, statement of trumpeter John Martin to Walter Camp.

26. Nichols, *Reno Court of Inquiry*, 633–35, see exhibit 1 of Major Reno to the president of the court-martial board, June 22, 1878, and attachment no. 1 to the exhibit contains a news release with a copy of the scurrilous accusations of Frederick Whittaker dated May 18, 1878; Reno, *Reno and Apsaalooka*, 156, 171–72, 288; Nichols, *In Custer's Shadow*, 362; King, *Massacre*, 29.

27. Nichols, *Reno Court of Inquiry*, testimony of Lt. Luther Hare, 295–97, Lt. George Wallace, 52; John Gray, *Custer's Last Campaign*, 289.

28. King, *Massacre*, 29.

29. Darling, *Final Hours*, 9–10.

30. See Ladenheim, *Custer's Thorn*, 197.

31. Graham, *Custer Myth*, undated letter of Capt. R. G. Carter, 302–5.

32. Clausewitz, *On War*, 271; see also Graham, *Custer Myth*, 311–13, letter of Graham dated March 30, 1925, supporting Reno's decisions and actions; cf. letter of Sgt. John M. Ryan, dated June 22, 1923, at 243–45.

33. Transporting the wounded was a slow, painful, and laborious affair. After the battle ended, one writer noted that, "transport by hand litter took 150 men six hours just to move the first three miles, with the injured shrieking in agony." Ladenheim, *Custer's Thorn*, 197.

34. Graham, *Custer Myth*, 116.

35. John Gray, *Custer's Last Campaign*, 185–89.
36. Hammer, *Custer in '76*, 92.
37. Utley, *Cavalier in Buckskin*, 186.
38. Nichols, *Reno Court of Inquiry*, testimony of Capt. Frederick Benteen, 404.
39. Hammer, *Custer in '76*, 93.
40. Utley, *Cavalier in Buckskin*, 186; comment overheard by the messenger Kanipe.
41. Ibid., 185.
42. Hammer, *Custer in '76*, 99–105, Camp's two interviews of the trumpeter, John Martin.
43. Ibid., 153; statements by George B. Herendeen, quoted by Graham, *Custer Myth*, 260.

## Chapter 11

1. McLaughlin, *My Friend*, 166. Beautiful White Cow was also called "Pretty White Buffalo" by other translators.
2. Hardorff, *Indian Views*, 35 (Crazy Horse, May 24, 1877); 45 (White Bull, Brave Wolf, and Hump, June 27, 1878); Hammer, *Custer in '76*, 197–216 (Foolish Elk, Turtle Rib, Black Bear, He Dog, Flying By, White Bull, Tall Bull, and Standing Bear); Jensen, *Indian Interviews*, 203 (Black Bear), 205 (He Dog).
3. Jensen, *Indian Interviews*, 310 (Standing Bear [the Lakota]).
4. Hardorff, *Lakota Recollections*, 164.
5. Ibid., 179.
6. Ibid., 188.
7. McLaughlin, *My Friend*, 172.
8. Hardorff, *Lakota Recollections*, Eli Ricker interview of Hunkpapa warrior Black Hawk, 63–64.
9. DeMallie, *Sixth Grandfather*, 180–81.
10. Graham, *Custer Myth*, 75.
11. Michno, *Lakota Noon*, 25.
12. Hammer, *Custer in '76*, 203–4.
13. Scott, Fox, and Harmon, *Archaeological Insights*; Scott, Fox et al., *Archaeological Perspectives*.
14. DuMont, *Custer Battle Guns*, 58.

## Chapter 12

1. Service, *Complete Poems*, 228.
2. Scott and Bleed, *Good Walk*, 36; Collins et al., *Sioux Wars*, map no. 23.

3. Greene, *Evidence*, 20–23.

4. Scott and Bleed, *Good Walk*, 36–37, 40.

5. Greene, *Evidence*, 27.

6. See map 10.

7. Fox, *Archaeology, History*, 280.

8. Utley, *Cavalier in Buckskin*, 182, 196; John Gray, *Centennial Campaign*, 147; McDermott, *Guide to the Indian Wars*, 49, 51–52, 55.

9. The aerial map was prepared at the author's request in 2007, utilizing information obtained from the 1984–1985 archaeological surveys of the Little Big Horn Battlefield by Douglas C. Scott, then chief of the Rocky Mountain Research Division, Midwest Archaeological Center, National Park Service, Lincoln, Nebraska.

10. Fox, *Archaeology, History*, figures 6-12 and 6-13; Scott, Fox, et al., *Archaeological Perspectives*, 120, 122, figures 37 and 38.

11. John Gray, *Custer's Last Campaign*, 371–72.

12. We are indeed fortunate to have the results of brilliant archaeological studies conducted in 1983, 1984, and 1985. The results are displayed, mapped, and analyzed by Scott, Fox, and Harmon in *Archaeological Insights*. The boundary areas surrounding the Custer and Reno-Benteen Battlefields are addressed by Scott and Bleed, *Good Walk*.

13. Scott, Fox, et al., *Archaeological Perspectives*, 26–32.

14. Scott, Fox, and Harmon, *Archaeological Insights*, 55–81.

15. Ibid., xii.

16. Prepared by locating the four corners of the marble headstones shown on map 15 in relation to Calhoun Coulee, Calhoun Hill, and Last Stand Hill.

17. Scott, Fox, et al., *Archaeological Perspectives*, chapter 5.

18. Ibid., 88.

19. Hardorff, *Lakota Recollections*, 30.

20. Michno, *Lakota Noon*, 183; Fox, *Archaeology, History*, 278–79 et seq.

21. Clausewitz, *On War*, 357.

22. Ibid., 404–8.

23. Scott, Fox et al., *Archaeological Perspectives*, 123.

24. Ibid., 130.

25. Nichols, *Reno Court of Inquiry*, 417.

26. John Gray, *Custer's Last Campaign*, 372.

27. Scott, Willey, and Connor, *They Died With Custer*, 12–13.

28. Scott, Fox et al., *Archaeological Perspectives*, 278; Jensen, *Indian Interviews*, 310 (Standing Bear [the Lakota]), 314 (Iron Hawk).

29. Marquis, *Wooden Leg*, 232–33; Hammer, *Custer in '76*, 202 (Turtle Rib), 199 (Foolish Elk).

30. See Michno, *Lakota Noon*, 279, 281, naming twenty-one Indians killed and identifying the Indian informant.
31. Hardorff, *Hokahey!*
32. Hardorff, *Camp*, 84, interview with Hunkpapa warrior Good Voice[d] Elk.
33. John Gray, *Custer's Last Campaign*, 290.
34. Michno, *Lakota Noon*, 287–92.
35. Rankin, *Legacy*, 121.
36. Service, "The Quitter," *Complete Poems*, 228.

## Chapter 13

1. John Gray, *Centennial Campaign*, 181.
2. At Reno's request, the army convened a court of inquiry on January 13, 1879, to inquire into the conduct of Major Reno at the Little Big Horn. Reno Court of Inquiry, abstract of proceedings convened at Chicago, IL, on November 25, 1878, by direction of the president on the application of Maj. Marcus A. Reno in Graham, *Reno Court of Inquiry*, iv–vii.
3. John Gray, *Centennial Campaign*, 181.
4. Graham, *Custer Myth*, 145, narrative of Gen. Edward S. Godfrey.
5. Reno, *Reno and Apsaalooka*, 149.
6. Hardorff, *Indian Views*, 69, from an interview appearing in the *Leavenworth Times* on August 14, 1881.
7. Nichols, *Reno Court of Inquiry*, 646, exhibit no. 5.
8. Reno, *Reno and Apsaalooka*, 152.
9. Ibid., 153.
10. Ibid., 151.

## Chapter 14

1. Clausewitz, *On War*, 204.
2. The basic fundamentals of combat operations, the "general rules to aid commanders . . . throughout all stages of tactical planning and in the execution of combat operations," are summarized in detail in *Theory and Dynamics*, 25–61. Combat maneuvers are contained in Craighill, *1862 Pocket Companion*, 76–83.
3. *Revised Regulations of 1861*.
4. Ibid., paras. 656, 658, and 678.
5. Hardee taught during Custer's fifth-, fourth-, and third-class years (1858–1860), and Mahan's materials were used all four years (1857–1861). See

*Official Register*, June 1861, p. 19; June 1859, p. 18; June 1860, p. 18; May 1861, p. 18; May and June 1861, p. 17.

6. Mahan, *Elementary Treatise*, 57, para. 143.

7. Ibid., para. 144.

8. Ibid., 58, para. 145.

9. Ibid., 105, para. 292.

10. Ibid., para. 293.

11. Ibid., 114, para. 320.

12. Kautz, *1865 Customs of Service*.

13. Ibid., 56, para. 95.

14. Ibid., 327, para. 671.

15. Ibid., 332, para. 684.

16. Ibid., 335, para. 691.

17. Ibid., 368, para. 774.

18. Information on Custer's courses of study and textbooks obtained from the *Official Register* for the years 1860 and 1861.

19. Jomini, *Art of War*, 275.

20. Clausewitz, *On War*, 117.

21. Ibid., 204.

22. Ibid., 198.

23. Ibid., 170.

24. Ibid., 171.

25. Sun Tzu, *Art of War*.

26. Ibid., 65.

27. Sides, *Ghost Soldiers*.

28. Ibid., 24.

29. All the information concerning the rescue was taken from ibid.

30. Prange, *Miracle at Midway*, 17–20; Symonds, *Battle of Midway*, 133.

31. Morrison, *Coral Sea*, 4: 78.

32. Symonds, *Battle of Midway*, 178–79.

33. Fuchida and Okumiya, *Midway*, 7.

34. Symonds, *Battle of Midway*, 248.

35. Fuchida and Okumiya, *Midway*, 188.

36. Symonds, *Battle of Midway*.

37. Ibid., 295–307.

38. Ibid., 212.

39. Salter, *Recon Scout*.

40. Ibid., 19–20.

41. Eisenhower, *So Far from God*, 258–65.

42. Ibid., 272–74.
43. Bauer, *Mexican War*, 267–68; Eisenhower, *So Far from God*, 283.
44. Eisenhower, *So Far from God*, 277–78.
45. Elliott, *Winfield Scott*, 503.

**Chapter 15**

1. Wagner, *Organization and Tactics*, 280.
2. Upton, *Cavalry Tactics*, 476–78; see comments in McDermott, *Crook's 1876 Campaign*, 142–43, discussing the evolution of the army's infantry and cavalry tactics in the nineteenth century.
3. Upton, *Cavalry Tactics*, 478.
4. Nye, "Marching with Custer," 113–14.
5. Bourke, *On the Border*, 352–53.
6. Wagner, *Organization and Tactics*, 280.
7. Cooke, *Cavalry Tactics*, 1: 163.
8. Information obtained from interviews with Charles Martin of Bigfork, Montana, a recognized expert in competitive mounted-action firing; see also Wolf and Wolf, *Loading Cartridges*, 45–70.
9. Ibid.
10. Vaughn, *With Crook*, 213. Undoubtedly there were more Indian casualties, including wounded warriors who died later, but in any event, marksmanship was poor.
11. Buecker, *Fort Robinson*, 57.
12. Shockley, *Trap-Door Springfield*, 16.
13. Cooke, *Cavalry Tactics*, 65–66, 110.
14. Ibid., 117.
15. Kautz, *1865 Customs of Service*, 339–40.

**Chapter 16**

1. See Prange, *Miracle at Midway*, 376; this was "a convenient framework to evaluate any military or naval battle."
2. See Custer's letters to the news media and Libbie on June 22, John Gray, *Centennial Campaign*, 146; Elizabeth Custer, *Boot and Saddles*, 275.
3. Kennedy, *On the Plains*, 146n2.
4. Clausewitz, *On War*, 213.
5. Murdock, "Principles of War."
6. Nichols, *Reno Court of Inquiry*, 417 et seq.
7. Carroll, *General Custer*, 76.

8. Coughlan, "Little Big Horn," 13.

9. Karcher, *Victory Disease*, 7.

10. Ibid., v.

11. Ibid., 39.

12. Ibid., 41–42.

13. Mangum, *Battle of the Rosebud*, 98–99.

14. Cohen and Gooch, *Military Misfortunes*, 26.

15. Collins, et al., *Sioux Wars*.

16. Robbins, *Last in Their Class*, ix.

17. Greiner, *General Phil Sheridan*, 357.

## Chapter 17

1. Bourke, *On the Border*, 393.

2. Greene, *Slim Buttes*, 33.

3. Ibid., 57–58.

4. McDermott, *Crook's 1876 Campaigns*, 75.

5. Greene, *Lakota and Cheyenne*, 87.

6. Greene, *Battles and Skirmishes*, 160–61, article written by Lt. Frank D. Baldwin.

7. McDermott, *Crook's 1876 Campaigns*, 91. McDermott's work is thorough, detailed, and accurate, documented by almost every primary and secondary source available.

8. Bourke, *On the Border*, 291–92.

9. McDermott, *Crook's 1876 Campaigns*, 100.

10. Bourke, *On the Border*, 393.

11. Ibid., 393.

12. Greene, *Lakota and Cheyenne*, 120.

13. McDermott, *Crook's 1876 Campaigns*, 115–44.

14. Robinson, *Bad Hand*, 228.

15. Bray, *Crazy Horse*, 269–85.

16. Miles, *Personal Recollections*, 243.

17. McBlain, "Lame Deer Fight," 205.

18. Opinion of U.S. District Judge Elmer S. Dundy in *United States ex rel. Standing Bear v. Crook*, 25 F. Cas. 695 (1879).

19. Wishart, *Unspeakable Sadness*, 208.

20. Starita, *I Am a Man*, 105–10.

21. *United States ex rel. Standing Bear v. Crook*, 25 F. Cas. 695 (c.c.d. Neb. 1879).

22. Wright, "Standing Bear," 4–9.

23. House Executive Document No. 1, 46th Congress, 3rd Sess., serial 1959, pp. 3–4, 11–13.

24. Jensen, *Indian Interviews,* 35; attributed by Ricker to interpreter William Garnett, who lived on the northern plains and had personal contact with the army and the Plains Indians.

25. Buecker, *Fort Robinson*, 125; probably the most thoroughly researched and carefully documented account of the Cheyenne Outbreak.

26. Ibid., 135.

27. Grinnell, *Fighting Cheyennes*, 419.

28. Buecker, *Fort Robinson*, 135.

29. Ibid., 147.

30. Wishart, *Unspeakable Sadness*, 207–16.

31. McDermott, *Crook's 1876 Campaigns*, 93.

32. Greene, *Morning Star Dawn*, 164.

33. McDermott, *Crook's 1876 Campaigns*, 150.

34. Ibid.

35. Ellis, *General Pope*, 201–4.

36. Wooster, *Nelson A. Miles*, 185, 330, citing the 1891 annual report of the secretary of war, 49.

## Chapter 18

1. *Elk v. Wilkins*, 112 U.S. 94 (1884).

2. Memmi, *Dominated Man*, 186, cited by Williams, *Loaded Weapon*, 116; Robertson, *Conquest by Law*, 103–6.

3. *Johnson v. M'Intosh*, 21 U.S. 543, 574 et seq.

4. Ibid., 590.

5. Ibid.

6. Robertson, *Conquest by Law*, 95–99.

7. Northwest Ordinance, article 3, adopted by the Second Continental Congress on July 13, 1878, reaffirmed with slight modification by the U.S. Congress on August 7, 1789, intended to be unalterable except by common consent.

8. Article VI of the Constitution of the United States.

9. Banner, *How the Indians*, 178–88.

10. Wunder, *Retained by the People*, 213.

11. *Cherokee Nation v. State of Georgia*, 30 U.S. 1 (1831).

12. Associate Justice Robert Jackson, dissenting in *Korematsu v. United States,* 323 U.S. 214, 1944.

13. *Cherokee Nation v. State of Georgia*, 30 U.S. 1 (1831).

14. Satz, *American Indian Policy*.

15. *Elk v. Wilkins*, 112 U.S. 94 (1884).

16. *Lone Wolf v. Hitchcock*, 187 U.S. 553 (1903).

17. *United States v. Sioux Nation of Indians*, 448 U.S. 371 (1980).

18. *Cobell v. Salazar*, 573 F. 3d 808 (D.C. Cir. 2009).

19. Annual Report of the Secretary of War, 1875, p. 76. See also report of Maj. Gen. Schofield while in command of division of the Pacific, ibid., p. 122.

20. Abstracted from *Army Navy Journal* 15, no. 52, Whole No. 780, August 3, 1878. Grierson papers 1861–1890.

# GLOSSARY

A list defining key terms arranged by sections, related to:
1. Fifth Amendment due process rights of the Sioux and Cheyenne Indians involved in the Great Sioux War;
2. General Orders No. 100, the U.S. Army's laws of war;
3. The specific duties of President Grant, his cabinet officers, and the officers of the U.S. Army officers he commanded; and
4. Miscellaneous terms.

## Section 1

The Fifth Amendment rights of the Sioux and Cheyenne Indians who were involved in the Great Sioux War

*Annihilate*—To destroy completely, a deprivation of life.

*Capture*—To deprive one of liberty.

*Citizen*—A person who is a qualified member of a sovereign state, entitled to its protection and subject to its laws. See definition of *person*.

*Due process*—Requires a fair and impartial legal proceeding that protects individual rights.

*Extermination*—To drive out or destroy, a deprivation of life or liberty.

*Fifth Amendment due process clause*—Provides that "no person" shall be deprived of life, liberty, or property without due process of law. Since the Lakota and Cheyenne Indians were persons, they were and continue to have the Fifth Amendment's due process rights.

*Forcible removal*—The use of military force or intimidation to cause the relocation of individuals or groups of Indian persons against their will, a deprivation of liberty.

*Freedom*—The power of acting, according to the dictates of the will, subject to conditions imposed by just and necessary laws. See definition of *liberty*.

*Hostile*—The enemy in a state of open war.

*Kill*—To cause the death of a person.

*Kill or capture*—Tactical orders of Generals Sherman and Sheridan to Lt. Colonel Custer in launching the mission that resulted in the attack by eleven companies of the Seventh Cavalry Regiment on the village of Cheyenne Peace Chief Black Kettle at the Washita River in November 1868, resulting in loss of life for some and loss of liberty and property for others.

*Law of war*—That branch of international law that prescribes the rights and obligations of belligerents, or—more broadly—those principles and usages that, in time of war, define the status and relations not only of enemies—whether or not in arms—but also of persons under military government or martial law and persons simply resident or being upon the theater of war, and authorizes the trial and punishment of offenders.

*Liberty*—Includes freedom from all restraints except those imposed by impartial and just laws, taken from the Sioux and Cheyenne Indians in the Great Sioux War.

*Massacre*—The indiscriminate, merciless killing of a number of human beings, a deprivation of life.

*Murder*—The unlawful killing of another; also includes premeditated murder, intentional murder, and murder induced by malice or illegal purpose, a deprivation of life without due process.

*Overall strategic objective*—The end and the complete result to be achieved in the pursuit of a war or general conflict. Thus in World War II, it was the unconditional surrender of the Axis powers, and in the Civil War it was to prevent the secession of the Confederate states from the Union and end slavery. The overall strategic objective of the Great Sioux War was to conquer those Sioux and Cheyenne Indians who were off their designated agencies, kill as many as necessary, strip the balance of their food, shelter, ponies, and firearms, and force them against their will to return to and remain on sites designated by the U.S. government, a deprivation of life, liberty, and property without any due process.

*Person*—A living human being.

*Pursuit of happiness* (from the Declaration of Independence)—Includes personal freedom, exemption from oppression, the right to follow one's preference in choice of occupation and use of one's energies, liberty of conscience, and the right to enjoy the domestic relations and privileges of the family and the home.

*War*—World-renowned theorist Carl von Clausewitz came to the point where he defined war as "an act of force to compel our enemy to do our will." American courts have defined war as hostile contention by means of armed forces, carried on between nations, states, or rulers, or between parties in the same nation or state. A common dictionary defines war as open armed conflict between countries or within factions in the same country. It is not necessary to precede the noun "war" with subjective and imprecise adjectives ("total" and "hard") in order to convey its meaning.

## Section 2

General Orders No. 100 (also known as the "Lieber Code") and the subsequent codification of the laws and rules of international law

*Atrocity*—Brutal, cruel, and outrageous behavior, violating the laws of war.

*Attempted crime*—An attempt to commit a crime is also a crime even if the attempt fails or is incomplete.

*De facto*—Being such in actual fact, though not by legal establishment.

*De jure*—By right or legal establishment.

*General Orders No. 100* (the "Lieber Code")—At the direction of President Lincoln, Prussian immigrant Franz Lieber, a professor of political science and history at Columbia, with a board of army officers chosen by the president, drafted a code of humanity and ethics for the "government of the Armies of the United States in the Field." Becoming effective on April 24, 1863, General Orders No. 100 codified the public international rules and principles observed by civilized peoples and regulated the conduct of armies in the field in the conduct of a public war. The Lieber Code was subsequently used as the primary source document for the Hague Convention of 1907 and the subsequent Geneva Conventions in the 1940s and Resolution 1674 adopted by the United Nations General Assembly on April 28, 2006. After it was drafted and approved, President Lincoln commanded that the Lieber Code be published for the information of all concerned. Shortly thereafter, the Confederate states adopted an identical code applicable to the Confederate Army. The code contained 157 separately stated and numbered orders organized into ten sections, dealing, inter alia, with the doctrine of "military necessity," humane treatment of prisoners and noncombatants, punishment of crimes against inhabitants of hostile countries, avoiding intentional cruelty, wanton violence, and directions regarding the giving of quarter, condemning internecine war, and honoring a bona fide truce. The following numbered orders of the Lieber Code relate to violations involving conflicts between the U.S. Army and various Indian tribes, particularly the battles of the Great Sioux War of 1876–77:

Order No. 28. Retaliation shall never be resorted to as a measure of revenge except after careful inquiry into the character of misdeeds that may demand retaliation.

Order No. 37. The United States acknowledge and protect, in hostile countries occupied by them, "morality . . . private property . . . the persons of the inhabitants, especially those of women. . . . Offenses to the contrary shall be rigorously punished."

Order No. 44. All wanton violence committed against persons in the invaded country, all destruction of private property not commanded by the authorized officer, all robbery, pillage or sacking, all rape, wounding or killing of such inhabitants, are prohibited and subject to the penalty of death. An officer or soldier who disobeys an order to cease and desist may be killed on the spot.

Order No. 47. "Crimes punishable by all penal codes, such as arson, murder, maiming, assaults . . . theft . . . and rape, if committed by an American soldier in a hostile country against its inhabitants, are not only punishable at home, but in all cases in which death is not inflicted, the severer punishment shall be inferred."

Order No. 68. "Modern wars are not internecine wars in which killing of the enemy is the object. . . . Unnecessary or revengeful destruction of life is not lawful."

Order No. 71. "Whoever intentionally inflicts intentional wounds on an enemy already disabled . . . or who encourages soldiers to do so, shall suffer death; if duly convicted."

Each of the foregoing Security Council resolutions is consistent with the provisions of Orders 4, 11, 16, 17, 19, 20, 22, 23, 25, 28, 30, 38, 40, 44, 47, 48, 66, 68, 71, and 72 of the Lieber Code, which were in effect the laws of war governing the actions of the U.S. Army, including the president and the officers serving in the army from April 24, 1863, for the balance of the nineteenth century.

*Genocide—The Convention on the Prevention and Punishment of the Crime of Genocide*, adopted by the General Assembly of the United Nations on December 9, 1948, defines genocide as "any of the following acts committed with intent to destroy, in whole or in part, a national, ethnical, racial or religious group, as such:

a. Killing members of the group;

b. Causing serious bodily or mental harm to members of the group;

c. Deliberately inflicting on the group conditions of life calculated to bring about its physical destruction in whole or in part."

The following crimes can be punished under this Convention:

a. Genocide;

b. Conspiracy to commit genocide;

c. Direct and public incitement to commit genocide;

d. Attempt to commit genocide;

e. Complicity in genocide.

The definition of genocide is broad enough to include the crimes of murder (including intentional and premeditated murder), extermination, massacre, forcible removal, false imprisonment, and annihilation.

*Impunity*—Freedom or exemption from punishment, penalty, or harm.

*Internecine war*—Full of slaughter and destruction; fits the description of Sherman's and Sheridan's orders to combat units ordered to seek out and attack Indian villages in the wintertime when the temperature was cold, food was scarce, and the ponies were undernourished.

*Military necessity*—The following numbered orders of General Orders No. 100 state the mandatory actions that are required of the U.S. Army engaged in war. Order No. 14 of General Orders No. 100 defines "military necessity" as "those measures which are (1) indispensable for securing the ends of the war, and (2) lawful according to modern law and usages of war." Order No. 15 allows the destruction of armed enemies, the destruction of travel ways as well as the destruction of the enemy's sustenance and means of life, as long as the actions do not break good faith, positively pledged, or existing under the rules of modern war. Order No. 16 does not permit "military necessity to be exercised in a cruel manner, i.e., to inflict suffering for the sake of suffering (often a part of the orders of Generals Sherman and Sheridan), for revenge, or maiming or wounding except in fight. "In general, military necessity does not include any act of hostility which makes the return to peace unnecessarily difficult."

It should be noted that an army officer attempting to use "military necessity" as an excuse for outrageous conduct banned by one or more of General Orders No. 100 is (1) admitting the unlawful conduct and (2) has the burden of proving that his soldiers' actions were in compliance with Orders No. 14, 15, and 16 noted above. For instance, Generals Crook and Terry were violating the provisions of the 1868 Treaty of Fort Laramie when they trespassed upon the Lakotas' Great Sioux Reservation and unceded treaty lands as they moved toward the Little Big Horn River and also thereafter when they continued to pursue and attack these same Indians as they moved south and east through their treaty lands, where white men were prohibited from trespassing. Similarly, when the forces under Crook and Terry pursued and attacked the Sioux and Cheyenne Indians in their scattered villages, they were killing innocent noncombatants and destroying their food stores and shelter in a wanton and cruel manner in order to complete the forcible removal of these Indians from these treaty lands on which these Indians had the right under their treaty to exclusive and perpetual occupancy. The rights of the Lakotas to treaty lands, the fact of the actions of the U.S. Army in attacking the Sioux and Cheyennes in a cruel manner, and the fact that President Grant and his generals started the war and created the belligerency in violation of a solemn treaty and for an illegal purpose would destroy any claim of military necessity that might be made for the purpose of validating the army's wrongful strategy of forcible removal by death or illegal military force.

*Necessity*—Military necessity, as defined in Order No. 14 of General Orders No. 100, "consists in the necessity of those measures which are indispensable for securing the ends of the war and are lawful according to the modern law and usages of war." The instigation of war by President Grant, the genocidal attacks on Lakota and Cheyenne villages, the premeditated and intentional murder of Indians in the villages and encampments, the forcible removal of the Indians from their treaty lands, and the destruction of their shelter, food stores, and ponies, and the confiscation of their firearms were all illegal war crimes subject to the Fifth Amendment's constitutionally protected property rights and constituted flagrant violations of the 1868 Treaty of Fort Laramie. These numerous violations were not for a military purpose and lacked any due process of law. Since the purpose of the genocidal attacks was to take the Indians' treaty lands from them, the plea of "military necessity" could never be proved—and was therefore never an issue in judging the conduct of President Grant and his generals who carried out the Great Sioux War.

*Reprisal*—Retaliation for an injury inflicted by another.

*Retaliation*—To strike back, injury for injury.

*Revenge*—To inflict damages, injury, or punishment in return for an injury.

*Total war and hard war*—The terms "hard war" and "total war" are neither relevant nor accurate to a description of the strategy of President Grant and Generals Sherman, Crook, and Sheridan in utilizing the U.S. Army to attack the Sioux and Cheyenne Indians and remove them from their treaty lands in 1876–1877.

*Wanton*—Recklessly or arrogantly ignoring justice, decency, and disregard of human rights.

*War crimes*—Any crimes committed in violation of international law or accepted laws of war, or assumed norms of humane behavior, committed in connection with a war, as by a member of a belligerent nation's military forces or government. When President Grant ordered the U.S. Army to attack the camps of the Lakota and Cheyenne Indians located on their "treaty lands," killing some and removing all others, he and the army he commanded were committing *war crimes* as defined in General Orders No. 100, as well as the accepted laws of war and assumed norms of humane behavior. As described in this book, the *war crimes* committed by the U.S. Army were:

1. Acts of violence committed against the Lakota and Cheyenne Indians,
2. committed by soldiers of the U.S. Army,
3. in violation of General Orders No. 100,
4. that were not justified by military necessity, and
5. involved armed attacks of unusual cruelty and devastation, targeting women, children, and noncombatants. (See Article 6(c) of the Constitution of the International Military Tribunal–annex to the agreement for protection and punishment of the major war criminals of the European Axis, August 8, 1945; the Lieber Code, General Orders No. 100 for the Government of the Armies of the U.S. in the Field, effective April 24, 1863.)

In order to have the military-necessity rule apply, two requirements must be met:

1. The measures utilized by the U.S. Army must be indispensable for securing the ends of the war, and
2. They must also be lawful according to modern law and usages of war.

On April 28, 2006, the United Nations Security Council unanimously adopted Resolution 1674, recalling that deliberately targeting civilians and protected persons in armed conflict is a "flagrant violation of international humanitarian law . . . demanding that all parties immediately put an end to such practices."

Resolution 1674 of the United Nations Security Council unanimously adopted on April 28, 2006 (excerpts):

*Recalling* the particular impact that armed conflict has on women and children . . . [and]

*Reaffirming* that parties to armed conflict bear the primary responsibility to take all feasible steps to ensure the protection of affected civilians . . . [and]

*Recalls* that deliberately targeting civilians and other protected persons as such in situations of armed conflict is a flagrant violation of international humanitarian law, *reiterates* its condemnation in the strongest terms of such practices, and *demands* that all parties immediately put an end to such practices;

*Reaffirms* the provisions of paragraphs 138 and 139 of the 2005 World Summit Outcome Document regarding the responsibility to protect populations from genocide, war crimes, ethnic cleansing and crimes against humanity;

*Demands* that all parties concerned comply strictly with the obligations applicable to them under international law, in particular those contained in the Hague Conventions of 1899 and 1907 and in the Geneva Conventions of 1949 and their Additional Protocols of 1977, as well as with the decisions of the Security Council;

*Reaffirms* that ending impunity is essential if a society in conflict or recovering from conflict is to come to terms with past abuses committed against civilians affected by armed conflict and to prevent future such abuses . . . [and]

*Emphasizes* in this context the responsibility of States to comply with their relevant obligations to end impunity and to prosecute those responsible for war crimes, genocide, crimes against humanity and serious violations of international humanitarian law . . . [and]

*Notes* that the deliberate targeting of civilians and other protected persons, and the commission of systematic, flagrant and widespread violations of international humanitarian and human rights law in situations of armed conflict, may constitute a threat to international peace and security, and, *reaffirms in this regard* its readiness to consider such situations and, where necessary, to adopt appropriate steps.

## Section 3

The specific duties of President Grant, his cabinet officers, and the officers of the U.S. Army officers he commanded

*Honor code*—The United States Military Academy currently has an honor code stating that, "a cadet will not lie, cheat, steal, or tolerate those who do." Originally dealing only with lying, it was subsequently modified to include cheating, stealing, and intolerance. Enforcement was not always strict or uniform until Gen. Douglas MacArthur formalized the system after World War I. Custer was guilty of cheating and stealing while a cadet.

*Oath of office of a commissioned officer of the U.S. Army*—Commencing on July 2, 1862, every officer of the U.S. Army was and is required to take an oath to support and defend the Constitution of the United States, a Constitution that prohibited taking the life, liberty, or property of any person without due process. In addition, any officer who "shall disobey any lawful command of his superior officer shall be punished." In later times the term "lawful order" was defined in the Uniform Code of Military Justice as follows: "An order requiring the performance of a military duty may be inferred to be lawful and it is disobeyed at the peril of the subordinate. This inference does not apply to a patently illegal order, such as one that directs the commission of a crime."

*Oath of office* of President Grant—"I do solemnly swear (or affirm) that I will faithfully execute the office of President of the United States, and will to the best of my ability, preserve, protect, and defend the Constitution of the United States." The actions of President Grant in instigating a state of war against portions of the Sioux and Cheyenne tribes violated the due process clause of the Fifth Amendment of the Constitution in that the actions that Grant instigated took the lives, liberty, and property of the Sioux and Cheyenne Indians without any due process of law.

*Power to declare war*—Article I, Section 8 of the U.S. Constitution gives Congress the power to declare war. While President Grant lacked the power to declare war in 1875 and 1876, he was commander in chief of the U.S. Army, with the power to use the army to defend the United States and repel aggression. In an effort to deprive the Sioux Nation of its treaty lands and remove them to designated reservations, President Grant directed the commissioner of Indian affairs to order all Sioux and Cheyenne Indians hunting on their treaty lands to return to their respective reservations by January 31, 1876, or be treated as "hostile"—a conditional, but de facto, declaration of war. At the time the declaration of hostility was declared, the Indians were not attacking or committing acts of aggression or threatening the security of the United States, and President Grant was acting in violation of the U.S. Constitution and the hallowed doctrine of separation of powers between the three branches of the United States government.

## Section 4

Miscellaneous terms

*Dead reckoning*—(relative to Custer's movements at Little Big Horn). A mathematical calculation of the location of a person or object based upon a known starting point, utilizing direction, speed, and time to estimate a new location, or relative locations of two or more separate objects.

*In extremis*—At the point of death.

*Wasicu*—Lakota word for white person.

# BIBLIOGRAPHY

## Manuscripts and Other Collections

Center for Great Plains Studies. Lincoln, Nebraska. John and Elizabeth Christlieb Manuscript Collection.

Combat Studies Institute. Fort Leavenworth, Kansas. Various collections.

Douglas County Historical Society. Omaha, Nebraska. General George Crook Collections.

Fort Stephen Watts Kearny State Historical Park. Kearney, Nebraska. Archives and Documents.

Museum of the Fur Trade. Chadron, Nebraska. Various collections.

National Park Service. Midwest Archaeological Center. Lincoln, Nebraska.

Nebraska State Historical Society. Eli Ricker Files.

Nebraska State Historical Society. Fort Robinson Museum.

Omaha Public Library. Omaha, Nebraska. Reinhardt Photograph Collection.

United States Cavalry Association. Fort Riley, Kansas. Memorabilia and various published and unpublished materials.

United States Military Academy. West Point, New York. Various sections.

University of Nebraska–Lincoln College of Journalism and Mass Communications. *Native Daughters: Who They Are, Where They've Been, and Why Indian Country Could Never Survive without Them*. 2010 in-depth report.

Wagmatcook Culture and Heritage Center. Cape Breton Island, Nova Scotia, Canada.

## Books and Articles

Abrams, Mark. *Sioux War Dispatches: Reports from the Field, 1866–1877*. Yardley, PA: Westholme Publishing, 2012.

Agonito, Rosemary, and Joseph Agonito. *Buffalo Calf Road Woman: The Story of a Warrior of the Little Bighorn*. Helena, MT: Globe Pequot Press, 2006.

Allen, J. A. *History of the American Bison, Bison Americanus*. Charleston, SC: Nabu Press, 2010.

Ambrose, Stephen E. *Crazy Horse and Custer: The Parallel Lives of Two American Warriors*. New York: Doubleday, 1975.

Andrist, Ralph K. *The Long Death*. Norman: University of Oklahoma Press, 1964.

Abstract. *Army Navy Journal* 15, no. 52 (August 3, 1878). Grierson papers 1861–1890.

Athearn, Robert G. *William Tecumseh Sherman and the Settlement of the West*. Norman: University of Oklahoma Press, 1995.

Axelrod, Alan. *Chronicle of the Indian Wars*. New York: Prentice Hall, 1993.

Bailyn, Bernard. *The Ideological Origins of the American Revolution*. Cambridge, MA: Harvard University Press, 1967.

Banner, Stuart. *How the Indians Lost Their Land: Law and Power on the Frontier*. Cambridge, MA: Belknap Press of Harvard University Press, 2007.

Barnard, Sandy, Brian G. Pohanka, and James S. Brust. *Where Custer Fell, Photographs of the Little Bighorn Battlefield Then and Now*. Norman: University of Oklahoma Press, 2005.

Barnett, Louise. *Touched By Fire: The Life, Death, and Mythic Afterlife of George Armstrong Custer*. New York: Henry Holt, 1996.

Bauer, K. Jack. *The Mexican War, 1846–1848*. Lincoln: University of Nebraska Press, 1974.

Beck, Paul N. *The First Sioux War: The Grattan Fight and Blue Water Creek, 1854–1856*. Lanham, MD: University Press of America, 2004.

———. *Inkpaduta: Dakota Leader*. Norman: University of Oklahoma Press, 2008.

Bennett, Ben. *Death, Too, for the Heavy Runner*. Missoula, MT: Mountain Press Publishing, 1982.

Berry, John M. *Roger Williams and the Creation of the American Soul: Church, State, and the Birth of Liberty*. New York: Penguin Group, 2012.

Berthrong, Donald J. *The Southern Cheyennes*. Norman: University of Oklahoma Press, 1986.

Bettelyoun, Susan Bordeaux, and Josephine Waggoner. *With My Own Eyes: A Lakota Woman Tells Her People's History*. Lincoln: University of Nebraska Press, 1988.

Bourke, John G. *On the Border with Crook*. New York: Charles Scribner's Sons, 1891; Reprint Alexandria, VA: Time Life Books, 1980.

Bradley, John. *Lidice: Sacrificial Village*. New York: Ballentine Books, 1972.

Bray, Kingsley M. *Crazy Horse: A Lakota Life*. Norman: University of Oklahoma Press, 2006.

———. I Belong to the Northern Nation: Crazy Horse and Lakota Leadership. Paper delivered at the 4th Fort Robinson History Conference, April 2002.

———. Teton Sioux Population History, 1655–1881. *Nebraska History*, Summer 1994.

Brininstool, E. A. *Troopers with Custer*. New York: Bonanza Books, 1952.

Britten, Thomas A. *American Indians in World War I: At War and at Home*. Albuquerque: University of New Mexico Press, 1998.

Brown, Barron. *Comanche*. New York: S. Lewis, 1973.

Brown, Dee. *The Fetterman Massacre*. Lincoln: University of Nebraska Press, 1962. Originally published as *Fort Phil Kearny: An American Saga*.

Brown, Mark H. *The Plainsmen of the Yellowstone: A History of the Yellowstone Basin*. New York: G. P. Putnam's Sons, 1961.

Buecker, Thomas R. *Fort Robinson and the American West, 1874–1899*. Lincoln: Nebraska State Historical Society, 1999.

Bugnet, Charles. *Foch Talks*. London: Camelot Press, 1929.

Bunting, Josiah, III. *Ulysses S. Grant*. New York: Henry Holt, 2004.

Calloway, Colin G., ed. *Our Hearts Fell to the Ground: Plains Indian Views of How the West Was Lost*. Boston: Bedford/St. Martins, 1996.

———. *The Shawnees and the War for America*. New York: Viking, 2007.

Carroll, John M., ed. *The Benteen-Goldin Letters on Custer and His Last Battle*. Lincoln: University of Nebraska Press, 1974.

———. *General Custer and the Battle of the Little Big Horn: The Federal View*. Bryan, TX: J. M. Carroll, 1986.

Carter, Robert. *On the Border with Mackenzie*. Austin: Texas State Historical Society, 2007.

Carter, William H. *The U.S. Cavalry Horse*. Guilford, CT: Lyons Press, 1895; republished 2003.

Cate, Fred H., Dennis H. Long, and David C. Williams, eds. *The Court Martial of George Armstrong Custer*. Bloomington: University of Indiana School of Law, 2001.

Chaky, Doreen. *Terrible Justice: Sioux Chiefs and U.S. Soldiers on the Upper Missouri, 1854–1868*. Norman, OK: Arthur H. Clark, 2012.

Chalfant, William Y. *Hancock's War: Conflict on the Southern Plains*. Norman: University of Oklahoma Press, 2010.

Chandler, Melbourne C. *Of Garryowen in Glory: The History of the Seventh United States Cavalry Regiment*. London: Turnpike Press, 1960.

Clark, Blue. *Lone Wolf v. Hitchcock: Treaty Rights and Indian Law at the End of the Nineteenth Century*. Lincoln: University of Nebraska Press, 1999.

Clausewitz, Carl von. *On War*, translated and edited by Michael Howard and Peter Paret. Princeton, NJ: Princeton University Press, 1976.

Clow, Richmond L., ed. *The Sioux in South Dakota History*. Pierre: South Dakota State Historical Society Press, 2007.

Coffman, Edward M. *The Old Army: A Portrait of the American Army in Peacetime, 1784–1898*. New York: Oxford University Press, 1986.

Cohen, Eliot A., and John Gooch. *Military Misfortunes: The Anatomy of Failure in War*. New York: Vintage Books, 1991.

Cohen, Lucy Kramer, ed. *The Legal Conscience: Selected Papers of Felix S. Cohen*. New Haven, CT: Yale University Press, 1960.

Connell, Evan S. *Son of the Morning Star: Custer and the Little Bighorn*. New York: Harper and Row, 1984.

Coughlan, Timothy M. "The Battle of the Little Big Horn: A Tactical Study." *Cavalry Journal* 43, no. 181 (January–February 1934).

Cox-Paul, Lori. "John M. Chivington: 'The Reverend Colonel,' 'Marry-Your-Daughter,' 'Sand Creek Massacre.'" *Nebraska History* 88, no. 4 (Winter 2007).

Crawford, Lewis F. *The Exploits of Ben Arnold: Indian Fighter, Gold Miner, Cowboy, Hunter and Army Scout*. Norman: University of Oklahoma Press, 1999.

Custer, Elizabeth B. *Boots and Saddles or, Life in Dakota with General Custer*. Norman: University of Oklahoma Press, 1961.

———. *Tenting on the Plains*. New York: Charles L. Webster, 1889.

Custer, General George Armstrong. *My Life on the Plains: Or Personal Experiences with Indians*. Norman: University of Oklahoma Press, 1962.

Daddis, Gregory. *No Sure Victory: Measuring U.S. Army Effectiveness and Progress in the Vietnam War*. New York: Oxford University Press, 2011.

Darling, Roger. *Benteen's Scout to the Left: The Route from the Divide to the Morass, June 25, 1876*. El Segundo, CA: Upton and Sons, 2000.

———. *General Custer's Final Hours: Correcting a Century of Misconceived History*. Vienna, VA: Potomac-Western Press, 1992.

———. *A Sad and Terrible Blunder: Generals Terry and Custer at the Little Big Horn: New Discoveries*. Vienna, VA: Potomac-Western Press, 1992.

DeMallie, Raymond J. *The Sixth Grandfather: Black Elk's Teachings Given to John G. Neihardt*. Lincoln: University of Nebraska Press, 1984.

de Vattel, Emer. *The Law of Nations: Or, Principles of the Law of Nature, Applied to the Conduct and Affairs of Nations and Sovereigns*, edited by Joseph Chitty. New York: Cambridge University Press, 2011.

Dippie, Brian W. "Custer the Indian Fighter." In Paul Andrew Hutton, *The Custer Reader*. Lincoln: University of Nebraska Press, 1993.

———. *Nomad: George A. Custer in "Turf, Field and Farm."* Austin: University of Texas Press, 1980.

Drinnon, Richard. *Facing West: The Metaphysics of Indian-Hating and Empire Building*. Norman: University of Oklahoma Press, 1997.

DuMont, John S. *Custer Battle Guns*. Ft. Collins, CO: Old Army Press, 1974.

Dustin, Fred. *The Custer Tragedy: Events Leading Up to and Following the Little Big Horn Campaign of 1876*. Ann Arbor, MI: Edwards Brothers, 1939.

Edwards, Charles S. *Hugo Grotius: The Miracle of Holland: A Study in Political and Legal Thought.* Chicago: Nelson-Hall, 1981.

Eisenhower, John S. D. *So Far from God: The U.S. War with Mexico, 1846–1848.* Norman: University of Oklahoma Press, 2000.

Elliott, Charles Winslow. *Winfield Scott: The Soldier and the Man.* New York: Macmillan, 1937.

Ellis, Richard N. *General Pope and U.S. Indian Policy.* Albuquerque: University of New Mexico Press, 1970.

Farr, William E. *Blackfoot Redemption: A Blood Indian's Story of Murder, Confinement and Imperfect Justice.* Norman: University of Oklahoma Press, 2012.

Fifer, Barbara. *Montana Battlefields, 1806–1877.* Helena, MT: Far Country Press, 2005.

Fitzgerald, Judith, and Michael Oren Fitzgerald, eds. *The Spirit of Indian Women.* Bloomington, IN: World Wisdom, 2005.

Foner, Eric. *Reconstruction: America's Unfinished Revolution 1863–1877.* New York: Harper-Collins, 2005.

Foreman, Grant. *Indian Removal: The Emigration of the Five Civilized Tribes of Indians.* Norman: University of Oklahoma Press, 1972.

Fox, Richard Allan, Jr. *Archaeology, History, and Custer's Last Battle.* Norman: University of Oklahoma Press, 1993.

Frost, Lawrence A. *The Court-Martial of General George Armstrong Custer.* Norman: University of Oklahoma Press, 1987.

Fuchida, Mitsuo, and Masatake Okumiya. *Midway, the Battle That Doomed Japan: The Japanese Navy's Story.* Annapolis, MD: Naval Institute Press, 2001.

Gaustad, Edwin S. *Liberty of Conscience: Roger Williams in America.* Valley Forge, PA: Judson Press, 1999.

Godfrey, E. S. *An Account of Custer's Last Campaign, and the Battle of the Little Big Horn.* Palo Alto, CA: Lewis Osborne, 1968.

———. "Custer's Last Battle." In Paul Andrew Hutton, ed., *The Custer Reader.* Lincoln: University of Nebraska Press, 1992.

Graham, W. A. *The Custer Myth: A Source Book of Custeriana.* Lincoln: University of Nebraska Press, 1986.

———. *The Reno Court of Inquiry.* Harrisburg, PA: Stackpole, 1954.

Gray, John S. *Centennial Campaign: The Sioux War of 1876.* Norman: University of Oklahoma Press, 1988.

———. *Custer's Last Campaign: Mitch Bouyer and the Little Bighorn Reconstructed.* Lincoln: University of Nebraska Press, 1991.

Gray, Paul Bryan. *A Clamor for Equality: Emergence and Exile of Californio Activist Francisco P. Ramirez.* Lubbock: Texas Tech University Press, 2012.

Greene, Jerome A., ed. *Battles and Skirmishes of the Great Sioux War, 1876–1877: The Military View.* Norman: University of Oklahoma Press, 1993.

———. *Evidence and the Custer Enigma: A Modern Study of Custer's Last Stand Based on Indian Testimony and on Indian and Army Artifacts Discovered on the Battlefield since 1876.* Reno, NV: Outbooks, 1979.

———. *Fort Randall on the Missouri, 1856–1892.* Pierre: South Dakota State Historical Society Press, 2005.

———. "The Hayfield Fight: A Reappraisal of a Neglected Action." *Montana, the Magazine of Western History* 22, no. 4 (October 1972).

———. *Lakota and Cheyenne: Indian Views of the Great War, 1876–1877.* Norman: University of Oklahoma Press, 1994.

———. *Morning Star Dawn: The Powder River Expedition and the Northern Cheyennes, 1876.* Norman: University of Oklahoma Press, 2003.

———. *Slim Buttes, 1876: An Episode of the Great Sioux War.* Norman: University of Oklahoma Press, 1982.

———. *Washita: The U.S. Army and the Southern Cheyennes, 1867–1869.* Norman: University of Oklahoma Press, 2004.

———. *Yellowstone Command: Colonel Nelson A. Miles and the Great Sioux War, 1876–1877.* Lincoln: University of Nebraska Press, 1991.

Greene, Jerome A., and Douglas D. Scott. *Finding Sand Creek.* Norman: University of Oklahoma Press, 2004.

Greiner, Henry C. *General Phil Sheridan as I Knew Him: Playmate–Comrade–Friend.* Chicago, J. S.: Hyland, 1908.

Grimsley, Mark. *The Hard Hand of War: Union Military Policy toward Southern Civilians, 1861–1865.* Cambridge: Cambridge University Press, 1997.

Grinnell, George Bird. *The Cheyenne Indians.* Vol. 1. Lincoln: University of Nebraska Press, 1972.

———. *The Fighting Cheyennes.* Madison: University of Wisconsin, Cooper Square Publishers, 1962.

Grotius, Hugo. *Prolegomena to the Law of War and Peace,* translated by Francis W. Kelsey. New York: Liberal Arts Press, 1957.

Guice, John D. W. *The Rocky Mountain Bench: The Territorial Supreme Courts of Colorado, Montana and Wyoming, 1861–1890.* New Haven, CT: Yale University Press, 1972.

Haley, James L. *The Buffalo War: The History of the Red River Indian Uprising of 1874.* Abilene, TX: State House Press of McMurry University, 1976.

Halleck, Henry W. *International Law and Laws of War; or, Rules Regulating the Intercourse of States in Peace and War.* San Francisco, CA: Painter, 1865.

Hammer, Kenneth, ed. *Custer in '76: Walter Camp's Notes on the Custer Fight.* Norman: University of Oklahoma Press, 1976.

Hanson, James A. *Northwest Nebraska's Indian People*. Chadron, NE: published by the author, 1983.

Hardee, W. J. *Hardee's Rifle and Light Infantry Tactics, for the Instruction, Exercises and Maneuvers of Riflemen and Light Infantry, including School of the Soldier and School of the Company, Also including the Articles of War*. New York: J. O. Kane, 1862.

Hardorff, Richard G. *Camp, Custer and the Little Bighorn*. El Segundo, CA: Upton and Sons, 1997.

———. *Hokahey! A Good Day to Die! The Indian Casualties of the Custer Fight*. Spokane, WA: Arthur H. Clark, 1993.

———. *Indian Views of the Custer Fight*. Norman: University of Oklahoma Press, 2005.

———. *Lakota Recollections of the Custer Fight: New Sources of Indian-Military History*. Lincoln: University of Nebraska Press, 1991.

———. *Washita Memories: Eyewitness Views of Custer's Attack on Black Kettle's Village*. Norman: University of Oklahoma Press, 2006.

Hart, B. H. Liddell. *Sherman: Soldier, Realist, American*. New York: Da Capo Press, 1929.

Hartigan, Richard Shelly. *Military Rules, Regulations and the Code of War: Francis Lieber and the Certification of Conflict*. New Brunswick, NJ: Transaction Publishers, 2011.

Hassrick, Royal B. *The Sioux: Life and Customs of a Warrior Society*. Norman: University of Oklahoma Press, 1964.

Hedren, Paul L. *After Custer: Loss and Transformation in Sioux Country*. Norman: University of Oklahoma Press, 2011.

———. *Battles and Skirmishes of the Great Sioux War, 1876–77: The Military View*. Norman: University of Oklahoma Press, 1993.

———. "Carbine Extractor Failure at the Little Big Horn: A New Examination." *Military Collector and Historian* (Summer 1973).

———. *Fort Laramie and the Great Sioux War*. Norman: University of Oklahoma Press, 1998.

———. *Great Sioux War Orders of Battle: How the United States Army Waged War on the Northern Plains, 1876–1877*. Norman: University of Oklahoma Press, 2011.

———. *Traveler's Guide to the Great Sioux War: The Battlefields, Forts and Related Sites of America's Greatest Indian War*. Helena: Montana Historical Society Press, 1996.

———. *We Trailed the Sioux: Enlisted Men Speak on Custer, Crook and the Great Sioux War*. Mechanicsburg, PA: Stackpole Books, 2003.

Heizer, Robert F. *The Destruction of California Indians*. Lincoln: University of Nebraska Press, 1993.

Her Many Horses, Emil, George Horse Capture, National Museum of the American Indian, eds. *A Song for the Horse Nation: Horses in Native American Cultures.* Golden, CO: Fulcrum Publishing, 2006.

Hirshson, Stanley P. *The White Tecumseh: A Biography of General William T. Sherman.* Hoboken, NJ: John Wiley and Sons, 1997.

Hofling, Charles K. *Custer and the Little Big Horn: A Psychobiographical Inquiry.* Detroit, MI: Wayne State University Press, 1981.

Hoig, Stan. *The Battle of the Washita: The Sheridan-Custer Indian Campaign of 1867–69.* Lincoln: University of Nebraska Press, 1976.

———. *The Sand Creek Massacre.* Norman: University of Oklahoma Press, 1961.

Holley, Francis C. *Once Their Home or Our Legacy.* Chicago: Donohue and Henneberry, 1890.

Horsman, Reginald. *Expansion and American Indian Policy 1783–1812.* Norman: University of Oklahoma Press, 1992.

Hutton, Paul A., ed. *The Custer Reader.* Lincoln: University of Nebraska Press, 1992.

———. *Phil Sheridan and His Army.* Rev. ed. Norman: University of Oklahoma Press, 1999.

Hyde, Anne F. *Empires, Nations and Families: A History of the North American West, 1800–1860.* Lincoln: University of Nebraska Press, 2011.

Hyde, George E. *Indians of the High Plains.* Norman: University of Oklahoma Press, 1959.

———. *Red Cloud's Folk: A History of the Oglala Sioux.* Norman: University of Oklahoma Press, 1987.

Irving, Washington. *The Adventures of Captain Bonneville, U.S.A.: In the Rocky Mountains and the Far West.* Norman: University of Oklahoma Press, 1986.

Isenberg, Andrew C. *The Destruction of the Bison.* Cambridge: Cambridge University Press, 2000.

Jackson, Helen Hunt. *A Century of Dishonor: The Early Crusade for Indian Reform.* New York: Harper and Row, 1965.

Jacoby, Karl. *Shadows at Dawn: A Borderlands Massacre and the Violence of History.* New York: Penguin Press, 2008.

Jamieson, Perry D. *Crossing the Deadly Ground: United States Army Tactics, 1865–1899.* Tuscaloosa: University of Alabama Press, 2004.

Jensen, Richard E., ed. *The Indian Interviews of Eli S. Ricker.* Lincoln: University of Nebraska Press, 2005.

Johnson, Randy, and Nancy Allan. *A Dispatch to Custer: The Tragedy of Lieutenant Kidder.* Missoula, MT: Mountain Press, 1999.

Johnson, W. Fletcher. *Life of Sitting Bull and History of the Indian War of 1890–91.* Philadelphia, PA: Edgewood Publishers, 1891.

Jomini, Antoine Henri de. *The Art of War*. London: Greenhill Books, 1992; originally published in 1838 by the author.

Karcher, Timothy. *Understanding the "Victory Disease" from the Little Big Horn to Mogadishu and Beyond*. Fort Leavenworth, KS: Combat Studies Institute Press, 1967.

Kautz, August V. *The 1865 Customs of Service for Officers of the Army*. Mechanicsburg, PA: Stackpole Books, 2002.

Keegan, John. *Intelligence in War: Knowledge of the Enemy from Napoleon to Al-Qaeda*. New York: Alfred Knopf, 2003.

Keenan, Jerry. *The Wagon Box Fight: An Episode of Red Cloud's War*. Conshohocken, PA: Savas Publishing, 2000.

Kelman, Ari. *A Misplaced Massacre: Struggling over the Memory of Sand Creek*. Cambridge, MA: Harvard University Press, 2013.

Kennedy, W. J. D. *On the Plains with Custer and Hancock: The Journal of Isaac Coates, Army Surgeon*. Boulder, CO: Johnson Books, 1997.

Killoren, John J. *Come Blackrobe: De Smet and the Indian Tragedy*. Norman: University of Oklahoma Press, 1995.

King, W. Kent. *Massacre: The Cover-up*. El Segundo, CA: Upton and Sons, 1989.

Knight, Orville. *Following the Indian Wars*. Norman: University of Oklahoma Press, 1990.

Koch, Amy. *High Plains Archaeology*. Lincoln: Nebraska State Historical Society, 2000.

Kvasnicka, Robert M., and Herman J. Viola, eds. *The Commissioners of Indian Affairs, 1824–1977*. Lincoln: University of Nebraska Press, 1979.

Ladenheim, Jules C. *Custer's Thorn: The Life of Frederick W. Benteen*. Westminster, MD: Heritage Books, 2007.

Latimer, Jon. *Buccaneers of the Caribbean: How Piracy Forged an Empire*. Cambridge, MA: Harvard University Press, 2009.

LaVelle, John. "Rescuing Paha Sapa." *Great Plains Resources Journal* 5, nos. 1 and 2 (Spring/Summer 2001).

Lazarus, Edward. *Black Hills/White Justice: The Sioux Nation versus the United States, 1775 to the Present*. New York: Harper Collins, 1991.

Lee, Kimberli A., ed. *"I Do Not Apologize for the Length of This Letter": The Mari Sandoz Letters on Native American Rights, 1940–1965*. Lubbock: Texas Tech University Press, 2009.

Lehman, Tim. *Bloodshed at Little Bighorn: Sitting Bull, Custer, and the Destinies of Nations*. Baltimore, MD: Johns Hopkins University Press, 2010.

Leiker, James N., and Ramon Powers. *The Northern Cheyenne Exodus in History and Memory*. Norman: University of Oklahoma Press, 2012.

Lemkin, Raphael. *Totally Unofficial: The Autobiography of Raphael Lemkin.* New Haven, CT: Yale University Press, 2013.

Lewis, Lloyd. *Sherman: Fighting Prophet.* New York: Harcourt Brace, 1932.

Libby, O. G. *The Arikara Narrative.* New York: Sol Lewis, 1973.

Longacre, Edward C. *The Cavalry at Gettysburg.* Lincoln: University of Nebraska Press, 1993.

Lubetkin, John. *Jay Cooke's Gamble: The Northern Pacific Railroad, the Sioux, and the Panic of 1873.* Norman: University of Oklahoma Press, 2006.

Magid, Paul. *George Crook: From the Redwoods to Appomattox.* Norman: University of Oklahoma Press, 2011.

Mahan, Dennis Hart. *Advanced-Guard, Out-Post, and Detachment Service of Troops, with the Essential Principles of Strategy and Grand Tactics.* New York: John Wiley, 1864; first published in 1847.

———. *An Elementary Treatise on Advanced-Guard, Out-Post, and Detachment Service of Troops, and the Manner of Posting and Handling Them in Presence of an Enemy, with a Historical Sketch of the Rise and Progress of Tactics, &c., &c. Intended as a Supplement to the System of Tactics Adopted for the Military Service of the United States, and Especially for the Use of Officers of Militia and Volunteers.* New York: John Wiley, 1862.

Mangum, Neil C. *Battle of the Rosebud: Prelude to the Little Bighorn.* El Segundo, CA: Upton and Sons, 1987.

Mapp, Paul W. *The Elusive West and the Contest for Empire, 1713–1763.* Chapel Hill: University of North Carolina Press, 2011.

Marquis, Thomas Bailey. *Wooden Leg: A Warrior Who Fought Custer.* Lincoln: University of Nebraska Press, 1962.

Marshall, Joseph M., III. *The Day the World Ended at Little Bighorn: A Lakota History.* New York: Penguin Group, 2007.

———. *The Lakota Way: Stories and Lessons for Living.* New York: Penguin Putnam, 2001.

Marshall, S. L. A. *Crimsoned Prairie: The Indian Wars.* New York: Da Capo Press, 1972.

Matthiessen, Peter. *In the Spirit of Crazy Horse.* New York: Penguin Books, 1991.

McAulay, John D. *Carbines of the U.S. Cavalry 1861–1905.* Lincoln, RI: Andrew Mowbray, 1996.

McBlain, John F. "The Lame Deer Fight." In *Battles and Skirmishes of the Great Sioux War, 1876–1877: The Military View,* edited by Jerome A. Greene. Norman: University of Oklahoma Press, 1993.

McChristian, Douglas C. *An Army of Marksmen.* Ft. Collins, CO: Old Army Press, 1981.

———. *Fort Laramie: Military Bastion of the High Plains*. Norman, OK: Arthur H. Clark, 2008.

McClernand, Edward J. *On Time for Disaster: Rescue of Custer's Command*. Lincoln: University of Nebraska Press, 1989.

McDermott, John D. *Circle of Fire: The Indian War of 1865*. Mechanicsburg, PA: Stackpole Books, 2003.

———. "Custer and the Little Big Horn Story." In Charles E. Rankin, ed., *Legacy: New Perspectives on the Battle of the Little Bighorn*. Helena: Montana Historical Society Press, 1996.

———. *General George Crook's 1876 Campaigns: A Report Prepared for the American Battlefield Protection Program*. Sheridan, WY: Frontier Heritage Alliance, 2000.

———. *Gold Rush: The Black Hills Story*. South Dakota State Historical Society, Dec. 2001.

———. *A Guide to the Indian Wars of the West*. Lincoln: University of Nebraska Press, 1998.

———. *Red Cloud's War*, 2 vols. Norman: University of Oklahoma Press, 2010.

McLaughlin, James. *My Friend, the Indian*. Lincoln: University of Nebraska Press, 1989.

McMurtry, Larry. *Custer*. New York: Simon & Schuster, 2012.

Memmi, Albert. *Dominated Man: Notes toward a Portrait*. New York: Orion Press, 1968.

Merington, Marguerite, ed. *The Custer Story: The Life and Intimate Letters of General George A. Custer and His Wife Elizabeth*. Lincoln: University of Nebraska Press, 1987.

Michno, Gregory F. *Lakota Noon: The Indian Narrative of Custer's Defeat*. Missoula, MT: Mountain Press Publishing Co., 1997.

Miles, Nelson A. *Personal Recollections and Observations of General Nelson A. Miles*. Vol. 1. Lincoln: University of Nebraska Press, 1992.

Miller, Robert J. *Native America, Discovered and Conquered: Thomas Jefferson, Lewis and Clark, and Manifest Destiny*. Westport, CT: Praeger, 2006.

Monaghan, Jay. *Custer: The Life of General George Armstrong Custer*. Boston: Houghton Mifflin, 1959.

Monnett, John H. *Where a Hundred Soldiers Were Killed: The Struggle for the Powder River Country in 1866 and the Making of the Fetterman Myth*. Albuquerque: University of New Mexico Press, 2010.

Mooney, James. *The Aboriginal Population of America North of Mexico*. Smithsonian Miscellaneous Collections 80, no. 7. Washington, DC: Smithsonian Institution, 1928.

Mooney, Michael J. "From Garryowen in Glory." *Army and Navy Life Magazine,* 39, no. 2 (February 1989): 58–64.

Morrison, Samuel Eliot. *Coral Sea: Midway and Submarine Actions, May 1942–August 1942*. Vol. 4. Edison, NJ: Castle Books, 1949.

Neff, Stephen C. *Justice in Blue and Gray: A Legal History of the Civil War*. Cambridge, MA: Harvard University Press, 2010.

Nichols, Ronald H. *In Custer's Shadow: Major Marcus Reno*. Fort Collins, CO: Old Army Press, 1999.

———, ed. *Reno Court of Inquiry: Proceedings in a Court of Inquiry in the Case of Major Marcus A. Reno Concerning His Conduct at the Battle of the Little Big Horn River on June 25–26, 1876*. Hardin, MT: Custer Battlefield Historical and Museum Association, 1996.

Nye, Elwood L. "Marching with Custer." In Barron Brown, Elwood L. Nye, and Ernest A. Garlington, *Comanche*. New York: S. Lewis, 1973.

Olson, James C. *Red Cloud and the Sioux Problem*. Lincoln: University of Nebraska Press, 1975.

Orth, John V. *Due Process of Law: A Brief History*. Lawrence: University Press of Kansas, 2003.

Ostler, Jeffrey. *The Lakotas and the Black Hills: The Struggle for Sacred Ground*. New York: Viking, 2010.

———. *The Plains Sioux and U.S. Colonialism from Lewis and Clark to Wounded Knee*. New York: Cambridge University Press, 2004.

Owens, Robert M. *Mr. Jefferson's Hammer: William Henry Harrison and the Origins of American Indian Policy*. Norman: University of Oklahoma Press, 2007.

Pope, Dennis C. *Sitting Bull, Prisoner of War*. Pierre: South Dakota State Historical Society Press, 2010.

Pound, Roscoe. *The Development of Constitutional Guarantees of Liberty*. New Haven, CT: Yale University Press, 1957.

Powell, Peter J. *Sweet Medicine*. Vol. 1. Norman: University of Oklahoma Press, 1998.

Power, Samantha. *A Problem from Hell: America and the Age of Genocide*. New York: Basic Books, 2013.

Powers, Thomas. *The Killing of Crazy Horse*. New York: Alfred A. Knopf, 2010.

Poyer, Joe, and Craig Riesch. *The .45-70 Springfield*. Tustin, CA: North Cape Publications, 1999.

Prange, Gordon W. *Miracle at Midway*. New York: McGraw-Hill, 1982.

Prucha, Francis Paul. *American Indian Treaties: The History of a Political Anomaly*. Berkeley: University of California Press, 1994.

———. *Documents of United States Indian Policy*. Lincoln: University of Nebraska Press, 2000.

Punke, Michael. *Last Stand: George Bird Grinnell, the Battle to Save the Buffalo, and the Birth of the New West.* New York: Harper Collins, First Smithsonian Books, 2007.

Rankin, Charles E., ed. *Legacy: New Perspectives on the Battle of the Little Bighorn.* Helena: Montana Historical Society Press, 1996.

Remini, Robert V. *Andrew Jackson and His Indian Wars.* New York: Penguin Putnam, 2001.

Reno, Ottie W. *Reno and Apsaalooka Survive Custer.* Danvers, MA: Rosemont, 1997.

Richardson, Heather Cox. *Wounded Knee: Party Politics and the Road to an American Massacre.* New York: Basic Books, 2010.

Rickey, Don, Jr. *Forty Miles a Day on Beans and Hay: The Enlisted Soldier Fighting the Indian Wars.* Norman: University of Oklahoma Press, 1983.

Ritchie, Robert. *Captain Kidd and the War against Pirates.* Cambridge, MA: Harvard University Press, 1989.

Robbins, James S. *Last in Their Class: Custer, Pickett and the Goats of West Point.* New York: Encounter Books, 2006.

Robertson, Lindsay. *Conquest by Law: How the Discovery of America Dispossessed Indigenous Peoples of Their Lands.* New York: Oxford University Press, 2005.

Robinson, Charles M., III. *Bad Hand: A Biography of General Ranald S. Mackenzie.* Abilene, KS: State House Press, 2005.

———, ed. *The Diaries of John Gregory Bourke.* Vol. 1, *November 20, 1872–July 28, 1876.* Denton: University of North Texas Press, 2003.

———. *General Crook and the Western Frontier.* Norman: University of Oklahoma Press, 2001.

Ruby, Robert H. *The Oglala Sioux: Warriors in Transition.* Lincoln: University of Nebraska Press, 2010.

Rushmore, Elsie Mitchell. *The Indian Policy during Grant's Administrations.* New York: Marion Press, 1914.

Salter, Fred H. *Recon Scout: A True Adventure, World War II.* Kalispell, MT: Scott Publishing, 1994.

Sandoz, Mari. *Cheyenne Autumn.* Lincoln: University of Nebraska Press, 1992.

Satz, Ronald N. *American Indian Policy in the Jacksonian Era.* Norman: University of Oklahoma Press, 1975.

Scott, Douglas D. *Uncovering History: Archaeological Investigation at the Little Bighorn.* Norman: University of Oklahoma Press, 2013.

Scott, Douglas D., and Peter Bleed. *A Good Walk around the Boundary: Archeological Inventory of the Dyck and Other Properties Adjacent to Little Bighorn Battlefield National Monument.* Lincoln: Nebraska State Historical Society, 2nd printing, 1997.

Scott, Douglas D., Richard A. Fox, Jr., and Dick Harmon. *Archaeological Insights into the Custer Battle: An Assessment of the 1984 Field Season.* Norman: University of Oklahoma Press, 1987.

Scott, Douglas D., Richard A. Fox, Jr., Dick Harmon, and Melissa A. Connor. *Archaeological Perspectives on the Battle of the Little Bighorn.* Norman: University of Oklahoma Press, 1989.

Scott, Douglas D., P. Willey, and Melissa A. Connor. *They Died with Custer.* Norman: University of Oklahoma Press, 1998.

Secrest, William B. *When the Great Spirit Died: The Destruction of the California Indians, 1850–1860.* Fresno, CA: Craven Street Books, 2003.

Service, Robert W. *The Complete Poems of Robert Service.* New York: Dodd, Mean, 1950.

Seymour, Flora Warren. *Indian Agents of the Old Frontier.* New York: Octagon Books, 1975.

Shockley, Philip M. *The Trap-Door Springfield in the Service.* Aledo, IL: World-Wide Gun Report, 1958.

Sides, Hampton. *Blood and Terror.* New York: Doubleday, 2006.

———. *Ghost Soldiers: The Forgotten Epic Story of World War II's Most Dramatic Mission.* New York: Doubleday, 2001.

Simonin, Louis L. *The Rocky Mountain West in 1867,* translated and annotated by Wilson O. Clough from *Le grand-ouest des Etats-Unis.* Lincoln: University of Nebraska Press, 1966.

Skelton, William B. *An American Profession of Arms: The Army Officer Corps, 1784–1861.* Lawrence: University Press of Kansas, 1992.

Smith, Jean Edward. *John Marshall: Definer of a Nation.* New York: Henry Holt, 1996.

Smith, Rich. *Fifth Amendment: The Right to Fairness (The Bill of Rights).* Edina, MN: ABDO Publishing, 2008.

Smith, Shannon D. *Give Me Eighty Men.* Lincoln: University of Nebraska Press, 2008.

Smythe, Douglas. *Guerrilla Warrior: The Early Life of John J. Pershing.* New York: Charles Scribner's Sons, 1973.

Stabler, Hollis. *No One Ever Asked Me: The World War II Memoirs of an Omaha Indian Soldier,* edited by Victoria Smith. Lincoln: University of Nebraska Press, 2005.

Stands in Timber, John, and Margot Liberty. *Cheyenne Memories.* 2nd ed. New Haven, CT: Yale University Press, 1998.

Starita, Joe. *I Am a Man: Chief Standing Bear's Journey for Justice.* New York: St. Martin Press, 2008.

Stevenson, Joan Nesbeth. *Deliverance from the Little Big Horn: Doctor Henry*

*Porter and Custer's Seventh Cavalry*. Norman: University of Oklahoma Press, 2012.

Stewart, Edgar I. *Custer's Luck*. Norman: University of Oklahoma Press, 1967.

St. Germain, Jill. *Broken Treaties: United States and Canadian Relations with the Lakotas and the Plains Cree, 1868–1885*. Lincoln: University of Nebraska Press, 2009.

Sun Tzu. *The Art of War: The Essential Translation of the Classic Book of Life*, translated and with commentary by John Minford. New York: Viking, 2002.

Sweeney, Edwin R. *Cochise: Chiricahua Apache Chief*. Norman: University of Oklahoma Press, 1991.

———. *From Cochise to Geronimo: The Chiricahua Apaches, 1874–1886*. Norman: University of Oklahoma Press, 2010.

Symonds, Craig L. *The Battle of Midway*. New York: Oxford University Press, 2011.

Tate, Michael L. *Indians and Emigrants: Encounters on the Overland Trails*. Norman: University of Oklahoma Press, 2006.

Thorndike, Rachael Sherman. *The Sherman Letters*. New York: Charles Scribner's Sons, 1894.

Trafzer, Clifford E., and Joel R. Hyer, eds. *Exterminate Them: Written Accounts of the Murder, Rape and Enslavement of Native Americans during the California Gold Rush, 1848–1868*. East Lansing: Michigan State University Press, 1999.

Upton, Emory. *Cavalry Tactics, United States Army, Assimilated to the Tactics of Infantry and Artillery*. New York: D. Appleton, 1874.

Urofsky, Melvin, and Paul Finkelman. *A March of Liberty: A Constitutional History of the United States*. Vol. 1, *From the Founding to 1900*. New York: Oxford University Press, 2011.

Utley, Robert M. *Cavalier in Buckskin: George Armstrong Custer and the Western Military Frontier*. Rev. ed. Norman: University of Oklahoma Press, 2001.

———. *Frontier Regulars: The United States Army and the Indian, 1866–1891*. New York: Macmillan, 1973.

———. *The Lance and the Shield: The Life and Times of Sitting Bull*. New York: Henry Holt, 1993.

———, ed. *Life in Custer's Cavalry: Diaries and Letters of Albert and Jennie Barnitz*. New Haven, CT: Yale University Press, 1977.

VanDevelder, Paul. *Savages and Scoundrels: The Untold Story of America's Road to Empire through Indian Territory*. New Haven, CT: Yale University Press, 2009.

Vaughn, J. W. *The Reynolds Campaign on Powder River*. Norman: University of Oklahoma Press, 1961.

———. *With Crook at the Rosebud*. Mechanicsburg, PA: Stackpole Books, 1956.

Vigil, Ralph H., Frances W. Kaye, and John R. Wunder, eds. *Spain and the Plains: Myths and Realities of Spanish Exploration and Settlement on the Great Plains*. Boulder: University Press of Colorado, 1994.

Wagner, Arthur Lockwood. *Organization and Tactics*. Kansas City, MO: Hudson-Kimberly, 1902.

Waite, M. D. "Bud," and B. D. Ernst. *Trap-Door Springfield*. Highland Park, NJ: Gun Room Press, 1980.

Walker, L. G., Jr. *Dr. Henry R. Porter: The Surgeon Who Survived Little Bighorn*. Jefferson, NC: McFarland, 2008.

Wallace, Anthony F. C. *Jefferson and the Indians: The Tragic Fate of the First Americans*. Cambridge: Belknap Press of Harvard University Press, 1999.

Watson, Samuel J. *Jackson's Sword: The Army Officer Corps on the American Frontier, 1810–1821*. Lawrence: University Press of Kansas, 2012.

Wert, Jeffry D. *Custer: The Controversial Life of George Armstrong Custer*. New York: Simon and Schuster, 1996.

Wheelan, Joseph. *Terrible Swift Sword: The Life of General Philip H. Sheridan*. Cambridge, MA: Da Capo Press, 2012.

White, Richard R. "The Winning of the West: The Expansion of the Western Sioux in the Eighteenth and Nineteenth Centuries." *Journal of American History* 65 (1978).

Wilkins, David E., and K. Tsianina Lomawaima. *Uneven Ground: American Indian Sovereignty and Federal Law*. Norman: University of Oklahoma Press, 2001.

Willbanks, James. *The Tet Offensive: A Concise History*. New York: Columbia University Press, 2007.

Willert, James, ed. *The Letters of General Alfred Howe Terry to His Sisters*, 1980.

Williams, Robert A., Jr. *Like a Loaded Weapon: The Rehnquist Court, Indian Rights, and the Legal History of Racism in America*. Minneapolis: University of Minnesota Press, 2005.

Winthrop, William. *Military Law and Precedents*. Vol. 2. Washington, DC: Beard Books, 2000.

Wishart, David J. *An Unspeakable Sadness: The Dispossession of the Nebraska Indians*. Lincoln: University of Nebraska Press, 1994.

Wolf, J. S., and Pat Wolf. *Loading Cartridges for the Original .45.70 Springfield Rifle and Carbine*. Sheridan, WY: Wolf's Western Traders, 1996.

Woodard, Colin. *The Republic of Pirates: Being the True and Surprising Story of the Caribbean Pirates and the Man Who Brought Them Down*. New York: Harcourt Press, 2008.

Wooster, Robert. *Nelson A. Miles and the Twilight of the Frontier Army*. Lincoln: University of Nebraska Press, 1996.

Wright, Charles E. "Standing Bear: A Long Walk for Liberty; A Firm Step for Justice." *Nebraska Lawyer* (August 2005).

Wunder, John R. *"Retained by the People": A History of American Indians and the Bill of Rights (Bicentennial Essays on the Bill of Rights)*. New York: Oxford University Press, 1994.

Wyman, Walker D. *The Wild Horse of the West*. Lincoln: University of Nebraska Press, 1966.

Zucchino, David. *Thunder Run: The Armored Strike to Capture Baghdad*. New York: Grove Press, 2004.


## Government Documents and Publications

American Articles of War, Article 41, enacted June 22, 1874.

Annual Report of the Secretary of War, 1875.

*Biographical Register of the Officers and Graduates of the U.S. Military Academy.* 1857–1862.

Bogy, L. V., *1866 Report of Commissioner of Indian Affairs*. Washington, D.C.: Government Printing Office, 1966.

Collins, Charles D., Jr., William Glenn Robertson, Jerold E. Brown, William M. Campsey, Scott R. McMeen, comps. *Atlas of the Sioux Wars*. Ft. Leavenworth, KS: Department of the Army, 1992.

Convention on the Prevention and Punishment of the Crime of Genocide, adopted by Resolution 260 (III) A, of the United Nations General Assembly on December 9, 1948.

Cooke, Philip St. George. *Cavalry Tactics, or Regulations for the Instruction, Formations and Movements of the Cavalry of the Army and Volunteers of the United States*. Prepared under the Direction of the War Department and approved and adopted by the Secretary of War. Vol. 1, November 1, 1861.

Craighill, William P. *The 1862 Army Officer's Pocket Companion: A Manual for Staff Officers in the Field*. Entered according to act of Congress in 1861, by D. Van Nostrand in the clerk's office of the District Court of the United States for the Southern District of New York.

1868 Treaty of Fort Laramie, April 29, 1868, with the Sioux Nation of Indians. In Prucha, Francis Paul, *Documents of United States Indian Policy*. Lincoln: University of Nebraska Press, 2000, 109–13.

Elsea, Jennifer K. and Richard F. Grimmett. Declaration of War and Authorizations for the Use of Military Force: Historical Background and Legal Implications. Congressional Research Serivce, RL31133, March 17, 2011. www.crs.gov.

House Executive Document No. 1, 46th Congress, 3rd Sess., serial 1959.

House Executive Document No. 2, 32nd Congress, 1st Sess., serial 636.

House Executive Document No. 97, 40th Cong., 2d Sess., serial 1337. Report of the Indian Peace Commission. January 7, 1868.

House Executive Document No. 184. Report of E. C. Watkins. "Military Expedition against the Sioux Indians." November 9, 1875.

*Journals of the Continental Congress*, 32: 340–41.

Kappler, Charles J., ed. *Indian Affairs: Laws and Treaties.* 5 vols. Washington, DC: United States Government Printing Office, 1904–1941.

*Manual for Courts-Martial.* United States Defense Department, Committee on Military Justice. Government Printing Office, Washington, DC: 2008.

Mooney, James. *The Aboriginal Population of America North of Mexico.* Washington, DC: Government Printing Office, 1928.

Morris, Scott R. "The Laws of War: Rules by Warriors for Warriors." DA-PAM 27-50-301. *Army Lawyer* (December 1997).

Murdock, Paul. "Principles of War on the Network-Concentric Battlefield: Mass and Economy of Force." *Parameters* (Spring 2002).

*Official Register of the Officers and Cadets of the U.S. Military Academy.* West Point, NY. 1858–1861.

*Revised United States Army Regulations of 1861, with an Appendix Containing the Changes and Laws Affecting Army Regulations and Articles of War to June 25, 1863.* Washington, DC: Government Printing Office, 1863.

Senate Executive Document No. 5, 34th Congress, 3rd Sess., serial 875.

Senate Report No. 156, 39th Cong., 2d Sess., serial 1279. Report of the Joint Special Committee of Congress, the "Doolittle Committee." January 26, 1867.

Sheridan, P. H. *Record of Engagements with the Hostile Indians, within the Military Division of the Missouri from 1868 to 1882.* Washington, DC: Government Printing Office, 1882.

*Small Wars Manual: United States Marine Corps, 1940.* Washington, DC: United States Government Printing Office, 1940.

*Theory and Dynamics of Tactical Operations: Department of the Army ROTC Manual* (ROTCM 145-60). Washington, DC: Headquarters, Department of the Army, March 1972.

United Nations Security Council. Resolution 1674 on protection of civilians in armed conflict. Adopted unanimously on April 28, 2006. S/Res/1674 (2006).

*United States Army Tactics—Cavalry.* Entered as General Orders No. 6. Published for the information and guidance of the Army. William W. Belknap, Secretary of War. July 17, 1873, by command of General Sherman, entered according to act of Congress in the year 1874, in the Office of the Libraries of Congress at Washington.

United States Cavalry Association. *The Cavalry School.* Washington, DC: Judd and Detweiler, 1921.

*United States Infantry Tactics for the Instruction, Exercise, and Manoeuvres of the United States Infantry, including Infantry of the Line, Light Infantry and Riflemen.* Prepared under the direction of the War Department and approved and adopted by the Secretary of War. May 1, 1861.

United States War Department. *The 1863 Laws of War.* Mechanicsburg, PA: Stackpole Books, 2005.

## Case Law

*Cherokee Nation v. State of Georgia,* 30 U.S. 1 (1831).

*Cobell v. Salazar,* 573 F.3d 808 (2009).

*Elk v. Wilkins,* 112 U.S. 94 (1884).

*Johnson v. M'Intosh,* 21 U.S. 543 (1823).

*Jones v. Meehan,* 175 U.S. 1 (1899).

*In re Yamashita,* 327 U.S. 1 (1946).

*Korematsu v. United States,* 323 U.S. 214 (1944).

*Lone Wolf v. Hitchcock,* 187 U.S. 553 (1903).

*Olmstead v. United States,* 277 U.S. 438 (1928).

*Sioux Nation of Indians v. United States,* 601 F.2d 1157 (1979).

*United States v. Sioux Nation,* 207 Ct. Cl. 234 (1975).

*United States v. Sioux Nation of Indians,* 448 U.S. 371, 100 S.Ct. 2716 (1980).

*United States ex rel. Standing Bear v. Crook,* 25 F. Cas. 695 (c.c.d. Neb. 1879).

*Washington v. Fishing Vessel Ass'n.,* 443 U.S. 658 (1979).

# INDEX